JOURNAL

OF THE

WATERLOO CAMPAIGN

KEPT THROUGHOUT THE CAMPAIGN OF 1815

by the late

GENERAL CAVALIÉ MERCER

COMMANDING THE 9TH BRIGADE ROYAL ARTILLERY

Introduction
by
the Hon. SIR JOHN FORTESCUE

New afterword
by
PHILIP J. HAYTHORNTHWAITE

DA CAPO PRESS

Library of Congress Cataloging in Publication Data

Mercer, Cavalié, 1783-1868.
 Journal of the Waterloo campaign kept throughout the campaign of, 1815 /
by Cavalié Mercer; introduction by John Fortescue; new afterword by Philip J.
Haythornthwaite.—1st Da Capo Press ed.
  p.   cm.
 ISBN 0-306-80651-7
  1. Mercer, Cavalié, 1783-1868—Diaries. 2. Waterloo, Battle of, 1815—Personal narratives, British. 3. Great Britain, Army—History—Napoleonic Wars,
1800-1815—Sources. I. Title.
DC241.5.M4A3   1995
940.2′7—dc20   95-4813
                                                                   CIP

First Da Capo Press edition 1995

This Da Capo Press paperback edition of *Journal of the Waterloo Campaign* is an
unabridged republication of the edition published in London in 1927, with the
addition of a new afterword by Philip J. Haythornthwaite.

New afterword copyright ©1995 by Philip J. Haythornthwaite

Published by Da Capo Press
A Member of the Perseus Books Group
http://www.dacapopress.com

Manufactured in the United States of America
10 9 8 7 6 5 4

CONTENTS

CONTENTS

CHAPTER XIX

CHAPTER XX

CHAPTER XXI

CHAPTER XXII

CHAPTER XXIII

CHAPTER XXIV

INTRODUCTION

REMINISCENCES and memoirs of the old campaigns written by officers and men who have taken part in them are, in the British Army, confined principally to the infantry. This, of course, is natural, seeing that the infantry greatly outnumber the other arms; and yet the dearth of such volumes among the cavalry is striking, for, among the very few that do exist, the diary of Colonel Tomkinson of the Sixteenth Light Dragoons is of peculiar interest and value. But the artillery were the most silent of all until in 1854 they produced an officer of exceptional literary gifts in the person of Captain E. B. Hamley. His book on the campaign of Sebastopol appeared in 1855, and not until fifteen years later was published Captain Cavalié Mercer's *Journal of the Waterloo Campaign*, the writer meanwhile having risen to the rank of general, and died at a great age in 1868.

It is noticeable that the officers who write the stories of their campaigns generally belong to the regiments which have most highly distinguished themselves in the course of the operations described. Thus, in Marlborough's Wars the Royal Irish (now disbanded) have almost a monopoly among the regimental authors, while in the Peninsula officers of the Light Division, and in particular of the Rifle Brigade, supply far more than their due proportion of volumes. This being the case, the silence of the gunners is the more remarkable; for, if I were asked which regiment in the army could show the finest record of invariable good service, I should answer without hesitation the Royal Artillery.

But the gunners, until within the memory of living men, were a peculiar people. They were not, like the cavalry and infantry, subject to the Commander-in-Chief, but to the Master-General of the Ordnance. And this was not their only nor most important distinction. For their officers could not purchase their commissions; their promotion also was by seniority and not by purchase; their colonels had not the privilege of clothing the men, that business being undertaken by the Board of Ordnance; and lastly, they had ever since 1741 been taught their business as cadets at the Royal Military Academy. Now, since the Royal Military College for officers of cavalry and infantry was not founded until 1802, it follows that for two whole generations the officers of the artillery were practically unique in the army, through the fact that every one of them had passed through a regular professional training. Their only rivals were the Engineers—another child of the Board of Ordnance—but they for long were a corps of officers only, and, having no men to teach, stood upon a different footing, and were supposed to concern themselves only with fortifications and sieges. Gunners and guns, on the other hand, were as essential as infantry to any expedition of the slightest importance, and consequently were engaged all over the world. Having studied the art of war, the officers were naturally superior as a body to their brethren of the cavalry and infantry; and the fact was generally, if sometimes rather grudgingly, admitted. Still, they were treated as a separate body, and not without jealousy. In the course of the American War the question was seriously raised whether an artillery officer of great ability and distinction, who had risen to General rank, could take command of cavalry and infantry; and it was decided that he could and should. But it was not until the Artillery had been transferred, after the Crimean War, from the control of the Master-General of the Ordnance to that of the Commander-in-Chief, that its officers began to stand upon exactly the same footing with those of the cavalry and infantry.

The horse-artillery, of which Mercer commanded a troop, was a comparatively recent recreation. They began life in January, 1793, at the outbreak of the Great War, with two companies, as they were then called, a number which by 1801 had swelled to ten troops. They very quickly made their mark by extraordinary smartness and efficiency; and as early as in 1797 Sir John Moore, after watching a troop at drill, declared that he could conceive of nothing in higher order. In the Peninsula the great name among horse-artillery officers was that of Norman Ramsay, who at Fuentes

de Oñoro galloped two of his guns straight through a mass
of French cavalry and brought them safely off. As a rule,
a troop consisted of five 6-pounder guns and one howitzer;
but, as Mercer tells us, there was considerable variety among
the nine troops that served in the Waterloo campaign, one
of them being composed wholly of howitzers. The fact is
that the British artillery had enjoyed since 1803 a missile
of peculiar power, in the shape of the shell recently invented
by Major Shrapnel. The projectiles in ordinary use at the
time were the solid round-shot, grape- or case-shot—a bag
or case of bullets which burst at the muzzle and was effective
up to a range of two hundred yards,—and the common shell.
Shrapnel's shell was a spherical iron case filled with bullets,
which was exploded by a time-fuse, and produced the effect
of grape at a range of eight hundred, a thousand, and, as
Mercer himself shows us, even twelve hundred yards. Of
course, with the erratic flight of a spherical projectile from
a smooth-bore howitzer, the bullets were not always very
destructive. A French general at Bussaco had his face
plastered with shrapnel-bullets, which were picked out of
his skin like currants off the top of a bun, leaving him considerably the uglier but otherwise little the worse. But in
a general way the shrapnel-shell gave the British a decided
advantage. Common shell, bursting into a few fragments,
was more terrifying than damaging, and was never very
accurate. A simple shrapnel-shell had been known to kill
every horse in a gun-team, even at long range; and it was
a really destructive projectile. The French hated it because
they could not reply to it. Napoleon had great numbers of
12-pounders, which he fondly called his "pretty girls," and
which were of greater range and calibre than the English
guns; but they could not compete with shrapnel-shell at
eight hundred yards. Shrapnel, in fact, had a great deal
more to do with beating the French than he receives credit
for.

All these things must be remembered before we follow
Mercer into his first and last actions on the 17th and 18th
of June, 1815. Nor must it be forgotten that Wellington,
in the Peninsula, had not got on well with his artillery officers.
In fact, he had in 1813 placed at their head Alexander Dickson, who was no more than a captain in the regiment and

a very young lieutenant-colonel in the army, and in 1815 was the titular commander of Mercer's troop. This had not made Wellington popular with the gunners, and his extreme severity to Norman Ramsay, for another officer's fault, after Vittoria, had still further embittered their feelings against him. Mercer had never yet served under the Duke, and could only listen with reverence to the stories of the Peninsula told by his brother-officers.

The opening pages of the Journal, amid a great deal of purely descriptive writing, contain some curious little pictures. There is first the naval transport officer, insisting upon the hasty landing of everything, no matter at what damage, so that he may gain the credit of energy and promptitude—a common type in all services. However, the troop was landed, "their clothes all soiled with mud and wet, their sabres rusty, and the bearskins of their helmets flattened down by the rain." The horse-artillery, it must be explained, wore at this time the Light Dragoons' helmet of black leather, with a band, called a turban, folded round its base, a great comb of fur running fore and aft over the top, and a plume at the side—a rather foolish head-dress, being so top-heavy that it generally fell from the men's heads in a charge and, as Mercer tells us, needed to be held on with the hand during a high wind. A short blue jacket and "pepper-and-salt" booted trousers completed the horse-gunner's costume.

It did not take long for Mercer to repair damages and put flesh on his horses, and then we find his troop evoking unbounded admiration alike from the French officers on the Duc de Berri's staff and from Blücher himself. Wellington, it seems, directed the old warrior's particular attention to it, but, while asking the name of its commander, did not condescend to look at him. For weeks the troop led a comfortable life, until suddenly on the 16th of June it received orders to march at once; and then Mercer found himself, through his own carelessness, in rather an awkward position. All of his officers were absent on leave; two of his guns were also at a distance, and the whole of his supply-waggons were wanting. It was therefore some hours before the troop could march, even then without its supply-waggons; and in order to make up for lost time and make quicker progress over the road, he marched away from his ammunition-waggons also. Finally, on reaching his appointed place, he omitted to feed his horses, and found himself obliged to march them on with their stomachs empty to Nivelle. There he heard the firing at Quatre Bras, and reached the field when the action was over. He had, as he frankly acknowledges, been guilty of very serious mistakes, such as had been cured among the old Peninsular officers years before.

From this point Mercer's narrative becomes of quite peculiar interest. He had not yet discovered the cavalry-brigade to which his troop was attached, but he found himself told off to work with the cavalry of the rear-guard while the army retreated from Quatre Bras to Waterloo. Before he moved, he caught sight of Napoleon himself, and then, after firing a few rounds he was hurried back by Lord Uxbridge in person. His picture of Uxbridge, general-in-chief of the cavalry, behaving like a cornet, leading the guns into a narrow lane and leaving them to get themselves out, would be incredible were it not far too strange to have been invented. Meanwhile a terrific thunderstorm had burst, and through cataracts of rain and peals of thunder which drowned the reports of the guns, the troop galloped away to the rear with the French cavalry galloping after them. At Genappe, three miles from Quatre Bras, he found himself in an empty village, but came into action again just beyond it, engaging a French battery effectively with "spherical case"—otherwise shrapnel. Having exhausted his ammunition, he left the work to the rocket-troop; and here we catch a glimpse of Strangways, who had been with that troop at the battle of Leipsic—the only English contingent present at the battle of the nations—and was killed forty years later at Inkerman. We also catch a glimpse of rockets in action, though Wellington did not believe in them, and had wished to substitute guns for them. When told that such a change would break the heart of the troop commander, the Duke had answered only, "Damn his heart; let my order be obeyed"; and yet there the rockets were—very erratic, as dangerous to friends as to foes, fully justifying Wellington's dislike of them.

Mercer's account of the retreat is by far the most graphic and valuable that we possess. On both sides, so far as he could see, all was "blunder and confusion"; and French writers have used his narrative to prove to their own satisfaction that Wellington's retreat to Waterloo was virtually a flight, because a single troop of horse-artillery or a few squadrons, at the very tail of the army, held their ground for a little too long, and galloped away at top-speed for perhaps two miles. The truth seems to be that human nerves and human arrangements were utterly upset for the time, both among pursuers and pursued, by a great electric disturbance.

There was little rest for the troop that night, and not much food until the morning of the 18th, when an old bombardier, who had been despatched to fetch ammunition, appeared with beef, biscuit, and rum, which he had picked up abandoned on the road, returning, to his infinite credit, sober himself and with every man of his detachment sober likewise. Considering the habits of the English, military and civil, at the time, this fact avouches marvellous discipline in the horse-artillery.

While Mercer was thinking about food, the battle of Waterloo began, and he found himself alone in his bivouac without orders of any kind for some time, until he at last was directed to the extreme right of the Allied line, where little was doing. He gives a very pathetic account of a wounded horse, which would not be driven away from its companions, and, from what he could see after the battle had lasted four hours, had little else to think about beyond a general impression that the day was going badly. Then suddenly he was summoned to the very centre of the fight. "Left limber up—gallop!" and away the troop went in beautiful order, and unlimbered between two unsteady squares of Brunswick infantry. From that point there can be no abridgment of Mercer's story. It must be read as he wrote it, with no vision of the battle beyond his guns in the centre and the two Brunswick squares on either flank, until he found himself almost alone on the field with the wreck of his beautiful troop.

From beginning to end of the volume the professional bitterness of the gunner and the personal bitterness of the man against Wellington show themselves repeatedly. There is some excuse for it. Wellington after Waterloo wrote a report on the behaviour of the artillery which the gunners have never forgiven. It was one of those sweeping condemnations to which the Duke in moments of irritation was far too prone, but which, once pronounced, he would never revoke. He placed Mercer under arrest for a trifling matter later on, and never attempted to procure him any recognition of his services; but Mercer was only one of many sufferers from the Duke's extreme sensitiveness to anything that seemed to savour of insubordination. We may now pass over such things. If Wellington's orders were disobeyed, and rightly disobeyed, by Mercer at Waterloo, let us be content that the humble captain did his duty, though unrewarded, and that when his troop galloped up to its place Wellington was compelled to exclaim, "Ah! that's the way I like to see horse-artillery move." We can now bury all bygone grievances—every war produces a huge crop of them—and be content to enjoy the epic—for such it is—of G Troop Royal Horse Artillery.

J. W. FORTESCUE.

PREFACE

THIS work—the *Journal of the Campaign of* 1815—was written by my father in its present form about forty years ago, from rough notes jotted down every evening after the scenes and events of the day were over. It has no pretension to be an account of the military operations of the war, but merely a diary of the writer's own impressions—what he saw and felt while with the army, from the first landing in Belgium to the final embarkation for England. Of the great battle, no other description than that of the part taken in it by his own troop of Horse Artillery, or those corps in his immediate vicinity, is given; but from its very nature as a diary, the tedium of out-quarters, the fatigues of the march, and the hardships of the bivouac, are made present, as it were, to the reader. My father having been a very good amateur artist, was much struck, of course, by new and picturesque scenes, consequently has described them *con amore*, and in considerable detail. The author himself belonged to a military race; all his family were either in the army or navy. He was the second son of General Mercer of the Royal Engineers, who, after serving on Sir H. Clinton's staff during the American War of Independence, was more than twenty years commanding engineer in the West of England, where his honourable character procured him many friends. My father (also a general officer at the time of his death) was born in 1783, and passing as usual through the Military Academy at Woolwich, obtained a commission in the Royal Artillery at sixteen, and was sent to Ireland at the time of the Rebellion. In 1808 he went to the river Plate to join Whitelock's unfortunate expedition, and covered the retreat from Buenos Ayres. This proved a most unhappy affair for him; for having been in South America, he was prevented from partaking in the glorious campaigns of the Peninsula, and only saw foreign service again in the campaign of Waterloo.   After the peace, he was placed upon half-pay. In 1824 he was ordered to Canada, having the brevet rank of major (I should have noticed that at Waterloo he only held the rank of second captain, although commanding a troop— Sir Alex. Dickson, whose troop it was, being otherwise employed).   In 1837, being then a lieutenant-colonel, he was again sent to North America, and commanded the artillery in Nova Scotia at the time when the Maine boundary-line threatened to terminate in a war between this country and the United States.   He subsequently commanded the garrison at Dover, after which he retired from active service, although, being colonel-commandant of the 9th Brigade of Royal Artillery, he was never placed on the retired list. From that time to the period of his death, at the advanced age of eighty-five, he continued to reside at Cowley Cottage, near Exeter.

Another addition to the numerous books which have been published about Waterloo will hardly seem out of place at a time when the subject has been revived both here and in France.   It would seem that men's interest in this great "World Battle" is as strong now as fifty years ago; and although this little contribution will not elucidate any of the questions that are agitated, still (as far as memory serves) it is the first account of the campaign given to the world by an artillery officer, and may add another stone to the cairn raised to the glory of the British army and its immortal chief.   At any rate, the surviving veterans of this stirring epoch will rejoice to go again over the scenes of their younger days; while the lovers of peace will congratulate themselves on the cessation of such strife between two noble nations, whose last (and may it continue to be the last) hostile rencontre took place upon the plain of Waterloo.

CAVALIÉ A. MERCER.

TRIPOLI, SYRIA.

JOURNAL OF
THE WATERLOO CAMPAIGN

CHAPTER I

THE return of Napoleon from Elba, though a surprise to many, was far from being so to those who, well aware of his restless disposition, his insatiable ambition, and the enthusiastic attachment of the French soldiery to his person and fortunes, had scarcely expected that he would have remained so long as he actually did without some new attempt at disturbing the general peace.

The steps taken on this occasion by the different European Powers—their preparations for a renewal of the bloody scenes so lately ended—are out of my province. They belong to the historian, and not to the simple journalist, whose affair it is to confine himself strictly to those transactions in which he was himself a participator; or at most to glance at those more general subjects, merely to give connection to his narrative and make it better understood.

At the time the news of this extraordinary event arrived, the troop of horse-artillery which I commanded was stationed at Colchester; and the reductions necessary to put us on a peace-establishment had already commenced, when the order arrived for our being immediately equipped again for foreign service. To do this effectually, another troop, then in the same barracks, was broken up, and we got the picked horses of both, thus making it the finest troop in the service; and such diligence was used, that although our equipment fell little short of a complete reorganisation, Major Sir A. Fraser, commanding the horse-artillery in Colchester, was enabled to report on the third day that the troop was ready to march at a moment's warning.

Meantime the town of Colchester (situated as it is on the

great road from Harwich to London) presented a scene of bustle and anxiety seldom equalled—couriers passing to and fro incessantly, and numerous travellers, foreign and English, arriving day and night from the Continent, many travelling in breathless haste, as if fearful, even here, of Napoleon's emissaries.

The reports spread by these fugitives were various and contradictory, as might be expected.

According to some, Louis XVIII. had been arrested in Paris; according to others, he had sought refuge in the Pays Bas; and again, it was asserted that his Majesty was at Ostend, awaiting permission to pass the sea and return to his old and secure quarters in England.

In the midst of all this, on the 8th April, the post brought our order to march forthwith to Harwich, there to embark for Ostend—an order received with unfeigned joy by officers and men, all eager to plunge into danger and bloodshed, all hoping to obtain glory and distinction.

On the morning of the 9th, the troop paraded at half-past seven o'clock with as much regularity and as quietly as if only going to a field-day; not a man either absent or intoxicated, and every part of the guns and appointments in the most perfect order. At eight, the hour named in orders, we marched off the parade. The weather was fine, the scenery, as we skirted the beautiful banks of the Stour, charming, and the occasion exhilarating.

Near Manningtree we halted a short time to feed our horses, and then, pursuing our route, arrived at Harwich about three o'clock in the afternoon. Here we found the transports—the *Adventure*, *Philarea*, and *Salus*, in which last I embarked—awaiting us; but the tide being unfavourable, although we immediately commenced operations, we only succeeded in embarking the horses of one division and those of the officers; the remainder were therefore put up in the barracks for the night. As might be expected, the little town of Harwich presented a most animated spectacle. Its narrow streets of modest houses, with brick *trottoirs*, were crowded with soldiers—some, all over dust, just arrived; some, who had already been a day or two in the place, comparatively at home, lounging about in undress; others, about to embark, hurrying along to the beach with baggage and stores; sailors marketing, or rolling about half-seas-over; country-people bringing in vegetables and the like, and towns-people idling at their windows, or in groups at corners of the streets—in short, the usual picture incident on such occasions.

The morning of the 10th was foggy, which much retarded us, since it was necessary to embark the horses in flats to be taken off to the transports, not easily found in the fog. However, by noon all were on board, and without any serious accident, although a sailor was somewhat hurt in endeavouring to recover a horse that had fallen overboard. In the afternoon our guns, carriages, etc., were embarked; but as the wind blew right into the harbour, the agent would not attempt to get out, and we adjourned to Mr Bull's comfortable house (the Three Cups), there to pass our last evening in England in the enjoyment of a good dinner, and perhaps for the last time to sleep in good beds.

About 2 p.m. on the 11th, a light breeze from the N.W. induced our agent to get under way, and we repaired on board our respective ships with every prospect of a good and speedy passage. In this, however, we were disappointed, for the breeze dying away as the sun went down, we anchored, by signal, at the harbour's mouth, just as it got dark.

The evening was splendid. A clear sky studded with myriads of stars overhead, and below a calm unruffled sea, reflecting on its glassy surface the lights of the distant town, the low murmuring sounds from which, and the rippling of the water under the ship's bows, were the only interruptions to the solemn stillness that prevailed after the people had retired to their berths. In our more immediate neighbourhood stretched out the long, low, sandy tract, on the seaward extremity of which the dark masses of Landguard fort could just be distinguished.

With daybreak on the morning of the 12th came a favourable wind, though light, and again we took up our anchors and proceeded to sea. For some distance, after clearing the harbour, our course lay along the Suffolk coast, and so near in that objects on shore were plainly discernible. To us, who had long been stationed at Woodbridge, only a few miles inland, this was highly interesting. We knew every village, every copse, every knoll—nay, almost every tree. There were the houses in which we had so oft been hospitably entertained; there were the sheep-walks on which we had so often manœuvred; and there in the distance, as we passed the mouth of the Deben, our glasses showed us the very barrack on the hill, with its tiled roofs illumined by the noon-tide sun. About Bawdsey we left the coast, and steered straight over, with a light but favourable wind: the low sandy shores of Suffolk soon sank beneath the horizon. At noon fell in with a fleet of colliers bound for the river, and soon after saw the Sunk-Sand Light; when, as the wind had died away and the tide was setting us towards the bank, we anchored until the flood-tide. During the night a light breeze right aft, and smooth water, enabled us to make good progress; but towards morning (13th) the wind had very considerably increased, and although the coast was not in sight, we were sensible of its neighbourhood from the number of curious heavy-looking boats plying round us in all directions, having the foremast, with its huge lug-sail, stuck right up in the bow, or rather inclining over it. From one of these boats we soon procured a pilot—a little sturdy fellow, with a full, good-humoured countenance, and his breast decorated with a silver medal bearing the impress of an anchor, like our porters' tickets, the badge of his calling.

The poor fellow was hardly on deck ere he was surrounded and assailed by innumerable questions—"Where is Buona-parte?" "Where is the French army?" "What are the English about?" "Has there been any fighting?" etc. etc. Of this he understood or heard only the word "Buonaparte," and therefore to all kept repeating, "Il est capôte," accompanied by a significant motion of the hand across the throat, at the same time showing much anxiety to get rid of his tormentors and proceed to business, which he did with such earnestness as soon gave us to understand there must be more than ordinary difficulty in entering the port of Ostend. The first and principal care was the getting up a hawser and coiling it on deck, the use of which we were soon to learn.

Meanwhile we had been approaching the coast, which, though still invisible, the pilot informed us was not distant. The first intimation of the truth of this was the appearance of the church tower and lofty lighthouse of Ostend; and we had brought about half their height above the horizon before

land began to show itself, which it did in a number of isolated
and rounded yellow hummocks, and at the same time the
houses of the town became distinctly visible. With that impatience and excessive curiosity always felt upon approaching for the first time a strange land, especially under the
present interesting state of things, all our glasses were
directed to the coast, which we were rapidly nearing and
hoped soon to reach, when, to our great disappointment, the
pilot ordered the vessel to be hove to, and we found that
the tide would not permit our running for the port before
2 p.m. Numbers of ships, brigs, and schooners were lying-to
as well as ourselves, and others continually arriving.

Nothing, certainly, could be more repulsive than the
appearance of the coast—sand-hills as far as the eye could
reach, broken only by the grey and lugubrious works and
buildings of Ostend, and further west by the spires of Mit-
telkerke and Nieuport, peering above the sand-hills. The
day, too, was one little calculated to enliven the scene. A
fresh breeze and cloudy sky; the sea black, rough, and
chilly; the land all under one uniform cold grey tint, presenting scarcely any relief of light and shadow, consequently no
feature. Upon reconnoitring it, however, closer, we found
that this forbidding exterior was only an outer coating to a
lovely gem. Through the openings between the sand-hills
could be seen a rich level country, of the liveliest verdure,
studded with villages and farms interspersed amongst
avenues of trees and small patches of wood. An occasional
gleam of sunshine breaking out and illumining it, communicated to it a dreamy appearance that was very pleasing,
and tended to revive our spirits, drooping from the gloomy
aspect of the coast.

A black-looking mass of timber rising from the waters off
the entrance of the harbour, and which we understood to be
a fort, now became the principal object of our attention. As
the tide rises the depth of water is announced by different
flags hoisted on this fort; and we were delighted when at
last that (a red one) indicating the necessary depth for our
ship was hoisted, and we bore up for the harbour mouth.

The harbour of Ostend is an artificial one, formed by
jetées of piles projecting as far as low-water mark. The right,
on entering, is merely a row of piles running along in front

of the works of the town; but on the left is a long mole or *jetée*, on the extremity of which is a small fort.   Behind this mole, to the north-east, the shore curving inwards forms a bight presenting an extent of flat sandy beach on which the water is never more than a few feet deep, even at the highest tides.   A tremendous surf breaks on this whenever it blows from the westward.   As the flood-tide sets past the harbour mouth with great rapidity, a vessel attempting to enter with a westerly wind is in danger of being swept beyond it and thrown on the beach just mentioned.   And this we now discovered was the cause of the anxiety displayed by our pilot, and for which we could not before account.   In approaching the harbour, we steered as if going to run the ship ashore on the broad stone glacis of the town, which extended into the water all along the sea-front.   Even with this precaution we were drifted so much to leeward that, instead of shooting into the harbour, we went bump upon the *jetée*.[1]   The poor pilot raved and jumped about like a madman, but there still was method in his madness; and now we discovered the use of the hawser he had coiled upon deck, for passing the end of this to the Belgic soldiers, who upon the shock immediately ran out of their guard-room, the vessel was saved from swinging round (as she otherwise would have done) and falling ashore on the beach beyond, stern foremost, and soon dragged within the influence of the current setting up the harbour.

Our attention, before engaged by our perilous situation, was now directed to new and exhilarating objects on the other side, where the works of the town arose immediately from the sands.   These were crowded with spectators, and, being Sunday, all in their best; so that the sun, just peeping out as we shot along, imparted to the scene quite an air of gaiety; and to us it was also a novel one.   I remember being mightily struck with the head-dress of the women, so different from what we had been accustomed to see at home, and the comparison was certainly not in favour of my fair compatriots. With these the fashionable coiffure was a large low *poke-bonnet*, which I had always fancied very becoming; but there is no describing how this sunk into meanness and deformity

---

[1] The port of Ostend is what people usually term a " dry harbour." It is dry at low tide, but the flood brings in about 16 or 18 feet water.

in a moment when I cast my eyes on the elegantly tapering, high-crowned straws of the *belles* on the rampart, encircled sometimes with two, and even three, rows of gay ribbon or artificial flowers. These gave them such a lofty commanding air, and withal was so light and graceful. But bonnets were not allowed long to occupy my attention. Followed by a crowd of other craft of all sorts and sizes, we shot rapidly along towards that part of the harbour where a dense assemblage of shipping filled up its whole breadth, and forbade further progress, so that one wondered what was to become of the numerous vessels in our wake. The mystery was soon explained, for each having attained the point, turning her prow to the town, ran bump on the sands, and there stuck fast. Those immediately above us had just arrived, and from them a regiment of Light Dragoons was in the act of disembarking by throwing the horses overboard, and then hauling them ashore by a long rope attached to their head-collars. What a scene! What hallooing, shouting, vociferating, and plunging! The poor horses did not appear much gratified by their sudden transition from the warm hold to a cold bath.

CHAPTER II

OUR keel had scarcely touched the sand ere we were abruptly boarded by a naval officer (Captain Hill) with a gang of sailors, who, *sans cérémonie*, instantly commenced hoisting our horses out, and throwing them, as well as our saddlery, etc., overboard, without ever giving time for making any disposition to receive or secure the one or the other. To my remonstrance his answer was, "I can't help it, sir; the Duke's *orders are positive that no delay is to take place in landing the troops as they arrive, and the ships sent back again ; so you must be out of her before dark.*" It was then about 3 p.m.; and I thought this a most uncomfortable arrangement.

The scramble and confusion that ensued baffle all description. Bundles of harness went over the side in rapid succession, as well as horses. In vain we urged the loss and damage that must accrue from such a proceeding. "Can't help it—no business of mine—Duke's orders are positive," etc. etc., was our only answer. Meantime the ebb had begun to diminish the depth of water alongside, and enabled us to send parties overboard and to the beach to collect and carry things ashore, as well as to haul and secure the horses. The same operation commenced from the other vessels as they arrived, and the bustle and noise were inconceivable. The Dragoons and our men (some nearly, others quite, naked) were dashing in and out of the water, struggling with the affrighted horses, or securing their wet accoutrements as best they could. Some of the former were saddling their dripping horses, and others mounting and marching off in small parties. Disconsolate-looking groups of women and children were to be seen here and there sitting on their poor duds, or roaming about in search of their husbands, or mayhap of a stray child, all clamouring, lamenting, and materially increasing the babel-like confusion, amidst which Erin's brogue was everywhere predominant. Irish beggars swarm

8

everywhere and in all quarters of the globe. Even here they pestered us to death, and one young bare-legged rascal, when he found his whining and cant unavailing, suddenly changing his tone, tried to excite our liberality by a dirty joke on the Flemish pronunciation of their word horse (*pferd*). Add to all this crowds of people from the town idling about—some as spectators, others watching for windfalls; some bringing cakes, beer, etc., for sale, others teasing the officers with various offers of service, and these not always of the most respectable kind.

It was not without difficulty that I succeeded at last in impressing upon Captain Hill the necessity of leaving our guns and ammunition waggons, etc., on board for the night —otherwise his furious zeal would have turned all out to stand on the wet sand or be washed away. Meantime, although we were on shore, we were without orders what to do next. Not an officer, either of the staff, the garrison, nor even of our own corps, came near us. Night approached, and with it bad weather evidently. Our poor shivering horses and heaps of wet harness could not remain on the sands much longer, when the flood began to make again; and it was necessary to look about and see what could be done. With this intent, therefore, leaving the officers to collect their divisions, I got one of my horses saddled and rode into the town. Here was the same bustle (although not the same confusion) as on the sands. The streets were thronged with British officers, and the quays with guns, waggons, horses, baggage, &c.

One would hardly expect to meet with any delay in finding the commandant of a fortress, yet such was my case; and it was not until after long and repeated inquiry that I discovered Lieutenant-Colonel Gregory, 44th Regiment, to be that personage, and found his residence. From him, however, I could obtain nothing. He seemed hardly to have expected the compliment of reporting our arrival, and stated that he had no other orders but that the troops of every arm should march for Ghent the moment they landed, without halting a single day in Ostend.

Strange to say, neither I nor the Colonel recollected there was such a person in Ostend as an Assistant-Quartermaster-General, who should be referred to on such an occasion. Yet this was the case; and that officer, instead of attending the debarkation of the troops, or making himself acquainted with the arrivals, kept out of sight altogether.   Baffled at all points I was returning to the sands when I met Major Drummond on the Quai Impérial, and related my story.   He had been here some time, and was consequently acquainted with the locale. His advice was to march to Ghystelle (a village about six miles from Ostend), and after putting up there for the night, to return and disembark my guns, etc., in the morning. Whilst speaking, however, some one (I forget who) came up with the agreeable information that Ghystelle was already fully occupied by the 16th Dragoons.   He, however, gave me directions for some large sheds about a mile off, where his own horses had passed the preceding night.   This was some consolation; so riding off immediately to reconnoitre the place and the road to it, I returned to the beach just as it got dark; and a most miserable scene of confusion I there found. Our saddles, harness, baggage, etc., were still strewed about the sand, and these the flood, which was now making, threatened soon to submerge.   *Pour surcroît de malheur*, the rain came down in torrents, and a storm, which had been brewing up the whole afternoon, now burst over us most furiously.   The lightning was quite tremendous, whilst a hurricane, howling horribly through the rigging of the ships, was only exceeded in noise by the loud explosions and rattling of the incessant claps of thunder.

Our people, meantime, blinded by the lightning, had borrowed some lanterns from the ship, and were busily employed searching for the numerous articles still missing. The obscurity, however, between the vivid flashes was such that we were only enabled to keep together by repeatedly calling to each other, and it was not without difficulty and great watchfulness that we escaped being caught by the tide, which flowed rapidly in over the flat sands.   At length, having collected as many of our things as was possible, and saddled our horses (some two or three of which had escaped altogether), we began our march for the sheds a little after midnight, with a farrier and another dismounted man carrying lanterns at the head of our column.   The rain continued pouring, but flashes of lightning occurred now only at intervals, and the more subdued rolling of the thunder told us that it was passing away in the distance. Our route lay through the town, to gain which we found some advanced ditch to be crossed by a very frail wooden bridge. Half the column, perhaps, might have cleared this, when "crack" down it went, precipitating all who were on it at the moment into the mud below, and completely cutting off those in the rear. Here was a dilemma. Ignorant of the localities, and without a guide, how was the rear of the column to join us, or how were the people in the ditch, with their horses, to be extricated? Luckily none were hurt seriously, and the depth was not great—not more, perhaps, than six or eight feet; but that was enough to baffle all our attempts at extricating the horses. Some Belgic soldiers of a neighbouring guard, of which we were not aware, fortunately heard us, and came to our assistance; and one of them, crossing the ditch, undertook to guide the rear of our column and those below to another gate, whilst one accompanied us to the Quai Impérial, where, after waiting a while, we were at length assembled, drenched with rain and starving of cold and hunger. The Quai was silent and dark; the only light gleamed dimly through the wet from a miserable lamp over the door of a café, in which people were still moving; and the only sounds that broke the stillness of the quarter were the splashing of the rain and the clattering of our steel scabbards and horses' feet as we moved dejectedly on—winding our way through unknown avenues (for in the dark I found it impossible to recognise the narrow streets through which I had so hurriedly passed in the afternoon), occasionally illuminated by a solitary lamp, the feeble light of which, however, was somewhat increased by reflection on the wet pavement. After following for some time this devious course, I began to fear I had missed the road, when again we stumbled upon a Belgic guard, by whose direction and guidance we at length reached the outer barrier. Here we again came to a standstill, the officer in charge refusing to let us out. Some altercation ensued: I forget the particulars, but it ended in his opening the gate.

Once clear of the town, we hoped soon to reach our lodging; but had scarcely advanced a hundred yards ere we found that result was more distant than we had fancied, and that patience was still requisite. The rain had rendered the fat soil so slippery that our horses could scarcely keep their legs, and the road running along the narrow summit of a dyke, with ditches on each side, rendered precaution and slow movement imperative. Every moment the fall of some horse impeded the column; our lanterns went out; and after wandering a considerable time, we at length ascertained, by knocking up the people at a house by the wayside, that we had overshot our mark, and it was not until two in the morning that we succeeded in finding the sheds. These were immensely long buildings attached to some sawmills, for what use I know not, unless to store planks, etc., for they were now empty; but they were admirably adapted to our purpose, since we could range all our horses along one side, whilst the men occupied the other, in one of them. A quantity of hay, and some straw, left by our predecessors, was a valuable acquisition to man and beast under such circumstances. All our enjoyments are the effect of contrast. It would be considered miserable enough to be obliged to pass the night under such equivocal shelter as these sheds afforded, and that, too, in wet clothes; yet did we now, after twelve hours of harassing work and exposure to the weather, look upon them as palaces, and, having cared for our poor beasts as far as circumstances would permit, proceeded to prepare for that repose so necessary and so longed for.

I was already ensconced in some hay, when Lieutenant Leathes, who had been reconnoitring, brought intelligence that the people were still up in an adjoining miller's house, and that they were willing to give us shelter until morning. Thither, therefore, we repaired; and being ushered into the kitchen, quite a pattern of neatness, found the good woman and one of her men already busy making a fire and preparing some coffee for us—unlooked-for luxury! To this kindness she added the offer of two beds, which were eagerly and thankfully accepted by Lieutenants Ingleby and Bell. For my part, I preferred not pulling off my wet clothes and putting them on again in the morning, and therefore declined. Spite of our fatigue, we were all so refreshed by the coffee, that a pleasant hour was passed chatting to our kind hostess and joking with her man Coché, a sort of good-humoured, half-witted Caliban. At last sleep began to weigh heavily on our eyelids. The lady retired to her chamber, Coché hid himself somewhere, and, sinking back in our old-fashioned, high-backed chairs, we were soon unconscious of everything.

14*th*.—Awoke from my slumbers just as the grey dawn began to render objects visible in the kitchen. My companions still slept soundly, so without disturbing them I quietly explored my way to the door, and soon found myself in a pretty little garden, ornamented and intersected by high hedges or walls of verdure, the young leaves of which, scarcely yet fully developed, were of the brightest green. These screens, effectually protecting the beds, in which many an early flower already blossomed, I thought delightful. It was the first time I had seen these *brise-vents*, or hornbeam hedges, which I subsequently found so common. The air of the morning was delicious, and my clothes having dried during my repose, I again felt comfortable and happy as I sauntered about the garden, enjoying the morning song of the little birds, with which the whole neighbourhood resounded. I could have stayed for ever in this tranquil and, as I then thought it, lovely retreat. By and by my companions turned out, and we lost no time in getting again under way in order to reach the gates of Ostend as soon as they opened.

Sass, or Schlickens, where we had passed the night, is the port of the Bruges canal, and hence the Treckschuyt from Ostend for that city takes its departure. It cannot be called a village, there being only a few small houses connected with the canal business, and some sawmills and others worked by wind. Surrounded by marsh, it is a dreary comfortless place, although this was hidden from me in the early morning by the verdant screens in the miller's garden.

Our road back to the town, now we had daylight, appeared very short, and having dried considerably, was not so slippery as last night. The gates were not yet opened when we arrived; a crowd of workmen of different kinds had already assembled and were waiting for admission, as were we, for a few minutes. At last they opened, and we proceeded to the harbour in search of our ship. The Quais, beach, etc., were thronged as on the day before, and we added to the bustle in disembarking our guns and carriages, etc. This was completed by eleven o'clock, and we were ready to march forward; but the commissariat detained us waiting the issue of our rations until 3 p.m.—four mortal hours, considering our eagerness to get on and explore this new country, and the bore of being confined to one spot, since it was impossible to wander about the town, seeing that we could not calculate the moment when these gentry might find it convenient to supply us. Of our horses two were still missing, as were some saddle-bags and a number of smaller articles; and this is not to be wondered at when the scandalous manner in which they were thrown overboard, the badness of the weather, the darkness of the night, together with the ebbing and flowing of the tide, are taken into consideration.

The appearance, too, of the troop was vexatious in the extreme. Our noble horses, yesterday morning so sleek and spirited, now stood with drooping heads and rough staring coats, plainly indicating the mischief they had sustained in being taken from a hot hold, plunged into cold water, and then exposed for more than seven hours on an open beach to such a tempest of wind and rain as that we experienced last night. Here was a practical illustration of the folly of grooming and pampering military horses, destined as they are to such exposures and privations. As for our men, they looked jaded, their clothes all soiled with mud and wet, the sabres rusty, and the bear-skins of their helmets flattened down by the rain. Still, however, they displayed the same spirit and alacrity as that which has always been a characteristic of the horse-artillery, more particularly of G troop.

Whilst thus awaiting our rations, we had ample leisure to look about us, and amuse ourselves with the varied groups collected on the quay and the novelty of the scene. To be sure, the principal of these were English, and mostly soldiers too. Some were drinking at the doors of the cabarets, knapsacks on their backs, and prepared to start; others already in movement, escorting baggage; near us a battery of field-artillery parked, with their horses picketed in a long line along the rear of the carriages, quietly eating their corn out of hair nosebags, which ever and anon they would toss in the air, the better to get at the few remaining grains of their food; gunners and drivers lying about ready to fall in or mount at the shortest notice. Here they had passed the night, and the remains of their fires were still glowing in some rudely constructed fireplaces of loose stones or bricks. Such objects were familiar to our eyes, but they were intermixed with

others which were not.   These were the Flemish peasantry,
with their heavy countenances, walking by the side of their
long, narrow waggons, and guiding their noble horses with
admirable dexterity through the throng by long reins of small
(very small) cord passing through holes in the clumsy highly
ornamental collars or haims.   Long blue smock-frocks,
decorated with embroidery in coloured worsted about the
breast and shoulders; their skulls ensconced in night-caps,
red or white; many with long thick queues—and all in clumsy
wooden shoes.   Women, with hard weather-beaten features,
in long-eared caps, enormous gold pendants in their ears, a
small cross on the breast, suspended from the scraggy neck
by a strip of black velvet, thick petticoats, giving great swell
to the hip, and from their shortness exhibiting a pair of stout
understanders cased in coarse blue stockings and terminating
in heavy sabots, enriched about the instep by a rabbit's skin
clumped about in all directions.   From time to time a patrol
of the gendarmerie, in plain blue uniforms, with large white
grenades on the skirts and the ends of their valises, broad
belts, and high, stiff, well-polished boots, passed quietly
through the assembled crowds; their quick inquiring eyes
cast searchingly about as they moved leisurely along.   At the
corner of the quay was a group of boatmen (not much
differing in outward appearance from our own of the same
class) listlessly reclining on the pavement, or lounging up
and down with folded arms, amusing themselves with the
bustling anxiety of a score of soldiers' wives, who, loaded
with children or bundles, their ample grey or faded red
cloaks flying out loosely behind them, struggled through all
impediments opposed to their progress with an activity,
perseverance, and volubility which seemed highly diverting
to the mariners, many of whom, in broken English, were
bantering these amazons, or exchanging coarse jokes with
them; at which play, however—the ladies being mostly from
the Green Isle—the gentlemen came off second best.

   Such were the scenes we contemplated, when a loud cry
of dismay suddenly pervaded the crowd, and all simultaneously rushed to the ramparts.   I followed this movement.   The morning, though somewhat overcast, had been
fine, and the wind moderate; but as the day advanced, and
the flood-tide set in, the south-westerly breeze had gradually

increased to a gale. On reaching the rampart, I immediately observed that the flat shore to the northward, as far as the eye could reach, was covered with a sheet of white foam from the tremendous surf breaking on it; whilst the spray, rising in clouds and borne along before the blast, involved the whole neighbourhood in a thick salt mist. Nothing could be more savage and wild than the appearance of the coast. In the offing, numerous vessels under small sail were running for the harbour One small brig had missed, and before assistance could be given, had been whirled round the *jetée*, and cast broadside on amongst the breakers. Her situation was truly awful. The surf broke over her in a frightful manner, sending its spray higher than her masts, and causing her to roll from side to side until her yards dipped in the water, and induced a belief every moment that she must roll over. Every now and then a huge wave, larger than its predecessor, would raise her bodily, and then, rapidly receding, suddenly let her fall on the ground again with a concussion that made the masts bend and vibrate like fishing-rods, and seemed to threaten instant annihilation. Of her sails, some were torn to rags, and others, flying loose, flapped and fluttered with a noise that was audible from the rampart, despite the roaring of the surf. The people on board appeared in great agitation, and kept shouting to those on shore for assistance, which they were unable to give. Intense anxiety pervaded the assembled multitude as the shattered vessel alternately rose to view or was buried in a sea of foam. Numbers ran down to the sands opposite to her; and from them she could not have been twenty yards distant, yet could they not afford the despairing crew the slightest aid. Whilst thus attending in breathless expectation the horrid catastrophe, the return of our quartermaster with the rations summoned us unwillingly from the rampart to commence our march. We afterwards learnt that a boat from the harbour had succeeded in saving the crew (she had no troops on board); but the unfortunate pilot who thus gallantly risked his own life for them was killed by the boat rising suddenly under the vessel's counter as he stood in the bow, which dashed his brains out.

Of Ostend I have little to say, my whole time and mind being fully occupied during the few hours of my stay in it.

The impression it made on me was a dismal one. Narrow
dirty streets; gloomy, old-fashioned, low, mean houses; the
whole surrounded by marsh, sand-hills, or sea; and that sea,
from its muddy colour, detracting nought from the lugubrious
effect of the scene. Of the fortifications I saw still less than
of the town; yet, from what little I did see, it would appear
that Ostend depends more upon water than earth or stone—
its great protection consisting in the facility of inundating the
neighbouring marshes. On the Blanckenberg side, situated
upon an eminence (I think of sand), we had a glimpse of Fort
Napoleon, and working parties were busy constructing a
redoubt among the sand-hills toward Nieuport. We had no
leisure, however, to visit either.

CHAPTER III

RIGHT glad were we to find ourselves at last *en route* from this dismal place. In passing through the streets towards the barrier, soon after leaving the quays, we found that we had likewise left all the bustle, crowd, and confusion behind us. Few people were moving about in any of them, and some were totally deserted. The prospect which presented itself on issuing from the gates was as *triste* and repulsive as can well be conceived. In front and to the left marsh! marsh! for miles, and looking black, dreary, and pestilential; the distance obscured by a red haze, occasioned by the clouds of sand blown inland by the gale from a range of sand and sandhills (the dunes) extending all along the coast. A straight, ill-paved, and muddy road, running away in long perspective between two wide ditches filled with stagnant stinking water, bordered here and there by a few stunted willows bending to the blast, and their usual cold colour rendered still more cold by thus exposing the whitish backs of their young leaves. Such was the scene, in which our column (men, horses, and carriages, soiled, and looking miserable; the mounted gunners leaning to windward, with one hand generally upraised holding on their helmets; the limber-gunners sitting sideways, turning their backs to the gale) formed an appropriate accompaniment, as it proceeded slowly along the causeway. About half-way to Ghystelles,[1] at a barrier, we were rejoiced at finding the horses that had escaped from us on the sands. The man said they had been there all night.

After traversing these marshes for about five or six miles, we entered on a country almost as flat, but of a very different character, highly cultivated and well wooded. The road became an avenue, whilst the adjoining fields were interspersed everywhere with patches of copsewood, and rows of tufted bushes serving here and there as boundaries in place

---

[1] *Ghistel*, according to the map of Maillart, etc.

of hedges; the scenery, of course, much more pleasing, although not seen to advantage under the still gloomy, overcast sky.

It was late when we reached Ghistel, the appearance of which, however, was consolatory, and promised some comfort.

Before we could seek that, a troublesome task still remained to be performed. Our men could not understand their billets, some of which were on isolated farms a mile or two from the village; neither could they inquire their way. It therefore became necessary for us to accompany and see them safely housed ere we could resign ourselves to the enjoyments of our auberge. In the village itself they were soon put up, for many of the people spoke or understood a little English.

At length, as night set in, our business was finished, and we all assembled at our auberge, which, though humble, was delightfully clean, and to us, after last night's adventure, appeared luxurious. No less so was the excellent dinner to which we soon sat down; whilst doing justice to which we could not help laughing at its spread, for it was composed, not of solid joints, etc. etc., but of an immense multitude and variety of little dishes of stews and all sorts of nameless (to us) things. A bottle of good port would have rendered us superlatively happy, but that was not to be thought of in Ghistel; so having amused ourselves, and puzzled the neat, pretty, black-eyed girl who officiated as *garçon* by our inquiries for this our national, but by her unheard-of, beverage, we were fain to make ourselves comfortable, and pass the evening in social chat over the poor, thin, though well-flavoured liquor that the house afforded. Some of our number, to be sure, were unreasonable enough to grumble, and one actually got the stomach-ache, but whether from the wine or last night's wetting it is difficult to say, though he swore it was the former.

I shall not easily forget my delight on retiring, when I found a most clean, enticing bed prepared for me, in a pretty little room, the window of which looked into a quiet well-kept garden. The enormous pillow at first took me aback. Such a thing! It seemed to occupy half the bed. I, however, soon made acquaintance with it, and enjoyed a most delicious sleep. The first steps in a new country are to me always a source of pleasurable sensations. Everything one sees is striking, interesting, and makes a lasting impression. This evening and its enjoyments will long remain a bright spot in my memory.

15th.—A fine, mild, grey morning. Our people paraded in much better order, and very much higher spirits, than yesterday, and all seemed pleased with their entertainment. The novelty amused them, and every one had some tale to relate of last night's adventures. Their hosts had generally been very kind to them, and allowed them to take as much forage for their horses as they chose. The poor animals, therefore, had passed the night equally well. In marching out of Ghistel, I noticed many houses of a superior description to the rustic dwellings which alone I saw last night. Some of these had much the appearance of stage scenery, having façades painted to represent pilasters, urns, wreaths, festoons, etc. etc., all in very childish taste. These, no doubt, were the villas or *lusthausen* of the Ostend citizens.

Our march to Bruges (about twelve miles) was through a country perfectly flat, but rich and highly cultivated; and from the numerous little woods, farms, and substantial villages—added, again, to the charm of novelty—it was far from uninteresting.

About noon we entered the city by a fine, broad, airy street, rendered pleasing by the intermixture of foliage with its picturesque buildings, and swarming with people. By and by we came to narrower streets and more antiquated-looking houses; winding our way amongst which we at last reached the cavalry barrack, situated in a narrow, dirty back lane at the farther extremity of the town—a large, heavy, inelegant mass of masonry, more like some old storehouse than a barrack. Here, in the extensive yard, we parked our guns, and put our men into the barrack, the rooms of which were large, lofty, and vaulted, but extremely filthy, so that our people had to regret the clean comfortable billets and kind hospitality which they would have enjoyed amongst the inhabitants. A range of ruinous wooden sheds, extending along two sides of the yard, served as stabling, and received all our horses.

Having arranged affairs at the barrack, and called on Sir F. Lyons, the British commandant, we betook ourselves to our billet at the Hôtel de Commerce, which, however, we had some difficulty in finding. As this was the first large hotel we had been in, it had the recommendation of novelty, and everything in it became subject of curiosity. The large dreary hall; the comfortless bar adjoining, and separated from it by an immense window or glazed partition, so unlike the cheerful snug-looking bar of an English inn; the equally comfortless and gloomy saloon behind it, into which we were shown; the squalid, dirty appearance of the domestics (men or boys), in filthy cotton jackets and *bonnets de nuit*—all served to chill one on first entering. Our arrival, followed by orderlies and servants carrying portmanteaus, etc. etc., caused a sensation in the establishment, every member of which, not excepting the chef, was assembled to greet us in the hall. For some minutes a scene of bustle ensued, which ended in mounting the stairs to inspect our dormitories. These contrasted strangely with the vast apartments below. From the head of the staircase a long corridor ran right and left the whole length of the house, off which a number of doors opened into as many little cells, each barely large enough to contain bed, chair, and a small table. The beds (without curtains) were very homely, but quite clean, the furniture and utensils of the commonest kind. The attend-ants, having shown us our rooms, withdrew, and with the sound of their departing footsteps ended the bustle of the day. When I again stepped out on the gallery, the stillness of the place astonished me—hall, staircase, bar, all deserted; not a soul to be seen, nor a sound heard except that of my own tread over the creaking floor; no ringing of bells; no calls for chambermaid, boots, or waiter; no running to and fro;— in short, the place appeared altogether abandoned, and I hastened into the street to lounge away the time until dinner, of which, however, I had my misgivings.

Bruges is a highly interesting town at all times; but after being shut out from the Continent so many years, the novelty of everything one saw enhanced this interest amazingly. My ramble led me through streets of lofty, whimsically con-structed houses, the upper parts of which sometimes pro-jected in the manner one frequently sees in our old midland towns, the projections decorated with drop-balls on fretwork; immense windows sometimes occupied the whole front of each floor; ample portals, the lofty folding doors of which were occasionally studded with iron, like those of a fortress or dungeon; gables, with high pointed roofs, presented almost everywhere to the street; chimneys of bizarre and fantastic forms, and surmounted by a finish of semicircular tiles rising pyramidally over each other; here and there towers or turrets with high conical roofs;—such were the architectural peculiarities that attracted my attention. The long streets running in wavy lines, and of unequal breadth, between these grotesque buildings, exhibited specimens of costume as novel, and frequently not less grotesque, which, intermingling with the scarlet and blue uniforms of our soldiers, very much heightened the picturesque effect. It was only in the principal thoroughfares and business parts of the town that all this animation was met with. In those quarters principally inhabited by the richer citizens the streets were as dull, solitary, and scrupulously clean as it is possible to conceive. In these I frequently found myself the only animated being visible—not a loiterer at a door, not even a head at a window. Many of even the best houses appeared absolutely uninhabited. Could this have always been the case? Was this the state of things when Bruges was the central mart for the whole Pays Bas, and saw merchants from every nation in Europe crowding to its fairs in search of its linen and woollen cloth, and of the naval stores and rich productions of India continually arriving from the north, the Venetian and other Italian States, when the splendid dress and magnificent palaces of its citizens were sufficient to excite the indignation and envy of a queen? Surely not. These grass-grown streets, now so solitary, then exhibited very different scenes. Many a plumed and portly burgher then trod their pavement, and many a fair bejewelled dame graced the numerous windows of its palaces, now so silent. This decay and depopulation dates from the moment when these wealthy merchants arrogantly resisted their sovereign, Maximilian, who, aided by Antwerp and Amsterdam, shut up its port of Sluys, and thus diverting its commerce into other channels, inflicted on it that punishment the effects of which are so perceptible even after a lapse of more than three hundred years. From these melancholy monuments of fallen grandeur, and the death-like silence of these deserted streets, I suddenly emerged into the midst of bustle in the Grand Place, where crowds of peasantry were assembled apparently for the sole purpose of buying and selling little earthen pots of a peculiar form (*terrines*), the number of which, disposed in long rows on the ground, really surprised me. The Stadthouse stands in this place. It has a lofty square tower, surmounted by another of nearly equal height of an octagonal form. This certainly possesses no beauty, but the singularity of the construction attracts notice. From the Place I wandered to the *Cathédrale*,[1] the very lofty spire of which, I am told, serves as a landmark for vessels approaching Ostend, though certainly I do not recollect having seen it there. It is even *said* by some to be visible from the *banks of the Thames*—a pretty long view! Entering the temple, I found the garish light of broad day exchanged for a mysterious twilight, and the busy hum of high market for a solemn silence, scarcely interrupted by the light step of some veiled female (of males only a few, very old men, were there) as she glided to the spot chosen for her devotions, where, rapidly crossing herself, she sank on her knees before a shrine in some side chapel. At the high altar, priests in embroidered robes were celebrating mass with a solemnity which rendered still more ridiculous their repeated genuflexions, the extinction from time to time of a taper, and the removal of a crucifix from one end of the altar to another, only to bring it back the next moment, whilst ever and anon they would bow, cross themselves, and bow again.

The nave of the church was not spoilt, as ours are, by pews. A number of plain chairs were assembled round the pillars, and these served the worshippers to kneel upon—that is, the men, for the women invariably sank on the pavement in most picturesque attitudes. Of the latter, most seemed in earnest; but with the former, a duty was hurried through, in which the heart had evidently little or no concern. Some certainly placed both knees on the chairs, and, leaning over the backs with clasped hands, kept their eyes steadily on the altar, whilst the rapid motion of their lips betrayed the hurried manner in which they prayed. Others, however, with one knee only on the chair, and the body half-turned,

---

[1] The Church of Notre Dame ceased to be a cathedral 1801, when it was united to the diocese of Ghent.

gazed about them whilst mumbling over their daily portion
of prayer.   People were continually coming in and going out,
which seemed to disturb no one, but rather served as amusement to the gazers just mentioned.   However lukewarm the
frequenters of the temple might evince themselves, yet was
there something very impressive in the scene.   In a pictorial
point of view it was most interesting, for the building is a fine
Gothic structure, and the interior of these always affords
picturesque scenery, even without such accessories as those
furnished by the various kneeling groups, more particularly
of females.   Some good pictures I saw, but did not like to
stop and examine them.   A striking feature in this church
are the colossal statues of the Apostles perched upon shelves,
one to each column of the nave: the effect is not good.   The
pulpit, and staircase leading up to it, are a most elaborate
and ingenious example of sculpture in wood.   The impression
on me was one of wonder at the inexhaustible patience of the
artist.   Sauntering about the church, near the great door I
stumbled upon something not unlike a sentry-box; it was
a confessional!   In this sat a sleek-looking priest, head resting on his left hand, and the ear inclined to a little grated
aperture in one side, through which a female on her knees,
and shrouded in a black veil, poured out her heart in a loud
whisper.   The holy man received the communication with
becoming gravity, though it was easy to divine, by a short
perusal of his countenance, that he was receiving nothing but
commonplace, or at best no very important, intelligence.
Everything in this religion appears most childish mummery;
what more so than this?   Leaving Notre Dame, I sought the
ramparts.   These no longer exist in a military sense, but the
high grassy mounds which remain, being planted with trees,
serve at once as a pretty promenade, and diversify the views
of the city from without.   The moat in most places still
remains green—almost as the meadows—with aquatic plants.
Some of the ancient gateways, also, are still there to tell a tale
of other times.   These, with their sombre grey towers,
roofed with tile, are eminently picturesque, and harmonise
well with the other buildings of the town.   These towers,
with high conical roofs, which one meets almost everywhere
throughout the Continent, particularly in this country, form
a characteristic feature, distinguishing its scenery from that

of the British Islands, where the ruins of ancient castles have
almost invariably their round or square towers terminated by
a castellated parapet and flat roof. True it is that the Irish
round towers have such roofs; but they are low, and form a
very small portion in the general aspect of the building: as
also those solitary square towers seen along the Scottish
Border, and sprinkled here and there over the soil of Ireland
—the dwellings or keeps of petty chieftains—were also surmounted by high, but not conical roofs.

Tired of rambling about the streets, I returned to our
hotel, where, to my surprise, an excellent dinner awaited me,
exceedingly well served, and the attendants (who had made
themselves clean) very active and obliging. Among these a
boy of fifteen or sixteen was a perfect beauty—so much so as
to excite universal admiration. Nor must I forget another
beauty of a far different kind—some very old and genuine
cognac. It was quite a liqueur; and we were so pleased with
it, that each secured a small stock to carry forward with him.
In short, we went to bed in better humour with the Hôtel
de Commerce.

CHAPTER IV

16th.—Marched through a country very similar to that of yesterday—that is, flat rich soil, highly cultivated, very populous, and diversified with patches of wood, etc.—to Eccloo (*chéf lieu du canton*), a neat little village consisting of two broad streets forming a sort of place at the point of union, here we parked our guns, despite the objections of the inhabitants, who were woefully afraid of an explosion. The Duke of Wellington, *en route* to Ostend, passed as we were forming up, and scrutinised us pretty closely, but said nothing, although I afterwards learned that it was positively against orders to park ammunition of any kind in a village.

The landlord of the only auberge was so very insolent that we formed a mess for the day in one of our billets, our own servants cooking for us. The fare was not sumptuous, but *en revanche,* very cheap, consisting entirely of our rations. My own billet here was in the house of a widow, who kept a hardware shop—humble, but, as usual in this country, a pattern of cleanliness. Returning from the mess, I joined the old lady and her daughter in their little parlour behind the shop, and two or three neighbours coming in, the conversation became animated. The subject was the return of Napoleon and the probable consequences. According to their ideas, our cause was hopeless. Last year our hostess had lodged an officer of Cossacks, whom she described as a most gentlemanly man.

17th.—The same description of country accompanied us to Ghent. At the large village of Lovendeghem the road joined the canal; and here we obtained the first view of this celebrated city, the birthplace of Charles V., and the scene of so many interesting events in the history of the Middle Ages, forming with its numerous towers a fine termination to the long vista of the canal.

Nearer the coast the trees had been small and somewhat

26

stunted; indeed, most of the woods we had seen were merely coppice. Here, however, they assumed a different character, being of large size and great luxuriance, giving a much higher interest to the landscape as they bordered the fine meadows lying along either side of the canal, on the bank of which our road lay. The scenery now became further enriched and enlivened by the frequent occurrence of country-seats, generally of brick, and embowered in foliage; a lawn stretching down to the canal, and terminated by a terrace with a low parapet-wall and a summer-house at one end of it. The only boat, however, we met was the packet going to Bruges; and the road itself was so solitary that, had not our eyes convinced us to the contrary, we should never have imagined ourselves approaching so rich and populous a city.

About 2 p.m. we reached the canal harbour, separated from the city by a handsome *barrière* (*grille*) or iron railing in imitation of spears, the shafts painted light blue, with gilded blades. A small building, with the word "*Octroi*" in large letters over the door, stood on one side of the gate by which we now entered the capital of Flanders, and immediately found ourselves in a fine broad street, with large and stately houses on either side. Yet the very first impression was that of disappointment. The street was lonely, almost deserted, and nearly every second house exhibited a board bearing a notice in French and Flemish that it was to sell or let—"Maison à louer," "Huys zu heuer," or "Maison à vendre," etc. etc. Curious it is that two languages should be indispensably necessary; but such seems to be the case here, for I observed that all proclamations and public notices of any kind were invariably in French and Flemish. We proceeded some way through the same sort of quiet and (apparently) depopulated region; but at last, crossing a broad canal, or, may be, one of the several rivers which here unite, we came at once into the very heart of bustle, business, fine shops, and crowds of people, continuing on nearly a mile, through all which we at last reached the cavalry barracks (our destination), quite at the farther extremity of the town, near the Barrière de Bruxelles, where we parked our guns and put up our horses; but there was no room for the men, consequently they were billeted.[1] Nothing could be more in-

[1] M'Donald's troop had arrived ten days before us.

convenient than this arrangement, though I believe it could not be helped, the place being already crowded with troops, English and French—for this was the headquarters of Louis XVIII.'s phantom of an army.   Upon ascertaining the situation of our billets, too, we found things still worse, these being generally in the Quartier de Bruge, a distance of nearly one and a half miles from the barrack, and some still farther off—one detachment being billeted at La Barqué, a cabaret on the canal harbour, and another at some village still farther off. A serious inconvenience this for horse-soldiers, whose duties required them to be so continually at the barrack, and most harassing when it is recollected that the distance from barrier to barrier is reckoned three miles—the whole distance over an execrable pavement.   It was not without some trouble that I succeeded in finding my own billet in Bruge Straet, a respectable house, but nowise remarkable either for size or architecture.   My host, a stout cheerful-looking old gentleman, whose bearing and dress bespoke the opulent citizen, met me in the gateway, and with great cordiality (recognising my billet) ushered me into a large room by the side of the brick-paved entry, announcing it as mine during my stay, at the same time offering me the use of his whole establishment, particularly of his cook.   This last I accepted with pleasure, having arranged with my officers that our mess should be in my quarter, wherever that might be.   Meantime, my baggage-cart having been drawn up the narrow yard and the horses dismissed, the great gates reclosed, and the bustle of arrival subsided, everything sank into silence—a silence as predominating in the street without as within the house.

My apartment was a large, lofty, long room, running back from the street, towards which two high windows admitted such insufficient light that even in fine weather it was particularly gloomy.   At the farther end two folding-doors cut off a portion of its length, and this was fitted up as a bed-chamber—dark enough.   The furniture of the *salle* consisted of a few common chairs and a large table covered with oilcloth.   The floor was without carpet, as the windows were without either blinds or curtains.   How the rest of the house might have been fitted up I am ignorant, having seen no more of its interior than the kitchen, which opened into the yard, and that was certainly the neatest and cleanest I ever saw, with its red floor and red stoves and highly polished brass pans, etc. etc. Nor did I ever see much more of the inhabitants; for, with the exception of two females in the kitchen, the house seemed deserted. A man-servant certainly assisted at our dinner, but we rarely saw even him at any other time. Not a voice—not a footfall—not a sound of any kind, unless emanating from ourselves, ever disturbed the death-like silence that reigned through this establishment. Mine host was, I believe, a merchant, and went out every morning to his business, whence he returned not until the evening, at least as far as I could ascertain. I saw nothing more of him from my first reception until I called to take leave and thank him for his attentions and hospitality. These consisted in the assistance of his servants and the use of his beer-cask, on which we drew for our daily supply.

During the seven days we remained in Ghent, our time was so occupied by duties that there was little leisure to look about us. Twice every day it was necessary to be at the barracks, so that a very great portion of my time was spent in walking backward and forward between them and Bruge Straet.

Amongst other duties it fell to our lot to furnish a guard of honour to Louis XVIII., then residing in Ghent, his own troops having been sent to Alost to make room for the British, which were continually passing through. Our subalterns were very well pleased with this arrangement, for the duty was nothing. They found an excellent table, and passed their time very agreeably with the young men of the *garde du corps*, some of whom were always in attendance. Many of these were mere boys, and the anteroom of his most Christian Majesty frequently exhibited bolstering matches and other amusements, savouring strongly of the boarding-school; however, they were good-natured, and always most attentive to the comforts of the officer on guard. The royal stud was in the barrack stables, and consisted principally of grey horses, eighteen or twenty of which had been purchased in England at a sale of *cast horses* from the Scots Greys.

We frequently met French officers of all ranks, and formed acquaintance with many gentlemanly, well-informed men. At the Lion d'Or and Hôtel de Flandre we found there was a table d'hôte every night at eight o'clock, and by way of passing

the evening, usually resorted to one or the other for supper.
Here we were sure of meeting many Frenchmen, and as the
same people were generally constant attendants, we became
intimate, and discussed the merits of our national troops
respectively over our wine or *ponche*.   It was the first time
most of them had had an opportunity of inspecting British
troops closely, though many had often met them in the field;
and they were very curious in their inquiries into the organisation, government, and equipment of our army.   Although
allowing all due credit to the bravery displayed by our troops
in the Peninsula, and the talents of our General (the Duke),
yet were they unanimous in their belief that neither would
avail in the approaching conflict, and that we must succumb
before their idol and his grand army;   for though these
gentlemen had deserted Napoleon to follow the fortunes of
Louis XVIII., it was evident they still revered the former.
Their admiration of our troops, particularly of the cavalry,
was very great;   but they expressed astonishment at seeing
so few decorations.   It was in vain we asserted that medals
were rarely given in the British army, and then only to
commanding officers, etc.   They shook their heads, appeared
incredulous, and asked, "Where are the troops that fought in
Spain?"   There might have been something more than mere
curiosity in all this.   There might have been an anxiety to
ascertain whether their countrymen were about to cope with
veterans or young soldiers.   It might have been thrown out
as a lure, to provoke information relative to the present
employment of those veteran bands.   Moreover, I shrewdly
suspected many of these gentlemen were actually spies.
Amongst others who had followed Louis XVIII. was Marmont.   I think it was the day after our arrival, passing over
the open space near the Place d'Armes, by the river, I saw a
French general officer exercising a horse in the *manège*, and
learnt with astonishment that this was Marmont;   for the
man in question had *two* good arms—whereas, for years past,
I had, in common with most people in England, looked upon
it as a fact that he had left one at Salamanca.   French
deserters, both officers and privates, were daily coming in;   it
was said they deserted by hundreds.   Be that as it may, I
one day saw a column of thirty march up to the Bureau des
Logemens.   They were in a most miserable plight—all in

rags—and apparently half-starved. All these deserters, as well as the rest, were forwarded without delay to Alost. The Commissaire des Logemens told me that, after the departure of the French troops to Alost, there still remained more than three hundred of his Majesty's immediate followers for whom it was necessary to provide in Ghent.

The huzzars of the K.G. Legion, stationed about Detto, and toward the frontier, frequently sent intelligence of hostile movements; but except this, we were in perfect ignorance of the positions either of our own or the French army. Regiments arrived from England, halted a night, and were off again we knew not where.

Meantime we lived well, and saw as much of the place as our scanty time would permit. The markets were most abundantly supplied with everything, and very cheap; so that with the assistance of our *bourgmestre's* cook we kept an excellent table at a moderate rate. As for our horses, although they had exhibited symptoms of having felt their exposure on the sands at Ostend when we first arrived, yet rest and good forage soon restored their original appearance and we began to get tired of Ghent, and long for a forward move.

I cannot, however, bid adieu to Ghent without recording a few notes, which my confined means of observation enabled me to preserve; and be it remembered that, at that period, the continent of Europe was almost a *terra incognita* to Englishmen, to whom everything, therefore, even trifles, bore a degree of interest, which our present intimate acquaintance may cause to appear puerile at the present day.

I need not say that Ghent is a large and populous city, standing upon ground generally flat, intersected and divided into numerous islands by three or four rivers, besides canals, which hold their course through it, nor that it is the birthplace of the Emperor Charles V.; but I may add that Ghent, independent of its historical recollections, is, and ever must be, a most interesting place, particularly to the artist; for where can we see such picturesque street-scenes as are exhibited here? The streets, bordered by lofty houses generally of a quaint style of architecture, wind their devious way—now narrow, now spreading out to an ample breadth—with an irregularity that certainly leaves no room to complain of sameness. This irregularity attaches as much to the houses as to the streets. These are of every variety—high stepped gables towards the street, little turrets with pointed roofs, others with large French windows, and, again, others all window, as at Bruges. These, intermingled with, and partially seen through the foliage of the trees, which in many places border the canals, etc., offer most picturesque morsels, precisely such as one sees in the pictures of the old Flemish painters, so that they appeared quite familiar. This effect is considerably heightened by the deep embrasures of the windows, lofty grotesquely ornamented portals, and, above all, the rich deep tone of colouring that pervaded the whole. Chapels and churches, too—some in the Gothic, others Italian, or still more modern styles—intervened continually, the whole forming rich perspectives, animated by the varied and bustling crowds of citizens, peasants, soldiers, etc. One peculiarity struck me as savouring much of indolence and curiosity combined: almost every house, at one or more windows of the first floor, had small square mirrors, sometimes single, sometimes double, so arranged that persons seated within the room could see the passengers on the *trottoir* below without stirring from their seats. In English towns one constantly sees heads peeping over the blinds; here, no one is seen at the windows.

Near the centre of the city is the Place d'Armes, a large square, having the area ornamented by rows of well-grown linden trees, and its houses of a superior character to those in the adjoining quarters. This is the focus of business, and in this neighbourhood one sees all the best shops, some of which astonished us by the profuse display of Indian goods, particularly silk pocket-handkerchiefs, which we found of the very finest quality, and at about half the price they sold at in England. The Place d'Armes is, however, spoiled in a great measure by the shabby wooden railing enclosing the promenade.

In this square was a magnificent hotel, at least as far as outward appearance went. The Duc de Berri had his quarters in it; and one day, as I returned from the barrack, I saw him set off for Alost. This was the first travelling equipage I had seen in the country; and consequently I was much amused with the coxcombry and costume of the postilions—their glazed hats stuck on one side; queues, each with the side-hair neatly plaited in; short, very short jackets; and, above all, the enormous jackboots. But if the costume amused, the dexterity with which they handled their whips astonished me—"klang-klang-klang,"—between them they almost made music. The rapid and dexterous manner in which, flourishing their whips over their heads, they crack them—before, behind, right, and left—is of a piece with that manual dexterity with which our laboratory-boys make ball-cartridges, and our drummers, by quickly repeated but distinct taps, produce a rolling sound in which the most delicate ear cannot detect a break. But to return from this digression.

The very little time I had to myself did not admit of seeing half the place, and my wanderings were pretty much confined to the neighbourhood of the line between Bruges Straet and the barrack. Sometimes, however, I did extend a little to the right and left, and in one of these excursions got a glimpse, but no more, of some pleasant gardens—public, I suppose—in which numerous walks, overarched with verdure, intersected each other, and presented, as the weather was hot, most inviting retreats. At another time I wandered as far as the Citadel—I suppose the one built by William III. of England, not that of Charles V., of which not a vestige remains. It must have been but an insignificant work;—the plan, I think, a parallelogram. The mounds of the ramparts remain entire, and the wet ditch. At present it is completely overlooked by the neighbouring houses. From this work, which is situated just without the *barrière* of the road to Thermonde, one commands a prospect, perhaps of its kind unrivalled. Here are no picturesque or romantic features, but the eye wanders unimpeded over a region as flat as the ocean, and, like it, only terminating in the distant horizon. This region is amongst the richest in the world, and, spite of its flatness, offers to our view a scene at once pleasing and astonishing. Verdant meadows, enamelled with myriads of yellow and white flowers, amidst which graze innumerable herds of the finest cattle, extend for miles from the city, and then, intermingled with corn-fields, groves, and thickets, amidst which are seen everywhere villages, farms, and scattered houses, melt gradually away into the blue distance. In the immediate foreground, a singular hillock, crowned by a little chapel and environed by trees, rears its form and enhances the picture by variety of feature and the interesting peeps admitted between the openings of the foliage. The road from Thermonde passes through this grove, and, covered as it generally is (or was, when I saw it) with groups of market-people, carts, and cattle, etc., throws a charming animation into the scene. The lengthened perspective, too, of this road running away in a straight line bordered by trees, and gradually diminishing until lost in the distance, breaks the unvaried flatness of the meadows, and prevents one feeling them monotonous. Returning from the Citadel, I joined the rustic crowd pouring in through the *barrière*, and, following the stream, was brought by it into an extensive square surrounded by lofty and antique-looking houses, apparently the exclusive abode of the humbler classes of merchants or artisans. The crowd here was immense; and it was not without difficulty that I made my way through it. I think this is the Marché aux Grains. Not far from thence I stumbled on the great gun, called the Basilisc,[1] said to have been cast by order of Charles V., to overawe the Ghentois. As far as I could see, this enormous piece, which reposes on a mass of brickwork in an open space at the turn of the street, is a plain unornamented cylinder of iron (wrought). It was too high for minute inspection. The pedestal upon which it rests serves also as a public fountain, about which are usually groups of gossiping women with their pitchers under their arms, or noisy boys.

Amongst the buildings of Ghent, interesting from their style, the ancient Gothic Hôtel de Ville stands pre-eminent, with its rich and elaborately ornamented façades. This venerable pile is said to have been built, at least the older part of it, in the beginning of the seventh century. Another remnant of antiquity, perhaps still more old, I discovered in my own neighbourhood—this was the ancient castle, Castrum Ganda (?), a small open space, in the corner of which are the remains of thick walls and one tower still nearly entire—its

---

[1] La Folle Marguerite (?), 18 feet long and 3 feet in diameter, near the Marché de Vendredi ; it is called the Mannekens Aert. It is named after a Countess of Flanders celebrated for the violence of her temper. It is also designated the Wonder of Ghent, is made of malleable iron, and, according to another account, was used by Philip Van Arteveldt at the siege of Oudenarde in 1382.—Quin's *Moselle*, etc., vol. i. p. 160.

different stories affording lodgment to several poor families, from whom, however, I sought in vain for any information respecting these ruins. From the direction of the patches of wall, I conjectured that the open space was once the inner court of the castle.

In the same quarter was one of the markets, through which I passed every day in going to and coming from the barrack; it was for meat and vegetables, etc. The latter were exposed for sale in the open air in baskets, as with us; and here, as everywhere else, one could not but be struck with the great abundance and fine quality of every produce of this rich country. One vegetable seemingly in great request was the tender root of the hop plant. This, when peeled and stewed in milk, is really delicious. We had it every day on our table, and it was a general favourite. A principal occupation of the market-women was peeling these roots, which were then thrown into a basin of cold water to keep them fresh, and thus exposed for sale. The meat-market adjoining was under cover and closed in, like the central avenue of Covent Garden, forming a long street of stalls, each full of the finest meat imaginable, cut up into joints, etc., whilst overhead, suspended under the roof, were innumerable whole carcasses of bullocks, sheep, and pigs. Nothing could exceed the cleanliness of this place, or the neatness and propriety of dress of the butchers, their wives, and daughters. Unlike our markets, there was no loud talking, no confused gabbling of tongues; everything seemed conducted with the utmost quiet, order, and decency. The middle of the passage was thronged with well-dressed people of all classes and both sexes. On entering I was struck with a singular dull murmuring sound that pervaded the building, somewhat resembling the sound of a distant mill, which I soon perceived to be produced by the active industry of the women, who, instead of sitting idly waiting for custom, were all busily employed pounding sausage-meat. If ever I could relish a sausage it would be a Ghent one, for nothing can exceed the cleanliness of the operators and their operations, or the goodness of the materials of which they are made. One may form some idea of the abundance of this fine country from the fact that, having been all last year the seat of war, and now everywhere occupied by numerous foreign troops, still there appeared no diminution in the supplies, and the markets of every town exhibit as great a profusion as ever.

With the exception of a slight sandy eminence at Eccloo, the first undulations of the country we had yet seen were at Ghent. On the southern side of the town I ascended with pleasure a hill, which apparently was the commencement of a sort of rolling country extending towards Deynse. From its summit is an excellent view of the city and the fine country around it. Meadows of the liveliest green, intersected by numerous streams, exhibited everywhere immense quantities of linen exposed for bleaching—such was the scene immediately below. In the distance, as the plain became foreshortened, it seemed to be bounded by woods. The city itself was rendered a more pleasing object by having its sombre masses broken and relieved by large plots of garden-ground and the frequent intervention of foliage. On this hill stood a large square building, once a monastery, but suppressed during the Revolution, like many others. To what use it is now turned I could not guess, as not a living soul was to be seen in or about it of whom to make inquiry. The massive pile, with its numerous windows, high roof, and yawning portal, was not an unpicturesque object. I sauntered into its solitary court; grass had almost overgrown the pavement, and desolation was stamped on every feature. I could not look on all this without indulging in a dream, and in my mind's eye embodying fat and lazy monks strolling about the court, or lounging in idle converse on the stone benches against the sunny wall; again, some more venerable figure passing the corridors in silent meditation. On the road from the town, too, I conjured up groups of ascending and descending brothers, and though not approving of their vocation, could not but regret the absence of their picturesque costume. The only convent I saw besides this in Ghent was an inhabited one, and it is to be hoped always will be. This is the Beguinage, to which I hardly know whether the term "convent" should be applied, for it rather resembles a small town. Each of the sisters has a separate dwelling, with a little flower garden in front of it, much in the style of some of our better kind of almshouses in England. It appears an old building, and is surrounded by a moat.

The Cathedral of St Bavon being in our neighbourhood,

and not much out of the way of my daily walks, I frequently
went in to see what was going on; for one goes to these
Catholic ceremonies as to any other show. This church
makes no great appearance from without, but the interior is
imposing and beautiful, as all Gothic interiors are. The
panels of the choir over the stalls are a series of paintings
exceedingly well executed, representing the acts of St Paul,
I believe. The curiosities of the church are the crypt, the
tombs, and the pulpit. The former of these probably originated in the unsoundness of the ground rendering such a
foundation necessary. Its arches are semicircular, and
spring from low but very massive pillars. Mass is sometimes performed here, but only often enough, I should
imagine, to prevent its desecration. Of the tombs, there are
two of very admirable sculpture—the one in white, the other
in black marble—both, I think, of bishops. The pulpit is
like that of Bruges—an elaborate piece of carving in wood
—notable monument of patience and perseverance. One
evening, attracted by the chanting, I walked in, just as a
procession wound slowly from behind the choir, and advanced
with banners and lighted tapers down the side aisle. The
approaching twilight had thrown every part of the church
into a mysterious obscurity, harmonising well with such a
scene. Two boys in scarlet surplices, with shaven heads,
but beautiful faces, came first, swinging about large handsome censers of silver. The atmosphere was soon impregnated with the smoking frankincense, whose odour was
well calculated to aid the imposing effect. Two banners, in
form resembling the labarum, followed. To these succeeded
a train of priests, in variously coloured, rich, and picturesque
dresses, some bearing other banners of different shapes and
devices; and a number of boys, all habited like those already
mentioned, and equally fair, flanked the procession, and
enveloped it in a light haze by the fumes of their incessantly
swinging censers. The chant had just died away as I
entered the nave, and the procession, with solemn, silent
tread, moved slowly down the aisle—the only sound that
broke upon the ear being the grating rattle of the censer-lids
as they were drawn rapidly up and down the chains. Then
again the full impressive harmony of the chant filled the
vaulted roof with its sweet and solemn notes, died away, and

after another pause was again and again resumed; and thus, having made the circuit of the nave, the procession became gradually lost in the obscurity of the aisle as it slowly retired behind the choir, whence at intervals, softened by distance, the chant still rose over the dividing screen behind the high altar.

Puerile as these exhibitions may be, the effect on me was exciting; and as the last notes were faintly re-echoed through the building, I left it in a frame of mind far different from that in which I had entered.

On the Sunday we passed in Ghent a mass was celebrated expressly for Monsieur (le Comte d'Artois). Expecting something grand I repaired to the cathedral in company with several other officers. We were received with great civility by the functionaries of the establishment, and provided with seats in the stalls and organ-loft. Our party formed the whole congregation, for there were none of the inhabitants. We had not been long seated ere a slight movement and the shuffling of feet in the direction of the grand entrance announced the approach of the illustrious communicant; and Monsieur entered the choir, followed at a little distance by the gentlemen of his suite; a small man of good figure, but of no very distinguished appearance. He was dressed in a blue uniform coat with silver embroidery, white breeches, and silk stockings. He advanced with a quick pace to the steps of the high altar, where a single chair had been placed for him, bowed very low, crossed himself most devoutly, bowed again, and, kneeling on the chair with his arms resting on the back, buried his face in his hands, and in this attitude remained throughout the ceremony. His suite, military and civil, ranged themselves across the choir behind him. A few found chairs, and knelt on them, but the greater part remained standing, and seemed little interested in the service. At length, to my great joy, the last taper was extinguished, and, tired to death, I made my escape, resolved never again to attend a royal mass.

With the interior of the houses in Ghent I had little acquaintance, having seen no more of them than the rooms inhabited by our own officers. In our Quartier de Bruges were many very large and even magnificent ones—some of them in the modern style, with French windows, of three or four stories, or occasionally only one, with a basement entirely blank; others, again, in the heavy antique Flemish style, with large windows in deep embrasures (perhaps with little panes of glass set in lead, and divided by heavy stone mullions)—those on the ground-floor defended by an iron cage, as in Spain; lofty folding-doors, full of iron studs, surmounted by a cumbrous tasteless pediment, or an equally cumbrous escutcheon, looking gloomily magnificent. In all cases, however, the most scrupulous cleanliness and neatness were general characteristics; and as the street-doors usually stood wide open throughout the day, the eye of the passenger, as it glanced through the darkened perspective of the entrance-hall, was sure to be refreshed by the vivid verdure of vines and acacias decorating the interior court—a never-failing accompaniment, particularly to the older houses.

One of my officers, with whom I had established a breakfast mess, was billeted in a house (or rather palace) of the latter description in the Rue de Poivre (Pepper Straet). The rooms in this were of magnificent dimensions, wainscoted with some dark wood, the doorways and ceilings ornamented with arabesques. They were scrupulously clean, but very bare of furniture, the little there was (merely chairs and tables) clumsy and antique—folding-doors with their ornamented encasements reaching to the ceiling—neither door nor window frames painted. The whole house was as deserted and silent as I have described my own to be—gloomily obscure; but this, as the weather was hot, formed a recommendation, for it was deliciously cool. The only inhabitants ever seen either by my companion or myself were the lord of the mansion—a most precise, polite, frigid little sexagenarian, and an old domestic in cotton jacket and *bonnet de nuit*, who sometimes assisted Q.'s servant. The old gentleman was, however, most civil in going through the ceremony of offering everything his house afforded, but what that might be there were no means of ascertaining, for we never either saw or smelt his kitchen. The garden, an irregular area of no great dimensions, presented a grove of trees with thickets of underwood, threaded in all directions by narrow serpentine walks; and to prevent a sense of confinement, I suppose, the high boundary-wall was painted from top to bottom in distemper, with the representation of a distant country sky and all. The effect of this, in my opinion, was vastly inferior to that which would have been produced by covering it with

vines or flowering creepers.   Another of our people dwelt in
a house of quite a different description—it was one of those
already mentioned as having a blank basement, and giving
but a single row of large French windows to the street.   My
friend's apartments were truly luxurious.   The walls were
covered with French paper representing the scenery of some
tropical region, the furniture (of which there was even a
superfluity) all elegant;   the large windows, adorned by
ample draperies, looked out upon a lovely and luxuriant
garden, and the light that entered through them was broken
and tempered by festoons of vine leaves that hung across
them, whilst the air came redolent of delicious odours from
the ocean of flowers below, and the ear was entertained with
the sweet warbling of birds suspended in pretty cages of brass
wire in all parts of the house.   The family consisted of several
females—handsome, elegant, and simple in their dress;
women-servants, scrupulously neat and clean, but not a man.
These ladies must have been people of some consequence, if
we may judge from the number and respectability of their
visitors.   The general aspect of the population of Ghent, as
seen in the streets, etc., did not strike me as having anything
very peculiar in it to attract the attention of a foreigner; the
numbers, however, and to him novel appearance, of the
secular clergy form a feature not to be omitted.   An Englishman is totally unused to having the Church and its accessories
so constantly in his presence as he here finds it.   Both eyes
and ears remind him perpetually of one and the other.   The
carillons, and the irregular unmeaning jingle-jangle of the
bells from the numerous churches, continuing more or less
throughout the day—the monotonous nasal chant issuing
from every church one passes (and they constantly recur)—
the occasional rencontre of some procession, and the number
of priests to be seen everywhere in black cassocks and bands,
with very small three-cornered cocked-hats stuck formally on
their well-powdered heads—never allow one to forget Holy
Mother Church as a leading member of the commonwealth.
These priests all look sleek and in good case—they are
evidently well fed; and it is amusing to see some of them
(very young men) gliding along with downcast eyes (*vultus
dejectu*) and demure steps, whilst ever and anon a stealthy
sidelong glance announces that their thoughts are not

entirely abstracted in devotional meditation—that they are
not insensible to the excitement of the busy scene around
them. To these may be added the dowdy, homely figures
of the Beguines in their inelegant black dresses, as inelegant
and truly bizarre caps of snow-white linen floating like
enormous wings on either side of their heads. The remainder of the population, as I have said, offered nothing
very striking in the way of costume, at least as far as regarded
the higher classes. People everywhere now have adopted,
it may be said, a common uniform. All the male world wear
round hats, tail or frock coats of sober colours, and trousers.
The rich old *bourgmestres*, for instance, are precisely what
one would figure to himself a *bourgmestre* to be—fat, portly,
aldermanly men, often in cocked-hats and powdered wigs,
a sober or sad-coloured suit of good broadcloth, amply cut,
breeches ditto, silver knee-buckles, white or striped silk
stockings, clumsy, square-toed, but well-polished, high-
quartered shoes, with enormous silver buckles—quite
antiques; the finish, a handsome cane with golden knob,
sometimes ruffles, figured-silk waistcoats, etc. etc. The
peasantry frequenting the markets differed from our people
of the same class in the prevalence of short striped cotton
jackets, caps, and sabots. Many of them, like our rustics,
wore smock-frocks, much ornamented about the back,
breast, and shoulders by embroidery in coloured worsteds;
these frocks, however, are generally dark blue. The street
groups of the middle and lower classes were principally
characterised by the frequency of short jackets, generally
nankin or striped cotton, breeches of velveteen, with silver
knee-buckles and striped stockings; cloth, nankin, or a sort
of grey linen, foraging-caps of all shapes—some trimmed with
wool or fur, generally having long pendant tassels from the
top, and almost all having immense broad shades either of
leather, or of the same material as the cap.

Of the manners of a people it would be presumption to
speak on so short an acquaintance. The little intercourse
we had with them, however, made a favourable impression
on us. We found those of the upper classes obliging and
polite; the tradesmen civil and attentive; the labouring
classes quiet, orderly, and extremely respectful.

In point of religion, the men of the upper classes appeared

indifferent or lukewarm, the women very assiduous in the performance of ceremonies, in which it was obvious the heart frequently had little concern. The lower orders were superstitious, priest-ridden, and extremely punctual in the performance of their duties. The peasantry alone seemed quite in earnest. I may characterise the whole population, high and low, as priest-ridden; for, however indifferent the men of the former may be, they are not a whit the less subservient to these their spiritual, and generally temporal, masters.

It would be unjust to condemn as immoral a whole people for the vices found in their cities. We ought not, therefore, to pass unqualified censure on the Flemings because this was exhibited to us openly in the streets of their great cities. I allude to the barefaced manner in which we were tormented incessantly by a number of boys making the most impudent and depraved propositions, and that with a pertinacity not readily repulsed. An instance of moral and religious degradation, I am happy to say, we rarely met with afterwards until our arrival at that hotbed of vice—Paris.

Our last transaction in Ghent was the taking over a number of baggage-mules from Captain Clive's Brigade of the German Legion Artillery. These beautiful animals they had brought with them from Spain, and I shall never forget the grief and indignation with which they parted with them. Affection for, and care of, his horse, is the trait, *par excellence*, which distinguishes the German dragoon from the English. The former would sell everything to feed his horse; the latter would sell his horse itself for spirits, or the means of obtaining them. The one never thinks of himself until his horse is provided for; the other looks upon the animal as a curse and a source of perpetual drudgery to himself, and gives himself no concern about it when once away from under his officer's eye. The German accustoms his horse to partake of his own fare. I remember a beautiful mare, belonging to a sergeant of the 3d Hussars, K.G.L., which would even eat onions. She was one of the very few that escaped after the disastrous retreat of Corunna, and had been saved and smuggled on board ship by the sergeant himself. In the Peninsula the only means of enforcing some attention to their horses amongst our English regiments was to make every man walk and carry his saddle-bags whose horse died or was ill.

CHAPTER V

April 24.—Orders to march to-morrow morning to Thermonde. At a loss to know where this can be, but find it is Dendermonde. Whether this be in consequence of any movement of the French army, or only for the purpose of concentration, we are in the dark. The other troops of horse-artillery in Ghent have also received orders to march, but we move independently of each other. To-day passed in preparation, visiting, and leave-taking. Called on my host, whom I found in a handsome well-furnished drawing-room at the back of the house, looking over a very nice garden. Had no idea of so much cheerfulness and comfort existing under our roof, nor of the two good-looking women I found with him. After much complimenting we parted.

25th.—Fine morning. Marched early; leaving Ghent by the road already mentioned as passing under the Citadel, and crossing that flat but splendid country which I understand extends without interruption to Antwerp, or rather to the Tête de Flandre. This is the Pays de Waes, perhaps the highest cultivated land in Europe. It is said to have been once little better than moving sand, but that the great quantities of manure laid on it for so many successive centuries have completely changed its nature, and produced the fine rich black mould which is now everywhere of considerable depth. If this be true, it will in some measure account for the hillock already spoken of, which is entirely of sand. Passing close under this, I could not but be struck by the circumstance of this sandy mound standing in the midst of an otherwise unbroken level, and conjectured it must be artificial—one of those enormous tumuli erected as the tomb of departed warriors, or as a look-out, which was a common Roman custom, particularly in so flat a region. It is about the height of Silbury, perhaps less, but by no means of so regular a form; its slope, which is covered with trees and bushes, being excavated and broken in numerous places, probably for the sand. Standing as it does amidst a grove of trees, through the boles of which one catches pretty peeps of the blue distance, and crowned by the little chapel, independent of its historical or geological existence, it is really a very interesting object, and forms an admirable foreground to a picture of the Pays de Waes. Every one does not understand the beauty of a landscape, the principal feature of which is a dead level. Yet these, like others, have their beauties, which consist principally in the effect under which they are seen, and the delicious tones of the aerial perspective gradually melting into the purply tints of extreme distance. I have often found very exquisite beauty in these flat Flemish scenes, especially when relieved and animated by groups of men and cattle, such as one sees in Cuyp and all the Dutch and Flemish masters. Whether from the richness of the soil, or some peculiar quality of the atmosphere, I know not, but I always fancied the colouring here much more vivid than in England, and the distances much more purply—quite Italian. But I am halting under the hill; so to proceed. Our road led us through the midst of this magnificent Pays de Waes, everywhere exhibiting such crops and such pastures as it is difficult to form an idea of—the latter covered with fine beasts, which I understand are brought hither from Holland to fatten. We passed through several populous villages, particularly Locristy and Seven Eeke, and about fifteen miles from Ghent reached Lokeren, a large manufacturing town, having all the dirty, smoky, dismal appearance of our northern manufacturing places, to which the blackish-coloured stone—somewhat, in colour at least, resembling the slag used about Bristol as a building material—contributes not a little. The houses, of three and four stories, appeared tenanted each by many families; and the population had all the squalid, filthy character of our own manufacturing population, always excepting those of Stroudwater and the bottoms in Gloucestershire. Cloth is the article fabricated here, but of what quality I know not.

A strong column of Hanoverian infantry, composed of several battalions of militia, crossing our route, detained us at the entrance of the town more than half an hour, to the great amusement of a crowd of gazing weavers and dyers, with upturned sleeves and blue hands and arms, who surrounded us. The Hanoverians were fine-looking troops, generally very young, and completely English in dress and appointments, except that the officers wore parti-coloured sashes. Each battalion had a very good band, though rather noisy, from the number of jingling instruments entering into its composition—as cymbals, triangles, ottomans, etc. etc.—all which are much more patronised by foreigners than by us. The chaussée terminating at Lokeren, when we continued our march it was on a bad cross-road, which soon brought us to Zéle—a large populous manufacturing village, having a wide, clean street. Houses in the cottage style, and generally only of one floor. The whole population turned out to see us pass, with the *curé* at their head—a tall, respectable-looking old man, who, judging from the good-humoured countenance with which he scrutinised our column as it passed, and the air *empressé* with which he came forward to offer his advice respecting the road to Dendermonde, I set down either as a very amiable person, or very zealous in the cause of legitimacy: we were feeling our way without a guide, and therefore had to ask. The respectful, quiet, and contented air of his flock spoke also in his favour, and, together with the bright eyes of numerous pretty women among the crowd, left a favourable impression of Zêle.

Henceforward the scenery took a very different aspect, and we exchanged the smiling, populous, well-wooded country we had been hitherto traversing for a lugubrious, marshy tract, devoid of anything that could break its monotony—neither trees nor houses, and but few cattle, were to be seen, whilst the abominable road became so slippery that it was with difficulty our horses could keep their feet.

About half a league from Dendermonde we struck the Scheldt, but could see nothing of it or the opposite country for the high dyke by which the river is here confined, and along the foot of which, for some little distance, our road lay, until it brought us to a wooden bridge elevated nearly thirty feet above the water, and so tottering that it was necessary to pass by single divisions, and even then its vibrations were not pleasant. Our quartermaster, who had been sent in advance, met us here, with orders not to halt in Dendermonde, but to proceed on to St Gille, situated beyond it on

the Brussels road.   The appearance of things improved here,
from the number of trees about Dendermonde, which we
soon after entered by a long, straight, narrow, gloomy, mean-
looking street of low houses, built of the same dark stone
we had seen at Lokeren.   This led us to a spacious quay,
encompassing what I supposed to be the harbour, for the
water was very low, and the mud bare, like Bristol.   Passing
round the head of this, we soon left the town again, and almost
immediately found ourselves at St Gille, which consists of a
few mean houses scattered along the chaussée, the only
decent one being that of a *juge de paix*, on which I found
myself billeted.

In a country so carefully cultivated as this is, a piece of
waste land is a rarity, and therefore we had some difficulty
in forming our park, which at last was done in a small
enclosed cemetery, not without disturbing the ashes of the
dead, and running some risk of breaking our horses' legs and
our own necks, for the graves had all been so loosely filled in
that the horses sank to their shoulders in the light soil.   Our
men and horses were dispersed amongst the neighbouring
farms of the commune, and though rather widely scattered,
yet most comfortably put up everywhere.

Whilst employed at the park my servant had taken my
baggage to my billet, so that on repairing thither I found
Madame la Juge, *en habit de Dimanches*, already waiting at the
door to receive me.   A fine and handsome woman, perhaps
turned of thirty, and possessing a degree of *embonpoint* which,
whilst it added dignity to her air, detracted nothing from
the grace of her person.   She received me with more than
common politeness, with kindness and cordiality, which, as
an intruder, I felt I had no right to expect, and, conducting
me into the house, assured me that it should be her study to
render my stay at St Gille as agreeable as possible, ushering
me into an apartment destined for my use, and offering the
assistance of her servants—in short, the whole house was at
my disposal.   All this was not mere compliment, for in good
truth she kept her word to the very letter.   I never experienced greater kindness, or more sincere hospitality, and
under such circumstances soon felt myself perfectly at home
in my neat lodgings.

What a contrast was this to the gloomy billet I left in the

morning in the silent, solitary Rue de Bruges! Here everything was light, airy, and cheerful. But I must describe my
new home. The *apartment* consisted of a saloon of about
eighteen feet square, with a little cabinet or sleeping-room
adjoining and opening from it. Both were as clean as it was
possible to conceive anything could be, and the white walls
perfectly immaculate. Furniture of the simplest kind—
chairs of oak or walnut ranged along the walls, two tables
covered with oilcloth, neat but scanty window-curtains, with
draperies and fringe, and a most brilliant stove, *en faïence*,
ornamented with brass-work, standing out nearly in the
middle of the floor; that floor of red tiles, or brick highly
varnished, the coolness of which, in the present hot weather,
was highly grateful. I have designated this room as light and
airy, and truly it was so, for it was illuminated by no less than
six windows. Three of these in the front commanded a
pleasant view over the well-wooded and beautifully cultivated
country beyond the great Brussels road, which ran beneath
them—the fields more resembling extensive gardens than
anything else. As this part of the house projected beyond
the *porte cochère*, a window in the side afforded a peep up the
road, terminated by the town of Dendermonde, which hence
appeared embosomed in trees. Two fine acacias in front of
the gateway overshadowed this with their delicate pensile
foliage, and screened it from the hot rays of the afternoon
sun. The remaining two windows in the back looked into a
delicious and carefully kept garden, divided as usual by
those verdant hornbeam walls into different departments.
Such was my saloon. My bedroom, if so it may be called,
was equally neat and simple in its equipment: a low bedstead without curtains, bedding of humble materials, but so
clean that the most fastidious could have found no fault with
it, a chair or two, and a small dressing-table in the single
window, constituted its whole furniture. Having made
arrangements for establishing our mess here, I set off to visit
my people, who, as before mentioned, were scattered by
threes and fours all over the commune amongst the farmers;
and with these good and simple people I found them already
quite at home. In most houses I found them seated at
dinner with the family—at all they had been invited so to do;
and everywhere the greatest good humour and best possible

understanding prevailed between the host and guests. When I asked, "Ist der meister content mit den soldaten?"—gibberish coined for the occasion, as they understood no French, and I no Flemish—the answer was always a hearty "Yaw, mynheer—yaw! ist brav—ist goot"—at the same time good-naturedly slapping one of them on the back, and leering archly round at the others. Boys, women, and children would all swarm round me, exclaiming "Goot, goot, goot!" Then, anticipating my wish to see the horses, one of them would invite me to the stables, which, though dark, were all warm and comfortable. Here I found our cattle stowed away, perhaps, amongst half a dozen of their elephants of horses, literally living in clover, for their racks and mangers were full of it (the finest I ever saw), and their stalls of clean straw up to their bellies. These good people seemed quite proud of having made the lucky brutes so comfortable. I found afterwards from our Juge de Paix that this bounty was in some measure repaid by the dung, which is here so valuable that the production of one horse in four-and-twenty hours is worth at least three or four pounds of hay, and perhaps four times the quantity of clover.

These farming establishments were very much alike, generally speaking; embosomed in orchards, which in their turn are surrounded by lofty elms. The dwelling-house is usually of brick, only one floor, a high roof, under which are the dormitories with garret-windows, sometimes two tiers of them. On the ground-floor the windows are large and open in the French style, outside shutters almost invariably green. Commonly there are only two rooms on this floor, one on each side of the passage, the door of which opens on the yards, as do the windows. One of these rooms is the kitchen, or ordinary residence of the family, the other is a salle de cérémonie. In the first is the usual display of brass pans, kettles, crockery, etc., which, with some common benches and a large table or two, constitute its furniture. As everywhere throughout this country, the most perfect cleanliness prevails, and the metallic lustre of the brass is brought out as much as scrubbing can effect. The salle exhibits a collection of stiff old-fashioned chairs with rush bottoms and high upright carved backs, ponderous oaken

tables, snow-white window-curtains, and a series of very
common prints, in as common frames, suspended from the
walls. These usually represent saints, etc. On the chimney-
piece waxen or earthenware figures of animals, fruits, etc.;
and frequently affixed to the wall over the centre one sees a
kind of deep frame or box with glass front, in which, amongst
cut paper, moss, or shell-work, is either a crucifix or a portrait
of the Virgin and child. The barns, stables, cow-houses,
and other out offices, form the other three sides of a square of
which the front of the dwelling is the fourth. A rough pavement of about ten or twelve feet wide runs all round in front
of the building; the remainder of the area is one vast dung-
hill, having a reservoir in the centre to receive its drainings,
whilst it receives those of the cow-houses, stables, and dwelling by means of gutters constructed for the purpose. This
precious fluid is the great dependence of the Flemish agri-
culturist, as the principal fertiliser of his fields. When the
land is to be manured, it is carted out upon the grounds in a
large tub (like a brewing-tub). A boy leads the cart very
slowly all over the field, whilst a man, armed with a scoop,
keeps scattering it in all directions. It must be confessed
that the fields after this aspersion do not exhale the most
savoury odours, but then nothing can exceed their fertility.
The country about Dendermonde was, generally speaking,
laid out in long narrow patches, separated from each other
sometimes by a belt of turf, sometimes by a footpath, at
others by ditches, along the edge of which might be a growth
of alders, but no regular hedges anywhere. Towards the
Dender, ditches of water were the common division, and
these fields were fertilised by irrigation, not by the scoop,
and a more beautiful verdure could not be seen, all being
pastures; of the other fields or patches, each bore a different
crop, some flax, some wheat, some *trèfle* or clover, some
buckwheat, some hops—the whole district having the appearance of one vast garden. The soil in general was a light rich
mould, but degenerating into sand as it approached the
Scheldt, on the north side of St Gille. The absence of hedges
was fully compensated by the numerous copses that enriched
the scenery in all directions, together with the rows of trees
with which almost every road was bordered, so that, although
a dead level, nothing could be more pleasing than the

pictures it presented, except the tract towards the Scheldt, which was bleak enough.

My rounds finished, I returned to my billet, where I found our people all assembled, and we soon sat down to a most excellent dinner. The wine, which we had procured from the town, was thin, pale, almost white, but of a very piquant flavour, and over it we were enjoying ourselves, when a servant came in, and announced that M. le Juge, having that moment returned from the town, begged permission to pay his respects to M. le Commandant. Permission granted. Enter a little vulgar-looking man, about sixty years of age, whose coarse and by no means prepossessing physiognomy was not improved by the loss of an eye; nor was his person set off to the best advantage by his costume, consisting of a shabby blue frock, dark waistcoat sprigged over with golden flowers, and very long drab pantaloons, hanging about his legs in large folds, evidently unrestrained by any suspensatory process. His head was surmounted by a sort of forage-cap of dark-green velvet, with a band of silver lace, and a silver tassel falling over the crown. Doffing this, with a profusion of bows he casts his sharp single eye inquiringly round our party, exclaiming, "M. le Commandant?" I bow. "M. le Commandant, se trouve-t-il bien ici?" I assent, and express my gratitude to his better half for her attentions. "Da tout, M. le Commandant, da tout! Elle n'a rien fait que son devoir aupres de vous, M. le Commandant! Et de plus, je vous engage de considerer la maison and les domestiques tous à vôtre service, M. le Commandant—tous, tous, tous!" (pronouncing strongly the final s of the last word) "et si, par hazard, M. le Commandant aimerait la solitude, voilà la joli promenade là bas," pointing to the garden. All this passed with us as mere words; but we had formed a wrong estimate of our Juge, who fulfilled to the utmost his professions, and turned out a very worthy fellow. Whilst this colloquy was in progress, our friend had established himself at the table with less ceremony than might have been expected from so complimentary a gentleman, and the bottle, circulating briskly, had the usual effect of loosening tongues and tightening friendship. M. le Juge begged to know where we had obtained our wine, which he did not approve of; it was not such as we ought to drink;

begged permission to send for some of a very superior quality
from his own cellar.   The wine is brought accordingly, a
bottle drawn by Monsieur himself with great solemnity and
some grimace, relating at the same time its whole history.
Clean glasses are called for, Monsieur fills a bumper, and
after contemplating it for a moment against the light, hands
it to me with a profound inclination.   In colour it exactly
resembles what is on the table.   I taste it: there is not a
shade of difference in the flavour.   M. le Juge fills a glass
for each of my companions, and hands it to them with the
same ceremonious bow.   It was easy to see that their
opinions coincided with mine; but we did not wish to hurt
the good man, and so we one and all smacked our lips, and
pronounced it excellent.   He immediately ordered a further
supply, and insisted on our drinking nothing else.   However,
the bottles becoming mingled on the table, none of us could
distinguish the difference, and our friend himself I observed,
filled his own glass indiscriminately from the one and the
other.   He meant to treat us, and took this way of accom-
plishing it, no doubt.   We found him an intelligent,
facetious companion, although, as we got farther into the
night, he did get a little prosy with his anecdotes of the good
people of Dendermonde.   *En revanche*, he amused us much
with a description of the process of enrolling the militia then
going on; and droll pictures he drew of the peasantry who
were brought to him for that purpose every day by the
gens d'armés.   It would seem that these people were forced
into the service sorely against their will, being much attached
to Buonaparte, and quite averse to the new order of things.
This seemed to be the general feeling amongst the bourgeois
of Dendermonde, as far as we could learn; and it appeared
very doubtful whether our worthy host himself, although a
public functionary under the new Government, did not
participate in this rage for Napoleon and Impérialisme.   Be
that, however, as it may, he was so well pleased with our
society, that the first cocks crew ere he retired, his hiccough-
ing adieus and twinkling eye fully demonstrating that, for
him at least, the wine was not quite such watery stuff as we
had at first imagined.   To us *port-drinkers* it was innocuous.
The next day we had leisure to look about us, and visit
Dendermonde—a place, in my mind, inseparably connected

with Corporal Trim and Uncle Toby; and no little amusement was it to my good Juge and his spouse when I related to them the story. They thought it all true for a time.

Whilst my comrades sought the town, I turned to the country, which for me has infinitely more charms. The steeple of a village church peering above the trees about a mile from us, on the Brussels road, attracted me in that direction. The opulent village of Lebbeke, embowered in orchards, appeared peculiarly animated as I approached it. White tents, horses at picket in long lines, groups of artillerymen, peasants and their waggons bringing loads of hay, intermingled amongst the apple-trees, enlivened the scene. Three batteries of 9-pounders were parked in the orchards, and their people partly billeted in the farms, partly encamped near their guns. It was a curious medley of peace and war. Here a large barn by the roadside, its doors thrown wide open, and peasants within busily occupied in threshing, spoke of the former; the guns and their accompaniments in the opposite orchard, of the latter—the horses, looking cool and comfortable under the shade of a fine row of elms, quietly eating their hay, or playfully biting each other. Gunners and drivers, half undressed, were lounging about the tents, or sitting on the wall by the roadside, contentedly smoking their pipes; others busy cleaning their appointments, or raking up the hay in front of the horses.

Large, substantial-looking farmhouses principally formed the village street, and by their comfortable appearance aroused the taste for rural life; but this would be overset by the sight of an officer, his coat unbuttoned, forage-cap on head, and cigar in mouth, lolling listlessly out of a casement, as if perfectly at home—a sight directly antagonistic to the tranquillity of rural retirement. The Flemish waggons, with their teams and drivers, bringing loads of hay, amused me much—long-bodied, and on low wheels, drawn by four, and sometimes five, immense animals, overloaded with fat. The waggoner, walking beside the forewheels, guides his team with some dexterity by means of long reins of cord running through holes in the haims. The horses are harnessed two and two, if the team be of four—otherwise two in the wheel and three leaders abreast, always separated from the wheelers by exceedingly long traces; the pole invariably used. The richer farmers, as with us, affect great show in their teams, the harness being gay with fringes and tassels of coloured worsted, and the haims are always particularly fine. These are of wood, flat, about four or five inches broad, the edges frequently studded with brass nails, the front decorated with painted flowers, and often with the Imperial eagle. The overgrown horses are pampered like pet lapdogs, and never required to do one quarter of the work they are capable of. They are noble brutes.

However rich the scenery of this country may be from its cultivation, still, in an Englishman's eye, there is something wanting. Except on the pastures along the Dender, no cattle are ever seen animating the fields. The absence of hedges or other fences obliges the farmer to keep these shut up, except for a short period after the harvest, when they are turned out to pick up what they can along the borders and on the *tréf* layers.

The quantity of manure accumulated by keeping them up is considerable, and no doubt enters into the farmer's calculation. Sheep in small flocks (for I do not see that any large ones are kept) are taken out to pasture by a shepherd and two or three dogs—not at all resembling our sheep-dogs, except in sagacity, but small black curs with long tails. I have seen one of these shepherds dozing on a bank by the roadside, whilst his little flock, grazing in an adjoining slip of grass-land, was quite as efficiently watched as if the fellow had been wide awake. This slip was bounded on three sides by young wheat, and on each of the dividing borders was posted one of these curs. As the flock moved forward or backward so did the dogs; and whilst they fed, these intelligent animals kept incessantly running backwards and forwards on their post like sentinels, instantly darting at any sheep that attempted to break bounds, and driving it back into the grass-plot. The day was exceedingly warm, and their lolling tongues proclaimed that the little animals had no very light task of it, whatever their master's might be.

The town of Dendermonde (of which I saw but little) is situated on the right bank of the Scheldt, at the point where the little river Dender flows into it, as the name imports—Dender mond or mund—*Dender mouth*. This river flows through it, and, being backed up by sluices, forms the basin.

I noticed on the day of our arrival. It is not large, and its population might be about 5000 or 6000—manufacturers of linens, fustians, etc. etc. The fortifications have nearly disappeared, the only remnant that I saw being something like a ravelin on the Alost side. It is, however, so surrounded by water, and the country is so flat, that an extensive inundation could soon be formed to supply their place if necessary. The general aspect of the town is mean and gloomy, but on the side next to St Gille were several good-looking houses, though all built of the same dark stone. We saw here more pretty women, however, than we had yet met with, always excepting in Zêle.

CHAPTER VI

FINDING all quiet, and that our move hither from Ghent had only been for the purpose of bringing us nearer to the cavalry, whose headquarters were at Ninove, and into a more abundant country for forage, we now gave ourselves up to the amusements our situation afforded, as much as the requisite attention to military duties would allow. Some made excursions to Brussels and Antwerp; some passed their mornings knocking about the balls at a miserable billiard-table upon the rickety floor of an upstairs room in a neighbouring cabaret; whilst others made a sort of flirting acquaintance with some of the fair damsels of Dendermonde. The time flew quickly, because we were happy.

I was anxious to see Antwerp, and proposed going thither; but day after day something occurred to prevent me, and at last I had the mortifying reflection of having passed six idle days within eighteen miles of it, and yet never been there. My only excursion was to Alost, or Aulst, as they call it. On the 28th Leathes and I set off on this expedition. Until within a mile of Alost, the character of the country we traversed was much the same as that about Dendermonde, but the villages and farmhouses were less neat and more poor in their appearance—ragged thatch instead of slates and tiles, etc.—and the streets of the villages or hamlets narrower and dirtier. During the whole ride we saw but one house that appeared the residence of a gentleman, and that was a large heavy-looking brick building, standing in the midst of an old-fashioned garden, ornamented (if so it may be called) with painted statues of men and monsters quite in the Cockney style. *En effet*, this was the *lusthause* of a wealthy *bourgmestre* of the Ville de Gand. Approaching Alost, we found the character of the country changing, and having seen nothing but a dead-level ever since landing at Ostend, were agreeably surprised at finding ourselves ascending a gentle slope, and surrounded by a gently undulating country, yet so slightly so that we were not aware of it until on it. Passing a sort of advanced barrier, we soon reached the town, and rode into a respectable sort of square, where we dismounted at the Maison d'Autriche. No accommodation for horses here, so we were obliged to resort to a carrier's in an adjoining street, where we with difficulty got stableroom, all being crowded with horses of Louis XVIII.'s cavalry. Being tired when I returned to Dendermonde, I made no note of my visit to Aulst, and therefore can say little about it. All I remember is a fine broad street of handsome houses running up an ascent; a pretty public walk (*en berceau*) called L'Allée d'Amour (as we should say, *Love Lane*; and what town or village is there in England which has not its Allée d'Amour?); a fine church, in which was a series of paintings (good, I believe) representing the life and adventures of some saint; the canal harbour, full of boats laden with corn and hay for our cavalry, the contractors having established here their grand depot, etc. etc.; great crowding and bustling in the streets, occasioned partly by this circumstance, partly by the presence of the Duc de Berri and his troops, and partly by an unusual influx of travellers. Moreover, I remember that we got a most delicious omelet and bottle of very fine sauterne at the Maison d'Autriche, for which (*garçon* included) we paid only five francs; whilst, *en revanche*, as it were, we had to pay eight to the villain of a carrier for the feed of bad oats which our horses would not eat; that we saddled them ourselves, and sallied from Alost, expecting in due time and without contretemps, to reach St Gille; that we actually arrived within a mile of Lebbeke, the spire of whose church was closely seen by us above the trees, and towards which we attempted a short cut, which attempt ended in losing ourselves, and wandering about for an hour within 800 yards of St Gille, and always with the spire of Lebbeke in view, without being able to reach one place or the other; and that there we might have wandered till doomsday, had we not fortunately fallen in with a patrol (foot) of *gens d'armes*, who put us into the right way—such is the intricacy of this country, intersected as it is by lanes and ditches, like network, and the view confined to the neighbouring field by the multitudinous little woods. We got home! *Chez moi*, things went on so comfortably that I was quite happy, my worthy host and his spouse treating me and mine quite as part of the family. Of Monsieur, however, I did not see very much, for every morning, immediately after breakfast, he went to his office in Dendermonde, where he remained all day, and he never ventured another soirée with our party. The last year (1814) my position in their *ménage* had been occupied by a French colonel, of whom they spoke in the highest terms, always winding up with, "Ah! il était brave garçon, celui là." When taking leave of them, which the approach of English troops rendered necessary, he added to his adieux, "Mais pour l'année prochaine"; and both these good people confidently expected to see him again, setting it down as certain that the moment the Emperor advanced the English would hasten to their ships, never dreaming that we could resist *him*. So slipped time away, and my present comfort approached its end.

May 1st.—I still slept, when, at five o'clock in the morning, our sergeant-major aroused me to read a note brought by an orderly hussar. It was most laconic—*la voici*: "Captain Mercer's troop of horse-artillery will march to Strytem without delay. Signed," etc. etc.

Where is Strytem? and for what this sudden move? These were questions to which I could get no answer. The hussar knew nothing, and the people about me less. One thing was positive, and that was, that we must be under weigh instanter, and pick out Strytem as best we might. The sergeant-major, therefore, was despatched to give the alert; and having given the hussar a receipt in full for his important despatch, I proceeded to clothe my person for the journey, having hitherto been *en chemise*. As the trumpeter was lodged in a house close by with my own grooms, the "boot and saddle" quickly reverberated through the village, and set its whole population in movement. A gentle tap at my door announced a visitor. What was my surprise on opening it!—there was Madame la Juge *tout en déshabillé*, evidently just tumbled out of bed, and apparently much agitated. Such a scene I did not expect.

"Ah, Monsieur, vous allez partis!" and she actually began to sob and cry like a child. Was she serious, or was this acting? If the latter, she certainly played her part so well that I could not but give her credit for being in earnest.   It is so delightful to believe one's self interesting to a fine woman.   Advancing my toilette, I tried at the same time to moderate this outbreak of feeling.   She only wept the more. Meantime M. le Juge arrived on the stage, his old blue frock carelessly thrown on, and his nether garment occupying both his hands, one holding it up, and the other arranging it, the eternal green cap stuck on his head, hardly yet quite awake—unwashed, uncombed: the good man did not present the most amiable figure by the side of his neat consort.

Our people were not accustomed to delay, and the road in front of the house was already a scene of bustle from the assembling of the detachments lying nearer home.   Although still lachrymose, Madame did not stand idle; but, seeing my servant sufficiently employed packing my portmanteau, set about preparing breakfast, to which I soon sat down, whilst the worthy couple waited on me, recommending this and that, and pressing me to eat, much in the manner of two fond parents hanging over the early meal of their darling boy, about to return to school by the expected coach.   I could not but feel grateful for so much kindness, and consequently sorrow at so soon leaving them; and so this breakfast was rather a melancholy one, although the morning sun did shine so bright.   The good people were unceasing in their regrets, and repeatedly made me promise that, if I remained in the country, I would pay them another visit—a promise I was never able to fulfil, however.

To my questions respecting Strytem, Monsieur could give no satisfactory answers.   "It lay in a very fine country, somewhere in the neighbourhood of Brussels; and we had better take the road to that city in the first instance, and trust for further information to the peasantry as we went along."

These people are singularly ignorant in this respect, having no knowledge, generally speaking, of any place more than two or three miles from home.   Monsieur, however, invited me to follow him to his study—a small room all in a litter—over the gateway, and there, after some hunting amongst books, old clothes, etc. etc., he rummaged out the mutilated fragment of an old but very excellent map, which he insisted on my putting into my *sabretache*, which I did, and still keep for his sake.

At length the moment of departure arrived, the parade was formed, my horse at the door. The tears of Madame flowed afresh as she embraced me. Monsieur led me by the hand to the gateway. Here the great coarse Flemish cook, the corner of her apron applied to her eyes, for she also wept (at the departure of my groom, I suspect), came running out, her clumsy sabots with their trimmings of rabbit skin clattering along the stone passage like the hoofs of a cart-horse. My servant had made her a present for her assistance, in her eyes so magnificent that she could hardly express her gratitude, and so poured on me a shower of thanks and blessings, and recommendations to the protection of saints and saintesses, with a volubility which her usual taciturn, phlegmatic manner had not led me to expect. "*Prepare to mount!*" "*Mount!*" The trumpets sound a march, and waiving a last adieu to the group at the gate of my late home, I turn my back on it for ever, perhaps. The men were in high spirits, and horses fat as pigs and sleek as moles—thanks to rest, good stabling and abundance of *tréf*. Most of the peasants on whom many of our men had been billeted accompanied them to the parade, and it was interesting to witness the kindness with which they shook hands at parting, and the complacency with which, patting the horses on the neck, they scanned them all over, as if proud of their good condition. And yet these were Napoleonists, according to our Juge. For my part, I believe they were utterly indifferent as to whether they lived under the rule of Napoleon or the house of Orange, so long as their agricultural labours were not interrupted: and this alone, I suspect, was the cause of their aversion to being militiamen.

Passing through Lebbeke, we found the three brigades of 9-pounders also getting on march, and the whole village astir. The officers told us their orders were to march direct to Brussels, and they were fully persuaded the French army had advanced.

For about seven miles the road lay through a country differing little from what we had hitherto seen; but then it became suddenly hilly. Ascending the first long but not very steep ascent, we were assailed by a host of beggars, who had stationed themselves here to take advantage of the slow pace at which carriages were obliged to ascend the hill.

These were the first I recollect having seen in the country. The ragged boys accompanied the column to the top of the hill, endeavouring to excite, if not compassion, at least admiration of the agility with which they rolled themselves along alternately on hands and feet, like so many wheels—a feat that procured them some coppers.

The country had now totally changed its character; still fertile, highly cultivated, and abundantly populous, yet presenting scenery of a much more interesting nature. Fine swells enabled one to obtain, from time to time, most charming views of the rich distance, instead of, as hitherto, being confined to a few hundred yards of meadow, shut up, as the flat country was, by trees and small copses.

Villages and large farms appeared in all directions, intermingled with extensive woods; the fields exhibited the richest exuberance of crops—wheat, rye, hops, buckwheat, etc., with their lighter tints relieving the more sombre tones of the woodlands. Here the spire of a village church, there the conical roofs and quaint architecture of a chateau, peered above the foliage of the woods, and increased the interest of the scene. To me this change was delightful. I thought I had never seen anything half so rich as the fine landscape spread before me when I turned to look back on gaining the first summit. The height, however, was not sufficient to allow me, at this distance, in a country so thickly wooded, to see Dendermonde again, though my eye eagerly sought it. The large village of Assche (town, I should call it, being marked bourg in the map) crowned this hill, and here we found a battery of Belgian horse-artillery in quarters. The men lounging about in undress, or without their jackets, without any appearance of a move, induced us to believe our own was, after all, only another change of quarters—and we were right. The people here knew Strytem, which they said was only a few miles distant, to the southward of the road we were on. Accordingly I despatched an officer to precede us, and make the necessary arrangements for our reception; at the same time quitting the chaussée, we plunged into a villanous cross-road, all up and down, and every bottom occupied by a stream crossed by bridges of loose planks, which to us were rather annoying from their apparent insecurity, as well as from the boggy state of the ground for some yards at either end of them. However, if the road was bad, the beauty of the country through which it led made ample amends. Descending from the hill on which Assche is situated, we travelled for two or three miles through a bottom, between two nearly parallel ridges, whose slopes exhibited all the luxuriance of vegetation in splendid crops of grain, etc., and magnificent trees, so peculiar to this country, whilst an almost continued wood occupied their summits. This part of our route reminded me strongly of the valley in which High Wycombe lies, though there nothing like this exuberance is seen. About a mile, as it proved, from Strytem, for we had not as yet seen anything like a village, we ascended the hill again, and were continuing along the summit when a peasant, in blue smock-frock and white nightcap, came running after us with a scrap of paper in his hand, which he presented to me with a most profound bow, doffing at the same time his dirty cap. A few lines in pencil from Dr Bell informed me that the bearer would lead us to Strytem; and he by signs—for he spoke no French—gave us to understand that we must turn back, having passed the road leading thither. Accordingly a countermarch, by un-limbering, took place, and, following our guide, we descended into a most secluded little valley, green and lovely, the bottom being principally meadow, everywhere surrounded by stately elms. The road, however, became worse than ever—deep tenacious mud, sadly broken up. After march-ing a short distance we passed a wheelwright's shop; then came to a broader space, where stood a small mean-looking church, a miserable cabaret, a forge, two very large farm establishments, with a few wretched-looking cottages;—this, our guide gave us to understand, was Strytem. Bell's note spoke of a chateau at the point we were to make for, but here was nothing of the sort. All seemed disappointment, for the miserable place itself was so different from the fine spacious streets and substantial houses of all the villages we had hitherto seen, that one could scarcely imagine it to be the same country. Our guide, however, led on, and after passing this poor collection of dwellings, a high stone wall bounding the road to the left, with a wide gateway in the centre, announced the chateau, which was so completely shut in by the woods, etc., that the first glimpse we got of it was on entering these gates. A spacious green court sloped down to the building, a dreary-looking old pile of brick, forming three sides of a square, and surrounded by a broad moat—nearly as green as the court, from the aquatic weeds floating on its stagnant water. Arched doors; high but narrow windows, composed of small panes set in lead, and encased in heavy stone frames; lofty stepped gables, and a tower occupying one angle of the court, with a conical roof surmounted by an iron cross and weathercock, gave it a most venerable and somewhat imposing aspect. The sombre effect, however, was in some measure relieved by the lively tints of roses and rich verdure of the broad leaves of a vine trained over a trellis along the edge of the moat, as well as the fine fruit-trees everywhere covering the walls of the front court. A broad gravel-drive descended to the moat, which was crossed by a stone bridge, substantial, but not ornamental. On our right were stables, etc., for about half-way down the court; on the left the enormous roofs of barns and farm-buildings appeared over the wall, and beyond them, again, the rather inelegant spire of the village church. An arched doorway communicated on this side with the farmyard. Behind the chateau the view was bounded by the tufted and feathery masses of a superb avenue of beeches and a hill covered with wood seen through the few openings between them, relieving well the reddish sombre tone and formal out-lines of the building. Every feature of this place is strongly impressed on my memory as I then beheld it for the first time, not without emotions of disgust; for though rather a picturesque object to look at, I could not suppress a shudder at the idea of its becoming my habitation for an indefinite time. Nothing do I regret more than not having made a sketch of it from this side, although I did several from other points.

The road was so narrow, and the turn so sharp, that it required all the dexterity of our drivers to get decently into the court with their six-horse teams. They did, however, effect it without carrying away the gate-posts, to the no small amazement of some half-dozen boors, whom the novelty of arrival had drawn together, and we finally formed a very compact little park, three pieces and their ammunition waggons on each side of the central path. The *corps de*

garde was established in the loft over the stables in which
were lodged the officers' horses; and the rest of the troop
were billeted on the neighbouring farms, which, in general,
were so large that they took a subdivision, or thirty-two
horses, each, and, if I mistake not, that adjoining the chateau
a whole division of sixty-four horses. Having despatched
this business, we proceeded to examine our own quarters.
The old gardener, a tall meagre figure, with a venerable grey
head and good-humoured physiognomy, but somewhat bent
by age, accompanied by his daughter, a pale melancholy
looking young woman, met us on the bridge, the keys of his
fortalice in one hand and his dirty *bonnet de nuit* in the other.
(Be it here remarked that although neatness and cleanliness
characterise the dwellings of the Flemish peasantry, yet are
they not over and above particular in this respect as regards
their own persons.)   As he could speak nothing but Flemish,
Mademoiselle came to officiate as his interpreter, but the
patois in which she expressed herself was so unintelligible
that, after listening for some time to her long-winded story,
and comprehending nothing more of it than the constantly
recurring "Mon père dit," etc., our politeness gave way, and
we begged that the doors might be forthwith thrown open.
The burden of her song or chant, for such it was, seemed to
be an endeavour to dissuade us from our purpose of lodging
there, though I could not well comprehend why.   Leaving,
then, the good man to replace his bonnet, and Mademoiselle
to explain to him something or another, we proceeded to
examine the interior in order to select our rooms.   The
chateau had been uninhabited for many years, and, though
not ruinous, was in a very dilapidated state.   Nothing could
be more chillingly repulsive than the vast flagged hall into
which we first entered.   Several doors led from this, right
and left, into suites of apartments, and one, low and arched,
opposite the entrance, opened on a long bridge leading over
the moat to the garden and pleasure-grounds, etc.   This hall
was totally devoid of furniture.   We found the rooms on the
ground-floor large, lofty, and of good proportions, but only
feebly illuminated by high windows sunk deep in the wall,
and of which the heavy stone mullions intercepted nearly as
much light as entered between them.   The walls were hung
with tapestry so ancient and so much decayed that the figures,

landscapes, etc., by which it had once been ornamented, were nearly obliterated. In some rooms old family portraits occupied the places of the wainscot panels, particularly over the doors. The only furniture in any of them was a few ponderous tables, and some high-backed equally ponderous chairs, having both seats and backs stuffed and covered with tapestry. On the floor above, a large corridor or hall—for it was directly over and corresponded in size with the one below—was hung round with full-length portraits of the Van Volden family (to whom the domain belonged), male and female. Some of these were common enough; but there were others evidently the production of no ordinary pencil— one in particular, a lady habited in a costume such as prevailed about our Charles II.'s time—a splendidly beautiful creature of some two or three and twenty years of age, painted in a most masterly style; and, from being in a much more magnificent frame than any of the others, apparently a person of higher consideration. "*Mon-père-dit*" (as we had christened the gardener's pallid daughter), who accompanied us through the rooms, could give no information respecting this fair dame—all she knew was that she had been a person of very high rank, and, she believed, an ancestress of Madame la Baronne, the present proprietress. By the way, Madame Van Volden, Baronne Von Lombeke et Strytem (such were her titles), was at this time residing in Brussels, where she had a grand mansion—Rue de Dominicans. She possessed also another estate at or near Vilvorde, between which and her town residence she divided her time, so that her Strytem tenants saw her very rarely. Her son being *maire* of the commune, paid an occasional visit to the village, but then always put up at the farmhouse, so that the chateau had long been locked up and quite neglected. To return from this digression. Having visited the upper apartments, all which were as dismal as those below, we proceeded to choose our quarters, much to the chagrin of Mademoiselle *Mon-père-dit*, who had, no doubt, entertained hopes that the repulsive appearance of things would have deterred us from taking up our residence there. I selected a large salon, immediately off the hall, on the ground-floor. It might have been about 30 feet by 26 or 28, very lofty, with an immense gaping fireplace, but without grate. Two great stone-cased windows looked into the front court, a third across the moat and towards the woods behind the chateau. There were three visible doors—the one leading into the great hall, a second into a sort of vestibule or small hall, whence a staircase ascended to the apartments of the right wing, and the third into a long narrow, but lofty room, in one corner of which I placed my mattress on an old settee. There was also a door from this room into the vestibule, and beyond that another suite of apartments, in which our surgeon established himself. The walls of my salon, like most of the others, were covered with tapestry, and in the compartments between the windows, over the doors, etc., were grim-looking portraits of *ci-devant* Van Voldens, each having the name and date inscribed at the bottom of it, from which I learned that most of them were of considerable antiquity; some, I think, dating 1537.

I have said that there were three *visible* doors to this room. I had been in it some time ere, by accident, I discovered a fourth, concealed under the tapestry, leading into a very small chapel fitted up with great neatness (except the altar, which was rather gaudy), and evidently the only part of the mansion of which any care had been taken. Such was my new domicile, in which I was soon at home, although it contrasted as strongly with my late cheerful apartment at Dendermonde as that did with the gloomy hole at Ghent. Some of our people found a similar contrast, and could not refrain from grumbling. "By the Lord, gentlemen," said old Lieutenant Ingleby, "you ought to think yourselves very fortunate in getting such a quarter. In the Peninsula the Duke himself would have thought so, and was often glad to get so good a roof over his head." The grumblers were ashamed, and we heard no more of it. A large salon in the left wing we chose for our mess-room, and the other officers established themselves upstairs. Fires were soon lighted above and below; servants running up and down;—all was life and movement, and the old place had not been so gay for years before. Indeed, on returning to my room after visiting the billets, there was an appearance of home and comfort about it which I did not expect. A large wood-fire blazed and crackled in the great chimney. My servant had collected chairs enough to make a show, ranged round the walls; on one of the great antique tables in the centre he had placed my writing apparatus and one or two books, together with a map of the Pays Bas I had brought from Ghent, in the anticipation of country quarters. Clean linen was airing over the back of one of the tapestry chairs, with other preparations for dressing for dinner; whilst coiled up near the blazing hearth lay my old faithful dog and constant companion for the last ten years.

Our mess-room was as much changed, and the preparations for dinner had given it quite another air to what it had when first seen. Like most of the others, it was spacious, but, unlike them, inasmuch as the windows down to the floor were in the modern French style. Of these there were only two—one looking over the garden and woods, the other over a small field or lawn, bounded on two of its sides by double rows of noble beeches, and on the other two (round which ran the road or lane leading to Brussels) by orchards, hop-grounds, etc. etc. Each had an old iron balcony, so rust-eaten that they seemed ready to drop into the water of the moat which lay below them. Over the elaborately carved antique-looking chimney-piece was a large painting of a castle, with a number of men apparently employed clearing the ditch. The floor had been swept, chairs and tables collected from different parts of the house, and one of the latter covered by a clean tablecloth, and our canteen apparatus laid out for dinner—the whole looking so much more comfortable than we expected, that even our grumblers voted the old chateau not so bad after all, as they sat themselves down to the well-covered board. For the feast, not a despicable one, as well as the arrangement of the salon, we were indebted to the indefatigable activity and unrivalled skill of our friend Karl —a worthy whom I have not yet introduced; so, by way of episode, whilst we are enjoying the good viands of his preparation, let me do so.

On the memorable night of our landing at Ostend, whilst standing on the sands, I was accosted by a very handsome youth of about eighteen or twenty, who asked if I wanted a servant. His costume indicated that he meant himself, for he wore a green livery-coat with red cuffs and collar, and a glazed hat with a cockade in it. His history was, that he had lived some time with General Vandamme, and had accompanied him to Moscow; but on returning into Saxony, although he had been a great favourite with the General, this noble personage one day deserted him most unexpectedly, leaving him, not only without money, but also without a prospect of recovering the long arrears of wages due to him—[there was a mystery in this part of the story]—and after vainly waiting in hopes still that the General might return or send for him, he had set out and found his way thus far towards France, when the chance of getting employment amongst *les officiers Anglais* (and no doubt some of their *guinées*) had occurred to him, and I was the first he had addressed. His figure was rather under the middle size, extremely well made; face beautiful, and address perfect. Moreover, according to his own account, he was a pearl without price. He could speak five or six languages, and cook, cut and dress hair, and a thousand other things I have forgotten; but the great recommendation was a talent he had acquired, when with the French army, of *discovering* and *appropriating* the resources of a country—Anglicé, *plundering*. If Monsieur would but try him, he would find him so attentive, so faithful. For his part, he was sure he should soon love Monsieur—his countenance was so amiable. All would not do—I rejected him; but Leathes took a liking to and engaged him. So thenceforth he became one of us, and soon a general favourite; for although he had sounded his own trumpet, he had in nowise exaggerated his qualifications, nor even told us all, for in addition he was the merriest and most kind-hearted creature I ever met with. He had an inexhaustible fund of stories and songs, and sang beautifully, and in a most sweet and melodious voice; was an admirable mimic, and amongst other things mimicked so well two flutes, that one day, at Strytem, sitting smoking my cigar on the parapet of the bridge, I actually made sure two people were playing a duet in the kitchen; but upon going thither, found only Karl, who, seated on a table, was warbling out a favourite waltz, like a robin on the housetop.

Our language he had soon added to his stock, and being now a tolerable proficient, and evidently so well suited for the office, we had at once nominated him major-domo (spite of his youth) this morning on arriving, and placed all the other servants under his directions. But although understanding and speaking English sufficiently for all common purposes, and to communicate with the other servants, he never would address any of us but in French. To return again to the course of our narrative. Our cheerful meal had been discussed with many an encomium on the provider, and the circulation of the bottle had already produced a genial exhilaration amongst our party, when the door was abruptly thrown open, and in rushed our friend Karl, holding his sides, and unable to speak for laughter. "Why, Karl, what the devil's the matter now?" "C'est l'adjoint, monsieur, qui demande à vous parler." "Well, what of that? Is there anything very comical in this visit?"—"Excusez, monsieur, il est si drôle—est-ce que je lui ferai entrer, monsieur," and the merry young dog tried to compose his features. I was about to go out to meet this functionary and learn his business, but the whole mess cried out with one voice to bring him in—curiosity being excited by Karl's obstreperous laughter; so I desired him to be admitted. Karl soon returned, ushering in with most ludicrous gravity the worthy *maire*, and his cortège (for it appeared he had not come alone), who, each as he crossed the threshold, making a profound salaam, followed his leader until they were all drawn up in line across the end of the room. The appearance of the party was certainly comic, and for a few moments we contemplated each other in silent amazement. The principal figure of this group—he on the right of the line, Mynheer Jan Evenpoel, *adjoint-maire*—was a short, fat, square-built man, with a head like a pumpkin deeply set (*zabullida*, the Spaniards would say) between his broad high shoulders; countenance stolidity itself; little pig-eyes, half hid in the swell of his fat cheeks and the thick overhanging brow; nose pudsy, resembling a lump of brown clay thrown against his face more than a nose; a monstrous wide (now half-open) mouth, showing within a row of fangs standing apart like palisades; a great fat dew-lap; the whole phiz finished by two enormous projecting ears. Such was the object that had excited so powerfully the risible faculties of young Karl. Our silent gaze seemed to paralyse him. There he stood, evidently endeavouring to assume some sort of an air of office, but trembling visibly, and as visibly perspiring from his extreme nervousness, twirling his hat in his hand, looking timidly, first at me, then at the formidable party round the table, then inquiringly glancing at his own party. The poor man's evident anxiety must have excited pity, had it not more forcibly excited our risibility, as well as that of Karl.

Three peasants, heavy-looking men, with somewhat more intelligence in their countenances, yet decidedly equally alarmed, arranged themselves next to Mynheer Evenpoel. These, as well as their chief, were all arrayed in their roast-beef suits—jackets of cotton, unmentionables of black or bottle-green velveteen, blue-and-white-striped cotton stockings, clumsy silver knee- and shoe-buckles—such was their costume. The eternal *bonnet de nuit* for this time had given place to rather smart round hats, with a profusion of plush on them. Drawn up on their left stood the old gardener, his two sons—stout peasants, clad something like, though more humbly than, the rest—and Mademoiselle "*Mon-père-dit*," also in her best bib and tucker, trying to look amiable, but evidently most particularly anxious. Lastly, with a brisk, self-satisfied air, stepped in one of the most extraordinary-looking personages of the whole party—a diminutive spare figure with a complexion like mahogany, but upright, and of a most martial bearing. He was clad in a short green uniform coat, with large copper buttons decorated with the imperial eagle of France, green pantaloons, and an enormous leathern cocked-hat, which he touched by way of salute on entering, but, soldier-like, retained on his head. In his hand he carried a sort of javelin, or short hunting-spear. This dignitary, a person of most decided importance, passing the others, stepped briskly up and placed himself at the elbow of the trembling magistrate, who drew a long breath, and gave unequivocal testimony of satisfaction at seeing his tutelary genius by his side.

The important personage just described was the *garde-champêtre*—or *garde-village*, as he was more frequently called —a sort of police officer placed by Napoleon in every village of his empire. I never could ascertain precisely the position and duties of these people; they seemed to be chief police officers, and the *maires* paid them great deference, seldom acting in extraordinary cases without their advice and concurrence. They acted as gamekeepers and constables, billeted troops, and exercised a general surveillance in the commune. No doubt they noted and made reports of all they saw and heard, so that H.I. Majesty had an authorised spy in every village. They were well paid, and the situation appeared to be a comfortable retreat for old soldiers, for such we always found them to be. Our present friend (called familiarly by the peasantry Petit Jean) had served in a regiment of the line under Marshal Suchet in Catalonia, and although still only a middle-aged man, had been pensioned on account of having lost two fingers of his left hand, and placed here for life as *garde-village*. Well, the whole cortège has entered the room, and ranged themselves in line across the lower end of it, close to the wall; the shuffling of feet has ceased, and a profound silence prevails. We sit staring at them, and wondering what the deuce they interrupt us for. Bowing and scraping renewed spontaneously; again silence, but various glances are shot at and signs made to Mynheer Evenpoel, which in his fright he utterly disregards, and stands like an owl, without a movement except the evident shaking of his limbs. After a while old Ingleby, who had been leaning over the back of his chair eyeing the poor devil, utters in his usual gruff Yorkshire way, "*Well, sir?*" without reflecting on the fact of his English not being understood. The tone is enough, however, and it determines the party to bolder measures—the quaking magnate is actually shoved forward to the table. Petit Jean also advances, and again places himself at the poor man's elbow; his right arm, outstretched, bears upon the upright javelin, the butt of which he plants firmly, and with an air, on the floor; in his mutilated left hand he holds up to us an unfolded sheet of foolscap, which we soon ascertain to be inscribed by certain characters calculated to extract hay and corn, etc., from the lofts and granaries of our clients—in short, the requisition for forage and provisions, etc., of our quartermaster-general addressed to the commune of Strytem. The brown little warrior looks complacently round the company as though he would say, "And I also am a soldier; *Moi!*" After repeated applications of a very scanty blue cotton handkerchief to his front—*pour essuyer la sueur*—the worthy magistrate at length, in a trembling, hesitating voice, opens his oration, gains courage as he goes on, warms, and even becomes rather energetic towards the conclusion of nearly a quarter of an hour's talk, to which we have listened, but understood not a word. Mynheer salaams, wipes his front, and stands, mouth half-open, attending the applause due to his exertions, and our reply to his statements, whatever they may be. Petit Jean comprehends the dilemma, steps forward with a military salute, places himself again in an attitude, and, whilst Mynheer stares and seems to envy his self-possession, requests permission of *messieurs les officiers* to explain what M. l'Adjoint would wish to say, and goes off at score— "M. Evenpoel only expresses the sentiments of the whole commune when he assures *messieurs les officiers* that the arrival of the brave English has diffused throughout its population the most lively joy. *Les Anglais* are a people as generous as they are brave, and M. l'Adjoint rests satisfied that under the protection of M. le Commandant the peaceful tranquillity of the commune will remain undisturbed." Here, at a glance from Petit Jean, M. Evenpoel and the whole cortège salaam together, repeating with one consent, "Mais c'est vrai—c'est vrai! Oui, M. le Commandant, c'est vrai cà!" Petit Jean resumes. "*But*, M. le Commandant, we sensibly regret the poverty of our commune, and are *au déséspoir* that Milor Wellington should have sent his brave soldiers to so miserable a place—a place so incapable of affording them the good cheer (*bon traitement*) that they so richly merit, whilst the surrounding country abounds in rich and populous villages, fully adequate to lodge them comfortably (*convenablement*) and to supply all their wants. It was only *l'année passée* that this poor commune was oppressed and impoverished by being obliged to provide for a corps of Prussians during several months. These people, undisciplined and *bien méchants*, plundered us all without restraint, and wantonly consumed our whole substance—hardly leaving wherewithal to support our miserable existence. Thus ruined and impoverished, M. le Commandant, we feel assured, will see that, in spite of our good wishes, we are in an impossibility of supplying the immense rations of forage, etc., here demanded"; and here, taking off his chapeau and making a most profound salaam, he again flourishes before us the obnoxious sheet of foolscap, whilst M. l'Adjoint, beginning to fidget, indicates an inclination to renew his harangue amidst a general buzz of approbation, and a reiteration of "C'est vrai, mon commandant, c'est bien vrai." M. le Commandant silences them by observing, "That a soldier must obey orders—that it is for his general to think and investigate—that Milor Wellington, or those acting for him, had no doubt sufficiently informed themselves as to the resources of the country before they ordered troops thither — that, having done so, right or wrong, these troops must live— that it is evident from the good case of all present, particularly of M. le Maire, that the commune did produce something to eat and drink;—consequently, the gentlemen are invited to allow our partaking with them, or we must help ourselves, which would be *bien facheux.*" A general grunt—"Ah, mon Dieu!"—accompanied by deep sighs on the part of Mademoiselle "*Mon-père-dit.*" I should have stated that M. le Maire and a farmer named Walsdragen were the only two ignorant of French. The former of these had profited by an offered chair, and seated himself during the oration of Petit Jean and my answer. Hearing the concert of sighs and groans, he opens his little pig-eyes to the utmost, and casting them about on the surrounding group, seems to demand an explanation. Petit Jean communicates the awful purport of my answer. Agitation recommences, and I am conjured, for pity's sake, at least to delay until an express be sent to Brussels to acquaint Milor Wellington of the utter impossibility of so large a body of men and horses being supported by so poor a place. Poor simple people! I should like to have witnessed the reception of the delegate. M. le Commandant observes that M. le Maire may do as to him seemeth best, but cannot be so unreasonable as to expect that we and our horses should wait for supper until his messenger return—ergo, as it is already late, M. le Maire is again invited to lose no more time in talking, but to proceed forthwith in collecting the articles demanded. But, to make a long story short, after a deal of action and whispering in a corner of the room, they made a proposition to furnish one-half the quantity. And here it flashed across me, that these people must be dealt with like the Turkish rayah, who, after protesting his incapability to produce a single egg for a whole hour, at last, upon the application of the Mikmander's whip, brings out a whole store of good things. So I cut the matter short by sending Karl for the quartermaster, who was without awaiting the result of the Maire's visit. The old veteran enters, head erect, shoulders thrown back, and steel scabbard jangling on the floor as he advanced to the table, and silently made his salute. The assembled rustics gape and stare at him in evident alarm. Mynheer trembles, Petit Jean draws himself up, as if imitating old Hall's military bearing, whilst I, pointing him out to the assembled multitude, inform them that in five minutes he will proceed at the head of a foraging party to rummage their barns, granaries, and larders, and help himself. The quartermaster, having received his orders, makes his salute, without deigning even a glance at the Maire and party, amongst whom a precious scene of confusion now takes place, amidst which out they all trundle after old Hall, without even the ceremony of a parting salaam; and we, replenishing our glasses, drank success to our foray, rejoicing in having got rid of the noise. Our quiet, however, was of very short duration, for in the court Hall was already assembling his party, and neither understood their remonstrances nor attended to their grimaces; so with one accord back they came upon us, bursting into the room as unceremoniously as they had just left it, bellowing like so many bulls. A new negotiation opened, and terminated with a promise that everything should be brought in if I would give them *two hours*, after they had vainly struggled for daybreak—and away they went. The two hours had nearly elapsed, and we were still at table, when Petit Jean, foaming with rage, burst into the room unaccompanied: "Ah, mais ces faquins là bas—ils ne font que se moquer de vous et de vôtre bonté, Monsieur le Commandant. Mais excusez, monsieur, je suis militaire, moi! et je me suis indigne de voir des militaires se laisser tromper par des vilains paysans; qui qu'ils sont, connaissent très bien l'accueil q'ils auraient reçus à la main d'un officier Prussien, ou même Français. Avec permission, monsieur, je m'en vais amener avec moi vos fourrageurs faire un fourrage militairement"; and, without waiting for an answer, the little hero bolted, and following to the hall-door, there we saw him sure enough march out of the gate perched upon one of our immense gun-horses, looking for all the world like a monkey on a dromedary. In two hours bread, forage, and all—nay, more than we had demanded—were brought in.

Meantime our sergeant of the guard comes in for orders as to what he shall do with the mayor. "The mayor?— what have you to do with the mayor?" "Why, we have him safe in the guard-room, sir." "The devil you have! and by whose order?" "Why, sir, we thought it best to keep him until the foraging-party with *Pitty Jan* returned, least he might try to hinder 'em." Here was a dilemma, should the old man complain to headquarters. However, on sending an officer to release him, and explain the mistake, Mynheer was too frightened to think of anything but rejoicing at gaining his liberty. Perhaps conscience told him that he deserved punishment for the imposition he had attempted to practise on us.

Petit Jean from that moment became our great friend and ally. On almost all occasions he sided with the soldiers in any little difference between them and the boors. On one occasion a complaint had been made to me, by a man who lived near the gate, that one of our gunners had not only plundered his potato-garden, but had also otherwise ill-treated him. On my going to investigate the business on the spot, it turned out that he had struck the gunner. Petit Jean, who had accompanied me officially, on hearing this, turned suddenly on the fellow, "You sacré cochon! frapper un militaire; sacré vilain homme! Quoi!—un vil paysan frapper un militaire? Ah, que cela me révolte!"—and seizing a stake from the hedge, foaming with unfeigned anger, he fell on the poor devil, and fairly chased him out of sight, belabouring him all the way. What English soldier would ever take up the cudgels against his own countryman because the French soldier was his brother-in-arms? Whenever his patrol duty did not call him out, he was sure to be found in the guard-room, or somewhere amongst the men. He might certainly have been a spy in the camp, for Buonaparte had most accurate information respecting the state, positions, and numbers of our army, part of which no doubt was communicated by these *gardes-champêtres*, who, as before mentioned, were all old French soldiers, and did not conceal their attachment to the Emperor. Spy or no spy, Petit Jean was always extremely obliging, and frequently of most essential service to us. Our equipment was in every way too perfect to leave any care as to what might be reported of our state;

and as to future movements, we were as ignorant of them as
Napoleon himself. But to return to our story. The row
was all over, our mess-party broken up, and I retired to my
room; but, alas! on getting into bed I found sleep impossible
—the moat under my window was peopled with millions of
frogs, and such was the horrid croaking of these little
wretches, that sleep was out of the question, and the Van
Voldens were avenged.

CHAPTER VII

THE next morning a most superb breakfast was on my table when I returned from a stroll in the woods—the finest milk, eggs, and butter I ever saw in my life, and in profusion. My servant had procured them at the adjoining farm, and so cheap, that he had brought a large soup-plate full of eggs and an antique jug holding more than two quarts of milk. During our whole stay at Strytem there was never any difference in this respect—always abundance. After breakfast, the usual watering order parade took place in the grand avenue, under the shade of stately beeches. The contented countenances of the men, the sleek coats and frolicksome spirit of the horses, testified sufficiently that neither had fared indifferently. I found, however, that the chateau farm was rather crowded, and therefore detached the 1st division, officer and all, to a small village, with a pretty chateau on the hill, about a mile from us—Yseringen. This move made all hands completely comfortable, and so we went on. Nothing could exceed the delicious tranquillity I enjoyed in Strytem. For those who preferred more bustle and more society Brussels was at hand, and thither they frequently repaired; on the other side Ninove, the headquarters of Lord Uxbridge, who commanded the cavalry, was only three or four miles distant, and all the surrounding villages were full of cavalry or horse-artillery. Every one breakfasted in his own apartment. At 10 a.m. watering order parade and inspection of horses, etc. Then, after visiting the billets and getting through any casual business, I was at liberty, and, mounting my horse, employed the remainder of the morning in exploring the country. In the evening we all assembled to our social meal. Those who had been to Brussels (or, as we used to say, "Up to town") usually brought some news, or at least some gossip, which added zest to the excellent cheer almost always on our board.

How our table was furnished I do not exactly recollect, my notes on the subject being silent,[1] but believe the meat was ration brought from Ninove every day by our commissary (Mr Coates), so was the bread. Poultry, vegetables, etc. etc., we procured in abundance amongst our neighbours; our wine came from Brussels; candles, wood, etc., from Ninove. After dinner some took a short ride previous to seeing their horses done up for the night. For my part, I preferred enjoying the calm beauties of evening with my cigar under the splendid avenue of beech in rear of the chateau, and when night closed in, retired to my antique saloon, which a blazing fire of fagots and a couple of candles made tolerably comfortable. Here I busied myself in Madame de Genlis's *Life of Henri IV.*, sometimes until midnight, tranquil and happy. At times, as I occasionally look up from my book and cast my eyes round, no sound interrupting the solemn stillness save the ticking of my watch as it lay on the table before me, the croaking of the frogs, or the moaning of the wind as it eddied round the old hall, I could almost fancy the deep-toned portraits of *ci-devant* Van Voldens, in their sombre velvet suits and stiff ruffs, actually embued with life, and frowning on my intrusion; or fixing them on the door of the chapel, I would conjure up figures of warriors, *bourgmestres*, or damsels clad all in white, raising the tapestry, and——but then old Bal, getting up from his place before the fire to scratch himself, or the voice of the sentry in the outer court solemnly proclaiming "All's well," would suddenly recall me from my reverie to a consciousness that it was bedtime; and so to bed I hied me, to sleep as well as the eternal frog-concert would allow. Such was the general tenor of our life at Strytem, varied a little at times by circumstances to be related as they occurred, and sometimes disturbed for a moment by reports of hostile movements, or the low murmurs of a distant cannonade. This last, however, was heard so frequently, without being followed by any consequences, that we got accustomed to, and finally disregarded, it. Subsequently we found that it proceeded from the practice and exercising of the Belgic artillery at Mons, or somewhere

---

[1] The moat supplied us daily a dish of very fine carp, and the gardener's sons occasionally shot us a hare or two.

in that direction. My rides, after a time, brought me some-what acquainted with the neighbouring country, but only by slow degrees, for surely never was reconnaissance of any country more difficult,—it was a perfect labyrinth.

In the immediate neighbourhood of Strytem the ground arose in a succession of round-topped hills, of no very great height, and all very much alike. Of these, the summits, and frequently the slopes, were clothed with woods of oak, ash, beech, etc. etc., intermixed with coppice of the finest hazel I ever saw, thus forming a number of little valleys running into each other, but all from the profusion of wood and the overlapping (if I may use the term) of the flanks of the hills, presenting an appearance of the most perfect seclusion. Amongst these woods were scattered large tracts of cultivated ground, laid out in fields of wheat, rye, barley, buckwheat, hops, clover, etc. etc., frequently here enclosed by thick and lofty hedges; quite in the bottoms, and lying along a small stream of water, which ran through almost every one of these little valleys, were meadows of the liveliest verdure, whilst rows of magnificent elms fringed the banks and overshadowed the rippling waters of the rivulets. Villages and detached farms were of constant recurrence, and in all directions one saw the modest spires of the village churches rising above the massed and verdant foliage. Although these woods were, generally speaking, of no great extent—perhaps only a few acres—yet were there some of such extent as to entitle this to the appellation of a woody, or even forest, country. The Bois de Lieder-kerke, for instance, commenced near the village of Paemêle, and extended no less than four miles in the direction of Assche; everywhere two or three miles wide, including a great variety of ground, and in different directions were several others nearly of the same extent. At first, one is surprised at finding such vast tracts of woodland in a country so populous and so assiduously cultivated; but the thing is easily explained. In addition to the ordinary demands for small wood in husbandry, there are large and numerous hop-grounds requiring a continual supply of poles; but, above all, the enormous quantity of fuel required, not only by the peasantry, but also by the inhabitants of the towns, —wood being almost exclusively used for that purpose.

The kind of country I have been describing extended northward from us as far as Assche—perhaps much farther, but of that I know not—and eastward to Brussels. Towards the south the round hills gradually gave place to longer slopes and plateaux, and the woods became less frequent, but the villages were numerous, with the same careful cultivation everywhere. Toward the west, and only a few miles distant, we were bounded by the Dender, holding its course through extensive flat meadows covered with luxuriant crops of hay, or affording pasturage to herds of fine cattle. Beyond the river-valley the country assumed a different aspect: long and less abrupt slopes; woods fewer and thinner; a total absence of hedges; altogether presenting an aspect in many places bare and cheerless, strongly contrasting with the lovely scenery about Strytem—if I may call scenery lovely where we find neither rock, nor mountain, nor precipice, nor torrent; but it is home scenery, and its character simplicity, luxuriance, abundance, tranquillity, and repose. There one saw the rustic dwellings of the peasantry situated in secluded nooks, and embosomed in orchards and hop-grounds; the rural village with its modest church low down in the rich bottom, surrounded by smiling fields of grain or clover; a gentle rivulet slowly winding its devious way amidst the rank luxuriance of vegetation clothing its overhanging banks; the whole encased, as it were, by wavy heights, crowned with thick and verdant woods. One thing, however, was wanting to complete this picture of rural wealth and happiness—it wanted the animating presence of domestic animals, of herds and flocks dotting the fair surface of its fields. The farms in this country are not large as with us; the farmer does not live in a splendid mansion, still more splendidly furnished, nor does he idle away his time in shooting or fox-hunting. The Flemish farmer is a plain honest rustic, clad in homespun grey, a cotton nightcap on his head, wooden shoes on his feet, and the everlasting short pipe in his mouth; he himself holds the plough, guides his team, or assists in thrashing out his grain. Ignorance of their language prevented my acquiring more information concerning them and their affairs than what could be done by observation of outward appearance; therefore I could neither learn the extent of their farms, their ideas on agriculture, the amount of rents, length of leases, nor the value of land, etc. Coarsely fed and coarsely clad, still they are an industrious, hard-working, and contented race; not very intelligent, I allow, but perhaps they are the happier for it;—they are kind to their inferiors, affable and communicative with their equals, and respectful, almost to servility, to their superiors, or those they fancy such.[1]

Although many of the farming establishments in our neighbourhood resembled in plan and construction those already described about Dendermonde, yet were they not universally of this description. That adjoining the chateau was really a very fine one—substantial brick house, barns, outhouses of every kind, all on a great scale, and, as usual, surrounded by a spacious court. But others were very different from this; many were very humble abodes, constructed of wood or clay, with thatched roofs and small casement windows, standing along the edges of the fields, with their barn adjoining but not united, nor any courtyard for manure, etc., the outbuildings all on a small scale, as also, I suppose, were their farms. Others, standing likewise open in the fields, were again of a different character. These had high thatched roofs projecting several feet beyond the walls, and supported by rough posts, forming a sort of verandah; this is filled up to the eaves with firewood—some in logs, some in fagots—which gives to the exterior a very rude appearance, and must make the interior very dark, from the great depth of embrasure thus formed both to door and window; but to balance this, it keeps the house cool in summer and warm in winter. Although the actual village of Strytem consisted of no more than the chateau, the farm, and the few mean houses clustered round the church, yet the commune was extensive, comprising not only many fine farms, but also other and more important villages. The real *maire* was M. le Baron Von Volden, son

---

[1] Such crops I never before saw, particularly those vividly green crops of *trèf*, which really appeared so thick that one might walk on them without sinking to the ground. But to me the height attained by the rye was most astonishing. In one field which I rode through nearly every day it was as high as my head, when mounted on my little horse Cossack, about 14¾ hands high, so that it could not have been less than 7 or 8 feet, the ears remarkably full and looking well.

of the proprietress of our chateau. He, however, seldom came nearer the place than Brussels, leaving to his worthy *adjoint*, Jan Evenpoel, the care of administering the government, and at the time of our arrival either was in Paris, or had but just returned from it. Where the *maire* is thus vested in the person of the *châtelain*, the post seems to be one of much importance—not confined to the police of the village alone, but extending to a general superintendence over the welfare of the commune, the state of the roads, etc. etc. Whether owing to the baron being so much an absentee I know not, but the roads all about Strytem were hardly passable after heavy rain (of which we had a pretty good share), not only from their badness, having no foundations, and receiving little or no repair, but also from the unctuous and slippery soil, which makes riding absolutely dangerous immediately after rain. Some of the worst sloughs, which otherwise would be quite impassable, are repaired, as in Russia, Poland, and America, by laying logs transversely, and covering them with brushwood, and then earth; but these, after a little weathering and wear and tear, become absolutely dangerous from horses slipping in between the logs, sometimes up to the shoulder.

This was one of the drawbacks upon our enjoyment in this otherwise pleasant country; and, having confessed as much, I may as well admit that there were a few others which prevented us from living in a state of absolute and unalloyed happiness. One grievance was the cheapness of gin—a villanous kind of spirit manufactured in the country, and on which a man could get "royal" for twopence; for though our men were really fine fellows and generally very steady soldiers, yet, like other Englishmen, they could not resist a social glass nor avoid its consequences; and, indeed, if excuse it be, they were in a measure driven to the use of this pernicious spirit by the execrable quality of all the beer in the country, which more resembled a mixture of cow-dung and water than anything else. The sale of this poison took place in a small cabaret near the church, which was usually thronged with our people every evening after stable-hour; and, strange to say, where they mixed most sociably with the boors, to my no small astonishment. It is a curious fact, that upon inquiry of the sergeant-

major how they could understand each other, he replied
that the Yorkshire, Lancashire, and Lincolnshire men, who
spoke very broad, could make themselves understood pretty
well, and in like manner could comprehend the Flemish
of their boon companions.   Quarrels would sometimes arise
in this *tabagie*, which occasioned a temporary derangement
of our tranquil life.   But that was a trifle to another grievance
which stuck to us incessantly, and was the most serious
drawback we endured during our sojourn in the valley of
Strytem.   I allude to the infernal and eternal frog-concert
that nightly disturbed our rest more or less, and kept us in a
constant state of irritability.   For a few days we bore this
curse very philosophically, then began to war against the
wretches by pelting them with stones, firing at them with
small-shot, beating the water with poles, etc. etc., but all
to no purpose, for though we killed them by scores, yet did
their numbers never appear to thin nor their detestable
"quoah, quoah" to lessen in intensity.   Then we made
the wheeler construct a raft, and with this some one was
always cruising and slaying, yet still no alleviation to the
evil.   A council was held, and it was determined that
nothing short of draining the moat would avail, and therefore
drained it should be.   Curiosity had some hand in this
decision, for we had heard that the moat contained the
largest carp ever seen—a fish several feet in length, and
weighing I know not what.   The old gardener, when
acquainted with our resolve and ordered to make the
necessary preparations, was perfectly astounded, and (as
did Mademoiselle and the sons) used every sort of argument to turn us from it ;   amongst others, he assured us
that *l'année passée* the Prussians had attempted to drain the
moat merely to kill all the fish—"les sacré vilains hommes!"
but the stench arising from it when low, quickly obliged them
to desist.   It would not do—we were peremptory; and at
length the old man opened the voider, closed the feeder,
and to our delight the work of destruction began.   Day
after day the water gradually receded from the foot of the
old walls and from the opposite bank—already in many
places the oozy slime of the bottom began to appear—
already we rejoiced at the innumerable corpses of our
enemies lying on it everywhere; the upper part of the moat

was already, not dry, but waterless; and we were on the point of seeing the giant leviathan, when lo! the weather, hitherto cool and showery, became superb, and the heat almost insufferable. Decomposition, animal and vegetable, commenced with alarming rapidity, and the mephitic vapours thus produced pervading every creek and corner of the chateau, obliged us, *bongré malgrè*, to reclose the voider and reopen the feeder,—and thus terminated *la guerre aux grenouilles*. But, alas! our punishment for having resisted the entreaties and warnings of the old gardener was not to close with the sluices. The same hot sun had dried up nearly all the sources whence the moat had been fed, and many a long day of disgust and repentance had we to endure ere the waters again covered the odious slime sufficiently to relieve us from its nauseous stink, and to enable the frogs to renew their song, which, when they did, was to us a song of joy; and we had the further mortification of finding that, with a little patience, we might have saved ourselves all the trouble and suffering, for we had become so accustomed to it that it fell on our ear innocuous.

But the charms of a country life have so occupied my brain as to chase from it all recollection of being a soldier. To be sure, professional occupations did not consume a very great portion of our time, yet still there remain a few little items worthy of being recorded—*imprimis*, drills. So completely is the whole of this country (not occupied by wood) under tillage, that it was long after our arrival at Strytem ere we discovered a spot on which we could even draw out the troop, much less exercise it. At length, and I cannot recollect how, we found a piece of scrubby common of some acres in extent near the village of Denderhout, some miles off on the other side of the Dender, and not far from Alost. Thither, then, we repaired occasionally to practise ourselves, and prevent our people forgetting entirely their drills. Thither also came occasionally His Highness of Berri with his newly formed corps of cavalry to learn theirs. We frequently met, and as the ground was too confined to admit of both corps working at the same time, the last comers were obliged to dismount and wait until the others had done, for we continued our operations when first on the ground, regardless of the impatience of the royal drill-master, who, though he never said anything to us, did not fail to betray, by a thousand little pettish actions, the annoyance he felt at our want of due respect.   One day that they had got in possession and we were obliged to wait, I had a good opportunity of seeing this curious corps and its savage leader. The former presented a most grotesque appearance— cuirassiers, hussars, grenadiers à cheval, and chasseurs, dragoons and lancers, officers and privates, with a few of the new *garde de corps*, were indiscriminately mingled in the ranks.   One file were colonels, the next privates, and so on, and all wearing their proper uniforms and mounted on their proper horses, so that these were of all sizes and colours.   There might have been about two hundred men, divided into two or three squadrons, the commanders of which were generals.   The Prince, as I have said, was drill-master.   A more intemperate, brutal, and (in his situation) impolitic one, can scarcely be conceived.   The slightest fault (frequently occasioned by his own blunders) was visited by showers of low-life abuse—using on all occasions the most odious language.   One unfortunate squadron officer (*a general!*) offended him, and was immediately charged with such violence that I expected a catastrophe. Reining up his horse, however, close to the unhappy man, his vociferation and villanous abuse were those of a perfect madman; shaking his sabre at him, and even at one time thrusting the pommel of it into his face, and, as far as I could see, pushing it against his nose!   Such a scene!   Yet all the others sat mute as mice, and witnessed all this humiliation of their comrade, and the degradation of him for whom they had forsaken Napoleon.   Just at this moment one of our troop-dogs ran barking at the heels of the Prince's horse. Boiling with rage before, he now boiled over in earnest, and, stooping, made a furious cut at the dog, which, eluding the weapon, continued his annoyance.   The Duke, quitting the unfortunate *chef d'escadron*, now turned seriously at the dog, but he, accustomed to horses, kept circling about, yapping and snapping, and always out of reach; and it was not until he had tired himself with the fruitless pursuit that, foaming with rage, he returned to his doomed squadrons, who had sat quietly looking on at this exhibition.   While all this took place, I had made acquaintance with another general officer who appeared to be there in the capacity of aide-de-camp—a gentlemanly sort of man, who, having been many years in England with Louis XVIII., spoke English fluently. This man pleased me much at the time; he was then in adversity. I met him afterwards in prosperity—*nous verrons!*

Now that I have got on military affairs, it may be as well to record the manner in which this country was occupied—at least as far as my knowledge on the subject goes. First, then, headquarters of the cavalry and horse-artillery at Ninove, where was also the principal depot of forage and provisions. The reason for assembling the cavalry thus at some distance from the expected scene of operations was the great fertility of this part of Brabant, and the facility of communication with Alost, to which place, the Dender being navigable, advantage could be taken of the rich Pays de Waes. The villages, farms, etc., all round Ninove were full of troops.

Okegem.—Major M'Donald's troop   horse-artillery.
Paemêle.—Sir Robert Gardiner's   do.
Strytem and Yseringen.—Captain Mercer's   do.
Lombeke, Nôtre Dame.—Captain Sinclair's brigade of 9-pounders.
Lennik, St Martin.—Headquarters of Lieutenant-Colonel Hawker, Royal Artillery, commanding two batteries somewhere in his neighbourhood.
Beyond Ninove, westward, were the troops, horse-artillery, of Majors Bull, Ramsay, and Webber Smyth—forget names of villages.
Liederkerke, Denderlue, and vicinage.—Life Guards and Blues.
Schendelbeke and vicinage.—The three huzzar regiments, 10th, 15th, 18th.
Lerbeke, etc.—23d Light Dragoons.
Castre, etc.—16th   do.
Meerbeke.—Headquarters Sir O. Vandeleur with 12th and 13th Light Dragoons.
Grammont.—Foot Guards.
Enghien.—Foot Guards.
Schaepdale, etc.—Brunswick infantry ; all boys.
Brussels.—*The* headquarters—92d Highlanders, Rifles, Hanoverian infantry, and some Belgian dragoons and huzzars ;

grand depot of forage and provisions, and of artillery stores, etc. etc.

Mons.—English artillery and Dutch troops of different arms.

Assche.—Troop of Belgian horse-artillery.

Courtray, Atto, Tournay.—Believe huzzars of the K.G. Legion.

Visitors from England were at this time flocking over in great numbers, and travelling about amongst the cantonments; but ours was so secluded, being distant from every great road, that none of them found us out, until Sir G. A. Wood (our Colonel commanding), coming over to review the horse-artillery, brought with him the Knight of Kerry and another Irish gentleman (name forgotten), who passed a day with us in the old chateau, and were mightily pleased with our snuggery. The inspection took place on the little common at Denderhout. Six troops [1] were drawn out, and made a splendid show—for finer, as to equipment, men, horses, etc. etc., could not possibly be seen. Mine was generally allowed to be the finest (old G), though there was some hesitation in deciding between it and Webber Smyth's.

The line was scarcely formed when his Royal Highness of Berri arrived, and as usual got into a pet at finding himself forestalled. Sir Augustus Frazer, however, with his excellent manners and as excellent French, soothed him by expressions of regret, etc. etc., and stating that some of our people had come a long distance, and unless soon despatched, would hardly be able to get home before night. Roads bad, etc., otherwise, etc. etc. etc. The Duke cooled down, and condescended to accompany Sir G. Wood through the ranks. We then marched past, and off home.[2]

The French officers were all admiration and astonish-

---

[1] The *captains* were—viz. Lieutenant-Colonel Sir Hew D. Ross, Major Bull, —— Ramsay, Lieutenant-Colonel W. Smyth, Major M'Donald, Captain Mercer.

[2] The Duke of Wellington was so indifferent to the manner in which officers dressed, that they indulged in all sorts of fancies. I remember, at this inspection, Ramsay wore the light-cavalry belt instead of a sash ; Bull wore beard and mustache ; so did Newland ; I wore the mustache. The usual dress of hussars was frock-coat open, with a red waistcoat richly laced with gold. At that time our regimental pantaloons were *pepper-and-salt*, with straps of brown leather inside the legs and round the bottom, and a red stripe down outside seam.

ment: they had never seen anything so complete nor any troop so mounted.

At Waterloo, on the 18th June, there were present eight troops of British and two of Hanoverian horse-artillery. The British, as far as I can recollect, were: 1. Lieutenant-Colonel Sir Hew D. Ross's; 2. Major Bull's; 3. Major M'Donald's; 4. Major Ramsay's; 5. Lieutenant-Colonel Webber Smyth's; 6. Lieutenant-Colonel Sir Robert Gardiner's; 7. Major Beane's; 8. Lieutenant-Colonel Sir A. Dickson, *alias* Captain Mercer's; also Captain Whinyate's rocket troop. These were armed as follows: Major Bull's, six heavy $5\frac{1}{2}$-inch howitzers; Lieutenant-Colonel Gardiner's and W. Smith's, five light 6-pounders, and one light $5\frac{1}{2}$-inch howitzer—these two being attached to the hussar brigades; Captain Whinyate's rockets and light 6-pounders; each of the others had five 9-pounders and one heavy $5\frac{1}{2}$-inch howitzer; and these "heavy drags" (as we called them) were destined, by Sir Augustus Frazer, who commanded the horse-artillery, together with Bull's howitzers, to form a grand battery in reserve, to be applied as he might find occasion—a formidable reserve it would have been. However, it never came into play in that manner; for in the general orders of the army organising it, we were all posted to different brigades of cavalry, consequently Frazer's *grande batterie* vanished in smoke. In this allotment I fell to the first division, Lord Edward Somerset, composed of the three Household regiments, the Scots Greys, 1st Dragoon Guards, and 6th or Inniskillings. We continued, however, at Strytem, neither reporting to, nor receiving orders from, Lord Edward; nor did we ever join the division until 21st June, near Mons, whence we marched with them to Paris, and then again separated.

Of the field-artillery I know very little, but remember that, about the beginning of June, Sir Augustus Frazer, who was Sir G. Wood's *right-hand man*, told me that, including the horse-artillery, there were then twenty brigades of British artillery, or 120 pieces, ready to take the field. More arrived, I believe, after this; I know Beane's troop of horse-artillery did. What number of Hanoverian, Dutch, Belgic, etc., there might be, I never knew.

Whence it originated, I cannot conjecture, but, certes,

much indecision did exist about this time as to our armament. Shortly after our arrival at Strytem, we were ordered to send our light 6-pounders to Ghent, there to be exchanged for *heavies*. These, after a few days, were to be sent back and replaced by the 9-pounders, which eventually we kept.

These changes, whilst in progress, cost me considerable anxiety, from the dread of a move taking place whilst my guns were absent—an event the more to be dreaded, since the Duke never attended to any justification if anything went wrong; nor would he have looked to my superiors, but myself alone, and thus I should have borne the whole weight of his anger.

At length, about the beginning of June we were complete, when my troop establishment was as follows, viz.:—

5 guns, 9-pounders, and 1 heavy 5½-inch howitzer— 8 horses each	48
9 ammunition waggons—viz. 1 to each piece, and a spare one per division—6 horses each . . .	54
1 spare-wheel carriage—6 horses	6
1 forge, 1 curricle-cart, 1 baggage-waggon—4 horses each	12
Total in draught . . .	120
6 mounted detachments—8 horses each . . .	48
2 staff-sergeants, 2 farriers, 1 collar-maker . .	5
6 officers' horses, lent them by the Board of Ordnance	6
6 officers' mules, for carrying their baggage . .	6
Total	185
Additional horses unaccounted for above, spare, etc. .	30
General total of animals . .	215
Besides which, each officer had his own two horses, and the surgeon one, making 11 more—so that, including these, we had	226

The *personnel* consisted of—Second Captain, Mercer, commanding; Captain Pakenham (subsequently Newland) as Second Captain; Lieutenants Bell, Hincks, Ingleby, and Leathes—the former acting as adjutant to Sir A. Frazer, the latter as supernumerary; and before we left Strytem,

Ingleby exchanged with Lieutenant Breton, and joined Sir Robert Gardiner's troop; so that, finally, it stood: Breton, Hincks, Leathes—surgeon, Hitchins; 2 staff-sergeants, 3 sergeants, 3 corporals, 6 bombardiers, 1 farrier, 3 shoeing smiths, 2 collar-makers, 1 wheeler, 1 trumpeter, and 1 acting do., 80 gunners, 84 drivers—the 1 acting trumpeter not included. The organisation was in three divisions, of two subdivisions each—a subdivision being one piece of ordnance, with its ammunition waggon and detachment. Each division had one spare ammunition waggon and a proportion of the other carriages, etc. The division was commanded by a lieutenant, and the sub-divisions, the right of the division by a sergeant, the left by a corporal—a bombardier to each subdivision. On parade, the 5⅜-inch howitzer was the right of the centre division. Perhaps at this time a troop of horse-artillery was the completest thing in the army; and whether broken up into half-brigades under the first and second captains, or into divisions under their lieutenants, or subdivisions under their sergeants and corporals, still each body was a perfect whole.

CHAPTER VIII

I HAVE confessed a little further back that the happiness of our sojourn in this lovely country was not without some alloy; and having done so, I may add one or two more items to this balance, *per contra*.

Soon after our arrival at Strytem, an officer of the commissariat was attached to the troop, for the purpose of feeding us and our animals. His first care was to secure a sufficient number of country waggons, with their drivers and horses, intending to keep them together ready for a move. The farmers, finding this a grievance, besieged me, personally and through Mynheer Evenpoel, to allow them to remain at home until wanted. This Mr Coates (who, by the way, was an experienced and excellent commissary) strongly opposed, foretelling the consequences but too truly; however, I yielded, upon a solemn promise of M. l'Adjoint that they should be held ready to move at a moment's notice. Having committed this folly, I was well punished for it by the anxiety I experienced at every report of a move; and at last when the hour did come, they were called and found wanting, and poor Mr Coates had to mount and hunt them up, when they ought to have been loaded and on the road. This was a lesson to me.

Another misery I endured was the constant apprehension of falling under the Duke's displeasure for systematic plundering of the farmers by our people, which I could not well check without risk of incurring the same on another score—*i.e.* for not doing it! This is enigmatical; let me explain. Our allowance of forage, though sufficient to keep our horses in pretty good condition when idle, was not sufficient when they were hard worked; nor was it sufficient at any time to put on them that load of flesh, and give them that rotundity of form which Peninsular practice had established as the *beau ideal* of a horse entering on a campaign, the maxim being—"The more flesh a horse carries, the more he has to lose, and the longer he will be able to bear privation." To keep up this, therefore, it was necessary to borrow from the farmers; and at this time of the year the superb crops of the *trèfe* offered themselves most opportunely. The practice was general amongst cavalry and artillery, so that all the horses were equally in good case; and it would have been a most dangerous proceeding, by abstaining from it, to let your horses appear thinner than those of your neighbour. The quick eye of the Duke would have seen the difference, asked no questions, attended to no justification, but condemned the unfortunate victim of samples as unworthy of the command he held, and perhaps sent him from the army. We therefore, like others, plundered the farmers' fields; with this difference, however, that we did it in a regular manner, and without waste—whereas many of the cavalry regiments destroyed nearly as much as they carried away, by trampling about the fields. The dread of this being reported kept me continually in hot water, for my farmers (who, under the reign of the Prussians, would never have dared utter a complaint), hearing how strictly plundering was forbidden by the Duke, soon became exceedingly troublesome with their threats of reporting me.[1] How we escaped it is difficult to say, but certainly we continued helping ourselves; and latterly St Cyr, and some other farmers, getting more docile, would themselves mark out where we were to cut. Our neighbour at the chateau farm (Walsdragen) was the most troublesome. The Duke was not partial to our corps, which made it still more fortunate for me that these people never put their threats in execution. It is difficult to say why, but his Grace certainly treated us harshly, and on many occasions unjustly. Of his harshness *voici un exemple*. Captain Whinyates having joined the army with the rocket troop, the Duke, who looked upon rockets as nonsense, ordered that they should be put into store, and the troop supplied with guns instead. Colonel Sir G. Wood, instigated by Whinyates, called on the Duke to ask permission to leave him his

---

[1] A report *was* sent to Brussels, but it never reached the Duke, for the simple people went in the first instance to Sir G. Wood, and there it was strangled.

rockets as well as guns. A refusal. Sir George, however,
seeing the Duke was in a particular good humour, ventured
to say, "It will break poor Whinyate's heart to lose his
rockets." "D—n his heart, sir; let my order be obeyed,"
was the answer thundered in his ear by the Duke, as he
turned on the worthy Sir George. Let me return to the
country and its charms.

With me one of the most delightful occupations is the
exploring a new country; so that, whilst others could not
exist except in Brussels, I found abundant occupation for my
leisure riding about the neighbourhood of Strytem. One
of my first rides was, as in duty bound, to Ninove. Instead
of taking the main road from Brussels thither, which runs
through Meerbeke, I took a by-one to Liederkerke, and,
turning to the left a short distance from this place, crossed
the gently flowing Dender, opposite the little village of
Okegem, by a rustic bridge supported on posts, so narrow
and fragile that it was not without demur, and at last leading
my horse, that I ventured over. I found the officers of
the troop here very humbly lodged—in mere cottages, and
that of a poor description. Nothing here comparable to
our lordly tapestried saloons at Strytem—to the which, by
the way, we were becoming attached, more particularly since
the fine weather had set in, and taught us to appreciate their
coolness and refreshing *demi-jour*.

The country, after passing the river, was not interesting,
as I have mentioned elsewhere, but the scenery improved
somewhat on drawing near Ninove, which place, with the
immense monastery of white stone built on the higher part
of the ground, had a somewhat imposing appearance:
drawing still nearer, some fragments of old walls begin to
make their appearance amongst the trees, which now became
more numerous, and we enter the place under a dark-
browed picturesque arch, flanked by two circular towers,
partly in ruins and overgrown with ivy, the whole half
concealed, until one turns short upon it, by the clustering
foliage of some handsome elms and the thick shrubbery of
bushes growing out of the old walls. As my horse's feet
resounded under the archway, a flash of romance came across
me, and I thought of the counts of Burgundy and their
romantic court, and pictured in my mind's eye some lordly

pageant streaming from out the archway in all its glittering
array. Sober reality soon banished romance. A short
street brought me from the gate to the head of the principal
one—long, broad, clean; houses low, and of rather a humble
description; on the whole, looking more like the street of an
English country town than anything I had seen in the Pays
Bas here; and standing across it was the monastery which
had formed so conspicuous a feature in the aspect of the
town from without. This, instead of representing the sort
of ecclesiastical building one would expect a monastery to
be, was a magnificent modern-built house of three stories,
pierced with numerous large sashed windows, looking airy
and cheerful—anything rather than the house of sorrow,
repentance, and abstinence. It is, I suspect, a modern
restoration of the monastery of Premonstrantine monks
mentioned by Blau, and the only one he does mention. It
was suppressed in 1792. Wandering into the court, which
was overrun with grass and weeds, I met the only remaining
brother of the order, the dress of which he wore. His
appearance was venerable, but whether it was that he was
naturally morose, or because I was a heretic, he would
answer none of my questions, only making a waive of the
hand in answer to my inquiry whether I might walk over
the premises. That this reserve did not arise from ignorance
of French, his immediately turning and giving directions
to a labourer in that language testified. Lord Uxbridge
and his staff having taken up their abode here restricted my
observations to the exterior of the building. I saw enough,
however, to learn that the Premonstrantine monks had once
been lodged like princes, and so passed on to look at the
town.

Ninove is prettily situated on the left bank of the Dender,
from which its spacious street ascends by a gentle acclivity;
and at this time it presented a very gay and bustling appearance, from the presence of the cavalry staff and the active
operations of the commissariat. It may contain about 3000
inhabitants, and was once surrounded by a wall, with flanking
towers, of which some vestiges still remain. I believe much
weaving is done here, and I saw several mills and tanneries.
Blau says the ancient name was "Nienevem, Ninoviam,
Ninovam, *vulgus* Kandrorum; *nunc* Ninovam—Gallo belgæ

Ninof appellant; Belgia regalis," etc.   So much for Ninove.
For that time I bid it adieu, and passing the bridge at the
bottom of the street, took my road homewards through the
pretty and interesting country to the southward of it.   Old
Blau says there was some joke against the people of Ninove
connected with its ancient name Ninevem, which he com-
pares with the Nineveh of Assyria.   In my way home,
passing through Meerbeke, I saw a handsome chateau,
where Sir Ormsby Vandeleur had his divisional headquarters.
It was a picturesque object, and truly Flemish in style,
though in situation, etc., it resembled an English country-
house—two stories, with numerous large windows, and the
usual double tier of dormitory windows in the high roof.
It was flanked at either end by a round tower, with the
characteristic conical roof.   The grounds were quite English.
A level lawn of smooth and verdant turf extended from the
front to the road.   Shrubberies of laburnums, etc., surrounded
it on three sides, concealing the offices, and these were
backed by a thick wood of lofty forest trees.   To judge from
externals, an agreeable quarter.

   The great Bois de Liederkerke afforded me a fine field
for exploration, and many a delightful ride I took amongst
its grateful shades.   In one of these I discovered, in the
very heart of it, a cleared spot of a few acres, part of which
was occupied by the blackened ruins of some building, and
part exhibited the very melancholy appearance of a once
handsome garden, run wild and gone to decay—even the
very ruins were nearly overrun by brushwood and weeds.
A peasant, whom I met with after leaving the wood, told me
that although he had never seen these ruins, he supposed
they must be the remains of a convent of nuns which once
existed somewhere in the wood, but had been burned many
years ago.   Ignorance of his language prevented my understanding a long story he told me—partly in Flemish, partly
in French—but I picked out that the nuns of this convent
had all been ladies of considerable, some of very high, rank.

   The main road to Alost, by Liederkerke and Denderlue,
runs through this wood, and, emerging from it on that side,
one exchanges the gloomy obscurity of the forest and confined view amongst the trees for the broad light of day and
a wide expanse of fine meadows, covered with herds of

cattle, through which the Dender runs brawling and bubbling along over its pebbly bed, crossed at this point by a long wooden bridge, immediately beyond which is the village of Liederkerke, at the time of my visit full of our Household troops.

It was a curious sensation that of seeing Lifeguardsmen lounging about the street and before the houses—these people are so intimately associated in one's mind with London, the Park, Horse Guards, etc. Nor was the contrast between their tall full figures and rosy complexions and the gaunt awkward figures and sallow complexions of the Flemish peasantry—the smart tight-fitting scarlet or blue jackets of the one, with the coarse homely garbs and dingy-coloured smock-frocks of the other—less curious.

Both banks of the river, which here approach each other and are rather steep, are well clothed with trees, and form a picturesque scene. Immediately above and below the bridge, these banks, retiring from each other, leave between their bases and the river a wide level of meadow-land, which, being everywhere bounded by low thickly wooded hills, and, as before mentioned, thickly sprinkled with herds of fine cattle or luxuriant crops of hay, now almost ready for mowing, afford scenes of a different but not less pleasing character. On the right the hills, projecting like a promontory, and blending themselves with those on the left, enclose these fine meadows in an amphitheatre of beautifully variegated and tufted foliage, unbroken by buildings or any indication of the haunts of man; whilst the left bank, less thickly wooded, presents here and there intervening fields, the high thatched roofs of farms and cottages, and, pre-eminent amongst the whole, the spire of Denderlue peeping through the foliage. Amongst other excursions, one was of a more than commonly interesting nature, since it brought me acquainted, not only with a very lovely spot, but also with a singularly eccentric character—one whose history is of so romantic a nature, that I ever regret not having made myself master of it in all its details; I mean Paul Visconti, Marquis d'Acornati and Lord of Gaesbeke, the chateau of which he inhabits. The first notice we had of this singular man was from some officers of the 23d Light Dragoons, who had been cantoned in his village. On their first arrival the old gentleman was quite furious at the insult offered him in sending troops thither at all, but especially without his having been consulted. The officers, having quartered their men, proceeded to take up their own abode in the chateau, and the Marquis, being aware of this, closed his gates, and made preparations to resist. His garrison consisted of two or three ancient domestics and six or eight young boys. On approaching the gates, the officers were somewhat surprised at seeing guns pointed at them from several embrasures, and at the same time a venerable turbaned head, projecting from one of them, demanded, in good English, how they dared trespass on the property of the Marquis d'Acornati, peremptorily bidding them to depart, or take the consequences. The captain, a true English gentleman, having heard something of the Marquis's peculiarities from the villagers, instead of resenting the opposition, humoured the old man's whim, and commenced a parley in the true language and all the forms of chivalry. This was touching the Marquis in a tender point. The gates were thrown open, as were his arms, to these courteous strangers, whom he received and entertained with the hospitality of the olden times during their stay, mourned their departure, and never mentioned them afterwards but in the highest terms of praise. Some of my officers had already visited Gaesbeke, and their accounts excited my curiosity to see this extraordinary man. Accordingly one day mounting Nelly I set out. The road lay through the large village of Lennik St Martin, remarkable in the distance for its handsome spire, towering above the more humble ones of the surrounding villages. Here I found Lieutenant-Colonel Hawker and his adjutant, Lieutenant Anderson. The colonel commanded a division composed of two batteries, 9-pounders, which were cantoned in his immediate neighbourhood, but not in Lennik. Hence the country was exquisite—the scenery acquiring a greater degree of interest from the increasing height of the hills, though in luxuriance and verdure, both of arborific and cereal vegetation, it could not exceed that which I had left behind me.

At length, after a pleasant ride of about twelve miles, on attaining the summit of a hill, the noble Château de Gaesbeke

appeared in front, on the edge of a deep ravine, which
separated me from it, surrounded by thick woods, the sombre
verdure of which harmonised well with the mellowed tone
of its antique brick walls and towers, whilst their round
tufted tops were finely contrasted with its sharp angles and
pointed conical roofs. Crossing the ravine, I arrived on a
plateau of rich velvety turf, ornamented by a few clumps
of the most superb beech-trees I ever saw in my life, some
of their boles rising almost straight forty or fifty feet, without
a twig to break the smooth rounded surface of their glossy
grey bark. Fine as those composing the great avenue at
Strytem were, still they were far exceeded in size, luxuriance,
and beauty of form by these. Artificial means are employed
to produce these magnificent ornaments of the park or
pleasure-ground. Whilst the tree is young it is constantly
watched, and every bud carefully eradicated the moment it
pierces the bark, until, having attained a certain height,
nature is permitted to take her course and push out lateral
branches, leaving between them and the soil a stupendous
column of timber. A broad carriage-road, winding amongst
these clumps, led to the great gate of the chateau, now un-
suspicious of another military invasion, standing wide open.
It was approached by a stone bridge thrown over a ditch,
which, running along the front of the chateau, imperceptibly
lost itself in the steep declivity to the right and left. The
lofty arched portal was flanked by round towers, having
semicircular embrasures on the first floor, and above them
a row of arched windows with rusty iron balconies, extending
across the gateway also. Toward the right, the two tiers
of large French windows gave a more modern air to the
curtain (if I may so call it), which was terminated in that
direction by an immense elliptical tower, the steep roof of
which finished in a short ridge with ornamental ironwork,
and a weathercock at either end. To the left, the blank
wall ended in a round tower of smaller dimensions, and
without the usual conical roof, its picturesque antique form
only partially seen through the foliage of the trees, which
formed a screen before that front.

I entered the castle court without seeing a soul, or any indication of the place being inhabited. True, there was little
of ruin. The old walls appeared generally in good repair;

the glass in the windows was sound, not a pane broken—yet a forlorn deserted aspect reigned over all; and the bent iron ornaments of the roofs, the grass-grown court, and the shattered remains of two or three low-wheeled carriages, lying half buried in the rank vegetation of weeds which had sprung up around them, added not a little to the cheerless desolate aspect of the whole. To the right on entering was a long range of two stories (which, from the lofty windows, appeared to be the state apartments), terminating at either end with a tower. From the gateway into the angle on the same side similar features indicated other suites of apartments. To the left of the gateway, extending to the tower on that side, were stables and coach-houses. From this tower a parapet-wall followed the outline of the ground along the edge of the declivity, running out in semicircular bastions at intervals of about fifty yards, until, joining the tower at the extremity of the right wing, it completed the enclosure of the court, forming an area of an irregular figure, the low parapet allowing to the windows of the main building a most striking and extensive view over the rich country to the westward. The defence of this front was further increased by a range of casemated apartments, with narrow loopholes, probably intended for arrows; but whether they extended the whole length of the front, or only under the bastions, I forget. They are entered by a narrow staircase from the court above. In the centre of this court, upon a rude pedestal, was the fragment of a man in a sitting posture, of which the Marquis afterwards gave me a printed explanation, drawn up by himself, tending to show that this must be a remnant of the celebrated Torse de Belvedere, and that the whole constituted a figure of Ulysses, seated, and in the act of discharging an arrow from his bow. But to return. After taking a cursory glance at the general arrangement of the buildings, and finding that the sound of my horse's feet had no effect in extracting their inhabitants, I rode up to and thundered at a low-arched door which stood half open in the great tower. The appeal was answercd by a sallow-faced dirty boy of fifteen, with long uncombed flaxen locks hanging about his ears, and giving him a peculiarly wild and savage appearance as he stood staring at me with widely distended eyes. To my inquiry if the Marquis were at home, he only answered by a nod, and then disappeared in the gloom of the dark vaulted passage whence he had emerged. Returning almost immediately, he had found his tongue, and begged me to go to the principal entrance to the right wing (what had once been handsome panelled folding-doors), which he unbolted within, and, taking my horse as I dismounted, ushered me into a large and lofty vestibule of handsome proportions, but quite unfurnished, and in a miserable state of decay. On the opposite side of this, at the desire of my guide, I entered a fine lofty room, with a coved roof, painted in blue and white stripes in imitation of the interior of a Turkish tent, and at the corners, where the drapery was supposed to be gathered up, ornamented with an imitation of golden cords and tassels. Round the walls were suspended trophies formed of swords, daggers, pistols, etc., all richly mounted, and almost all Oriental. The furniture consisted of large ottomans, covered with a striped stuff to match the pattern of the tent. These were ranged round the walls, and there was neither chair nor table in the room, which was lighted by an arched window opening upon a clumsy wooden balcony, and commanding a beautiful view over the distant country and of the deep wooded ravine below. After waiting here about ten minutes, the object of my curiosity made his appearance, followed by a rather vulgar-looking fattish man, with whom he had been engaged, and whom I discovered to be a lawyer of Brussels, and his man of business. This gentleman soon took his leave, and left me *tête-à-tête* with his client. Let me draw his portrait, while still fresh in my memory: Below the middle size, and a little bent by age; thin, light, and active; a countenance embrowned by southern suns, if not natural; regular features, and a face that had evidently once been handsome; quick, sparkling, intelligent eyes giving to his physiognomy a vivacious expression, rather at variance with the wrinkled cheek of the *octogènaire*. His costume was completely Turkish. A white muslin turban, somewhat soiled, but plentifully beset with precious stones, covered his head; an ample caftan of blue cloth, vest and trousers of the same—the former tied across the chest with strings, the latter large and full-gathered, and at bottom stuffed into a pair of extremely short boots, strangers apparently to Day and Martin or their kindred of the Pays Bas. A crimson silk sash girded his waist, in which was stuck an Oriental poignard, having its handle entirely covered with precious stones, and scabbard tastefully enchased in silver filigree. In his right hand he carried a short hunting-spear, and in his left a small *cor de chasse.* His address, easy and affable, was evidently that of one accustomed to the best society. The reception he gave me was most flattering, and even affectionate; and he incessantly repeated his admiration of England and her sons. For my part, I told only half the truth in stating that the celebrity of his chateau and gardens had procured him the honour of this visit, never hinting how great a lion he was himself. After a short conversation, he proposed showing me his chateau, etc., and conducting me through several apartments on the ground-floor, we arrived at his own bedroom in the extremity of the building. Nothing can be conceived more desolate and cheerless. Superb as to dimensions and form, these apartments were completely unfurnished, and in a most melancholy state of dilapidation. The painting soiled and faded, the elaborately moulded ceilings and cornices coming down piecemeal and covering the floors with their fragments; these floors themselves rotten, and sinking in many places into holes. The shutters of the high and numerous windows, some closed entirely, others only half; others, again, with one leaf, perhaps, on the floor, and one hanging by a single hinge. Such was the appearance of these once lordly rooms. I shuddered as I traversed this scene of former splendour—of present degradation. The mind, always busy on these occasions, called up the beruffed slashed-sleeve cavalier of other days; the courtly dame, the stomacher resplendent with costly jewels, ebon locks falling in ringlets over her bare well-turned shoulders and swelling bosom. How changed the scene! The lordly *châtelain* has given place to the little curved Turkish figure before me; the brilliant assemblage of knights and dames to desolation and solitude.

The dormitory of mine host, where at least some comfort might have been expected, was only of a piece with the rest. Coarse, scanty, and not very clean-looking bedding, lying in a confused heap upon a low bedstead of common deal, without curtains—in short, such a bed as one sometimes sees in an ostler's room over the stables—a rickety deal table, and

a couple of old chairs. None of the appurtenances of the
toilet, nor any apparent means of stowing his wardrobe;
bare walls, and nought else. One might have imagined it
the abode of some poor devil whom charity had admitted to
occupy a nook in the deserted mansion. The Marquis
showed all with perfect *sang-froid*, unconscious that there
was anything strange in a man of his princely fortune living
like a pauper, and continued leading me from room to room,
until we arrived at one smaller than the rest, and a little less
dilapidated, which he announced as his study—a title to
which a huge table, occupying the greater part of it, and
covered with a heap of papers, pictures, and writing material,
all intermingled in most glorious confusion, seemed to give
some colour; and here were also two or three common chairs.
From amongst the litter on the table, after a little hunting,
he rummaged out a small miniature of a female, which he
thrust into my hand with an air of exultation, as much as to
say, "There!—what think you of that?" and evidently
supposing me as intimate with its features as himself, and as
evidently mortified at my asking who the original might be,
whilst, with rather a haughty air, he informed me that it was
the portrait of his dear mistress (kissing it respectfully), the
Empress Maria Theresa, whom he had had the honour to
serve as an officer of Hungarian hussars many years. Whilst
laying the miniature again on the table, he hurried out of the
room, motioning me to follow him. The old man was quite
chivalric when speaking on this subject, and apparently quite
in earnest.

Our next visit was to the kitchen, whither he took me to see
the thickness of the walls, which were no less than 10 feet.
Such a den as this never before sullied the respected name of
kitchen. From the smallness of the windows, or port-holes,
and the enormous thickness of the walls, it was, even at this
time of day, almost dark enough to require candles; spacious
and vaulted, with a floor all decayed—and no wonder, for it
was in great part covered by an immense heap of potatoes,
and quite devoid of furniture. Its occupants were a second
Dame Leonarda, and three or four dirty boys, lounging
indolently about. A wood-fire blazed on the ash-encumbered
hearth, over which was suspended an iron pot filled with
potatoes. He then led me through the casemates or sub-

terraneous defences on the western side, before mentioned; and having thus completed our survey of the castle, we sallied from the portal to visit the gardens and *pleasaunce*, the Marquis stepping out with all the briskness of youth. We had got about half-way over the lawn, under one of the magnificent clumps of beeches, when suddenly my conductor, stopping, put his horn to his mouth and blew such a peal as made the woods ring again. No result followed, and as he had not explained himself, I was at a loss to conjecture the meaning of this, unless it were to let me hear the echo. After waiting impatiently a few minutes, the sound was repeated, and an instant afterwards out came all the boys scampering through the portal and over the turf towards us, with an activity strongly contrasted with their former list-lessness. This, however, did not satisfy their master, who, rating them soundly for their inattention to his first summons, ordered them to bring out the *carriole*. In a few minutes one of the old carriages I had seen in the court was drawn out by a miserable half-starved-looking beast, hardly de-serving the name of a horse, and with harness to match—that is, old, rusty, broken, and mended with bits of cord, etc. Into the suspicious-looking vehicle we both got, and having exchanged his hunting-spear for a shabby whip, the Marquis proceeded to do coachman, and conducted me through his lovely domain; for lovely it really was, in spite of the neglect evident in all directions—a circumstance, however, that one scarcely regretted, since it threw such an air of wildness over the scenery as to make it most charming.

The ground on which the castle stood ran out in knolls, with very abrupt slopes, forming deep ravines, at the bottom of which streams of limpid water ran bubbling along, until finding their way to the main trunk, or great ravine, under the western front, they there united their waters and formed a small lake, whose placid surface was animated by swans and whole flocks of wildfowl, which here found an undis-turbed retreat. The whole of the ground above described, excepting the level lawn in front of the great gate, was thickly covered with wood—in some parts impervious from the thick shrubbery of undergrowth, in others clear from this encum-brance—affording splendid forest vistas between the boles of the magnificent trees—the ground beneath carpeted with the most beautiful variety imaginable of mosses and wild-flowers—innumerable creepers hanging in festoons from the branches, with here and there a venerable ruin, fallen against and only supported by its neighbours, increasing the wildness and charm of this enchanting scenery. At times, after following a path winding through the thick shrubberies, and overshadowed by the luxuriant branches of the forest-trees, so as to be in perfect twilight, we suddenly came upon a small cleared space, carpeted with turf, in the centre of which, perhaps, was a rustic altar, or the fragment of a column, the marble of which, stained by damps or the encroachments of variously coloured lichens, harmonised well with the tints of the sylvan scene around it. Some of these were simple cylinders; others were angular with projecting cornices. Offerings of flowers there were on many of them—evidence of the feelings and peculiar sentiments of the noble proprietor, and that, although neglectful as far as repairs went, he still had eyes to see and a heart to feel the beauties of his lovely domain. Again emerging from the *demi-jour* of the cool *berceau*, the road wound round the face of a knoll, affording a charming view of the distant country, with the lordly chateau towering in the foreground; then replunging into obscurity, it opened again on a scene as extensive but of a totally different character—the country towards Hal, with its long and more thinly wooded slopes and summits. In one place, a clearing of three or four acres, bearing a crop of potatoes, presented precisely such a scene as one meets with in America—the ground still encumbered with roots and branches, the lofty surrounding wall of grey stems, here and there a tree fallen against its neighbours, or hanging forward as if ready to come to the ground at a touch; in short, a scene of such savage wildness as one would hardly expect to meet in this land of culture and improvement.

After a delightful drive, we returned to the chateau, passing under the ramparts of the garden, which, lying on the slope of the hill, are banked up in such a manner as to form a succession of nearly level terraces. These are laid out in parterres, ornamented with statues and fragments, etc. In the centre of these, a circular wooden tower rises to a great height, forming a conspicuous object from all the neighbouring country, over which the gallery on its summit commands a most extensive view.   The walls of this tower are of open work, and, as well as the winding staircase within, are said to be a *chef d'œuvre* of carpentry.

As it was growing late, I was obliged to decline my host's invitation to visit his farm in the valley below; and having, with the assistance of one of his young pages, saddled my horse, I took leave, and returned to Strytem highly pleased with my excursion.

A few days afterwards the Marquis sent me a bundle of papers containing the history of Gaesbeke and its counts; but being unable from want of leisure to copy any of it, I can only remember that the chateau was built about the middle of the thirteenth century by one of the Counts of Brabant, of whom it long continued to be the principal residence.   Of the present proprietor I could learn little except what was imparted by himself during our ride, in substance as follows:—Paul Acornati Visconti, an Italian by birth, inherits Gaesbeke in right of his mother, and by the father's side is of the celebrated family of Visconti of Milan.   Early in life he entered the Austrian army, and served as lieutenant and captain of Hungarian hussars during the Seven Years' War. At the peace of 1763, finding himself free, and in possession of a princely fortune, he gave himself up to his vagabond propensities, and passed his time in wandering over Europe, etc. etc.   In this way he ran over all Germany, France, and much of Russia and Poland; traversed Denmark, Sweden, and Lapland as far as the North Cape.   Either Dr Clarke or Acerbi mentions meeting him at Tornea, or having heard of him there.   He then visited the British Islands, where he remained some time (I think he told me he had been twelve times to England), extending his wanderings to the remotest corners of Ireland, the Highlands of Scotland, and the Western Isles.   Here (in England) he became acquainted with many of our celebrated characters—civil, military, and literary—of whose intimacy he was not a little proud.   He was delighted with England and its inhabitants, but his fondness for both yielded to the unaccountable mania with which he was subsequently seized for Turkey, the Turks, their manners, their institutions, and everything belonging to them; and after a prolonged residence amongst them, only returned to his own country when the management of his extensive estates in Italy and the Pays Bas imperatively required his presence. What his religious sentiments might have been I know not, but in every other respect he had become a complete Turk, and so determined to remain; thus he has always dressed in the Oriental costume, as I found him, and in every other way conforms to their customs. I have already described the person of this curious character. His health and activity are remarkable; and although a little curved, there is nothing of the old man in his step which is firm, light, and active; his usual pace is a little trot. His manner of living is extremely simple; his diet, I believe, principally vegetable, and his beverage water. He seldom goes to bed before midnight, rising again at three o'clock in the morning; and to this habit of early rising he assured me he was indebted for his good health. Whether he had ever been married I know not, but that he had a daughter I know, since in the note of invitation to a fête he intended giving at Brussels, he particularly mentioned his wish to introduce me to her. Amongst the people of the neighbourhood I found he bore various characters, some ascribing his eccentricities to a deranged intellect, others to philosophy. Others believed him to be a magician, wherefore the peasantry in general stand in great awe of him. All, however, allow that he is a most charitable, good man. It is said that his liberality towards even his most distant relations is so great, that they amongst them enjoy more of his wealth than he does himself. That he is wealthy is out of the question; his property is immense. Besides the Gaesbeke estate, he possesses others both in the Pays Bas and in Italy. Most of the best houses in Brussels are his, and the Gaesbeke property alone comprises seventeen villages and parishes. His own house in Brussels is said to be a magnificent one; in it he gave the fête to which I was invited, which I afterwards heard was very splendid, the first people of the country and many of our most distinguished officers having been present. He seldom resides in Brussels for any length of time, nor are his visits to that city frequent, as he prefers retirement and the country.

The establishment at Gaesbeke consisted only of a gardener, an old woman as cook, &c., and some five or six boys, from twelve to sixteen years of age, whom he sometimes dressed in the Hungarian hussar uniform, at others as

Orientals—so said the people. Be that as it may, they all wore the usual dress of the country when I saw them. After this first visit the lovely domain of Gaesbeke became a favourite lounge, and I passed many a delicious morning wandering about its cool shady walks. Sometimes the Marquis was at home, sometimes not, but it made little difference—he always received me with the same kindness, and seemed not a little flattered at the pleasure I took in his favourite woods; but we neither of us interrupted the pursuits of the other, for if he were employed he continued his employment, otherwise he would sometimes accompany me himself, or send one of his young pages, if there were anything to be done or seen that required assistance or a guide. It was not without regret that, eventually, I was obliged to leave his neighbourhood without having had an opportunity of taking leave of him.

There was another extraordinary character—a man of great wealth, too—residing within a few miles of us, at Ternath, or St Ulris Capelle; but him I only heard of from Leathes, who had visited him, which I never had an opportunity of doing. This man differed from Acornati in having his chateau splendidly furnished and his pleasure-grounds, described as vieing in beauty with those of Gaesbeke, kept in most excellent order. He had, moreover, a choice collection of paintings.

CHAPTER IX

WHILST our army thus revelled in luxury in this fine country, that of the enemy, we understood, was concentrating on our frontier, preparatory to the grand blow which was to drive us into the sea. To meet the threatened invasion, it was generally understood in the army that the Duke had made choice of two positions in the neighbourhood of Brussels— the one a little beyond the village of Waterloo, the other at Hal, the point where the roads from Ath and Mons unite. In one or the other of these, it was said, he intended to await the attack, according as the enemy might advance. Frequently, attended only by an orderly dragoon, he would visit these positions, studying them deeply, and most probably forming plans for their occupation and defence. In confirmation, too, of the reports that the French army would shortly advance, we about this time received an order to divest ourselves of all superfluous baggage, and were given to understand that, in case of passing the frontier, the army must be prepared to forego all shelter but what would be carried with it, since the operations were to be of the most active nature. Curious to see these positions, I one day rode over to Hal, which was the nearest to us. The country through which I passed for a long way was like that about Strytem; but on approaching Hal it became more open, free from wood, and without any kind of enclosures. This little town is situated on the Senne, here a good deal interrupted in its course by mill-dams, etc., so that it forms numerous ponds in and about the place, only to be crossed by the stone bridge over which the road from Braine le Leud and Braine le Château, etc., passes, and in the town unites with the two great roads from Ath and Mons, which have previously crossed a small rivulet descending from the north-west, and thus ascends the steep street in the direction of Brussels. On this side the ground rises to a considerable height, giving a great command over the valley and roads winding through it, which may be seen at a considerable distance descending from the opposite hills, which recede so much to the southward as to be of no avail against the positions, although considerably higher.

The town, as already stated, lies on a steep slope; the houses are of stone, many of them large and of most respectable appearance; streets wide and airy; many mills, etc., in the lower part, and tan-yards.

I was obliged to content myself with a very superficial view of Hal; for, having miscalculated the distance from Strytem, I had no time for more than to ride through it and back again. The only thing I saw on the road worth notice was a very pretty villa, small, but exceedingly neat, standing in the midst of well-kept pleasure-grounds, quite unlike anything else in the country that I had hitherto seen.

I have as yet been so wrapped up in the country that I have passed over Brussels, to which, however, I had already made several visits, and to which I must now devote a page. So—to begin at the beginning—my first visit was about four or five days after our arrival at Strytem. The weather was particularly favourable. It was one of those lovely days of spring, succeeding rain, when all nature seems bursting into new life—when we are ourselves sensible of the renovating effects of the season, and the elasticity of our spirits is such, that everything appears beautiful to our sight—when all is exhilaration and delight, and we are disposed to be in good humour with everything around us. The country through which my route lay, rich in the bounties of nature, and exhibiting a pleasing variety of feature, made this ride peculiarly agreeable. About half-way, at the villages of Itterbeke and Dilbeke, the appearance of several riflemen in grey or black uniforms, round hats having the brim looped up on one side, and decorated with pendant green plumes, scattered about the fields, the roads, and posted behind trees, somewhat surprised me. Near the roadside, too, on the point of a green knoll, stood one of those rude Rembrandt-like mills, so common in this country; and on the wooden stairs leading up to the door sat several men, with their rifles in hand or lying across their knees, whilst their attention seemed steadily fixed on the surrounding country, as if something interesting was transacting there. A dropping

shot now and then re-echoing amongst the woods, seemed
to confirm the truth of my apprehensions that the French
army had advanced, and that I had no time to lose in regaining Strytem. The sergeant of the party on the mill-
steps, however, dissipated my apprehensions. These people
belonged to the Duke of Brunswick, and, being all young
soldiers, he obliged them to live in their cantonments, as if
in face of an enemy, with all their videttes and advanced-
posts out. The firing, I found, proceeded from a party
practising with their rifles at targets cut in the shape of,
and painted to resemble, French soldiers. This was my
first interview with men (*mere boys!*) with whom subsequently I had to stand shoulder to shoulder in the great
struggle. My approach to the city was announced by the
occurrence of several pretty country-houses or villas, much
in the same style as that I had seen on the road to Hal, but
no indication in the distance—no towers, spires, or lofty
building towering over the trees—until, passing the summit
of a hill, Brussels suddenly burst on my sight, covering the
slope of the hills on the opposite side of the valley—a
glorious picture, and one not readily to be erased from my
memory. From this point, and under such a sky, she showed
herself to the utmost advantage, and the atmosphere was so
pure that even from this distance every detail was distinctly
visible. The cathedral of St Gudule, standing upon a
terrace, formed a striking feature. The tufted verdure of
the trees on the ramparts enclosing the city enabled one
easily to follow their outline along the summit of the heights,
whilst on the face of the slope the ramparts themselves, with
their venerable grey towers, gave additional interest to the
scene; the houses, rising in terraces, as it were, tier above
tier, and everywhere intermingled with foliage; innumerable churches and chapels; palaces, too, amongst which,
most conspicuous, was that of Prince d'Aremberg and the
Cour de Flandres, and in the lower town the beautiful
Stadthuys; all united to form the glorious picture.

In the vale below, the river Senne wound its way slowly
along amidst green meadows, the surface of which was
broken by long stripes of white linen, spread there to bleach.
In the west and south it was closed by a belt of black forest
—the ever-memorable Forest of Soigney. The Senne was

ravishing—it seemed as if one could never tire of looking on it; and as I lingered to do so, the more prominent features in the history of that fair city came crowding on my mind, and, now that the scene of action lay before me, embodied themselves to my mind's eye. At first the city seems to have been confined to the borders of the marsh, and thence gradually to have crept up the hillside, until at last it was circumscribed by a rampart—the lower part of the town being evidently the older, and of a different style entirely from the upper.

Descending the hill, I entered this lower town by the Barrière de Gand and a long winding narrow street, bordered on either side by houses of black stone, three stories (generally) high, but of a mean appearance, without *trottoirs* for the foot-passengers, and the mud above my horse's fetlocks; a little farther on I passed the fish-market, and a fearful penance it was—for the strongest stomach, I should think, could hardly resist its noisome smell, arising from a fearful accumulation of garbage flung beneath the tables.

Passing along, I found the streets in this part of the town crowded with commissariat waggons, coming for or taking supplies to the neighbouring cantonments, so that between these and the multitude of Hanoverian soldiers it was not without difficulty that I made my way along and reached an expansion of the street where the Marché aux Herbes is held, much as it used to be in the fore street at Exeter ere the present market-place was built. The bustle, gaiety, groups of females, the colour and smell of flowers and herbs, etc., always make a vegetable-market an agreeable scene. This one was enhanced by the various uniforms of the British, Belgic, and Hanoverian soldiery, and the handsome shops surrounding it. These exhibited in their windows every variety of the choicest productions of India and Europe; and pre-eminent amongst them all were the jewellers and pipe-sellers, or tobacconists, with their splendid displays of meerschaums, Turkish pipes with amber mouthpieces, rich tobacco-pouches, etc. etc. The Montagne de la Cour, though restricted after passing the market, still a broad street, ascended right in front; and at the foot of this a large hotel (d'Angleterre) occurred so opportunely that I rode into its court, and, leaving my orderly in charge of my horse, set off at once, eager to explore this new and interesting ground.

My first impulse was to seek the park, of which I had so often heard, and instinctively I ascended la Montagne de la Cour, which proved the direct road to it. At the top of the ascent I found myself in a pretty little square (Place Royale) surrounded by handsome houses, but having very much the appearance of pasteboard. Turning thence into a broad street, I found myself in a most magnificent square, far exceeding in beauty, if not in size, any of ours in London— pretty lawns and thick shrubberies, with fine trees, etc., enclosed by a handsome iron railing, and surrounded by fine houses, the façades ornamented by Ionic pilasters, and painted in delicate tints of buff, green, etc., or white, and the whole forming a splendid spectacle and delicious spot. The park is laid out in walks winding through shrubberies and dingles, affording varied and pleasing scenery, some part of the ground being broken and uneven. In the centre is a sort of pavilion where refreshments are sold, and near it is a sheet of water, etc. *Park* is a misnomer; consider it a *square*, in our acceptation of the term, and it is one of the most beautiful in Europe. Its beauty is considerably increased by the old ramparts with their fine umbrageous trees overtopping by far those of the park, and completing one side instead of a row of houses. The glimpse I here got of those ramparts naturally attracted me thither, and I was delighted with the lovely, airy, and commanding promenade they afforded. This promenade round the ramparts is the most delightful imaginable, elevated as they are so much above the highest houses of the city (on the east and north-east sides), and overshadowed by stately elms, affording beautiful views over the city and neighbouring country, always having in the foreground some imposing and picturesque mass of ancient masonry, overrun with a rank vegetation of large-leaved weeds, etc.; some grey and venerable tower—a remnant of antiquity. Descending the hill on either hand, the height of these ramparts decreases to that of the ordinary fortifications of the Middle Ages; but here, in the lower part, the walls and towers in themselves are far more picturesque, and exhibit much greater antiquity. They are here, I suspect, the same that were built when the city was first fortified in 1044, whilst those above are the more modern fortifications of 1379. Above, as I have before mentioned, the ramparts present a stupendous mound, with large square towers, this elevation being there necessary to protect the city—lying as it does on a declivity—from the higher ground beyond; whilst here below they are only of moderate elevation and breadth, with round or octagonal towers, the masonry timeworn and sombre, almost to blackness, and eminently picturesque.

But this, my first visit, was too short, and there was too much to see to admit of lingering long on any one spot; so, reluctantly quitting the ramparts, I hurried with eager curiosity from street to street and square to square, catching a slight, and but a slight, glimpse of anything, yet delighted, and devouring all. There is a charm which I cannot describe in the contemplation of these heavy and old-fashioned yet picturesque structures, with their sculptures, pointed gables, and eccentric variety of windows, such as most of those (either Gothic, Flemish, or Spanish) with which La Grande Place is surrounded. Here, too, is that most beautiful building, the Hôtel de Ville, flanked by hexagonal towers, and surmounted by its celebrated belfry, rising to a height, it is said, of more than 360 feet; its construction is of open work, and it is impossible to imagine anything combining at once such majesty, grace, elegance, and lightness. One would scarcely imagine that a work so delicate could be enduring; and yet this lovely tower, even now in appearance fresh and perfect, has already stood more than three, nay, nearly four, centuries—having been built in 1445. The statue of St Michael which surmounts it would, in my opinion, be better away; yet this is a feature more vaunted than the elegant form of the building or its admirable workmanship. The saint stands upon one foot, and pirouettes with every breeze. The Hôtel de Ville was commenced in 1380. After a lapse of four centuries, and notwithstanding the boasted "march of intellect," where is the man who could now sit down and conceive such a structure? Many there are, perhaps, who by help of books and existing examples, might compile something of the sort, but I doubt whether any modern architect be capable of the *original conception*; and I am sure that, spite of the *Mechanic's*

Magazine and the present philosophical studies of our
masons, none of them could produce more perfect or better
work. Like painting, architecture has had its day. Sir
Christopher Wren himself acknowledged his astonishment
at the boldness of the arches of King's College Chapel,
Cambridge, and confessed his ignorance as to their construction and mode of placing the key-stones.

After all, the Hôtel de Ville is irregular in its construction,
and the placing the tower at one extremity of the façade
instead of the centre I have heard censured as a grievous
fault;—I like it—there is originality even in that. The
general effect is most imposing.

Nor is the varied throng frequenting this fine place on
market-days unworthy of it,—their quaint and original
costume harmonising well with the character of the architectural setting around. Many were my visits to Brussels,
and always was I delighted. If I did not see all that I now
speak of at that first one, *n'importe*. The effect of St
Gudule's (the cathedral) is in this respect very good, situated
upon a terrace to which one ascends by a broad flight of
stairs to the fine Gothic portal, flanked by two handsome
towers, and looking out over the city on the country beyond.
Up this flight of steps I did ascend with solemn pace and
slow, and into its beautiful nave: but the celebrated sculptured pulpit obtained from me no more observation or
admiration than those of Ghent and Bruges. The emotion
I feel on entering a Gothic cathedral is of a nature too
solemn to admit of dwelling upon, or even noticing, such
things.

How strikingly Spanish are the charming Bruxellaises in
their mantillas, gracefully crossed on the bosom! I have
often heard and read that they are so, but had no recollection of the circumstance at the moment the fact struck me.
The mantilla itself, so Spanish, has its testimony of their
ancestry confirmed by the brilliant black eyes sparkling
beneath it; and the prevalence of black dresses amongst
the groups frequenting the park, or *allée-verte*, complete
the illusion, and for a second we forget that these are not
Andalusians. Never having been in company with any of
the fair dames of Brussels, it would be presumption to say
more than what I saw of them in public; my say, therefore,

amounts to the having seen many lovely faces and graceful figures, though I had once foolishly fancied that all Flemish women must be of the same breed as Anne of Cleves, or the strapping wenches with whom Rubens and others have made us familiar—forgetting that, as the offspring of some of the finest men and handsomest women in Europe, the Austrians, Spaniards, and French, they ought to show well. From outward appearance it would be, perhaps, difficult to decide the origin; but in the ladies the Spanish blood generally seems to predominate.

In wandering about Brussels one is struck with the frequent occurrence of ecclesiastical ruins—these are generally the remains of monasteries suppressed at the Revolution in 1793. The extensive, and apparently once handsome, house of the Capucines exhibits now only a heap of rubbish, with about five or six feet of the massive walls here and there; another, of which the chapel remained pretty entire, was used by our commissariat as a magazine for hay, straw, etc. etc.

A more striking scene, perhaps, cannot be imagined than the *allée-vert*, with its long vista overarched by thickly clothed branches of the stately elms lining it in double rows on either hand, the broad expanse of calm water covered by crowded and gaily painted barges, ornamented with flags and streamers, and enlivened with music and singing. The spacious roads on each bank gay with carriages, equestrians, and numerous pedestrians—all apparently happy, consequently smiling and merry. I took this route one Sunday with the intention of visiting the Palace of Lavickens, but, alas! the luxury of lounging amidst the merry crowd under the shade of the elms, and amongst these joyous groups, detained one in suchwise that, on arriving at the first lock, time no longer served, and my project was necessarily abandoned. As I turned homeward, the well-known overture to *Lodoiska* resounding from a neighbouring cabaret attracted me thither, and what was my surprise at finding the orchestra by which it was performed to consist of two pretty girls, each with a violin, whilst the old mother accompanied them on the violoncello. I afterwards heard these girls at a café near the Park, where, the audience being more refined, their performance was more careful. I thought their music exquisite, as well as their singing, which they sometimes mingled with it. Had their expressive black eyes and coquettish *cornettes* of red-striped cotton anything to do with it? In my subsequent visits to Brussels, instead of continuing to frequent the Hôtel d'Angleterre, I found a brother officer whose horses were billeted on the Hôtel d'Aremberg, and who offered me stalls whenever I came to town—an arrangement so convenient that his Highness was patronised by me during the remainder of my sojourn at Strytem. I am not sure that I ever saw my princely host, but believe that a tall, thin, elderly man, with a powdered head, a most amiable countenance, and most gentlemanly bearing, who one day crossed the stable-yard whilst I was there, must have been the Prince. We looked at, but did not condescend to bow to, each other. His being on the wrong side of politics was the cause of his domain being thus invaded by strangers, and the billetmaster was careful to keep him full.

One of our lounges at Brussels now was the exhibition of paintings just opened—a pleasant thing enough, as all the world assembled, and there was a daily squeeze in the rooms. As for the articles we were supposed to come to look at, they were below mediocrity—mere daubs, mostly portraits, and many of British officers.

The 19th of May 1815 was with us a memorable day; our friend Sir Augustus Frazer gave a grand, and a very good, dinner to all the horse-artillery officers, English and German, on the occasion of his being appointed lieutenant-colonel of that arm. The dinner was at the Hôtel de la Paix, Place Royale; excellent claret, sauterne, and champagne flowed in abundance, and the utmost hilarity prevailed. Many of us then met for the first time, many after a separation of years, and many for the last time. My friend Bolton sat next to me. I had not seen him since we were cadets together, but a few weeks afterwards he was gathered to his fathers on the field of Waterloo. Frazer had promised me a bed at his friend's (Lieutenant-Colonel Maxwell, 21st) lodgings; accordingly, slipping away from the party, I found my way thither somehow or other, and his servant showing me my room I was soon fast asleep. From this I was aroused some time after by persons coming into the room, and, to my infinite horror, found that I had occupied the bed intended for Bob Cairns.

A long dialogue of regrets, etc. etc., ensued, but I continued obstinately to sleep, as indignant at having been deceived as they were at my usurpation; so in the morning I arose early, and left the house and explanation to Sir Augustus. A few days afterwards poor Bob also was gathered to his fathers. With an aching head I repaired to the beautiful promenade on the ramparts, and made the circuit of the city, lingering about in the fresh morning air until I thought people would be stirring, and then adjourned to my friend Bell's, where, being renovated by an excellent breakfast, I mounted my horse and returned to Strytem—to see Brussels no more.

For some time past it had been generally understood that our army would advance into the French territory on or about the 20th June, in anticipation of which event I sometimes amused myself speculating on the probable events of the campaign. I drew out a written plan, in which we were to fight three battles and arrive in sixteen days at Paris, finishing by a grand *embrâsement*. This, as will be seen, was in some measure prophetic, since three battles were fought (Quatre Bras, Waterloo, and St Denis by the Prussians), and we did arrive in sixteen days, and the catastrophe was with difficulty prevented by the Duke.

CHAPTER X

May 29th.—Grand cavalry review near Grammont, in the fine meadows on the banks of the Dender, for the use of which, it is said, as much as £400 or £500 were paid.

The day was lovely, and we marched from Strytem in the cool of the morning. The roads, although pretty good, were in places so cut up by the passage of other troops before us, that it became necessary at times to halt until our men filled up the holes with brushwood and earth. About noon we arrived on the ground, than which nothing could be more favourable for the purpose.

The Dender, flowing through a broad tract of rich meadow-land perfectly flat, makes a bend from Grammont to the village of Jedeghem, the ground on its left bank rising in a gentle slope, whilst on the right the meadows extend back for about half a mile, and then terminate at the foot of an abrupt wooded height, which forms, as it were, a chord of the arc described by the river. This was the arena chosen for the review, and a more favourable one could scarcely have been chosen. We were formed in three lines. The first, near the banks of the river, was composed of hussars in squadrons, with wide intervals between them, and a battery of horse-artillery (6-pounders) on either flank. Opposite the centre of this line was a bridge (temporary, I believe) by which the cortège was to arrive on the ground, descending from the village of Schendelbeke. The second line—compact, or with only the usual squadron intervals—was composed entirely of heavy dragoons, having two batteries—the one of 24-pounder howitzers, the other of 9-pounders—in front of the centre, and a battery of 9-pounders on either flank. The third was a compact line like the second, but entirely of light dragoons, supported also on either flank by a battery of 9-pounders.

It was a splendid spectacle. The scattered line of hussars

in their fanciful yet picturesque costume; the more sober, but far more imposing line of heavy dragoons, like a wall of red brick; and again the serviceable and active appearance of the third line in their blue uniforms, with broad lappels of white, buff, red, yellow, and orange—the whole backed by the dark wood of the declivity already mentioned— formed, indeed, a fine picture. There were, I understood, about 6000 men on the field; and as I looked and admired their fine appearance, complete equipment, and excellent horses, I wondered how any troops could withstand their attacks, and wished Napoleon and his chiefs could but see them as they stood. My wish was in part gratified, for we afterwards learned beyond all question that numbers of French officers had not only been present, but actually were so in full uniform (many of them of high rank), and had mingled in the cortège of the Duke, and so rode through the ranks—the safest plan they could have pursued, it being impossible to say whether they did or did not belong to the corps of the Duc de Berri, who, as I said, still wore the imperial uniforms in which they had come over to the royal party; and this was still more favoured by a ridiculous scene which occasioned the absence of the French party from the review. It was as follows: Arriving on the ground covered with dust, the different corps had no sooner formed in their position, and dismounted, than off went belts, canteens, and haversacks, and a general brushing and scrubbing commenced; for the Duke, making no allowance for dusty or muddy roads, expected to see all as clean as if just turned out: accordingly, we had not only brought brushes, etc., but even straw to wisp over the horses. The whole line was in the midst of this business, many of the men even with jackets off, when suddenly a forest of plumes and a galaxy of brilliant uniforms came galloping down the slope from Schendelbeke towards the temporary bridge. "The Duke!" "the Duke!" "the Duke's coming!" ran along the lines, and for a moment caused considerable bustle amongst the people; but almost immediately this was discovered to be a mistake, and the brushing and cleaning recommenced with more devotion than ever; whilst the cavalcade, after slowly descending to the bridge and debouching on the meadows, started at full gallop toward the saluting point already marked

out, the Duc de Berri, whom we now recognised, keeping
several yards ahead, no doubt that he might clearly be seen.
At this point he reined up and looked haughtily and impatiently about him; and as we were now pretty intimate
with his manner, it was easy to see, even from our distant
position, that he was in a passion. The brushing, however,
suffered no interruption, and no notice was taken of his
presence. One of his suite was now called up and despatched to the front. What further took place I know not,
but, certes! the messenger no sooner returned than his Highness was off like a comet, his tail streaming after him all the
way up the slope, unable to keep pace with him, for he rode
like a madman, whilst a general titter pervaded our lines as
the report flew from one to the other that Mounseer was off
in a huff because we did not give him a general salute. Many
were the coarse jokes at his expense; and I was amused at
one of my drivers, who, holding up the collar from his horse's
chest with one hand, whilst with the other he brushed away
under it, exclaimed, laughing aloud, "I wouldn't be one of
them 'ere French fellows at drill upon the common to-
morrow for a penny; if they're not properly bullyragged,
I'm d——." It turned out afterwards that he had sent his
aide-de-camp to claim the reception due to a prince of the
blood-royal, but Lord Uxbridge excused himself by saying
he had no instructions on that head, etc. etc. About two
o'clock the Duke of Wellington and Prince Blucher, followed
by an immense cortège, in which were to be seen many of
the most distinguished officers and almost every uniform
in Europe, arrived on the ground. Need I say that the
foreigners were loud in praise of the martial air, fine persons,
and complete equipment of the men and horses, and of the
strength and beauty of the latter? and my vanity on that
occasion was most fully gratified, for on arriving where we
stood, the Duke not only called old Blucher's attention to
"the beautiful battery," but, instead of proceeding straight
through the ranks, as they had done everywhere else, each
subdivision—nay, each individual horse—was closely scrutinised, Blucher repeating continually that he had never seen
anything so superb in his life, and concluding by exclaiming,
"Mein Gott, dere is not von orse in dies batterie wich is not
goot for Veldt Marshal": and Wellington agreed with him.

It certainly was a splendid collection of horses. However, except asking Sir George Wood whose troop it was, his Grace never even bestowed a regard on me as I followed from subdivision to subdivision. The review over, and corps dismissed, I resigned my command to my second captain, and proceeded direct to Ninove, Lord Uxbridge having invited all commanding officers to meet his illustrious guests at dinner. On repairing to the monastery, I found a numerous company assembled, comprising some of the most distinguished characters in Europe.

The room in which we assembled, as well as the dining-room, was of splendid dimensions, but totally void of ornament: plain white stuccoed walls, and no furniture in the one but a few travelling articles of our noble hosts; and in the other the dinner-table, chairs, and benches of the most ordinary kind, evidently brought in for the occasion. Long corridors running the whole length of the two wings (standing at right angles to each other), with numerous rooms of similar dimensions opening from them, seemed to be the plan of the building. I suppose the dining-room must have been nearly 100 feet long, nearly square, and about 18 or 20 feet high. In this the tables were laid horse-shoe fashion. In the centre of the cross-table sat Lord Uxbridge; on either hand Blucher and Wellington; then the Duke of Brunswick; the hereditary Prince of Orange; his brother Prince Frederick; Gneiseneau; Ziethen; Kleist; Dornberg; a Danish general whose name I forget; Sir Frederick Arentschild, K.G.L. (the Duke of Wellington's favourite old hussar); Sir Sidney Smyth; Lords Hill, Pack, Picton, Elly; and a host of illustrious names, foreign and British, but not one Frenchman that I recollect. (Perhaps the affair of the morning might have caused the absence of the Duc de Berri, etc.) What names!—names familiar to every ear in the history of those exciting times—names we pronounce with respect regarding those who bear them as being removed above everyday life. But to have sat at table with them, to have heard them called out in the familiarity of everyday conversation—how strange! One can hardly imagine himself thoroughly awake on such occasions. But to return.

It was my good fortune to sit between Colonel Sir F. Arentschild and another no less celebrated officer of the

German Legion, Lieutenant Strenuwitz, a Pole by birth, who had signalised himself on more than one occasion in the Peninsula by attacking and capturing outposts. We broke up at an early hour (too early, I think, for old Blucher, who seemed to enjoy himself much), and retired to another room, where coffee was served, and after some little conversation we dispersed. In leaving the dining-room the Duke of Wellington stopped for a few minutes to converse with old Arentschild, and, pinned in a corner by them, I had time to contemplate, well and closely, our great leader. At that time he certainly had not a grey hair in his head.

It was getting dusk when I mounted my horse to return home, and the people were beginning to discharge squibs and crackers on the street of Ninove; the houses were decorated with garlands of laurel and green boughs, so that everything wore an air of festivity.

May 30*th.*—How delightful the tranquillity of Strytem appears after the stir and bustle of yesterday! The fields look more gay, the woods and pleasure-grounds more lovely than ever. Yesterday morning was passed amidst the din of arms and pomp of war—amidst crowds of crested warriors and the clang of martial music—the evening in festivity, amidst magnates of the earth.

How differently has this lovely day glided by! The morning I passed in a quiet peaceable ride amidst the charming scenery of the neighbourhood—wandering through corn-fields, orchards, and hop-grounds, and exploring the shady recesses of the Bois de Liederkerke; the evening in voluptuous indolence, sauntering up and down under the magnificent beeches of the great avenue, indulging in fairy dreams, and listening to the rural sound that, from time to time, broke on the stillness of the hour, whilst the smoke of my cigar hung in wreaths around me as I occasionally stopped to contemplate the scene. No living soul interrupted the solitude, except once the gardener's son, in his blue smock-frock, wooden shoes, and dirty nightcap, with a long rusty old gun under his arm and a short pipe in his mouth, crossed the avenue, marched up the central path of the garden, and disappeared amongst the thickets of the *pleasaunce* beyond. He went, I knew (for he always said so), to the Chasse aux Lièvres for the supply of our table; but as that was badly supplied, we might have fancied our game-keeper a bad shot, had not our worthy doctor one evening (for what purpose he could best say) also taken a ramble in the said *pleasaunce*, where, to his infinite surprise, he stumbled upon our chasseur making love to his sister's *adjointe* (a great Flanderkin of a Maritornes), which instantly explained the deficiency of supply.   There he went then, as I said, for either purpose—his short pipe leaving a long gossamer-like film of smoke behind him.   And this digression brings me to the close of this delightful day.

The genial month of May thus terminated amidst the delightful enjoyments of a country life, and June commenced under happy auspices, little dreaming of the far different scenes we were destined to witness ere yet another month had passed.

The only event that marked this period of our tranquil, even-flowing existence was the removal of our 1st division from the chateau farm, in compliance with the urgent request of the farmer (Walsdragen), to the pretty village of Yseringen, about a mile off, on the hill above us.   I regretted this separation of the troop, but could not withstand the poor man's solicitations, who expected every hour his wife's *accouchement*.   As for the division, it benefited by the change. The officer (Leathes) got most excellent quarters in a comfortable well-furnished chateau, whilst his men and horses were equally well lodged in the adjoining farm.   Poor Walsdragen, however, could not enjoy this relief, for, a few days after, the impending event took place, and he lost his wife.   I shall not forget in a hurry this melancholy circumstance, for I charged myself with unkindness towards him in his affliction by having so long withstood his solicitation, to be relieved of our people.   I was walking in the avenue, as usual, after dinner, enjoying my weed; the evening was calm and serene, the sun just setting; no sound disturbed the stillness save the hum of insects or the croaking of the frogs.   Suddenly one of the most terrific shrieks I ever heard burst forth, until the woods rang again.   At first, startled as I was, there was no saying whence the sound came, and taking my cigar from my mouth, I had scarcely assumed a listening attitude when, again and again, it was repeated in a manner so appalling as to make my very flesh creep.   It evidently proceeded from the farm; but what could occasion such horrid cries? This time they were succeeded by loud lamentations of many voices, male and female. I hurried towards the farm, hardly knowing what to conjecture. The first idea that flashed on me was an irruption of some French party, who were plundering, murdering, etc. etc., and this, in the first instance, seemed in some measure borne out when several men, without hats, came rushing out of the farmyard with lamentable cries, and passing by me without notice, proceeded to the bridge of the chateau, and there, throwing themselves on their knees before an image of the Virgin and child standing in a niche outside the chapel already mentioned, commenced a most dolorous mixture of lamentation and half-chanted supplication—part of a litany, I presume. I stood somewhat puzzled. After a few minutes of this devotional exercise, one of them ran away and brought a spade, with which he cut a large sod, and the whole party hurried back to the house, carrying it with them. At this moment St Cyr (one of our farmers, and the best amongst them) came up, and, making Mynheer Walsdragen's compliments, reported from him, and at his desire, the death of his wife, which had just taken place—a strange piece of etiquette at such a moment. The sod, I learned, was to put under her head, an ancient practice invariably observed.

My first idea of an irruption of the enemy did not seem just now quite so improbable, for we almost daily heard a good deal of firing in the direction of Mons, and the peasantry were continually bringing accounts of movements of the French army, none of which ever proved true; and the firing, we afterwards learned, proceeded from the practice of the Dutch or Belgic artillery at Mons.

Our host, the Baron van Lombeke, paid us a visit about the beginning of this month for the first time. The ostensible motive for this visit was an inspection of the roads, which he said were immediately to be put in a complete state of repair. He stayed three or four days with us, during which his excursions never extended farther than the major's or the *curé's*, so that he saw but little of the roads—which, together with the circumstance of his having arrived only a few days before from Paris, induced a suspicion that his real business was of a very different nature—possibly to ascertain the strength and positions of our cavalry corps, or something of the sort.

It seemed odd enough receiving a man as a guest in his own house; our servants prepared a room for him, and he was waited upon by the old gardener. Of course he dined, or rather supped, with us ; for I believe he usually partook of the *curé's* dinner at one o'clock. Although what we should call rather vulgar-looking, yet we found M. le Baron exceedingly well informed, perfectly the gentleman in manners, and upon the whole an agreeable acquisition to our little party. His gardens, and everything about the place, he begged us to consider as our own. We had done so already; however, we took the thing as it was meant—a mere compliment; but we felt that there was more sincerity in the contrast he drew between ourselves and the Prussians, and the repeated assertions of his satisfaction in having his chateau occupied by us instead of by them.

Finding me in want of books, he kindly promised to send me some from Brussels; and I was agreeably surprised at his punctuality, when, a day or two after his departure, the old gardener brought me the five volumes of *The Hermit of the Chaussée d'Antin*—a work new to me, and to which I was indebted for several most agreeable evenings.

The day marked for our advance into France now approached; and although no confirmation of the rumour reached us, yet we began to prepare for it as confidently as if already given out in general orders. Meantime, as will be seen, our friends beyond the border were scrutinising our intentions pretty closely.

It was on the evening of the 15th June, and about sunset or a little later, that an officer of hussars rode into the village of Yseringen, Leathes being at the time at dinner with me at our chateau. He was dressed as our hussars usually were when riding about the country—blue frock, scarlet waistcoat laced with gold, pantaloons, and forage-cap of the 7th Hussars. He was mounted on a smart pony, with plain saddle and bridle; was without sword or sash, and carried a small whip; in short, his costume and *monture* were correct in every particular. Moreover, he aped to the very life that "devil-may-care" nonchalant air so frequently characterising our young men of fashion. Seeing some of our gunners standing at the door of a house, he desired them to go for their officer, as he wished to see him. They called the sergeant, who told him that the officer was not in the village. In an authoritative tone he then demanded how many men and horses were quartered there, whose troop they belonged to, where the remainder of the troop was quartered, and of what it consisted? When all these questions were answered, he told the sergeant that he had been sent by Lord Uxbridge to order accommodation to be provided for two hundred horses, and that ours must consequently be put up as close as possible. The sergeant replied that there was not room in the village for a single additional horse. "Oh, we'll soon see that," said he; pointing to one of the men who stood by, "Do you go and tell the *maire* to come instantly to me." The *maire* came, and confirmed the sergeant's statement, upon which our friend, flying into a passion, commenced in excellent French to abuse the poor functionary like a pick-pocket, threatening to send a whole regiment into the village; and then, after a little further conversation with the sergeant, he mounted his pony and rode off just as Leathes returned to the village. Upon reporting the circumstance to the officer, the sergeant stated that he thought this man had appeared anxious to avoid him, having ridden off rather in a hurry when he appeared, which, together with a slight foreign accent, then for the first time excited a suspicion of his being a spy, which had not occurred to the sergeant before, as he knew there were several foreign officers in our hussars, and that the 10th was actually then commanded by one— Colonel Quentin. The suspicion was afterwards confirmed, for upon inquiry I found that no officer had been sent by Lord Uxbridge on any such mission. Our friend deserved to escape, for he was a bold and clever fellow. A brother emissary, however, who visited Lombeke Notre Dame the same evening, was not quite so prudent nor so fortunate, for he was caught by the sentinel in the act of examining the guns of Sinclair's Brigade by aid of a dark-lantern and made prisoner; but in the hubbub of marching the next morning made his escape, and was heard of no more. We afterwards learned that a number of officers had been sent the same evening into our cantonments to ascertain whether we remained quiet, etc. etc.

Spite of my eagerness for more active service, it was not without regret that I saw the time approach when I expected to leave for ever the tranquil abode of Strytem; and some such thoughts occupied me this very evening (15th), as I sauntered about the great avenue after Leathes had left me. Most of the other officers had gone to the ball at Brussels, and I remained quite alone.   The balmy softness of the air, the beauty and repose of the scenery, were, I thought, more exquisite than ever; and I continued in the avenue until the increasing obscurity of the evening drove me in to enjoy an hour or two with *The Hermit of the Chaussée d'Antin* ere I retired for the night.

CHAPTER XI

June 16*th.*—It would appear that our Quartermaster-General of the cavalry took a peculiar pleasure in disturbing people at very unseasonable hours. He served me so at Dendermonde and now he has done precisely the same at Strytem. As on that occasion, I was sound asleep when my servant, bustling into the room, awoke me *en sursaut.* He brought a note which an orderly hussar had left, and ridden off immediately. The note had nothing official in its appearance, and might have been an invitation to dinner; but the unceremonious manner in which the hussar had gone off without his receipt looked curious. My despatch was totally deficient in date, so that time and place were left to conjecture; its contents pithy—they were as follows, viz.:—

"Captain Mercer's troop will proceed with the utmost diligence to Enghien where he will meet Major M'Donald, who will point out the ground on which it is to bivouac to-night.

Signed,   *   *   *
D.A.Q.M.-Gen."

That we were to move forward, then, was certain. It was rather sudden, to be sure, and all the whys and wherefores were left to conjecture; but the suddenness of it, and the importance of arriving quickly at the appointed place, rather alarmed me, for upon reflection I remembered that I had been guilty of two or three imprudences. First, all my officers were absent; secondly, all my country waggons were absent; thirdly, a whole division (one-third of my troop) was absent at Yseringen. "Send the sergeant-major here," was the first order, as I drew on my stockings. "Send for Mr Coates" (my commissariat officer), the second, as I got one leg into my overalls. "William, make haste and get breakfast," the third, as I buttoned them up. The sergeant-major soon came, and received his orders to turn out instanter, with the three days' provisions and forage [1] in the haversacks and on the horses; also to send an express for the first division. He withdrew, and immediately the fine martial clang of "boot and saddle" resounded through the village and courts of the chateau, making the woods ring again, and even the frogs stop to listen.

The commissary soon made his appearance. "What! are we off, sir?" "Yes, without delay; and you must collect your waggons as quickly as possible." "I fear, Captain Mercer, that will take some time, for St Cyr's are gone to Ninove." My folly here stared me full in the face. Mr Coates said he would do his utmost to collect them; and as he was a most active, intelligent, and indefatigable fellow, I communicated to him my orders and determination not to wait, desiring him to follow us as soon as he possibly could. My first-enumerated care was speedily removed, for I learned that the officers had just arrived and were preparing for the march, having known of it at Brussels ere we did. The two divisions in Strytem were ready to turn out in a few minutes after the "boot and saddle" had resounded, but, as I feared, the first kept us waiting until near seven o'clock before it made its appearance. This delay allowed us time to make a hearty breakfast; and, in the uncertainty of when we should get another meal, we each stowed away a double portion of Walsdragen's fine eggs. At length the first division arrived, and the animating and soul-stirring notes of the "turnout" again awoke the echoes of the hills and woods. Up jumped my old dog Bal, and away to parade and increase the bustle by jumping at the horses' noses and barking, as parade formed. Away went the officers to inspect their divisions, and Milward is leading my impatient charger Cossack up and down the court. I linger to take a last look of my antique apartment, and bid farewell to my mute companions the Van Voldens.

The gardener, his son, and Mdlle. Mon-père-dit, with her pale face rendered still paler by the agitation of the morning, stand drawn up in the court, precisely in the same

---

[1] We had been ordered nearly a fortnight ago to keep this quantity ready, and the hay rolled, etc. etc.

order and on the same ground as on the day of our arrival.
With a profusion of blessings, etc., they thank me for the
great care we have taken of the chateau, and for the very
liberal gratuity which our paymaster, the doctor (Hitchins),
had bestowed upon them. They wish me all manner of
success, but fear we shall have bloody work. The old man
mutters something about Buonaparte *capôte*, which I do
not understand, but take for granted is something friendly,
so return thanks, mount my horse, and, once more, adieu
Strytem.

We had cleared the village and marched some miles well
enough, being within the range of my daily rides; but, this
limit passed, I was immediately sensible of another error—
that of having started without a guide, for the roads became
so numerous, intricate, and bad, often resembling only
woodmen's tracks, that I was sorely puzzled, spite of the
map I carried in my *sabretache*, to pick out my way. But
a graver error still I had now to reproach myself with, and
one that might have been attended with fatal consequences.
Eager to get on, and delayed by the badness of the roads,
I left all my ammunition waggons behind, under charge
of old Hall, my quartermaster-sergeant, to follow us, and
then pushed on with the guns alone, thus foolishly enough
dividing my troops into three columns—viz. the guns,
ammunition waggons, and the column of provision waggons
under the commissary. For this piece of folly I paid dearly
in the anxiety I suffered throughout this eventful day which
at times was excessive.

Rid of all encumbrances, we trotted merrily on whenever
the road permitted, and, arriving at Castre (an old Roman
legionary station), found there the 23d Light Dragoons just
turning out, having also received orders to march upon
Enghien. A Captain Dance, with whom I rode a short
distance, told me he had been at the ball at Brussels last
night, and that, when he left the room, the report was that
Blucher had been attacked in the morning, but that he had
repulsed the enemy with great slaughter, was following up
the blow, and that our advance was to support him. The
road for the last few miles had been upon a more elevated
country, not so wooded—a sort of plateau, consequently
hard and dry; but immediately on passing Castre, we came

to a piece which appeared almost impassable for about a hundred yards—a perfect black bog, across which a corduroy road had been made, but not kept in repair, consequently the logs, having decayed, left immense gaps. The 23d floundered through this with difficulty, and left us behind. How we got through with our 9-pounders, the horses slipping up to the shoulders between the logs every minute, I know not; but through we did get, and without accident, but it took time to do so. About noon, after threading our way through more mud and many watery lanes, doubtful if we were in the right direction, we came out upon a more open and dry country close to a park, which, upon inquiry, proved to be that of Enghien. To the same point various columns of cavalry were converging, and under the park wall we found Sir Ormsby Vandeleur's brigade of light dragoons, dismounted and feeding their horses. Here we also dismounted to await the arrival of Major M'Donald; and as I looked upon the day's march as finished, deferred feeding until our bivouac should be established—another folly, for an officer in campaign should never lose an opportunity of feeding, watering, or resting his horses, etc. Attracted by the novelty of the scene and the fineness of the day, we had numerous gay visitors here—ladies and gentlemen—who had stationed themselves within the park, enhancing by their presence the gaiety of the scene, for we had halted immediately under the park wall, and at the point where the road to Braine le Comte by Steenkerke branched off from the one we were on. All the corps as they arrived, I observed, took this road, and continued onwards, which made me somewhat impatient lest I should have halted short of my destination. Having waited a good half-hour, and no Major M'Donald appearing, I began to look about for some one who could give me information, but no staff-officer was to be seen, and no one else knew anything about the matter. Corps after corps arrived and passed on, generally without even halting, yet all professing ignorance of their destination. Pleasant situation this! Sir Ormsby's dragoons were by this time bridling up their horses and rolling up their nosebags, evidently with the intention of moving off. Seeing this, I sought out the general, whom I found seated against the bank, that, instead of a hedge, bordered the road. Whether naturally a savage, or that he feared committing himself, I know not, but Sir Ormsby cut my queries short with an asperity totally uncalled for. "I know nothing about you, sir! I know nothing at all about you!" "But you will perhaps have the goodness to tell me where you are going yourself?" "I know nothing at all about it, sir! I told you already I know nothing at all about *you*!" and starting abruptly from his seat, my friend mounted his horse, and (I suppose by instinct) took the road towards Steenkerke, followed by his brigade, leaving me and mine alone in the road, more disagreeably situated than ever. I now began to reflect very seriously on the "*to stay*" or "*not to stay*." In the former case I bade fair to have the ground all to myself, for although everybody I spoke to denied having any orders, yet all kept moving in one and the same direction. In the latter case, my orders in writing certainly were to stay; but circumstances might have occurred since to change this, and the new order might not have reached me. Moreover, it was better to get into a scrape for fighting than keeping out of the way, so I made up my mind to move forward too. Accordingly I had already mounted my people when Sir H. Vivian's brigade of hussars, followed by Major Bull's troop of our horse-artillery, passed. Bull I found was, like myself, without orders, but he thought it best to stick close to the cavalry, and advised me to do the same, which I did, following him and them on the road to Steenkerke. The country about this place appeared more bare and forbidding than any I had yet seen in the Pays Bas. Just as we moved off, the column of Household troops made its appearance, advancing from Ninove, and taking the same direction.

It was now that the recollection of my absent waggons began to torment me, and I actually feared never to see them again. However, there was no help for it now, and I continued onward.

A few miles farther we crossed the Senne by an old stone bridge, and about four in the afternoon arrived at Braine le Comte, almost ravenous with hunger, and roasted alive by the burning sun under which we had been marching all day. The country had improved and become more wooded, so that the town looked pretty, surrounded as it is by gardens and trees.   We were not allowed (why, I know not) to see more; for on arriving at one end of it we turned into a road on the left, and so, making a circuit round the back of the gardens, came out at the other end on a piece of bare ground, where we found several regiments drawn up in close columns, dismounted and feeding.   It was somewhere between Eng-hien and Braine le Comte that we met an aide-de-camp (I believe one of the Duke's) posting away as fast as his poor tired beast could get along, and dressed in his embroidered suit, white pantaloons, etc. etc., having evidently mounted as he left the ball-room.   This, I remember, struck us at the time as rather odd, but we had no idea of the real state of our affairs.

We had formed up, and were feeding also, but the nose-bags were scarcely put on the poor horses' heads than the cavalry corps, mounting again, moved off, one after the other, and we were constrained to follow ere the animals had half finished.   Here, as before, I could obtain no intelligence respecting our march, the direction and meaning of which all I spoke to professed a profound ignorance.   Whilst halt-ing, Hitchins, slipping into the town, brought us out a couple of bottles of wine, the which we passed round from one to the other without any scruple about sucking it all out of one muzzle.   This renewal of our march was a sad disappoint-ment, for on finding the cavalry assembled here, we made sure they were only waiting until the different bivouacs could be arranged, when we should settle ourselves for the night.

In marching round the town, many of the houses had a sort of gallery behind them, which were filled with spectators, particularly many priests.   The gardens were very pretty, and I could not but contrast the comparative luxury of these people, snug and comfortable, and sure of their bed when night came on, with our own vagabond situation.

The country beyond Braine le Comte was pretty, the usual rich and wooded champaign extending to the foot of an abrupt ridge of hills, covered with forest to the summit, and toward which our road lay.

A little hamlet (Long Tour, I think) lay at the foot of the hills, the straggling street of which we found so crowded with baggage-waggons of some Hanoverian or other foreign corps, that for a long while we were unable to pass.   The cavalry, therefore, left us behind, for they broke into the adjoining fields until they had cleared the impediment. Although annoyed at being thus hindered, I could not but admire the lightness, and even elegance, of the little waggons, with their neat white tilts, and as neat and pretty *jungfrauen* who were snugly seated under them. We found the ascent of the hills more difficult than we expected, the road, which went up in a zigzag (indeed, it could not have been otherwise), little better than a woodman's track, much cut up, and exceedingly steep—so much so, that we found it necessary to double-horse all our carriages, by taking only half up at once. This delayed us considerably; but, impatient as I was to get on, I was pleased at not being hurried through this charming forest-scenery. The hills, as I said, rose abruptly, and with a very steep acclivity, their sides being covered with noble forest-trees, amongst the boles of which the eye ranged without impediment—there being little or no underwood—occasionally catching glimpses through the foliage of the rich and varied plain which we had left, and of the grey buildings of Braine le Comte embosomed in verdure. Groups of dragoons and hussars, mingling with our guns, etc., all scrambling up the steep ascent, seen amongst the gigantic trunks of the trees and by the softened light of the forest, presented delicious pictures. Nor were these less interesting from the accompanying sounds—the dull tramp of the horses, the rattling of sabres, and the voices of command, all magnified by the echo of the forest, which was such that one might have fancied himself speaking under a vault.

At length the whole of our carriages were on the summit, but we were now quite alone, all the cavalry having gone on; and thus we continued our march on an elevated plateau, still covered with forest,[1] thicker and more gloomy than ever— here and there passing a farm and small clearing of a few fields, and then again plunging into the cool dark woods. At one of these farms I got a draught of new milk—very grateful after such a hot march and long fast. At length we had crossed the forest, and found ourselves on the verge of a declivity which stretched away less abruptly than the one we had ascended, consequently presenting a more extensive slope, down which our road continued. A most extensive view lay before us; and now for the first time, as emerging

[1] I believe this is the Bois de la Houssier.

from the woods, we became sensible of a dull, sullen sound that filled the air, somewhat resembling that of a distant water-mill, or still more distant thunder. On clearing the wood, it became more distinct, and its character was no longer questionable—heavy firing of cannon and musketry, which could now be distinguished from each other plainly. We could also hear the musketry in volleys and independent firing. The extensive view below us was bounded towards the horizon by a dark line of wood, above which, in the direction of the cannonade, volumes of grey smoke arose, leaving no doubt of what was going on. The object of our march was now evident, and we commenced descending the long slope with an animation we had not felt before.

It was here that Major M'Donald overtook us, and without adverting to the bivouac at Enghien, of which probably he had never heard, gave me orders to attach myself to the Household brigade, under Lord Edward Somerset, but no instructions where or when. I took care not to tell him they were in the rear, lest he might order us to halt for them, which would have been a sore punishment to people excited as we now were by the increasing roar of the battle evidently going on, and hoped that by marching faster they might soon overtake us. Just at this moment a cabriolet, driving at a smart pace, passed us. In it was seated an officer of the Guards, coat open and snuff-box in hand. I could not but admire the perfect nonchalance with which my man was thus hurrying forward to join in a bloody combat—much, perhaps, in the same manner, though certainly not in the same costume, as he might drive to Epsom or Ascot Heath. The descent terminated in a picturesque hollow, with a broad pool, dark and calm, and beyond it an old mill, perfectly in keeping with the scene. The opportunity of watering our poor brutes was too good to be missed, and I accordingly ordered a halt for that purpose. Whilst so employed, an aide-de-camp, descending from a singular knoll above us, on which I had noticed a group of officers looking out with their glasses in the direction of the battle, came to summons me to Sir Hussey Vivian, who was one of them.

On ascending the knoll, Sir Hussey called to me in a hurried manner to make haste. "Who do you belong to?" said he. I told him, as also that the brigade was yet in the rear. "Well," he replied, "never mind; there is something serious going on, to judge from that heavy firing, and artillery must be wanted; therefore bring up your guns as fast as you can, and join my hussars: can you keep up?" "I hope so, sir." "Well, come along without delay; we must move smartly." In a few minutes our people, guns and all, were on the hill. The hussars mounted, set off at a brisk trot, and we followed. Alas! thought I, where are my ammunition waggons? Neither this anxiety, however, nor the excitement of the moment, were sufficient to shut my eyes to the beautiful picture on that knoll. Conceive a point of ground standing forth with precipitous slopes over the hollow already mentioned, with its picturesque mill and calm glassy pool; on this ground, happily grouped, a band of warriors, in dresses not less picturesque, beneath a huge cross of the rudest workmanship; a few Salvator-like trees complete the foreground, the distance presenting a rich and varied scene of corn-fields (now yellow), and pastures of the liveliest green, and sombre wood—the whole extending away till in the distance all the features are massed and mellowed into indistinctness and purply vapour. Such was the scene. The hussars, to lighten their horses, untied the nets containing their hay, and the mouths of their corn-bags, which falling from them as they trotted on, the road was soon covered with hay and oats. We did not follow their example, and, although dragging with us 9-pounders, preserved our forage, and also our place in the column.

By and by a large town appeared in front of us, and the increasing intensity of the cannonade, and volumes of smoke about the trees, led us to suppose the battle near at hand, and on the hill just beyond the town. This town was Nivelle.

Another beautiful scene, and one full of excitement, now presented itself. We were descending by a gentle slope toward Nivelle, which lay spread out before us—its towers and masses of building, especially what appeared to be the ruins of an ancient castle, sweetly touched by the golden light of the setting sun, whilst the greater part lay in deep-toned purple obscurity. Fine trees, with dark overhanging foliage, bordering the road, formed a foreground and frame, as it were, to this picture. Beyond the town the ground rose, also in shadowy obscurity, crowned with sombre woods, over which ascended the greyish-blue smoke of the battle, now apparently so near that we fancied we could hear the shouts of the combatants—a fancy strengthened by crowds of people on the heights, whom we mistook for troops—inhabitants of Nivelle, as we soon discovered, seeking to get a sight of the fearful tragedy then enacting.   Before entering the town we halted for a moment, lighted our slow-matches, put shot into our leathern cartouches, loaded the guns with powder, and stuck priming wires into the vents to prevent the cartridges slipping forward, and, thus prepared for immediate action, again moved on.

On entering the town what a scene presented itself!   How different from the repose of the country we had been traversing all day!   There all was peace and tranquillity, undisturbed—absolutely undisturbed, except by the hurried march of successive columns along the highroad.   There the rustic pursued his wonted labours as in profound peace, the mill went its rumbling round, the birds carolled on the spray. True, the sounds of battle came borne on the evening breeze —the brattle of musketry and the boom of cannon shook the air; but it was distant—very distant—and might be heard, and the ascending smoke seen, with that sort of thrilling sensation with which we witness the progress of the storm when we ourselves are secure from its effects.   Here, on the contrary, all was confusion, agitation, and movement.   The danger was impending; explosion after explosion startling from their vicinity, and clattering peals of musketry, like those lengthened thunder-claps which announce to us so awfully the immediate neighbourhood of the electric cloud. The whole population of Nivelle was in the streets, doors and windows all wide open, whilst the inmates of the houses, male and female, stood huddled together in little groups like frightened sheep, or were hurrying along with the distracted air of people uncertain where they are going, or what they are doing.   The scene was strangely interesting.   In a sort of square which we traversed, a few soldiers, with the air of citizens (probably a municipal guard), were drawn up in line, looking anxiously about them at the numerous bleeding figures which we now began to meet.   Some were staggering along unaided, the blood falling from them in large drops as they went.   One man we met was wounded in the head;

pale and ghastly, with affrighted looks and uncertain step, he
evidently knew little of where he was, or what passed about
him, though still he staggered forward, the blood streaming
down his face on to the greatcoat which he wore rolled over his
left shoulder. An anxious crowd was collecting round him
as we passed on. Then came others supported between
two comrades, their faces deadly pale, and knees yielding
at every step. At every step, in short, we met numbers,
more or less wounded, hurrying along in search of that
assistance which many would never live to receive, and others
receive too late. Priests were running to and fro, hastening
to assist at the last moments of a dying man; all were in
haste—all wore that abstracted air so inseparable from those
engaged in an absorbing pursuit. There were women, too,
mingling in this scene of agitation. Ladies, fair delicate
ladies, stood on the steps at the doors of several handsome
houses, their hands folded before them, as if in the agony of
suspense, and with an air of deprecation, their eyes wandering over the excited crowd, whilst ever and anon they would
move their lips as if in prayer. I thought as we passed along
they looked at us, and prayed for our safety and success.
I gave them credit for it, at least, and the very idea had
the effect of inspiration. Strange that the sight—nay, often
the recollection—of all that is tender and compassionate, of
woman, should have the effect of stimulating us to martial
deeds. The little knots of excited citizens assembled on our
route would cease their energetic declamations, and turn to
look at us as we passed along. Many would run up, and,
patting our horses' necks, would call down benedictions on
us, and bid us hasten to the fight ere it were yet too late, or
utter trembling and not loud shouts of "Vivent les Anglais!"
A few there were who stood apart, with gloomy discontented
looks, eyeing their fellow-citizens with evident contempt,
and us with scowls, not unmixed with derision, as they
marked our dusty and jaded appearance. Through all this
crowd we held our way, and soon began to ascend the hill
beyond the town, where we entered a fine chaussée bordered
by elms, expecting every moment to enter on the field of
action, the roar of which appeared quite close to us. It was,
however, yet distant.

The road was covered with soldiers, many of them

wounded, but also many apparently untouched. The numbers thus leaving the field appeared extraordinary. Many of the wounded had six, eight, ten, and even more, attendants. When questioned about the battle, and why they left it, the answer was invariably, "Monsieur, tout est perdu! les Anglais sont abimés, en déroute, abimés, tous, tous, tous!" and then, nothing abashed, these fellows would resume their hurried route. My countrymen will rejoice to learn that amongst this dastardly crew not one Briton appeared. Whether they were of Nassau or Belgians, I know not; they were one or the other—I think the latter. One redcoat we did meet—not a fugitive though, for he was severely wounded. This man was a private of the 92d (Gordon Highlanders), a short, rough, hardy-looking fellow, with the national high cheek-bones, and a complexion that spoke of many a bivouac. He came limping along, evidently with difficulty and suffering. I stopped him to ask news of the battle, telling him what I had heard from the others. "Na, na, sir, it's aw a damned lee; they war fechtin' yat an I laft 'em; but it's a bludy business, and thar's na saying fat may be the end on't. Oor ragiment was nigh clean swapt off, and oor Colonel kilt jist as I cam awa." Upon inquiring about his own wound, we found that a musket-ball had lodged in his knee, or near it; accordingly Hitchins dismounting, seated him on the parapet of a little bridge we happened to be on, extracted the ball in a few minutes, and, binding up the wound, sent him hobbling along towards Nivelle, not having extracted a single exclamation from the poor man, who gratefully thanked him as he resumed his way. A little farther on, and as it began to grow dusk, we traversed the village of Hautain le Val, where a very different scene presented itself. Here, in a large cabaret by the roadside, we saw through the open windows the rooms filled with soldiers, cavalry and infantry; some standing about in earnest conversation, others seated round tables, smoking, carousing, and thumping the board with clenched fists, as they related with loud voices—what?—most likely their own gallant exploits. About the door their poor horses, tied to a rail, showed by their drooping heads, shifting legs, and the sweat drying and fuming on their soiled coats, that their exertions at least had been of no trivial nature.

CHAPTER XII

THE firing began to grow slacker, and even intermitting, as we entered on the field of Quatre Bras—our horses stumbling from time to time over corpses of the slain, which they were too tired to step over. The shot and shells which flew over our line of march from time to time (some of the latter bursting beyond us) were sufficient to enable us to say we had been *in* the battle of Quatre Bras, for such was the name of the place where we now arrived, just too late to be useful. In all directions the busy hum of human voices was heard; the wood along the skirts of which we marched re-echoed clearly and loudly the tones of the bugle, which ever and anon were overpowered by the sullen roar of cannon, or the sharper rattle of musketry; dark crowds of men moved in the increasing obscurity of evening, and the whole scene seemed alive with them. What a moment of excitement and anxiety as we proceeded amongst all this tumult, and amidst the dead and dying, ignorant as yet how the affair had terminated! Arrived at a mass of buildings, where four roads met (*les quatre bras*), Major M'Donald again came up with orders for us to bivouac on an adjoining field, where, accordingly, we established ourselves amongst the remains of a wheat crop.

Our men dismounted, and the horses tied up to the wheels of the carriages, every one was despatched with canteens and water-buckets to a well at the farm, to procure water for themselves and horses. This being the only water in the immediate neighbourhood, the crowd of all arms was so great about it that our people were employed fully two hours after halting ere they had completed watering their horses. They were then fed with corn, whilst eating which, a patch of wheat still standing was discovered near our bivouac. This we immediately cut or pulled up, and thus saved our hay, for there was sufficient to employ the poor brutes all night, if they preferred eating to sleeping.

Our animals cared for, the next consideration was ourselves. The men had provisions ready cooked in their haversacks, and therefore soon made themselves comfortable; but we had nothing, could procure nothing, and were likely to go supperless to bed. We had assembled in a little circle, discussing the events of the day previous to lying down, when, to our no small joy, the doctor made his appearance, followed by one of the servants bearing the remnant of a large meat-pie that yesterday had formed *part* of our dinner at Strytem, and which he, with laudable zeal and presence of mind, had in the hurry-scurry of the morning thrust into our little cart, thinking, good man, it might prove useful. No one can doubt that it did so in a degree; but the sixth part of the *remnant* of a pie went little way to satisfy the cravings of our stomachs, which had had so long a holiday. However, it was something, and we were grateful for it, and thankful to our worthy Esculapius for having been so provident. The meal ended and cigars lighted, we sat enveloped in our cloaks, chatting and listening to the Babel-like confusion at the well, where crowds were still struggling for water, until, one by one, we sank on the ground, overcome by sleep, which for my part remained unbroken until the grey dawn began to peep of the

17th June, when a popping fire of musketry, apparently close at hand, aroused me again to consciousness of my situation. At first I could not imagine where I was. I looked straight up, and the stars were twinkling over me in a clear sky. I put out a hand from beneath my cloak, and felt clods of damp earth and stalks of straw. The brattle of musketry increased, and then the consciousness of my situation came gradually over me. Although somewhat chilly, I was still drowsy, and, regardless of what might be going on, had turned on my side and began to doze again, when one of my neighbours started up with the exclamation, "I wonder what all that firing means!" This in an instant dispelled all desire to sleep; and up I got too, mechanically repeating his words, and rubbing my eyes as I began to peer about. One of the first, and certainly the most gratifying, sights that met my inquiring gaze, was Quartermaster Hall, who had arrived during the night with all his charge safe and sound. He had neither seen nor heard, however, of Mr Coates and his train of country waggons, for whom I began now to entertain serious apprehensions. From whatever the musketry might proceed we could see nothing—not even the flashes; but the increasing light allowed me to distinguish numberless dark forms on the ground all around me, people slumbering still, regardless of the firing that had aroused me. At a little distance numerous white discs, which were continually in motion, changing place and disappearing, to be succeeded by others, puzzled me exceedingly, and I could not even form a conjecture as to what they might be. Watching them attentively, I was still more surprised when some of these white objects ascended from the ground and suddenly disappeared; but the mystery was soon explained by the increasing light, which gave to my view a corps of Nassau troops lying on the ground, having white tops to their shakos. Daylight now gradually unfolded to us our situation. We were on a plateau which had been covered with corn, now almost everywhere trodden down. Four roads, as already mentioned, met a little to the right of our front, and just at that point stood a farmhouse, which, with its outbuildings, yard, etc., was enclosed by a very high wall. This was the farm of Quatre Bras. Beyond it, looking obliquely to the right, the wood (in which the battle still lingered when we arrived last night) stretched away some distance along the roads to Nivelle and Charleroi, which last we understood lay in front, but far out of sight. Along the continuation of the Charleroi road, and in the direction of Brussels, a little in rear of our right, a few cottages scattered along it had their little gardens enclosed by banks, with here and there an elder or some such bush growing on them; and these were the only enclosures to be seen, all the rest being a wide extent of corn-land without hedge or wall. On the farther side of the road, beyond the cottages, the fields were interspersed with thickets of underwood and a few clumps of trees, which shut in the view in that direction. To the rear the country appeared perfectly naked and open. To the left (I always speak with reference to the enemy whom we fronted) the ground descended very gradually for about two miles, where it appeared bounded by a long wood extending far away towards Brussels. In front it descended more abruptly; and then there was a plain about a mile in breadth extending along our front, from the wood on the left to that on the right.

The great road from Nivelle to Namur, crossing that from
Brussels to Charleroi at Quatre Bras, ran along this plain,
whilst the direction of the latter was nearly perpendicular to
our position. Beyond this plain the ground rose again to a
height somewhat superior to that on which we stood, and
another large wood extended on it from opposite the one on
our left, apparently half-way to that on the right, having the
declivity towards us laid out in fields enclosed by pretty
thick hedges. Between these two woods the opening gave
us an extensive view over the country, in the direction of
Gembloux and Namur.

On the Charleroi road and in the plain was a small village
(Frasnes), with its church, just beyond which the road
ascended the heights, on the open part of which, between
the road and the wood towards the left, was the bivouac of
the French army opposed to us. Its advanced posts were
in the valley near Frasnes, and ours opposite to them—our
main body occupying the ground between Quatre Bras and
the wood on the left. A smart skirmish was going on
amongst the hedges, etc., already mentioned, and this was
the firing we had heard all the morning. Our infantry were
lying about, cleaning their arms, cooking, or amusing themselves, totally regardless of the skirmish. This, however,
from our position, was a very interesting sight to me, for the
slope of the ground enabled me to see distinctly all the
manœuvres of both parties, as on a plan. After much firing
from the edge of the wood, opposite which our riflemen
occupied all the hedges, I saw the French chasseurs suddenly
make a rush forward in all directions, whilst the fire of our
people became thicker and faster than ever. Many of the
former scampered across the open fields until they reached
the nearest hedges, whilst others ran crouching under cover
of those perpendicular to their front, and the whole succeeded
in establishing themselves—thus forcing back and gaining
ground on our men. The fire then again became sharper
than ever—sometimes the French were driven back; and
this alternation I watched with great interest until summoned
to Major M'Donald, who brought us orders for the day.
From him I first learned the result of the action of yesterday
—the retreat of the Prussians, and that we were to do so too.
His directions to me were that I should follow some corps of

infantry, or something of the sort; for what followed caused me to forget it all: "Major Ramsay's troop," he said, "will remain in the rear with the cavalry, to cover the retreat; but I will not conceal from you that it falls to your turn to do this if you choose it." The Major looked rather conscience-stricken as he made this avowal, so, to relieve him, I begged he would give the devil his due and me mine. Accordingly all the others marched off, and as nothing was likely to take place immediately, we amused ourselves by looking on at what was doing. Just at this moment an amazing outcry arose amongst the infantry at the farm, who were running towards us in a confused mass, shouting and bellowing, jostling and pushing each other. I made sure the enemy's cavalry had made a dash amongst them, especially as the fire of the skirmishers became thicker and apparently nearer, when the thing was explained by a large pig, squealing as if already stuck, bursting from the throng by which he was beset in all directions. Some struck at him with axes, others with the butts of their muskets, others stabbed at him with bayonets. The chase would have been amusing had it not been so brutal; and I have seldom experienced greater horror than I did on this occasion when the poor brute, staggering from the repeated blows he received, was at last brought to the ground by at least half a dozen bayonets plunged into him at once.

All this time our retreat was going on very quietly. The corps at Quatre Bras had retired early in the morning and been replaced by others from the left, and this continued constantly—every corps halting for a time on the ground near Quatre Bras until another from the left arrived, these moving off on the great road to Brussels, ceding the ground to the new-comers.

At first every one, exulting in the success of yesterday—the having repulsed the enemy with a handful of men, as it were, unsupported by cavalry and with very little artillery—anticipated, now our army was united, nothing less than an immediate attack on the French position. We were sadly knocked down, then, when the certainty of our retreat became known. It was in vain we were told the retreat was only a manœuvre of concentration; the most gloomy anticipations pervaded every breast. About this time Sir Alexander

Dickson paid me a visit, having just arrived from New Orleans, where he commanded the artillery, to be our Deputy-Quartermaster-General. He only stayed a few minutes.

As the infantry corps on the plateau became fewer, the fire of the skirmishers amongst the hedges gradually relaxed, and at length ceased—the Rifles, etc., being withdrawn, and following the line of retreat. At last, about noon, I found myself left with my troop, quite alone, on the brow of the position, just by the farm of Quatre Bras—the only troops in sight being a small picket of hussars, near the village of Frasnes, in the plain below; a few more in our rear, but at some little distance, amongst the houses; and a brigade of hussars [1] far away to the left (about two miles), close to the wood in that quarter. Thus solitary, as it were, I had ample leisure to contemplate the scene of desolation around me, so strangely at variance with the otherwise smiling landscape. Everywhere mementoes of yesterday's bloody struggle met the eye—the corn trampled down, and the ground, particularly in the plain, plentifully besprinkled with bodies of the slain. Just in front of the farm of Quatre Bras there was a fearful scene of slaughter—Highlanders and cuirassiers lying thickly strewn about; the latter appeared to have charged up the Charleroi road, on which, and immediately bordering it, they lay most numerously.

In communicating to me the orders of our retreat, Major M'Donald had reiterated that to join Lord Edward Somerset's brigade without delay, but still he could not tell me where this brigade was to be found. Meantime Sir Ormsby Vandeleur's brigade of light dragoons having formed up in front of the houses, and supposing from this that all the cavalry must be nigh, as one step towards finding Lord Edward I crossed the road to the right of these dragoons, and rode towards the part where, as before stated, the light was intercepted by trees and bushes. On passing through these I had an uninterrupted view of the country for miles, but not a soldier or living being was to be seen in that direction. As I pushed on through the thickets my horse, suddenly coming to a stand, began to snort, and showed unequivocal symptoms of fear. I drove him on, however, but started myself when I saw, lying under the bush, the body of a man stripped naked.

[1] Sir Hussey Vivian's, I believe.

This victim of war was a youth of fair form, skin delicately white, and face but little darker; an embryo mustache decorated the upper lip, and his countenance, even in death, was beautiful. That he was French I conjectured, but neither on himself nor his horse was there a particle of clothing that could indicate to what nation he belonged. If French, how came he here to die alone so far in the rear of our lines? I know not why, but the rencontre with this solitary corpse had a wonderful effect on my spirits—far different from what I felt when gazing on the heaps that encumbered the field beyond. Seldom have I experienced such despondency—such heart-sinking—as when standing over this handsome form thus despoiled, neglected, and about to become a prey to wolves and carrion crows—the darling of some fond mother, the adored of some fair maid. His horse, stripped like himself, lay by—they had met their fate at once. Returning to my troop, I found Sir Augustus Frazer, who had come to order my ammunition waggons to the rear that the retreat might be as little encumbered as possible, and to tell me that what ammunition was used during the day would be supplied by my sending for it to Langeveldt, on the road to Brussels, where that to Wavre branches from it.

Thus divested of our ammunition, it was evident that our retreat must be a rapid one, since with only fifty rounds a-gun (the number in the limbers), it could not be expected that we could occupy any position longer than a few minutes. In the end, this measure had nearly led to very disagreeable results, as will be seen anon.

It was now about one o'clock. My battery stood in position on the brow of the declivity, with its right near the wall of the farm, all alone, the only troops in sight being, as before mentioned, the picket and a few scattered hussars in the direction of Frasnes, Sir O. Vandeleur's light dragoons two or three hundred yards in our rear, and Sir H. Vivian's hussars far away to the left. Still the French army made no demonstration of an advance. This inactivity was unaccountable. Lord Uxbridge and an aide-de-camp came to the front of my battery, and, dismounting, seated himself on the ground; so did I and the aide-de-camp. His lordship with his glass was watching the French position; and we were all three wondering at their want of observation and inactivity, which had not only permitted our infantry to retire unmolested, but also still retained them in their bivouac. "It will not be long now before they are on us," said the aide-de-camp, "for they always dine before they move; and those smokes seem to indicate that they are cooking now." He was right; for not long afterwards another aide-de-camp, scouring along the valley, came to report that a heavy column of cavalry [1] was advancing through the opening between the woods to the left from the direction of Gembloux. At the same moment we saw them distinctly; and Lord Uxbridge, having reconnoitered them a moment through his glass, started up, exclaiming, in a joyful tone, "By the Lord, they are Prussians!" jumped on his horse, and, followed by the two aides, dashed off like a whirlwind to meet them. For a moment I stood looking after them as they swept down the slope, and could not help wondering how the Prussians came there. I was, however, not left long in my perplexity, for, turning my eyes towards the French position, I saw their whole army descending from it in three or four dark masses, whilst their advanced cavalry picket was already skirmishing with and driving back our hussars. The truth instantly flashed on my mind, and I became exceedingly uneasy for the safety of Lord Uxbridge and his companions, now far advanced on their way down the valley, and likely to be irretrievably cut off. My situation now appeared somewhat awkward: left without orders and entirely alone on the brow of our position—the hussar pickets galloping in and hurrying past as fast as they could— the whole French army advancing, and already at no great distance. In this dilemma, I determined to retire across the little dip that separated me from Sir O. Vandeleur, and take up a position in front of his squadrons, whence, after giving a round to the French advance as soon as they stood on our present ground, I thought I could retire in sufficient time through his intervals to leave the ground clear for him to charge. This movement was immediately executed; but

---

[1] These appear to have been the cuirassiers of Milhaud, together with the light cavalry of the corps commanded by Count Lobau, sent to assist Ney in his attack on Quatre Bras.—See O'Meara's *Translation of Memoir of Napoleon*, lib. ix. cap. v. p. 109.

the guns were scarcely unlimbered ere Sir Ormsby came furiously up, exclaiming, "What are you doing here, sir? You encumber my front, and we shall not be able to charge. Take your guns away, sir; instantly, I say—take them away!" It was in vain that I endeavoured to explain my intentions, and that our fire would allow his charge to be made with more effect. "No, no; take them out of my way, sir!" was all the answer I could get; and, accordingly, I was preparing to obey, when up came Lord Uxbridge, and the scene changed in a twinkling. "Captain Mercer, are you loaded?" "Yes, my lord." "Then give them a round as they rise the hill, and retire as quickly as possible." "Light dragoons, threes right; at a trot, march!" and then some orders to Sir Ormsby, of whom I saw no more that day. "They are just coming up the hill," said Lord Uxbridge. "Let them get well up before you fire. Do you think you can retire quick enough afterwards?" "I am sure of it, my lord." "Very well, then, keep a good look-out, and point your guns well." I had often longed to see Napoleon, that mighty man of war—that astonishing genius who had filled the world with his renown. Now I saw him, and there was a degree of sublimity in the interview rarely equalled. The sky had become overcast since the morning, and at this moment presented a most extraordinary appearance. Large isolated masses of thundercloud, of the deepest, almost inky black, their lower edges hard and strongly defined, lagging down, as if momentarily about to burst, hung suspended over us, involving our position and everything on it in deep and gloomy obscurity; whilst the distant hill lately occupied by the French army still lay bathed in brilliant sunshine. Lord Uxbridge was yet speaking, when a single horseman,[1] immediately followed by several others, mounted the plateau I had left at a gallop, their dark figures thrown forward in strong relief from the illuminated distance, making them appear much nearer to us than they really were. For an instant they pulled up and regarded us, when several squadrons, coming rapidly on the plateau, Lord Uxbridge cried

[1] That this was Napoleon we have the authority of General Gourgand, who states that, irritated at the delay of Marshal Ney, he put himself at the head of the chasseurs (I think), and dashed forward in the hope of yet being able to catch our rear-guard.

out, "Fire!—fire!" and, giving them a general discharge, we quickly limbered up to retire, as they dashed forward supported by some horse-artillery guns, which opened upon us ere we could complete the manœuvre, but without much effect, for the only one touched was the servant of Major Whinyates, who was wounded in the leg by the splinter of a howitzer shell.

It was now for the first time that I discovered the Major and his rocket troop, who, annoyed at my having the rear, had disobeyed the order to retreat, and remained somewhere in the neighbourhood until this moment, hoping to share whatever might be going on. The first gun that was fired seemed to burst the clouds overhead, for its report was instantly followed by an awful clap of thunder, and lightning that almost blinded us, whilst the rain came down as if a waterspout had broken over us. The sublimity of the scene was inconceivable. Flash succeeded flash, and the peals of thunder were long and tremendous; whilst, as if in mockery of the elements, the French guns still sent forth their feebler glare and now scarcely audible reports—their cavalry dashing on at a headlong pace, adding their shouts to the uproar. We galloped for our lives through the storm, striving to gain the enclosures about the houses of the hamlets, Lord Uxbridge urging us on, crying, "Make haste!—make haste! for God's sake, gallop, or you will be taken!" We did make haste, and succeeded in getting amongst the houses and gardens, but with the French advance close on our heels. Here, however, observing the chaussée full of hussars, they pulled up. Had they continued their charge we were gone, for these hussars were scattered about the road in the utmost confusion, some in little squads, others singly, and, moreover, so crowded together that we had no room whatever to act with any effect—either they or us.

Meantime the enemy's detachments began to envelop the gardens, which Lord Uxbridge observing, called to me, "Here follow me with two of your guns," and immediately himself led the way into one of the narrow lanes between the gardens. What he intended doing, God knows, but I obeyed. The lane was very little broader than our carriages —there was not room for a horse to have passed them! The distance from the chaussée to the end of the lane, where it debouched on the open fields, could scarcely have been above one or two hundred yards at most. His lordship and I were in front, the guns and mounted detachments following. What he meant to do I was at a loss to conceive; we could hardly come to action in the lane; to enter on the open was certain destruction. Thus we had arrived at about fifty yards from its termination when a body of chasseurs or hussars appeared there as if waiting for us. These we might have seen from the first, for nothing but a few elder bushes intercepted the view from the chaussée. The whole transaction appears to me so wild and confused that at times I can hardly believe it to have been more than a confused dream—yet true it was;—the general-in-chief of the cavalry exposing himself amongst the skirmishers of his rear-guard, and literally doing the duty of a cornet! "By God! we are all prisoners" (or some such words), exclaimed Lord Uxbridge, dashing his horse at one of the garden-banks, which he cleared, and away he went, leaving us to get out of the scrape as best we could. There was no time for hesitation—one manœuvre alone could extricate us if allowed time, and it I ordered. "Reverse by unlimbering" was the order. To do this the gun was to be unlimbered, then turned round, and one wheel run up the bank, which just left space for the limber to pass it. The gun is then limbered up again and ready to move to the rear. The execution, however, was not easy, for the very reversing of the limber itself in so narrow a lane, with a team of eight horses, was sufficiently difficult, and required first-rate driving. Nothing could exceed the coolness and activity of our men; the thing was done quickly and well, and we returned to the chaussée without let or hindrance. How we were permitted to do so, I am at a loss to imagine; for although I gave the order to reverse, I certainly never expected to have seen it executed. Meantime my own situation was anything but a pleasant one, as I sat with my back to the gentlemen at the end of the lane, whose interference I momentarily expected, casting an eye from time to time over my shoulder to ascertain whether they still kept their position. There they sat motionless, and although thankful for their inactivity, I could not but wonder at their stupidity. It seemed, however, all of a piece that day—all blunder and confusion; and this last I found pretty considerable on regaining the chausée. His lordship we found collecting the scattered hussars together into a squadron for our rescue, for which purpose it was he had so unceremoniously left us. Heavy as the rain was and thick the weather, yet the French could not but have seen the confusion we were in, as they had closed up to the entrance of the enclosure; and yet they did not at once take advantage of it. Things could not remain long in this state. A heavy column of cavalry approached us by the chaussée, whilst another, skirting the enclosures, appeared pushing forward to cut us off. Retreat now became imperative. The order was given, and away we went, helter-skelter—guns, gun-detachments, and hussars, all mixed *pêle-mêle*, going like mad, and covering each other with mud, to be washed off by the rain, which, before sufficiently heavy, now came down again as it had done at first in splashes instead of drops, soaking us anew to the skin, and, what was worse, extinguishing every slow-match in the brigade. The obscurity caused by the splashing of the rain was such, that at one period I could not distinguish objects more than a few yards distant. Of course we lost sight of our pursuers altogether, and the shouts and halloos, and even laughter, they had at first sent forth were either silenced or drowned in the uproar of the elements and the noise of our too rapid retreat; for in addition to everything else the crashing and rattling of the thunder were most awful, and the glare of the lightning blinding. In this state we gained the bridge of Genappe at the moment when the thundercloud, having passed over, left us in comparative fine weather, although still raining heavily.

The town of Genappe stands on the slope of a hill rising immediately from the little verdant valley through which the Lys flows—here little better than a brook. Arrived at the bridge, we slackened our pace, and ascended leisurely the narrow winding street, in which not a living soul was visible. The shutters were all closed, and stream of water pouring from the roofs formed a perfect torrent of the gutter running down the middle of it. This solitude was rather a disappointment, for I had hoped here to have got fire to relight our slow-match.

For the last mile or so we had neither seen nor heard anything of our lively French friends, and now silently wound our way up the deserted street, nothing disturbing its death-like stillness save the iron sound of horses' feet, the rumbling of the carriages, and the splashing of water as it fell from the eaves,—all this was stillness compared with the hurly-burly and din from which we had just emerged.

On gaining the high ground beyond the town, we suddenly came in sight of the main body of our cavalry drawn up across the chaussée in two lines, and extending away far to the right and left of it.

It would have been an imposing spectacle at any time, but just now appeared to me magnificent, and I hailed it with complacency, for here I thought our fox-chase must end. "Those superb Life Guards and Blues will soon teach our pursuers a little modesty." Such fellows!—surely nothing can withstand them. Scarcely had these thoughts passed through my mind ere an order from his lordship recalled us to the rear. On debouching from the town, seeing nothing in the country right and left of us, and fearful of impeding the retreat, whilst our hussars retired skirmishing through the street (the French having again come up), we had continued onward to gain the position occupied by our heavy cavalry, from which we were still separated by a small dip of the ground. We returned then to the end of the town, where the flight of shot and shells over us (the road was here sunk between two high banks) gave very intelligible information as to the reason of our recall. The enemy's horse-artillery, having taken up a position in the meadows near the bridge, were annoying our dragoons as they de-bouched from the town. The ground was heavy from the rain, and very steep, so that it was only by great exertion that we succeeded at last in getting our guns into the adjoin-ing field. The moment we appeared the French battery bestowed on us its undivided attention, which we quickly acknowledged by an uncommonly well-directed fire of spherical case. Whilst so employed, Major M'Donald came up and put me through a regular catechism as to length of fuze, whether out of bag A or B, etc. etc. Although much vexed at such a schooling just now, yet the Major appeared so seriously in earnest that I could not but be amused; however, to convince him we knew what we were about, I directed his attention to our excellent practice, so superior to that of our antagonist, who was sending all his shot far over our heads. The French seemed pretty well convinced of this too, for after standing a few rounds they quitted the field, and left us again without occupation. The Major vanishing at the same time, I sent my guns, etc., to the rear, and set off to join Lord Uxbridge, who was still fighting in the street. Our ammunition was expended, the waggons having been taken away by Sir Augustus Frazer at Quatre Bras.

On regaining my troop, I found Major M'Donald and the rockets with it. They were in position on a gentle elevation, on which likewise were formed the lines of cavalry extending across the chaussée. Immediately on our left, encased in the hollow road, the Blues were formed in close column of half-squadrons, and it was not long ere Lord Uxbridge, with those he had retained at Genappe, came sweeping over the hill and joined us. They were closely followed by the French light cavalry, who, descending into the hollow, commenced a sharp skirmish with our advanced-posts. Soon squadron after squadron appeared on the hill we had passed, and took up their positions, forming a long line parallel to ours, whilst a battery of horse-artillery, forming across the chaussée, just on the brow of the declivity, opened its fire on us, though without much effect. To this we responded, though very slowly, having no more ammunition than what remained in our limbers. In order to amuse the enemy and our own cavalry, as well as to prevent the former noticing the slackness of our fire, I proposed to Major M'Donald making use of the rockets, which had hitherto done nothing. There was a little hesitation about this, and one of the officers (Strangways) whispered me, "No, no—it's too far!" This I immediately told the Major, proposing as a remedy that they should go closer. Still there was demur; but at last my proposition was agreed to, and down they marched into the thick of the skirmishers in the bottom. Of course, having proposed the measure myself, I could do no less than accompany them. Whilst they prepared their machinery, I had time to notice what was going on to the right and left of us. Two double lines of skirmishers extended all along the bottom—the foremost of each line were within a few yards of each other—constantly in motion, riding backwards and forwards, firing their carbines or pistols, and then reloading, still on the move. This fire seemed to me more dangerous for those on the hills above than for us below; for all, both French and English, generally stuck out their carbines or pistols as they continued to move backwards and forwards, and discharged them without taking any particular aim, and mostly in the air. I did not see a man fall on either side; the thing appeared quite ridiculous; and but for hearing the bullets whizzing overhead, one might have fancied it no more than a sham-fight.

Meanwhile the rocketeers had placed a little iron triangle in the road with a rocket lying on it. The order to fire is given — port-fire applied — the fidgety missile begins to sputter out sparks and wriggle its tail for a second or so, and then darts forth straight up the chaussée. A gun stands right in its way, between the wheels of which the shell in the head of the rocket bursts, the gunners fall right and left, and, those of the other guns taking to their heels, the battery is deserted in an instant. Strange; but so it was. I saw them run, and for some minutes afterwards I saw the guns standing mute and unmanned, whilst our rocketeers kept shooting off rockets, none of which ever followed the course of the first; most of them, on arriving about the middle of the ascent, took a vertical direction, whilst some actually turned back upon ourselves—and one of these, following me like a squib until its shell exploded, actually put me in more danger than all the fire of the enemy throughout the day. Meanwhile the French artillerymen, seeing how the land lay, returned to their guns and opened a fire of case-shot on us, but without effect, for we retreated to our ridge without the loss of a man, or even any wounded, though the range could not have been above 200 yards. As we had overtaken the rear of our infantry, it became necessary to make a stand here to enable them to gain ground. Major M'Donald therefore sent me in pursuit of my ammunition waggons, since all in our limbers was expended. Having before sent for these, we calculated that they could not now be very far off. In going to the rear I passed along the top of the bank, under which, as I have said, the Blues were encased in the hollow road. Shot and shells were flying pretty thickly about just then, and, sometimes striking the top of the bank, would send down a shower of mud and clods upon them.

The ammunition waggons I found coming up, and was returning with them when I met my whole troop again retiring by the road, whilst the cavalry did so by alternate regiments across the fields. The ground offering no feature for another stand, we continued thus along the road. The infantry had made so little progress that we again overtook the rear of their column, composed of Brunswickers—some of those same boys I used to see practising at Schäpdale in my rides to Brussels. These poor lads were pushing on at a great rate. As soon as their rear divisions heard the sound of our horses' feet, without once looking behind them, they began to crowd and press on those in front, until at last, hearing us close up to them, and finding it impossible to push forward in the road, many of them broke off into the fields; and such was their panic that, in order to run lighter, away went arms and knapsacks in all directions, and a general race ensued, the whole corps being in the most horrid confusion. It was to no purpose that I exerted my little stock of German to make them understand we were their English friends—a frightened glance and away, was all the effect of my interference, which drove many of them off. We, however, still kept on our way, and soon after passed a few houses by the roadside, which I afterwards found was La Belle Alliance. Hence we crossed another valley, and on rising the opposite hill I found a capital position on the top of an old gravel-pit, which I occupied without loss of time. Behind the ground on which my guns were formed was a long hedge [1] (a *rara avis* in this country), which prevented our seeing anything beyond; and as no troops were in sight except those following us across the valley, we had then no idea that we had arrived in the position where our whole army was assembled, nor that we then stood upon ground which, ere to-morrow's sun were set, would for ever be celebrated throughout all generations!

We did not long remain idle, for the guns were scarcely loaded ere the rear of our cavalry came crowding upon the

---

[1] This was the spot where Picton fell on the morrow, and in this hedge was the so well-known Wellington Tree.

infantry corps we had passed, and which were then only crossing the valley, the French advance skirmishing with these, whilst their squadrons occupied the heights. We waited a little until some of their larger masses were assembled, and then opened our fire with a range across the valley of about 1200 yards. The echo of our first gun had not ceased, when, to my astonishment, a heavy cannonade, commencing in a most startling manner from behind our hedge, rolled along the rising ground, on part of which we were posted. The truth now flashed on me; we had rejoined the army, and it is impossible to describe the pleasing sense of security I felt at having now the support of something more stanch than cavalry.

The French now brought up battery after battery, and a tremendous cannonading was kept up by both sides for some time. The effect was grand and exciting. Our position was a happy one, for all their shot which grazed short, came and struck in the perpendicular bank of our gravel-pit—and only one struck amongst us, breaking the traversing handspike at one of the guns, but neither injuring man nor horse. Our fire was principally directed against their masses as we could see them, which was not always the case from the smoke that, for want of wind, hung over them; then against their smaller parties that had advanced into the valley to skirmish with the rear-guard of our cavalry. Here for the second and last time I saw Napoleon, though infinitely more distant than in the morning. Some of my non-commissioned officers pointed their guns at the numerous cortège accompanying him as they stood near the road by Belle Alliance; and one, pointed by old Quartermaster Hall, fell in the midst of them. At the moment we saw some little confusion amongst the group, but it did not hinder them from continuing the reconnaissance.

Whilst we were thus engaged, a man of no very prepossessing appearance came rambling amongst our guns, and entered into conversation with me on the occurrences of the day. He was dressed in a shabby, old, drab greatcoat and a rusty round hat. I took him at the time for some amateur from Brussels (of whom we had heard there were several hovering about), and thinking many of his questions rather impertinent, was somewhat short in answering him, and he soon left us. How great was my astonishment on learning soon after that this was Sir Thomas Picton! The enemy, finding us obstinate in maintaining our position, soon slackened, and then ceased firing altogether; and we were immediately ordered to do the same, and establish ourselves in bivouac for the night. This we proceeded to obey as a most welcome order, and retiring from our position down the hill, came to a large farm, where, breaking through a quickset hedge, we formed our park in the adjoining orchard, preferring its green turf to the plashy, muddy fields around, that morning covered with fine crops of wheat, now little better than sloughs. We were not long, however, in discovering that it was only exchanging the frying-pan for the fire, since our smiling turf was nearly ankle-deep in water, the orchard lying low and hollow, somewhat below the level of the road. But it was already growing dark, consequently too late to hunt out another, so we were obliged to put up with it.

Thoroughly wet—cloaks, blankets, and all—comfort was out of the question, so we prepared to make the best of it.

Our first care was of course the horses, and these we had ample means of providing for, since, in addition to what corn we had left, one of our men had picked up and brought forward on an ammunition waggon a large sack full, which he found in the road near Genappe. Thus they, at least, had plenty to eat, and having been so well drenched all day, were not much in need of water. For ourselves we had nothing!—absolutely nothing! and looked forward to rest alone to restore our exhausted strength. Rather a bore going supperless to bed after such a day, yet was there no help for it.

But our poor animals were not all of them destined to repose, and much as they had undergone during the last six-and-thirty hours, some of them were yet obliged to pass the night on the road, and in harness. Completing our limbers with ammunition from two of the ammunition waggons, a non-commissioned officer was despatched with these, as soon as the horses had been fed, to Langeveldt near Brussels, where Sir Augustus Frazer had told me in the morning we should find a depot from whence to supply what had been expended during the day.

These cared for, came the care of ourselves. Our gunners,

etc., soon stowed themselves away beneath the carriages, using the painted covers as additional shelter against the rain, which now set in again as heavy as ever. We set up a small tent, into which (after vain attempts at procuring food or lodgings in the farm or its outbuildings, all of which were crammed to suffocation with officers and soldiers of all arms and nations) we crept, and rolling ourselves in our wet blankets, huddled close together, in hope, wet as we were, and wet as the ground was, of keeping each other warm. I know not how my bedfellows got on, as we all lay for a long while perfectly still and silent—the old Peninsular hands disdaining to complain before their Johnny Newcome comrades, and these fearing to do so lest they should provoke some such remarks, as "Lord have mercy on your poor tender carcass! what would such as you have done in the Pyrenees?" or "Oho, my boy! this is but child's play to what _we_ saw in Spain." So all who did not sleep (I believe the majority) pretended to do so, and bore their suffering with admirable heroism. For my part, I once or twice, from sheer fatigue, got into something like a doze; yet it would not do. There was no possibility of sleeping, for besides being already so wet, the tent proved no shelter, the water pouring through the canvas in streams; so up I got, and, to my infinite joy, found that some of the men had managed to make a couple of fires, round which they were sitting smoking their short pipes in something like comfort. The hint was a good one, and at that moment my second captain joining me, we borrowed from them a few sticks, and choosing the best spot under the hedge, proceeded to make a fire for ourselves. In a short time we succeeded in raising a cheerful blaze, which materially bettered our situation. My companion had an umbrella (which, by the way, had afforded some merriment to our people on the march); this we planted against the sloping bank of the hedge, and seating ourselves under it, he on one side of the stick, me on the other, we lighted cigars and became—comfortable. Dear weed! what comfort, what consolation dost thou not impart to the wretched!— with thee a hovel becomes a palace. What a stock of patience is there not enveloped in one of thy brown leaves! And thus we sat enjoying ourselves, puffing forth into the damp night air streams of fragrant smoke, being able now deliberately to converse on what had been, and probably would be. All this time a most infernal clatter of musketry was going on, which, but for the many quiet dark figures seated round the innumerable fires all along the position, might have been construed into a night-attack. But as these gentlemen were between us and the enemy, we felt assured of timely warning, and ere long learned that all this proceeded as before from the infantry discharging and cleaning their pieces. Our conversation naturally turned on our present position; and after discussing all the pros and cons, we made up our minds to recommence the retreat with to-morrow's sun; but when that retreat was to terminate, baffled all our powers of conjecture.

Whilst so employed, a rustling in the hedge behind attracted our attention, and in a few minutes a poor fellow belonging to some Hanoverian regiment, wet through like everybody else, and shivering with cold, made his appearance, and modestly begged permission to remain a short time and warm himself by our fire. He had somehow or other wandered from his colours, and had passed the greater part of the night searching for them, but in vain. At first he appeared quite exhausted, but the warmth reinvigorating him, he pulled out his pipe and began to smoke. Having finished his modicum, and carefully disposed of the ashes, he rose from his wet seat to renew his search, hoping to find his corps before daylight, he said, lest it should be engaged. Many thanks he offered for our hospitality; but what was our surprise when, after fumbling in his haversack for some time, he pulled out a poor half-starved chicken, presented it to us, and marched off. This was a god-send, in good truth, to people famished as we were; so calling for a camp-kettle, our prize was on the fire in a twinkling. Our comrades in the tent did not sleep so soundly but that they heard what was going on, and the kettle was hardly on the fire ere my gentlemen were assembled round it, a wet and shivering group, but all eager to partake of our good fortune —and so eager that, after various betrayals of impatience, the miserable chicken was at last snatched from the kettle ere it was half-boiled, pulled to pieces, and speedily devoured. I got a leg for my share, but it was not one mouthful, and this was the only food I tasted since the night before.

CHAPTER XIII

June 18*th.*—Memorable day! Some time before daybreak
the bombardier who had been despatched to Langeveldt
returned with a supply of ammunition. He reported that
he had been much impeded by the confusion on the road,
which was everywhere crowded with waggons, etc. Many
he had seen overturned, and many plundered, or being
plundered; but his account by no means justified those who
stated the road to be blocked up in such a manner as to be
impassable. Indeed, considering all things, he had performed his journey in sufficiently reasonable time.

With the providence of an old soldier, he had picked up
and brought on a considerable quantity of beef, biscuit, and
oatmeal, of which there was abundance scattered about
everywhere. Casks of rum, etc., there were, and having
broached one of these—he and his drivers—every one filled
his canteen—a most considerate act, and one for which the
whole troop was sincerely thankful. Nor must I omit to
remark that, amidst such temptations, his men had behaved
with the most perfect regularity, and returned to us *quite
sober!*

The rum was divided on the spot; and surely if ardent
spirits are ever beneficial, it must be to men situated as ours
were; it therefore came most providentially. The oatmeal
was converted speedily into stirabout, and afforded our
people a hearty meal, after which all hands set to work to
prepare the beef, make soup, etc. Unfortunately, we preferred waiting for this, and passed the stirabout, by which
piece of folly we were doomed to a very protracted fast as
will be seen. Whilst our soup was cooking, it being now
broad daylight, I mounted my horse to reconnoitre our
situation. During the night another troop (I think Major
Ramsay's) had established itself in our orchard, and just
outside the hedge I found Major Bean's, which had also

arrived during the night, direct from England. Ascending from the farm towards the ground we had left yesterday evening, the face of the slope, as far as I could see, to the right and left, was covered with troops *en bivouac*—here, I think, principally cavalry. Of these, some were cleaning their arms, some cooking, some sitting round fires smoking, and a few, generally officers, walking about, or standing in groups conversing. Many of the latter eagerly inquired where I was going, and appeared very anxious for intelligence, all expecting nothing less than to recommence our retreat. I continued on to the position we had occupied last, and thence clearly saw the French army on the opposite hill, where everything appeared perfectly quiet—people moving about individually, and no formation whatever. Their advanced-posts and vedettes in the valley, just beyond La Haye Sainte, were also quiet. Having satisfied my curiosity, I returned the way I came, communicating my observations to the many eager inquirers I met with. Various were the speculations in consequence. Some thought the French were afraid to attack us, others that they would do so soon, others that the Duke would not wait for it, others that he would, as he certainly would not allow them to go to Brussels; and so they went on speculating, whilst I returned to my people. Here, finding the mess not yet ready, and nothing to be done, I strolled into the garden of the farm, where several Lifeguardsmen were very busy digging potatoes— a fortunate discovery, which I determined to profit by. Therefore calling up some of my men, to work we went without loss of time.

Whilst thus employed, I noticed a very heavy firing going on in front, but this did not make us quit our work. Shortly, after, to my great astonishment, I observed that all the bivouacs on the hillside were deserted, and that even Ramsay's troop had left the orchard without my being aware of it, and my own was left quite alone, not a soul being visible from where I stood in any direction, the ground they had quitted presenting one unbroken muddy solitude. The firing became heavier and heavier. Alarmed at being thus left alone, when it was evident something serious was going on, I hastened back and ordered the horses to be put to immediately.

Away went our mess untasted. One of the servants was desired to hang the kettle with its contents under an ammunition waggon. The stupid fellow hung the kettle as desired, but first emptied it. Without orders, and all alone, the battle (for now there was no mistaking it) going on at the other side of the hill, I remained for a few minutes undecided what to do. It appeared to me we had been forgotten. All except only ourselves, were evidently engaged; and labouring under this delusion, I thought we had better get into the affair at once. As soon, therefore, as the troop was ready I led them up the hill on the highroad, hoping to meet some one who could give me directions what to do. We had not proceeded a hundred yards, when an artillery officer came furiously galloping down towards us. It was Major M'Lloyd, in a dreadful state of agitation—such, indeed, that he could hardly answer my questions. I learned, however, that the battle was very serious and bloody. Their first attack had been on that part of our position where his battery stood; but now the principal efforts were making against our right. All this was told in so hurried and anxious a manner, that one could hardly understand him. "But where are you going?" he added. I told him my plan. "Have you no orders?" "None whatever; I have not seen a soul." "Then, for God's sake, come and assist me, or I shall be ruined. My brigade is cut to pieces, ammunition expended, and, unless reinforced, we shall be destroyed." He was dreadfully agitated, and when I took his hand and promised to be with him directly, seemed transported with joy; so, bidding me make haste, he darted up the hill again, and went to receive that death-stroke which, ere long, was to terminate his earthly career. I trust before that termination he heard the reason why I never fulfilled that promise; for weeks elapsed ere he died, no doubt—otherwise he must have set me down for a base poltroon. My destiny led me elsewhere. My tutelary spirit was at hand: the eternal Major M'Donald made his appearance, and, giving me a sharp reprimand for having quitted my bivouac, desired me instantly to return to the foot of the hill, and there wait for orders. Sulkily and slowly we descended, and forming in line on the ground opposite the farm of Mont St Jean, with our left to the road, I dismounted the men that they might be a little less liable to be hit by shot and shells which, coming over the hill, were continually plunging into the muddy soil all around us. This was a peculiarly dismal situation—without honour or glory, to be knocked on the head in such a solitude, for not a living being was in sight.

It was while thus standing idle that a fine tall upright old gentleman, in plain clothes, followed by two young ones, came across our front at a gallop from the Brussels road, and continued on towards where we supposed the right of our army to be. I certainly stared at seeing three unarmed civilians pressing forward into so hot a fight. These were the Duke of Richmond and his two sons. How long we had been in this position, I know not, when at length we were relieved from it by our adjutant (Lieutenant Bell), who brought orders for our removal to the right of the second line. Moving, therefore, to our right, along the hollow, we soon began a very gentle ascent, and at the same time became aware of several corps of infantry, which had not been very far from us, but remained invisible, as they were all lying down. Although in this move we may be said to have been always under a heavy fire, from the number of missiles flying over us, yet were we still so fortunate as to arrive in our new position without losing man or horse. In point of seeing, our situation was much improved; but for danger and inactivity, it was much worse, since we were now fired directly at, and positively ordered not to return the compliment—the object in bringing us here being to watch a most formidable-looking line of lancers drawn up opposite to us, and threatening the right flank of our army. A scientific relation of this great struggle, on which the fate of Europe hinged, I pretend not to write. I write neither history, nor "Memoires pour servir à l'Histoire," etc. etc., but only pure simple gossip for my own amusement—just what happened to me and mine, and what I *did* see happen to others about me. Depend upon it, he who pretends to give a general account of a great battle from his own observation deceives you—believe him not. He can see no farther (that is, if he be personally engaged in it) than the length of his nose; and how is he to tell what is passing two or three miles off, with hills and trees and buildings intervening, and all enveloped in smoke? Busaco might have been tolerably described, but there are no Busacos in the Pays Bas. The back of the principal ridge on which our army was posted descended by a pretty regular slope in the direction of Waterloo, and but just in rear of its right another shorter and lower ridge ran a little way almost parallel to it. The highroad to Nivelle passed along the hollow between the two. Both ridges terminated in a ravine that enclosed our right flank, running down from the Château de Hougoumont (although it be pretended now that the name is "Goumont," I persist in the orthography which is found in all the old maps of this department) in the direction of Merke Braine; in short, a contracted continuation of the greater valley lying between the two armies and nearly at right angles to it.

The sides of this ravine (much steeper than any other ground near), as far as I can recollect, were partially covered with bushes; and, from the summit of the one opposite to us, the ground ascended by a very gradual slope for about 800 or 1000 yards; and there, on what appeared as the height of the land, there were several small clumps of wood. This slope itself was still covered with fine crops of standing corn. The crest was occupied by the long line of lancers already spoken of, whose movements I was ordered to watch, but on no account to interfere with, unless they attempted to pass the ravine.[1] Such was our front view.

To the right we looked over a fine open country, covered with crops and interspersed with thickets or small woods. There all was peaceful and smiling, not a living soul being in sight. To our left, the main ridge terminated rather abruptly just over Hougoumont, the back of it towards us being broken ground, with a few old trees on it just where the Nivelle road descended between high banks into the ravine. Thus we were formed en potence with the 1st line, from which we (my battery) were separated by some hundred yards. In our rear the 14th Regiment of infantry (in square, I think) lay on the ground. In our front were some light

---

[1] The light cavalry of the 2d Corps formed in three lines across the causeway from Nivelle, etc., nearly at the height of the first woods at Hougoumont, scouring all the plain by the left, and having main guards near Braine le Leude, and its battery of light artillery on the causeway of Nivelle.—*Memoir of Napoleon*, lib. ix. cap. vi. p. 134 ; O' Meara's translation.

dragoons of the German Legion, who from time to time detached small parties across the ravine. These pushed cautiously up the slope towards the line of lancers to reconnoitre. The corn, down to the edge of the ravine nearer the Nivelle road and beyond it, was full of French riflemen; and these were warmly attacked by others [1] from our side of the ravine, whom we saw crossing and gradually working their way up through the high corn, the French as gradually retiring. On the right of the lancers, two or three batteries kept up a continued fire at our position; but their shot, which could have been only 4-pounders, fell short—many not even reaching across the ravine. Some, however, did reach their destination; and we were particularly plagued by their howitzer shells with long fuses, which were continually falling about us, and lay spitting and sputtering several seconds before they exploded, to the no small annoyance of man and horse. Still, however, nobody was hurt; but a round-shot, striking the ammunition-boxes on the body of one of our waggons, penetrated through both and lodged in the back of the rear one, with nearly half its surface to be seen from without—a singular circumstance! In addition to this front fire, we were exposed to another on our left flank—the shot that passed over the main ridge terminating their career with us. Having little to occupy us here, we had ample leisure to observe what was passing there. We could see some corps at the end near us in squares—dark masses, having guns between them, relieved from a background of grey smoke, which seemed to fill the valley beyond, and rose high in the air above the hill. Every now and then torrents of French cavalry of all arms came sweeping over the ridge, as if carrying all before them. But, after their passage, the squares were still to be seen in the same places; and these gentry, who we feared would next fall on us, would evaporate, nobody could well say how. The firing still increased in intensity, so that we were at a loss to conjecture what all this could mean.

About this time, being impatient of standing idle, and annoyed by the batteries on the Nivelle road, I ventured to commit a folly, for which I should have paid dearly had our Duke chanced to be in our part of the field. I ventured to

---

[1] I believe Jägers of the Hanoverian corps.

disobey orders, and open a slow deliberate fire at the battery, thinking with my 9-pounders soon to silence his 4-pounders. My astonishment was great, however, when our very first gun was responded to by at least half-a-dozen gentlemen of very superior calibre, whose presence I had not even suspected, and whose superiority we immediately recognised by their rushing noise and long reach, for they flew far beyond us. I instantly saw my folly, and ceased firing, and they did the same—the 4-pounders alone continuing the cannonade as before. But this was not all. The first man of my troop touched was by one of these confounded long shot. I shall never forget the scream the poor lad gave when struck. It was one of the last they fired, and shattered his left arm to pieces as he stood between the waggons. That scream went to my very soul, for I accused myself as having caused his misfortune. I was, however, obliged to conceal my emotion from the men, who had turned to look at him; so, bidding them "stand to their front," I continued my walk up and down, whilst Hitchins ran to his assistance.

Amidst such stirring scenes, emotions of this kind are but of short duration; what occurred immediately afterwards completely banished Gunner Hunt from my recollection. As a counterbalance to this tragical event, our firing produced one so comic as to excite all our risibility. Two or three officers had lounged up to our guns to see the effect. One of them was a medico, and *he* (a shower having just come on) carried an umbrella overhead. No sooner did the heavy answers begin to arrive amongst us than these gentlemen, fancying they should be safer with their own corps, although only a few yards in the rear, scampered off in double-quick, doctor and all, he still carrying his umbrella aloft. Scarcely, however, had he made two paces when a shot, as he thought, passing rather too close, down he dropped on his hands and knees—or, I should rather say, hand and knees, for the one was employed in holding the silken cover most pertinaciously over him—and away he scrambled like a great baboon, his head turned fearfully over his shoulder, as if watching the coming shot, whilst our fellows made the field resound with their shouts and laughter.

I think I have already mentioned that it was not until

some days afterwards that I was able to resume my regular journal, consequently that everything relative to these three days is written from memory.   In trying to recollect scenes of this nature, some little confusion is inevitable; and here I confess myself somewhat puzzled to account for certain facts of which I am positive.   For instance, I remember perfectly Captain Bolton's brigade of 9-pounders being stationed to the left of us, somewhat in advance, and facing as we did, consequently not far from the Nivelle road. Bolton came and conversed with me some time, and was called hastily away by his battery commencing a heavy fire.   Query—Who, and what, was he firing at?   That he was himself under a heavy fire there is equally no doubt, for whilst we were not losing a man, we saw many, both of his men and horses, fall, and but a few minutes after leaving me, he was killed himself—this is a puzzle.   I have no recollection of any troops attempting to cross the ravine, and yet his fire was in that direction, and I think must have been toward the Nivelle road.   A distressing circumstance connected with this (shall I confess it?) made even more impression on my spirits than the misfortune of Gunner Hunt. Bolton's people had not been long engaged when we saw the men of the gun next to us unharness one of the horses and chase it away, wounded, I supposed; yet the beast stood and moved with firmness, going from one carriage to the other, whence I noticed he was always eagerly driven away. At last two or three gunners drove him before them to a considerable distance, and then returned to their guns.   I took little notice of this at the time, and was surprised by an exclamation of horror from some of my people in the rear.   A sickening sensation came over me, mixed with a deep feeling of pity, when within a few paces of me stood the poor horse in question, side by side with the leaders of one of our ammunition waggons, against which he pressed his panting sides, as though eager to identify himself as of their society—the driver, with horror depicted on every feature, endeavouring by words and gestures (for the kind-hearted lad could not strike) to drive from him so hideous a spectacle.   A cannon-shot had completely carried away the lower part of the animal's head, immediately below the eyes.   Still he lived, and seemed fully conscious of all around, whilst his full, clear eye seemed to implore us not to chase him from his companions. I ordered the farrier (Price) to put him out of misery, which, in a few minutes, he reported having accomplished, by running his sabre into the animal's heart. Even *he* evinced feeling on this occasion. Meantime the roar of cannon and musketry in the main position never slackened; it was intense, as was the smoke arising from it. Amidst this, from time to time, was to be seen still more dense columns of smoke rising straight into the air like a great pillar, then spreading out a mushroom-head. These arose from the explosions of ammunition waggons, which were continually taking place, although the noise which filled the whole atmosphere was too overpowering to allow them to be heard.

Amongst the multitudes of French cavalry continually pouring over the front ridge, one corps came sweeping down the slope entire, and was directing its course straight for us, when suddenly a regiment of light dragoons (I believe of the German Legion) came up from the ravine at a brisk trot on their flank. The French had barely time to wheel up to the left and push their horses into a gallop, when the two bodies came in collison. They were at a very short distance from us, so that we saw the charge perfectly. There was no check, no hesitation, on either side; both parties seemed to dash on in a most reckless manner, and we fully expected to have seen a horrid crash—no such thing! Each, as if by mutual consent, opened their files on coming near, and passed rapidly through each other, cutting and pointing, much in the same manner one might pass the fingers of the right hand through those of the left. We saw but few fall. The two corps reformed afterwards, and in a twinkling both disappeared, I know not how or where. It might have been about two o'clock when Colonel Gould, R.A., came to me, perhaps a little later. Be that as it may, we were conversing on the subject of our situation, which appeared to him rather desperate. He remarked that in the event of a retreat, there was but one road, which no doubt would be instantly choked up, and asked my opinion. My answer was, "It does indeed look very bad; but I trust in the Duke, who, I am sure, will get us out of it somehow or other." Meantime gloomy reflections arose in my mind, for though I did not choose to betray myself (as we spoke before the men), yet I could not help thinking that our affairs *were* rather desperate, and that some unfortunate catastrophe was at hand.   In this case I made up my mind to spike my guns and retreat over the fields, draught-horses and all, in the best manner I could, steering well from the highroad and general line of retreat.

We were still talking on this subject, when suddenly a dark mass of cavalry appeared for an instant on the main ridge, and then came sweeping down the slope in swarms, reminding me of an enormous surf bursting over the prostrate hull of a stranded vessel, and then running, hissing and foaming, up the beach.   The hollow space became in a twinkling covered with horsemen, crossing, turning, and riding about in all directions, apparently without any object.   Sometimes they came pretty near us, then would retire a little.   There were lancers amongst them, hussars, and dragoons—it was a complete *mêlée*.   On the main ridge no squares were to be seen; the only objects were a few guns standing in a confused manner, with muzzles in the air, and not one artilleryman.   After caracoling about for a few minutes, the crowd began to separate and draw together in small bodies, which continually increased; and now we really apprehended being overwhelmed, as the first line had apparently been.   For a moment an awful silence pervaded that part of the position to which we anxiously turned our eyes.   "I fear all is over," said Colonel Gould, who still remained by me.   The thing seemed but too likely, and this time I could not withhold my assent to his remark, for it did indeed appear so.   Meantime the 14th, springing from the earth, had formed their square, whilst we, throwing back the guns of our right and left divisions, stood waiting in momentary expectation of being enveloped and attacked.   Still they lingered in the hollow, when suddenly loud and repeated shouts (not English hurrahs) drew our attention to the other side.   There we saw two dense columns of infantry pushing forward at a quick pace towards us, crossing the fields, as if they had come from Merke Braine.   Every one, both of the 14th and ourselves, pronounced them French, yet still we delayed opening fire on them.   Shouting, yelling, and singing, on they came, right for us; and being now not above 800 or 1000 yards distant, it seemed folly allowing them to come nearer unmolested. The commanding officer of the 14th, to end our doubts, rode forward and endeavoured to ascertain who they were, but soon returned, assuring us they were French. The order was already given to fire, when, luckily, Colonel Gould recognised them as Belgians. Meantime, whilst my attention was occupied by these people, the cavalry had all vanished, nobody could say how or where.

We breathed again. Such was the agitated state in which we were kept in our second position. A third act was about to commence of a much more stirring and active nature.

It might have been, as nearly as I can recollect about 3 p.m., when Sir Augustus Frazer galloped up, crying out, "Left limber up, and as fast as you can." The words were scarcely uttered when my gallant troop stood as desired in column of subdivisions, left in front, pointing towards the main ridge. "At a gallop, march!" and away we flew, as steadily and compactly as if at a review. I rode with Frazer, whose face was as black as a chimney-sweep's from the smoke, and the jacket-sleeve of his right arm torn open by a musket-ball or case-shot, which had merely grazed his flesh. As we went along, he told me that the enemy had assembled an enormous mass of heavy cavalry in front of the point to which he was leading us (about one-third of the distance between Hougoumont and the Charleroi road), and that in all probability we should immediately be charged on gaining our position. "The Duke's orders, however, are positive," he added, "that in the event of their persevering and charging home, you do not expose your men, but retire with them into the adjacent squares of infantry." As he spoke, we were ascending the reverse slope of the main position. We breathed a new atmosphere—the air was suffocatingly hot, resembling that issuing from an oven. We were enveloped in thick smoke, and, *malgré* the incessant roar of cannon and musketry, could distinctly hear around us a mysterious humming noise, like that which one hears of a summer's evening proceeding from myriads of black beetles; cannon-shot, too, ploughed the ground in all directions, and so thick was the hail of balls and bullets that it seemed dangerous to extend the arm lest it should be torn off. In spite of the serious situation in which we were, I could not help being somewhat amused at the astonishment expressed by our kind-hearted surgeon (Hitchins), who heard for the first time this sort of music. He was close to me as we ascended the slope, and, hearing this infernal *carillon* about his ears, began staring round in the wildest and most comic manner imaginable, twisting himself from side to side, exclaiming, "My God, Mercer, what *is* that? What *is* all this noise? How curious!—how very curious!" And then when a cannon-shot rushed hissing past, "*There!—there!* What *is* it all?" It was with great difficulty that I persuaded him to retire: for a time he insisted on remaining near me, and it was only by pointing out how important it was to us, in case of being wounded, that he should keep himself safe to be able to assist us, that I prevailed on him to withdraw. Amidst this storm we gained the summit of the ridge, strange to say, without a casualty; and Sir Augustus, pointing out our position between two squares of Brunswick infantry, left us, with injunctions to remember the Duke's order, and to economise our ammunition. The Brunswickers were falling fast—the shot every moment making great gaps in their squares, which the officers and sergeants were actively employed in filling up by pushing their men together, and sometimes thumping them ere they could make them move. These were the very boys whom I had but yesterday seen throwing away their arms, and fleeing, panic-stricken, from the very sound of our horses' feet. To-day they fled not bodily, to be sure, but spiritually, for their senses seemed to have left them. There they stood, with recovered arms, like so many logs, or rather like the very wooden figures which I had seen them practising at in their cantonments. Every moment I feared they would again throw down their arms and flee; but their officers and sergeants behaved nobly, not only keeping them together, but managing to keep their squares closed in spite of the carnage made amongst them. To have sought refuge amongst men in such a state were madness—the very moment our men ran from their guns I was convinced, would be the signal for their disbanding. We had better, then, fall at our posts than in such a situation. Our coming up seemed to reanimate them, and all their eyes were directed to us—indeed, it was providential, for, had we not arrived as we did, I scarcely think there is a doubt of what would have been

their fate.[1] Our first gun had scarcely gained the interval
between their squares, when I saw through the smoke the
leading squadrons of the advancing column coming on at a
brisk trot, and already not more than one hundred yards
distant, if so much, for I don't think we could have seen so
far. I immediately ordered the line to be formed for action
—*case-shot*! and the leading gun was unlimbered and commenced firing almost as soon as the word was given: for
activity and intelligence our men were unrivalled. The very
first round, I saw, brought down several men and horses.
They continued, however, to advance. I glanced at the
Brunswickers, and that glance told me it would not do; they
had opened a fire from their front faces, but both squares
appeared too unsteady, and I resolved to say nothing about
the Duke's order, and take our chance—a resolve that was
strengthened by the effect of the remaining guns as they
rapidly succeeded in coming to action, making terrible
slaughter, and in an instant covering the ground with men
and horses. Still they persevered in approaching us (the
first round had brought them to a walk), though slowly,
and it did seem they would ride over us. We were a little
below the level of the ground on which they moved—having
in front of us a bank of about a foot and a half or two feet
high, along the top of which ran a narrow road—and this
gave more effect to our case-shot, all of which almost must
have taken effect, for the carnage was frightful.[2] I suppose

---

[1] One day, on the Marine Parade at Woolwich, a battalion coming
up in close column at the double march, Lieutenant-Colonel Brown,
who stood near me, remarked, "That puts me in mind of your troop
coming up at Waterloo, when you *saved* the Brunswickers." Until
this moment I never knew that our having done so had been remarked
by anybody ; but he assured me it was known to the whole army ; and
yet the Duke not only withheld that praise which was our due, but
refused me the brevet rank of major ; and, more than that, actually
deprived me of that troop given to me by Lord Mulgrave, the then
Master-General, *for* that action, as recommended by my commanding
officer, Sir G. Adams Wood.

That the Duke was not ignorant of their danger I have from Captain
Baynes, our Brigade-Major, who told me that after Sir Augustus Frazer
had been sent for us, his Grace exhibited considerable anxiety for our
coming up ; and that when he saw us crossing the fields at a gallop,
and in so compact a body, he actually cried out, " Ah ! that's the way
I like to see horse-artillery move." Another proof.

[2] The following extract, from a related account of a conscript, trans-
lated from the French and published by Murray, is so true and exact

this state of things occupied but a few seconds, when I observed symptoms of hesitation, and in a twinkling, at the instant I thought it was all over with us, they turned to either flank and filed away rapidly to the rear. Retreat of the mass, however, was not so easy. Many facing about and trying to force their way through the body of the column, that part next to us became a complete mob, into which we kept a steady fire of case-shot from our six pieces. The effect is hardly conceivable, and to paint this scene of slaughter and confusion impossible. Every discharge was followed by the fall of numbers, whilst the survivors struggled with each other, and I actually saw them using the pommels of their swords to fight their way out of the *mêlée*. Some, rendered desperate at finding themselves thus pent up at the muzzles of our guns, as it were, and others carried away by their horses, maddened with wounds, dashed through our intervals —few thinking of using their swords, but pushing furiously onward, intent only on saving themselves. At last the rear of the column, wheeling about, opened a passage, and the whole swept away at a much more rapid pace than they had advanced, nor stopped until the swell of the ground covered them from our fire. We then ceased firing; but as they were still not far off, for we saw the tops of their caps, having reloaded, we stood ready to receive them should they renew the attack.

One of, if not the first man who fell on our side was wounded by his own gun. Gunner Butterworth was one of the greatest pickles in the troop, but, at the same time, a most daring, active soldier; he was No. 7 (the man who sponged, etc.) at his gun. He had just finished ramming down the shot, and was stepping back outside the wheel, when his foot stuck in the miry soil, pulling him forward at

as to need no comment : " Through the smoke I saw the English gunners abandon their pieces, all but six guns stationed under the road, and almost immediately our cuirassiers were upon the squares, whose fire was drawn in zigzags. Now, I thought, those gunners would be cut to pieces ; but no, the devils kept firing with grape, which mowed them down like grass." It is pleasant, after all, to find we were observed and spoken of as we deserved, though not by those who ought to have done it. I may here mention that Sir James Shaw Kennedy in his book is, I think, mistaken in saying that the Brunswickers were saved by Major Bull's and Captain Mercer's batteries, since after the usual interval on the right of the Brunswick square occurred one of English and then Major Bull's battery, and the front of the French attacking column was only equal to our own.

the moment the gun was fired. As a man naturally does
when falling, he threw out both his arms before him, and they
were blown off at the elbows. He raised himself a little on
his two stumps, and looked up most piteously in my face.
To assist him was impossible—the safety of all, everything,
depended upon not slackening our fire, and I was obliged to
turn from him. The state of anxious activity in which we
were kept all day, and the numbers who fell almost immediately afterwards, caused me to lose sight of poor Butterworth;
and I afterwards learned that he had succeeded in rising and
was gone to the rear; but on inquiring for him next day,
some of my people who had been sent to Waterloo told me
that they saw his body lying by the roadside near the farm of
Mount St Jean—bled to death! The retreat of the cavalry
was succeeded by a shower of shot and shells, which must
have annihilated us had not the little bank covered and threw
most of them over us. Still some reached us and knocked
down men and horses.

At the first charge, the French column was composed of
grenadiers à cheval[1] and cuirassiers, the former in front. I
forget whether they had or had not changed this disposition,
but think, from the number of cuirasses we afterwards found,
that the cuirassiers led the second attack. Be this as it may,
their column reassembled. They prepared for a second
attempt, sending up a cloud of skirmishers, who galled us
terribly by a fire of carbines and pistols at scarcely forty yards
from our front. We were obliged to stand with port-fires
lighted, so that it was not without a little difficulty that I
succeeded in restraining the people from firing, for they
grew impatient under such fatal results. Seeing some
exertion beyond words necessary for this purpose, I leaped
my horse up the little bank, and began a promenade (by no
means agreeable) up and down our front, without even
drawing my sword, though these fellows were within speaking
distance of me. This quieted my men; but the tall blue
gentlemen, seeing me thus dare them, immediately made a
target of me, and commenced a very deliberate practice, to
show us what very bad shots they were and verify the old

---

[1] These grenadiers à cheval were very fine troops, clothed in blue
uniforms without facings, cuffs, or collars. Broad, very broad buff belts,
and huge muff caps, made them appear gigantic fellows.

artillery proverb, "The nearer the target, the safer you are." One fellow certainly made me flinch, but it was a miss; so I shook my finger at him, and called him *coquin*, etc. The rogue grinned as he reloaded, and again took aim. I certainly felt rather foolish at that moment, but was ashamed, after such bravado, to let him see it, and therefore continued my promenade. As if to prolong my torment, he was a terrible time about it. To me it seemed an age. Whenever I turned, the muzzle of his infernal carbine still followed me. At length bang it went, and whiz came the ball close to the back of my neck, and at the same instant down dropped the leading driver of one of my guns (Miller), into whose forehead the cursed missile had penetrated.

The column now once more mounted the plateau, and these popping gentry wheeled off right and left to clear the ground for their charge. The spectacle was imposing, and if ever the word sublime was appropriately applied, it might surely be to it. On they came in compact squadrons, one behind the other, so numerous that those of the rear were still below the brow when the head of the column was but at some sixty or seventy yards from our guns. Their pace was a slow but steady trot. None of your furious galloping charges was this, but a deliberate advance, at a deliberate pace, as of men resolved to carry their point. They moved in profound silence, and the only sound that could be heard from them amidst the incessant roar of battle was the low thunder-like reverberation of the ground beneath the simultaneous tread of so many horses. On our part was equal deliberation. Every man stood steadily at his post, the guns ready, loaded with a round-shot first and a case over it; the tubes were in the vents; the port-fires glared and sputtered behind the wheels; and my word alone was wanting to hurl destruction on that goodly show of gallant men and noble horses. I delayed this, for experience had given me confidence. The Brunswickers partook of this feeling, and with their squares—much reduced in point of size—well closed, stood firmly, with arms at the recover, and eyes fixed on us, ready to commence their fire with our first discharge. It was indeed a grand and imposing spectacle! The column [1] was

---

[1] Gourgand says : " Cette division de deux mille grenadiers à cheval, et dragons tous gens d'élite, s'étaient engagés sur le plateau, sans l'ordre

led on this time by an officer in a rich uniform, his breast covered with decorations, whose earnest gesticulations were strangely contrasted with the solemn demeanour of those to whom they were addressed. I thus allowed them to advance unmolested until the head of the column might have been about fifty or sixty yards from us, and then gave the word, "Fire!" The effect was terrible. Nearly the whole leading rank fell at once; and the round-shot, penetrating the column carried confusion throughout its extent. The ground, already encumbered with victims of the first struggle, became now almost impassable. Still, however, these devoted warriors struggled on, intent only on reaching us. The thing was impossible. Our guns were served with astonishing activity, whilst the running fire of the two squares was maintained with spirit. Those who pushed forward over the heaps of carcasses of men and horses gained but a few paces in advance, there to fall in their turn and add to the difficulties of those succeeding them. The discharge of every gun was followed by a fall of men and horses like that of grass before the mower's scythe. When the horse alone was killed, we could see the cuirassiers divesting themselves of the encumbrance and making their escape on foot. Still, for a moment, the confused mass (for all order was at an end) stood before us, vainly trying to urge their horses over the obstacles presented by their fallen comrades, in obedience to the now loud and rapid vociferations of him who had led them on and remained unhurt. As before, many cleared everything and rode through us; many came plunging forward only to fall, man and horse, close to the muzzles of our guns; but the majority again turned at the very moment when, from having less ground to go over, it were safer to advance than retire, and sought a passage to the rear. Of course the same confusion, struggle amongst themselves, and slaughter prevailed as before, until gradually they disappeared over the brow of the hill. We ceased firing, glad to take breath. Their retreat exposed us, as before, to a shower of shot and shells: these last, falling amongst us with very long fuses, kept burning and hissing a long time before they burst, and were a considerable annoyance to man and horse. The bank

de l'Empereur," etc., etc.—P. 88, ed. London. He speaks of the cavalry of reserve of the Guard. Could these be the people ?

in front, however, again stood our friend, and sent many over us innocuous.

Lieutenant Breton, who had already lost two horses and had mounted a troop-horse, was conversing with me during this our leisure moment. As his horse stood at right angles to mine, the poor jaded animal dozingly rested his muzzle on my thigh; whilst I, the better to hear amidst the infernal din, leant forward, resting my arm between his ears. In this attitude a cannon-shot smashed the horse's head to atoms. The headless trunk sank to the ground—Breton looking pale as death, expecting, as he afterwards told me, that I was cut in two. What was passing to the right and left of us I know no more about than the man in the moon—not even what corps were beyond the Brunswickers. The smoke confined our vision to a very small compass, so that my battle was restricted to the two squares and my own battery; and, as long as we maintained our ground, I thought it a matter of course that others did so too. It was just after this accident that our worthy commanding officer of artillery, Sir George Adam Wood, made his appearance through the smoke a little way from our left flank. As I said, we were doing nothing, for the cavalry were under the brow re-forming for a third attack, and we were being pelted by their artillery. "D—n it, Mercer," said the old man, blinking as a man does when facing a gale of wind, "you have hot work of it here." "Yes, sir, pretty hot"; and I was proceeding with an account of the two charges we had already discomfited, and the prospect of a third, when, glancing that way, I perceived their leading squadron already on the plateau. "There they are again!" I exclaimed; and, darting from Sir George *sans cérémonie*, was just in time to meet them with the same destruction as before. This time, indeed, it was child's play. They could not even approach us in any decent order, and we fired most deliberately; it was folly having attempted the thing. I was sitting on my horse near the right of my battery as they turned and began to retire once more. Intoxicated with success, I was singing out, "Beautiful!—beautiful!" and my right arm was flourishing about, when some one from behind, seizing it, said quietly, "Take care, or you'll strike the Duke"; and in effect our noble chief, with a serious air, and apparently much fatigued, passed close by me to the front, without

seeming to take the slightest notice of the remnant of the
French cavalry still lingering on the ground. This obliged
us to cease firing; and at the same moment I, perceiving a
line of infantry ascending from the rear, slowly, with ported
arms, and uttering a sort of feeble, suppressed hurrah—
ankle-deep in a thick tenacious mud, and threading their way
amongst or stepping over the numerous corpses covering
the ground, out of breath from their exertions, and hardly
preserving a line, broken everywhere into large gaps the
breadth of several files—could not but meditate on the
probable results of the last charge had I, in obedience to
the Duke's order, retired my men into the squares and
allowed the daring and formidable squadrons a passage to
our rear, where they must have gone thundering down
on this disjointed line. The summit gained, the line
was amended, files closed in, and the whole, including
our Brunswickers, advanced down the slope towards the
plain.

Although the infantry lost several men as they passed us,
yet on the whole the cannonade began to slacken on both
sides (why, I know not), and, the smoke clearing away a
little, I had now, for the first time, a good view of the field.
On the ridge opposite to us dark masses of troops were
stationary, or moving down into the intervening plain. Our
own advancing infantry were hid from view by the ground.
We therefore recommenced firing at the enemies' masses,
and the cannonade, spreading, soon became general again
along the line. Whilst thus occupied with our front, we
suddenly became sensible of a most destructive flanking fire
from a battery which had come, the Lord knows how, and
established itself on a knoll somewhat higher than the
ground we stood on, and only about 400 or 500 yards a little
in advance of our left flank. The rapidity and precision of
this fire were quite appalling. Every shot almost took effect,
and I certainly expected we should all be annihilated. Our
horses and limbers, being a little retired down the slope, had
hitherto been somewhat under cover from the direct fire in
front; but this plunged right amongst them, knocking them
down by pairs, and creating horrible confusion. The drivers
could hardly extricate themselves from one dead horse ere
another fell, or perhaps themselves. The saddle-bags, in

many instances, were torn from the horses' backs, and their contents scattered over the field. One shell I saw explode under the two finest wheel-horses in the troop—down they dropped. In some instances the horses of a gun or ammunition waggon remained, and all their drivers were killed.[1] The whole livelong day had cost us nothing like this. Our gunners too—the few left fit for duty of them—were so exhausted that they were unable to run the guns up after firing, consequently at every round they retreated nearer to the limbers; and as we had pointed our two left guns towards the people who were annoying us so terribly, they soon came altogether in a confused heap, the trails crossing each other, and the whole dangerously near the limbers and ammunition waggons, some of which were totally unhorsed, and others in sad confusion from the loss of their drivers and horses, many of them lying dead in their harness attached to their carriages. I sighed for my poor troop—it was already but a wreck.

I had dismounted, and was assisting at one of the guns to encourage my poor exhausted men, when through the smoke a black speck caught my eye, and I instantly knew what it was. The conviction that one never sees a shot coming towards you unless directly in its line flashed across my mind, together with the certainty that my doom was sealed. I had barely time to exclaim "Here it is then!"—much in that gasping sort of way one does when going into very cold water takes away the breath—"whush" it went past my face, striking the point of my pelisse collar, which was lying open, and smash into a horse close behind me. I breathed freely again.

Under such a fire, one may be said to have had a thousand narrow escapes; and, in good truth, I frequently experienced that displacement of air against my face caused by the passing of shot close to me; but the two above recorded, and a third which I shall mention, were remarkable ones, and made me feel in full force the goodness of Him who protected me among so many dangers. Whilst in position on the right of the second line, I had reproved some of my men for lying

[1] " The field was so much covered with blood, that it appeared as if it had been flooded with it," etc.—Simpson's *Paris after Waterloo*, etc., p. 21.

down when shells fell near them until they burst. Now my
turn came. A shell, with a long fuse, came slop into the mud
at my feet, and there lay fizzing and flaring, to my infinite
discomfiture. After what I had said on the subject, I felt
that I must act up to my own words, and, accordingly, there
I stood, endeavouring to look quite composed until the
cursed thing burst—and, strange to say, without injuring
me, though so near. The effect on my men was good. We
had scarcely fired many rounds at the enfilading battery when
a tall man in the black Brunswick uniform came galloping
up to me from the rear, exclaiming, "Ah! mine Gott!—mine
Gott! vat is it you doos, sare? Dat is your friends de
Proosiens; an you kills dem! Ah, mine Gott!—mine Gott!
vill you no stop, sare?—vill you no stop? Ah! mine Gott!
—mine Gott! vat for is dis? De Inglish kills dere friends
de Proosiens! Vere is de Dook von Vellington?—vere is
de Dook von Vellington? Oh, mine Gott!—mine Gott!"
etc. etc., and so he went on raving like one demented. I
observed that if these were our friends the Prussians they
were treating us very uncivilly; and that it was not without
sufficient provocation we had turned our guns on them,
pointing out to him at the same time the bloody proofs
of my assertion. Apparently not noticing what I said, he
continued his lamentations, and, "Vill you no stop, sare,
I say?" Wherefore, thinking he might be right, to pacify
him I ordered the whole to cease firing, desiring him to
remark the consequences. *Psieu, psieu, psieu*, came our
friends' shot, one after another; and our friend himself had
a narrow escape from one of them. "Now, sir," I said,
"you will be convinced; and we will continue our firing,
whilst you can ride round the way you came, and tell them
they kill their friends the English; the moment their fire
ceases, so shall mine." Still he lingered, exclaiming, "Oh,
dis is terreebly to see de Proosien and de Inglish kill
vonanoder!" At last darting off I saw no more of him.[1]

[1] At one time I thought this a French *ruse de guerre*. I remember
the man perfectly, with his silver arrow and chain attached to his black
shoulder-belt. In Sir John Sinclair's *Translation of Baron Muffling's
Account*, London, 1816, and at p. 29, I find that about 4 p.m., whilst
the cuirassiers, after charging through the 1st British line, were roaming
over the interval between it and the 2d, " the enemy advanced a battalion
on the plain of the platform, at hardly 500 yards' distance from the position,

The fire continued on both sides, mine becoming slacker and slacker, for we were reduced to the last extremity, and must have been annihilated but for the opportune arrival of a battery of Belgic artillery a little on our left, which, taking the others in flank nearly at point blank, soon silenced and drove them off. We were so reduced that all our strength was barely sufficient to load and fire three guns out of our six.

These Belgians were all beastly drunk, and, when they first came up, not at all particular as to which way they fired; and it was only by keeping an eye on them that they were prevented treating us, and even one another. The wretches had probably already done mischief elsewhere—who knows? My recollections of the latter part of this day are rather confused; I was fatigued, and almost deaf. I recollect clearly, however, that we had ceased firing—the plain below being covered with masses of troops, which we could not distinguish from each other. Captain Walcot of the horse-artillery had come to us, and we were all looking out anxiously at the movements below and on the opposite ridge, when he suddenly shouted out, "Victory!—victory! they fly!—they fly!" and sure enough we saw some of the masses dissolving, as it were, and those composing them streaming away in confused crowds over the field, whilst the already desultory fire of their artillery ceased altogether. I shall never forget this joyful moment!—this moment of exultation! On looking round I found we were left almost alone. Cavalry and infantry had all moved forward, and only a few guns here and there were to be seen on the position. A little to our right were the remains of Major M'Donald's troop under Lieutenant Sandilands, which had suffered much, but nothing like us. We were congratulating ourselves on the happy results of the day, when an aide-de-camp rode up, crying "Forward, sir!—forward! It is of the utmost importance that this movement should be supported by artillery!" at the same time waving his hat much in the manner of a huntsman laying on his dogs. I smiled at his

so as, perhaps, to establish his infantry on this side of the little wood of Hougoumont and in La Haye Sainte." Could this have been the one? At p. 35 he says, " The shot from Bulow's artillery reached the British, and the Duke was obliged to send notice of it." Query—Did the Duke observe this himself, or was it communicated to him by my black hussar?

energy, and, pointing to the remains of my poor troop, quietly asked, "How, sir?" A glance was sufficient to show him the impossibility, and away he went.

Our situation was indeed terrible: of 200 fine horses with which we had entered the battle, upwards of 140 lay dead, dying, or severely wounded. Of the men, scarcely two-thirds of those necessary for four guns remained, and these so completely exhausted as to be totally incapable of further exertion. Lieutenant Breton had three horses killed under him; Lieutenant Hincks was wounded in the breast by a spent ball; Lieutenant Leathes on the hip by a splinter; and although untouched myself, my horse had no less than eight wounds, one of which—a graze on the fetlock joint—lamed him for ever. Our guns and carriages were, as before mentioned, altogether in a confused heap, intermingled with dead and wounded horses, which it had not been possible to disengage from them. My poor men, such at least as were untouched, fairly worn out, their clothes, faces, etc., blackened by the smoke and spattered over with mud and blood, had seated themselves on the trails of the carriages, or had thrown themselves on the wet and polluted soil, too fatigued to think of anything but gaining a little rest. Such was our situation when called upon to advance! It was impossible, and we remained where we were. For myself, I was also excessively tired—hoarse, to making speech painful, and deaf from the infernal uproar of the last eleven hours. Moreover, I was devoured by a burning thirst, not a drop of liquid having passed my lips since the evening of the 16th; but although, with the exception of the chicken's leg last night, I may be said to have eaten nothing for two whole days, yet did I not feel the least desire for food.

The evening had become fine, and but for an occasional groan or lament from some poor sufferer, and the repeated piteous neighing of wounded horses, tranquillity might be said to reign over the field. As it got dusk, a large body of Prussian artillery arrived, and formed their bivouac near us. There was not light to see more of them than that their brass guns were kept bright, and that their carriages were encumbered with baggage, and, besides, appeared but clumsy machines when compared with ours. All wore their greatcoats, which apparently they had marched in.

As they looked at us rather scowlingly, and did not seem inclined to hold any communication with us, I soon returned to my own people, whom I found preparing to go supperless to bed—the two remaining officers, the non-commissioned officers and men having all got together in a heap, with some painted covers spread under and others drawn over them—at a distance from our guns, etc., the neighbourhood of which, they said, was too horrible to think of sleeping there. For my part, after standing all day amongst all these horrors, I felt no squeamishness about sleeping amongst them; so pulling down the painted cover of a limber over the footboard in the manner of a tent-roof, I crept under it, and endeavoured to sleep. The cramped situation in which I lay, and the feverish excitement of my mind, forbade, however, my obtaining that sound and refreshing sleep so much needed—I only dozed. From one of these dozes I awoke about midnight, chilled and cramped to death from the awkward doubled-up position imposed upon me by my short and narrow bed. So up I got to look around and contemplate a battle-field by the pale moonlight. The night was serene and pretty clear; a few light clouds occasionally passing across the moon's disc, and throwing objects into transient obscurity, added considerably to the solemnity of the scene. Oh, it was a thrilling sensation thus to stand in the silent hour of the night and contemplate that field—all day long the theatre of noise and strife, now so calm and still—the actors prostrate on the bloody soil, their pale wan faces upturned to the moon's cold beams, which caps and breastplates, and a thousand other things, reflected back in brilliant pencils of light from as many different points! Here and there some poor wretch, sitting up amidst the countless dead, busied himself in endeavours to stanch the flowing stream with which his life was fast ebbing away. Many whom I saw so employed that night were, when morning dawned, lying stiff and tranquil as those who had departed earlier. From time to time a figure would half raise itself from the ground, and then, with a despairing groan, fall back again. Others, slowly and painfully rising, stronger, or having less deadly hurt, would stagger away with uncertain steps across the field in search of succour. Many of these I followed with my gaze until

lost in the obscurity of distance; but many, alas! after
staggering a few paces, would sink again on the ground,
probably to rise no more. It was heart-rending—and yet
I gazed! Horses, too, there were to claim our pity—mild,
patient, enduring. Some lay on the ground with their
entrails hanging out, and yet they lived. These would
occasionally attempt to rise, but, like their human bedfellows, quickly falling back again, would lift their poor
heads, and, turning a wistful gaze at their side, lie quietly
down again, to repeat the same until strength no longer
remained, and then, their eyes gently closing, one short
convulsive struggle closed their sufferings. One poor
animal excited painful interest—he had lost, I believe, both
his hind legs; and there he sat the long night through on
his tail, looking about, as if in expectation of coming aid,
sending forth, from time to time, long and protracted melancholy neighing. Although I knew that killing him at once
would be mercy, I could not muster courage even to give the
order. Blood enough I had seen shed during the last six-
and-thirty hours, and sickened at the thought of shedding
more. There, then, he still sat when we left the ground,
neighing after us, as if reproaching our desertion of him in
the hour of need.

The Prussian bivouac near at hand offered a far different
and more cheering scene. There all was life and movement.
Their handsome horses, standing harnessed and tied to the
carriages, sent forth neighings of another character. Dark
forms moved amongst them; and by the bivouac-fires sat
figures that would have furnished studies for a Salvator.
Dark, brown, stern visages, rendered still sterner by the long
drooping mustache that overshadowed the mouth, from
which appended their constant companion, the pipe. Many
there were, too, busily occupied with the first great care of all
animals—cooking, or eating the mess already cooked. Save
these I have mentioned, no living being moved on the moonlit
field; and as I cast up my eyes at the lustrous lamp of heaven,
I thought on the thousand dear connections far, far away, on
whose peaceful dwelling it now looked down, their inmates
sleeping in tranquil security, ignorant as yet of the fatal blow
which had now for ever severed them from those they loved,
whose bodies encumbered the ground around me. And

here, even here, what a contrast between this charnel-house and the distant landscape within my ken!   Over it the same fair planet shed her mild beams, illuminating its groves and yellow corn-fields, its still and quiet villages, whose modest spires here and there arose from the horizon—emblems of peace, tranquillity, and repose.   Long I continued to gaze on this sad and solemn scene; and all this slaughter, I said, to gratify the ambition of one man, and that man—whom?— one who has risen from a station humble as my own, has already devastated Europe, and filled it with blood and mourning—who only recently left behind him 400,000 gallant men, a prey to the sword and the intemperance of a northern clime—fearful holocaust on the altar of that ambition!

At length I again crept into my cell, and again slept by fits and starts, until the first blush of day reddened the eastern sky, and aroused us all to new exertion.   As I emerged from under my cover a shudder crept over me, when the stronger light of day enabled me to see the corpse of one of my drivers lying mangled and bloody beneath my lair.

CHAPTER XIV

19th.—The cool air of the morning lasted not long; the rising sun soon burst in all his glory over our bloody bivouac, and all nature arose into renewed life, except the victims of ambition which lay unconscious of his presence. I had not been up many minutes when one of my sergeants came to ask if they might bury Driver Crammond. "And why particularly Driver Crammond?" "Because he looks frightful, sir; many of us have not had a wink of sleep for him." Curious! I walked to the spot where he lay, and certainly a more hideous sight cannot be imagined. A cannon-shot had carried away the whole head except barely the visage, which still remained attached to the torn and bloody neck. The men said they had been prevented sleeping by seeing his eyes fixed on them all night; and thus this one dreadful object had superseded all the other horrors by which they were surrounded. He was of course immediately buried, and as immediately forgotten. Our first care after this was to muster the remaining force, to disentangle our carriages from each other, and from the dead and dying animals with which they were encumbered. Many sound or only slightly-wounded horses, belonging to different corps of both armies, were wandering about the field. Of these we caught several in the course of the morning, and thus collected, with what remained of our own fit for work, sufficient to horse four guns, three ammunition waggons, and the forge. Of men we had nearly enough for these at reduced numbers, so we set to work equipping ourselves without delay. Although supplies of ammunition had been sent to us during the action, yet little remained. The expenditure had been enormous. A return had been called for yesterday evening just as we were lying down to rest, but, fatigued as we all were, it was impossible to give this correctly. As near as I could ascertain, we must have fired nearly 700 rounds per

gun.   Our harness, etc., was so cut to pieces, that but for
the vast magazines around us from which we could pick and
choose, we should never have got off the field.   Soon after
daybreak an officer came from headquarters to desire me to
send all my superfluous carriages to Lillois, where a park
was forming, and to inform me that a supply of ammunition
would be found in the village of Waterloo.   Accordingly the
carriages were sent without delay; but this requiring all
the horses, they were obliged to make a second trip for the
ammunition.   Whilst this was doing I had leisure to examine
the ground in our immediate vicinity. Books and papers,
etc., covered it in all directions.   The books at first surprised
me, but upon examination the thing was explained.   Each
French soldier, it appeared, carried a little accompt-book
of his pay, clothing, etc. etc.   The scene was now far from
solitary; for numerous groups of peasants were moving about
busily employed stripping the dead, and perhaps finishing
those not quite so.   Some of these men I met fairly staggering under the enormous load of clothes, etc., they had collected.   Some had firearms, swords, etc., and many had
large bunches of crosses and decorations; all seemed in high
glee, and professed unbounded hatred of the French.

I had fancied we were almost alone on the field, seeing only
the remains of Major Bull's troop of horse-artillery not far
from us (the Prussians had gone forward about, or a little
before, daybreak); but in wandering towards the Charleroi
road I stumbled on a whole regiment of British infantry fast
asleep, in columns of divisions, wrapped in their blankets,
with their knapsacks for pillows.   Not a man was awake.
There they lay in regular ranks, with the officers and sergeants
in their places, just as they would stand when awake.   Not
far from these, in a little hollow beneath a white thorn, lay
two Irish light-infantry men sending forth such howlings
and wailings, and oaths and execrations, as were shocking
to hear.   One of them had his leg shot off, the other a thigh
smashed by a cannon-shot.   They were certainly pitiable
objects, but their vehement exclamations, etc., were so
strongly contrasted with the quiet resolute bearing of
hundreds, both French and English, around them, that it
blunted one's feelings considerably.

I tried in vain to pacify them; so walked away amidst a

volley of abuse as a hard-hearted wretch who could thus leave two poor fellows to die like dogs. What could I do? All, however, though in more modest terms, craved assistance; and every poor wretch begged most earnestly for water. Some of my men had discovered a good well of uncontaminated water at Hougoumont, and filled their canteens; so I made several of them accompany me and administer to the most craving in our immediate vicinity. Nothing could exceed their gratitude, or the fervent blessings they implored on us for this momentary relief. The French were in general particularly grateful; and those who were strong enough, entered into conversation with us on the events of yesterday, and the probable fate awaiting themselves. All the non-commissioned officers and privates agreed in asserting that they had been deceived by their officers and betrayed; and, to my surprise, almost all of them reviled Buonaparte as the cause of their misery. Many begged me to kill them at once, since they would a thousand times rather die by the hand of a soldier than be left at the mercy of those villanous Belgic peasants. Whilst we stood by them, several would appear consoled and become tranquil; but the moment we attempted to leave, they invariably renewed the cry, "Ah, Monsieur, tuez moi donc! Tuez moi, pour l'amour de Dieu!" etc. etc. It was in vain I assured them carts would be sent to pick them all up. Nothing could reconcile them to the idea of being left. They looked on us as brother soldiers, and knew we were too honourable to harm them: "But the moment you go, those vile peasants will first insult, and then cruelly murder us." This, alas! I knew, was but too true. One Frenchman I found in a far different humour—an officer of lancers, and desperately wounded; a strong square-built man, with reddish hair and speckled complexion. When I approached him he appeared suffering horribly—rolling on his back, uttering loud groans. My first impulse was to raise and place him in a sitting posture; but, the moment he was touched, opening his eyes and seeing me, he became perfectly furious. Supposing he mistook my intention, I addressed him in a soothing tone, begging he would allow me to render him what little assistance was in my power. This only seemed to irritate him the more; and on my presenting him the canteen with water, he dashed it from him with such a passionate gesture and emphatic "*Non!*" that I saw there was no use in teasing, and therefore reluctantly left him. Returning towards our position, I was forcibly struck by the immense heap of bodies of men and horses which distinguished it even at a distance; indeed, Sir Augustus Frazer told me the other day, at Nivelles, that, in riding over the field, he "could plainly distinguish the position of G troop from the opposite height by the dark mass which, even from that distance, formed a remarkable feature in the field." These were his very words. One interesting sufferer I had nearly forgotten. He was a fine young man of the grenadiers à cheval, who had lain groaning near us all night—indeed scarcely five paces from my bed; therefore was the first person I visited as soon as daylight came. He was a most interesting person—tall, handsome, and a perfect gentleman in manners and speech; yet his costume was that of a private soldier. We conversed with him some time, and were exceedingly pleased with his mild and amiable address. Amongst other things he told us that Marshal Ney had led the charges against us. In this, however (if we understood him rightly), he must have been mistaken, since that Marshal is an infantry general. Be that as it may, we all felt deeply interested for our unfortunate prisoner, and did all in our power for him, which consisted in kind words and sending two careful men to lead him to the village—a most painful undertaking, for we now found that, besides one ball in the forehead, he had received another in his right thigh, which, together with his being barefooted, could not but render his journey both tedious and painful.

I now began to feel somewhat the effects of my long fast in a most unpleasant sense of weakness and an inordinate craving for food, which there were no means of satisfying. My joy, then, may be imagined when, returning to our bivouac, I found our people returned from Lillois, and, better still, that they had brought with them a quarter of veal, which they had found in a muddy ditch, of course in appearance then filthy enough. What was this to a parcel of men who had scarcely eaten a morsel for three days? In a trice it was cut up, the mud having been scraped off with a sabre, a fire kindled and fed with lance-shafts and musket-stocks; and old Quartermaster Hall, undertaking the cooking, proceeded to fry the dirty lumps in the lid of a camp-kettle. How we enjoyed the savoury smell! and, having made ourselves seats of cuirasses,[1] piled upon each other, we soon had that most agreeable of animal gratifications—the filling our empty stomachs. Never was a meal more perfectly military, nor more perfectly enjoyed.

We had not yet finished our meal, when a carriage drove on the ground from Brussels, the inmates of which, alighting, proceeded to examine the field. As they passed near us, it was amusing to see the horror with which they eyed our frightful figures; they all, however, pulled off their hats and made us low bows. One, a smartly dressed middle-aged man, in a high cocked-hat, came to our circle, and entered into conversation with me on the events of yesterday. He approached holding a delicately white perfumed handkerchief to his nose; stepping carefully to avoid the bodies (at which he cast fearful glances *en passant*), to avoid polluting the glossy silken hose that clothed his nether limbs. May I be pardoned for the comparison: Hotspur's description of a fop came forcibly to my mind as we conversed; clean and spruce, as if from a bandbox, redolent of perfume, he stood ever and anon applying the 'kerchief to his nose. I was not leaning on my sword, but I arose to receive him from my seat of armour, my hands and face begrimed and blackened with blood and smoke—clothes too. "I do remember when the fight was done," etc. etc. It came, as I said, forcibly to my mind as I eyed my friend's costume and sniffed the sweet-scented atmosphere that hovered round him. The perfumed handkerchief, in this instance, held the place of Shakespeare's "pouncet-box"—the scene was pleasant to remember! With a world of bows my man took leave, and proceeded, picking his steps with the same care as he followed the route of his companions in the direction of Hougoumont.

Having despatched our meal, and then the ammunition waggons to Waterloo, and leaving the people employed equipping as best they could, I set off to visit the chateau likewise; for the struggle that had taken place there yester-

---

[1] Here were more cuirasses than men; for the wounded (who could move), divesting themselves of its encumbrance, had made their escape, leaving their armour on the ground where they had fallen.

day rendered it an object of interest. The same scene of carnage as elsewhere characterised that part of the field over which I now bent my steps. The immediate neighbourhood of Hougoumont was more thickly strewn with corpses than most other parts of the field—the very ditches were full of them. The trees all about were most woefully cut and splintered, both by cannon-shot and musketry. The courts of the chateau presented a spectacle more terrible even than any I had yet seen. A large barn had been set on fire, and the conflagration had spread to the offices, and even to the main building. Here numbers, both of French and English, had perished in the flames, and their blackened swollen remains lay scattered about in all directions. Amongst this heap of ruins and misery many poor devils yet remained alive, and were sitting up endeavouring to bandage their wounds. Such a scene of horror, and one so sickening, was surely never witnessed.

Two or three German dragoons were wandering among the ruins, and many peasants. One of the former was speaking to me when two of the latter, after rifling the pockets, etc., of a dead Frenchman, seized the body by the shoulders, and, raising it from the ground, dashed it down again with all their force, uttering the grossest abuse, and kicking it about the head and face—revolting spectacle!—doing this, no doubt, to court favour with us. It had a contrary effect, which they soon learned. I had scarcely uttered an exclamation of disgust, when the dragoon's sabre was flashing over the miscreants' heads, and in a moment descended on their backs and shoulders with such vigour that they roared again, and were but too happy to make their escape. I turned from such scenes and entered the garden. How shall I describe the delicious sensation I experienced!

The garden was an ordinary one, but pretty—long straight walks of turf overshadowed by fruit-trees, and between these beds of vegetables, the whole enclosed by a tolerably high brick wall. Is it necessary to define my sensations? Is it possible that I am not understood at once? Listen then. For the last three days I have been in a constant state of excitement—in a perfect fever. My eyes have beheld nought but war in all its horrors—my ears have been assailed by a continued roar of cannon and cracking of musketry, the shouts of multitudes and the lamentations of war's victims. Suddenly and unexpectedly I find myself in solitude, pacing a green avenue, my eyes refreshed by the cool verdure of trees and shrubs; my ear soothed by the melody of feathered songsters—yea, of sweet Philomel herself—and the pleasing hum of insects sporting in the genial sunshine. Is there nothing in this to excite emotion? Nature in repose is always lovely: here, and under such circumstances, she was delicious. Long I rambled in this garden, up one walk, down another, and thought I could dwell here contented for ever. Nothing recalled the presence of war except the loopholed wall and two or three dead Guardsmen;[1] but the first caused no interruption, and these last lay so concealed amongst the exuberant vegetation of turnips and cabbages, etc., that, after coming from the field of death without, their pale and silent forms but little deteriorated my enjoyment. The leaves were green, roses and other flowers bloomed forth in all their sweetness, and the very turf when crushed by my feet smelt fresh and pleasant. There was but little of disorder visible to tell of what had been enacted here. I imagine it must have been assailed by infantry alone; and the havoc amongst the trees without made by our artillery posted on the hill above to cover the approach to it—principally, perhaps, by Bull's howitzer battery.

I had satisfied my curiosity at Hougoumont, and was retracing my steps up the hill, when my attention was called to a group of wounded Frenchmen by the calm, dignified, and soldier-like oration addressed by one of them to the rest. I cannot, like Livy, compose a fine harangue for my hero, and, of course, I could not retain the precise words, but the import of them was to exhort them to bear their sufferings with fortitude; not to repine, like women or children, at what every soldier should have made up his mind to suffer as the fortune of war, but, above all, to remember that they were surrounded by Englishmen, before whom they ought to be doubly careful not to disgrace themselves by displaying such

---

[1] In some accounts of the battle, and visits to the field, etc., it has been stated that this garden was a scene of slaughter. Totally untrue ! As I have stated in the text, I did not see above two or three altogether. There certainly might have been more concealed amongst the vegetation, but they could not have been many.

an unsoldier-like want of fortitude. The speaker was sitting
on the ground, with his lance stuck upright beside him—
an old veteran, with a thick bushy grizly beard, countenance
like a lion—a lancer of the Old Guard, and no doubt had
fought in many a field. One hand was flourished in the
air as he spoke, the other, severed at the wrist, lay on the
earth beside him; one ball (case-shot, probably) had entered
his body, another had broken his leg. His suffering, after
a night of exposure so mangled, must have been great; yet
he betrayed it not. His bearing was that of a Roman, or
perhaps of an Indian warrior, and I could fancy him concluding appropriately his speech in the words of the Mexican
king, "And I too; am I on a bed of roses?" I could not
but feel the highest veneration for this brave man, and told
him so, at the same time offering him the only consolation
in my power—a drink of cold water, and assurances that the
waggons would soon be sent round to collect the wounded.
He thanked me with a grace peculiar to Frenchmen, and
eagerly inquired the fate of their army. On this head I
could tell him nothing consolatory, so merely answered that
it had retired last night, and turned the conversation to the
events of yesterday. This truly brave man spoke in most
flattering terms of our troops, but said they had no idea in
the French army we should have fought so obstinately, since
it was generally understood that the English Government
had, for some inexplicable reason, connived at Napoleon's
escape from Elba, and therefore had ordered their army only
to make a show of resistance. After a very interesting conversation, I begged his lance as a keepsake, observing that it
never could be of further use to him. The old man's eyes
kindled as I spoke, and he emphatically assured me that it
would delight him to see it in the hands of a brave soldier,
instead of being torn from him, as he had feared, by those
vile peasants. So I took my leave, and walked away with
the lance in my hand.[1] Ever since, my groom (Milward) has

---

[1] During the remainder of the campaign Milward carried it; and
on returning to England I even rode into Canterbury followed by my
lancer—a novelty in those days. Whilst in retirement on half-pay, it
was suspended in my library; but on going to America in 1823 I deposited
it in the Rotunda at Woolwich. On my return in 1829 the lance was
gone. In 1823 or 1824 it seems Lieutenant-Colonel Vandaleur, of the
9th Lancers, came to Woolwich to look for a model. Mine pleased

been transformed into my lancer-orderly; and I propose, if ever I return to England, consecrating it to the memory of the interesting old hero. In passing Bull's bivouac it was my fate to witness another very interesting scene. A wounded hussar had somehow or another found his way there from another part of the field, and, exhausted by the exertion, had just fainted. Some of those collected round him cried out for water, and a young driver, who, being outside the throng, had not yet seen the sufferer, seized a canteen, and ran away to fill it. Whilst he was absent the hussar so far recovered as to be able to sit up. The driver returned at this moment, and, pushing aside his comrades, knelt down to enable the hussar to drink, holding the canteen to his lips, and in so doing recognised a brother whom he had not seen for years! His emotion was extreme, as may be supposed.

On regaining my own bivouac I found the ammunition arrived, and, what was still more satisfactory, Mr Coates with his whole train of Flemish waggons—our baggage and provisions. He had got intelligence in time of the battle of Quatre Bras and its results, and therefore altered his route to meet us on our retreat. On approaching the Charleroi road he had been swept away by the torrent of fugitives, and actually carried, *malgré lui*, beyond Brussels, some way on the road to Antwerp, before he could succeed in disentangling his train from the rabble rout, which he described as exceeding all imagination. As he brought the wherewithal, etc., of course his joining was hailed with joy by every one.

Since the order to send away my carriages I had received none; but as my diminished troop was completed as far as could be done here, I resolved to move off this horrid place;

him, and he took it to St John's Wood Riding-House, where it was tried against others in presence of the Duke of York, and approved of as a model for arming the British lancers. After a long hunt I at last found it at the Enfield manufactory, spoilt completely, the iron work and thong taken off, and flag gone. It cost me a long correspondence with the Board before I succeeded in getting it restored and put together. When I received it from him who had so long wielded it, the flag was dyed in blood, the blade notched, and also stained with blood ; inside the thong was cut Clement, VII., probably the number of his troop. [It is now in the possession of Dr Hall, an old Waterloo man, and sincere friend of my father.—ED.]

and accordingly, at 3 p.m., we joyfully took to the Nivelles road—by instinct, perhaps, for I knew nothing of the movements of the army, nor by what road they had gone forward.[1] About a mile or so from the field I formed our bivouac for the night in a sweet and wholesome orchard near the road, with a turf like velvet, and perfectly dry. This in itself was a luxury; it was a luxury to breathe pure uncontaminated air; it was a luxury to be out of hearing of groans, cries, and lamentations. This was not all. Mr Coates brought us a ham and a cheese; the neighbouring farmhouse supplied us with eggs, milk, and cider: so that in due time we sat down to an excellent dinner, seasoned with that sauce which no cook, however *scientific*, has yet learned to equal—hunger. Hilarity reigned at our board—if we may so term the fresh turf at the foot of an apple-tree; and over our grog and cigars we managed to pass a most pleasant evening. Previously, I had caused my servant to bring me a bucket of water, and prepared myself for our repast by the enjoyment of that first of luxuries, a thorough wash and clean clothes. This was the first time I had undressed since leaving Strytem —four whole days and three whole nights. It may be imagined with what joy I got rid of my bloody garments. Like the birds, we all retired to rest with the close of day, and the delicious sleep I enjoyed it is impossible to describe.

20th.—Awoke early, and at first could not imagine where I was. The cheerful sunbeams were playing amongst the leaves and branches overhead. The farmer's people were moving out with their cattle to commence their daily labours. All was peace and rural tranquillity. The events of the last four days passed across my recollection, and I could for a moment scarcely believe them other than a troubled dream; but I raised myself on my elbow, and there was the battle-field, still encumbered with the slain. Ah! there it lay, bathed in the full blaze of sunshine. Starting up, I roused our people, and would have immediately recommenced the march, but upon inquiry, found that, although the farriers had worked throughout the night, they had not yet completed

[1] Sir George Wood incurred the Duke's extreme displeasure for not securing and parking the French guns immediately after the action, for the Prussians got hold of many of them ; and it was only through the indefatigable activity of Sir Augustus Frazer that they were regained— partly by coaxing, partly by blustering. However, they were all recovered.

the shoeing. It was ten o'clock before they did so; and then we put ourselves in movement on the road to Nivelles, amidst crowds of stragglers, sutlers, etc., all pushing forward to overtake the army. It was like the highroad to some great fair. Every one appeared light-hearted, and it was delight to leave *that* field behind one.

Arrived at the gate of Nivelles, we found such a throng that there were no hopes of passing for at least some hours. I therefore drew up my troop in a pretty meadow by the roadside, where, besides being out of the dust, we could enjoy the cool shelter of the fine umbrageous elms by which it was surrounded, and water and feed our cattle. Mr Coates had preceded us and procured a fat cow, which one of our men slaughtered and cut up; and the meat being distributed, we were provided with the needful wherever we might bivouac. Up to this point I had no orders, nor did I know anything of the armies—English, Prussian, or French. We knew, to be sure, that the latter had been defeated on the 18th, and retired, followed by the other two; but we had no notion of the extent of the defeat, and therefore expected to find them again in position. Here I expected to get some information when I could get into the town; but the gate still continued so choked with waggons that it was impossible even for an individual to enter except in turn.

An order overtook us here to send back an officer to take charge of the guns and carriages we had left behind, until they could be rehorsed and forwarded to us again. Lieutenant Hincks, who rejoined us yesterday, being far from well, and suffering much from his contusion, I with some difficulty persuaded him to take this duty. On the opposite side of the road was a neat house, standing in a shrubbery, apparently deserted. Some of my men, wandering into the yard, discovered here three privates of the Guards. I forget what account they gave of themselves, but remember they complained of having eaten nothing for three days. We gave them a lump of beef and some bread, not reflecting at the time on the strange circumstance of their being thus left behind. I have since thought they remained here with the intention of deserting as soon as the coast was clear.

At length I effected my own entrance into the town, hoping to gain some information, or even meet some one who could give me orders. The first thing that struck me on passing the gates was the contrast the present aspect of the streets presented to that when we passed through on the evening of the 16th. Then all was sadness, despair, and lamentation; now all joy, confidence, and revel. The countenance of every one you met beamed exultation and triumph, Belgians as well as English. Men came up with frankness, took our hands, and paid us some compliment. The women, by smiles and kind looks, testified their sympathy; whilst the lower orders, in the joy of their hearts, would slap one on the thigh, *en passant*, with an emphatic "Bon!" "Brave garçon!" "Brave Anglais!" "Bon!" Or, if a number were collected at some corner, they would demonstrate their feelings by a cheer of "Vivent les Anglais!" The numerous cafés and cabarets (of which every door and window was open on account of the oppressive heat) were crammed with officers and soldiers of every arm and of every nation, eating, drinking, swearing, singing, and smoking. Music of some sort increased the *bouhara* in most of them. In many private houses, too, of the first appearance, large parties of officers were regaling themselves; and even in the streets many little assemblages of soldiers were to be seen enjoying their pipes and their beer in some shady corner. It was one complete scene of festivity. The streets were, moreover, crowded almost to suffocation with scattered soldiery: columns on their march; long files of country waggons laden with forage or provisions; together with the pretty little, low, light baggage-waggons of the German infantry, with their snow-white tilts. Here quartermasters and their attendants were running about chalking the doors of the houses (the head-quarters were here to-night) with the names of those who were to take up their temporary abode in them. "Lieutenant-Colonel ——" on one; "Deputy-Assistant-Adjutant-General" on another; "1st company of such a regiment" on another, and so on. Then several commissaries (followed by a swarm of Flemish waggoners) hurry along in search of the Magazin des Fourrages. Farther on, officers of the general staff are arranging the march of troops. Suddenly a loud shout announces something extraordinary even on this day of excitement. Every one hurries to the spot, pushing each other, jumping, shouting. "What can it mean?" I

inquired. "Monsieur l'Officier, c'est un convoi des prison-
niers que vient d'arriver," replied my man, doffing at the
same time his *bonnet de nuit* and making a most respectful
salaam. I stopped to see the convoy pass. The prisoners,
dressed in grey *capôtes* and *bonnets de fourrage*, march steadily
on. Some *vieux moustaches* look very grave, and cast about
furious glances at the noisy crowd which follows them with
the perseverance of a swarm of mosquitoes, *sacréeing* and
venting all kind of illiberal abuse on them and their b— of
an Emperor. Many, however, younger men, laugh, joke,
and return their abuse with interest, whilst the soldiers of
the escort (English) march doggedly along, pushing aside
the more forward of the throng, and apparently as if only
marching round a relief. The crowd passed on, and so did
I, until, meeting some of our own people, I learned that
Sir Augustus Frazer was here, and soon after found out his
billet. To find one's self in a quiet, genteel, well-furnished
room, after such scenes of bustle, etc., as had occupied our
last few days, is a pleasing change. Exactly such was that
in which I found Sir Augustus engaged with his adjutant.
He was in his slippers; his writing materials were arranged
on the table, and on another were some books and maps.
The open windows looked into a little shady garden gay
with flowers and flowering shrubs. There was an air of
cheerfulness, of home and home's comfort, about the place
that was quite refreshing. My visit was necessarily a short
one. I learned much more of our battle and its consequences than I had known before, and that I had better push
on with the crowd until I got orders, or fell in with Lord
Edward Somerset's division. Frazer and Bell told me
many flattering things about G troop, and considered it a
certainty that I should get the brevet—*nous verrons!*

Quitting them, I plunged again into the crowd and fought
my way towards the gate by which I had entered, but was
agreeably surprised at meeting my people in the street, Newland having pushed on the moment he observed the crowd at
the gate get somewhat thinner. Traversing the town with our
carriages proved a tedious operation; for in addition to what
I before found to struggle with, we now fell in with an endless
column of Belgic infantry marching the same route as ourselves—a most annoying obstruction. The march of these

people was a sort of triumphal procession: colours displayed; bands, with their clattering jangling cymbals, making a most martial noise; officers and men prancing along with short quick steps, bended knees, and stamping the pavement as if they wished to break holes in it, swaggering like turkey-cocks, and trying to appear indifferent, which was belied by the frequent upward glances at the fair dames in the windows, who certainly were doing all they could to blow up the vanity of these their brave countrymen by throwing out flowers on them, waving of handkerchiefs, clapping of hands, and faintly crying "Viva!"

We crept along the flank of this column of heroes, unnoticed and unknown, and soon after, clearing the Porte de Binche, got ahead and clear of them. The road was almost as much crowded as the streets of Nivelles, and I found it useless to expect to make rapid progress. For the first few miles the country was prettily wooded and interspersed with villages and neat houses; but then it began to get less wooded, less thickly inhabited, and in every way less interesting. Continued struggling on until towards evening, when our adjutant (Bell) overtook me with a little scrap of paper, on which was an order for me to bivouac either at Rœulx or Binche; but as we could not very well learn where these places were, and no guide was to be procured, and the evening began to close in, I determined on halting on a high and rather exposed piece of ground where we then happened to be. The bivouac was badly chosen—no water near, no house near, no wood near, no shelter of any kind near, and we were somehow all cross and out of humour. Set the men to work, scrubbing and cleaning appointments, this being the first opportunity of so doing. Went to sleep at nightfall. I think the nearest village to us was Haine. Some rustics who came to gape at us from a neighbouring farm told us that the King of Westphalia and another French general had passed the night of the 18th there with a few attendants, but that early on the morning of the 19th they had departed in a great hurry, evidently afraid of being overtaken.

21st.—Paraded early, and, considering all things, tolerably clean and neat. Descended to a lower country, equally dismal and uninteresting, without the one advantage which the other possesses—viz. that of commanding a distant

prospect, always more or less pleasing. At noon arrived in
the neighbourhood of Mons, where we overtook the Greys,
Inniskillings, Ross's troop of horse-artillery, and several
other corps, both of cavalry and infantry. We had, in short,
now rejoined the army. The Greys and the Inniskillings
were mere wrecks—the former, I think, did not muster
200 men, and the latter, with no greater strength, presented
a sad spectacle of disorganisation and bad discipline; they
had lost more than half their appointments. Some had
helmets, some had none; many had the skull-cap, but with
the crest cut or broken off; some were on their own large
horses, others on little ones they had picked up; belts there
were on some; many were without, not only belts, but also
canteens and haversacks. The enemy surely had not
effected in a single day so complete a disorganisation, and
I shrewdly suspect these rollicking Paddies of having mainly
spoilt themselves. The other corps all looked remarkably
well, although they, too, had partaken in the fight. We
overtook these corps about a mile from Mons, on a hill,
whence that place, with its old fortifications, looked venerable
and picturesque. Descending thence, the road crossed a
broad, flat, marshy piece of ground, which appeared nearly,
if not entirely, to surround the place. Here our further
progress was obstructed by a number of trees felled across
the road, and forming a sort of abatis, and we were consequently obliged to make a detour through the meadows, and
cross a rivulet by (I think the Trouille) a mill-dam, over
which the cavalry were obliged to file. This rendered it a
very tedious operation; and that part where at the mill we
had to pass our guns, etc., over a bridge of planks barely
broad enough, was a rather ticklish one. We crossed after the
Greys, and came with them on the main road to Maubeuge
at the moment a Highland regiment (perhaps the 92d),
which had come through Mons, was passing. The moment
the Highlanders saw the Greys an electrifying cheer burst
spontaneously from the column, which was answered as
heartily; and on reaching the road the two columns became
blended for a few minutes—the Highlanders running to
shake hands with their brave associates in the late battle.
This little burst of feeling was delightful—everybody felt
it; and although two or three general officers were present,

none interfered to prevent or to censure this breach of discipline. A few hundred yards farther on I found Lord Edward Somerset, with his brigade, formed in a field of clover by the roadside; and now, for the *first time*, I reported myself to him, and requested orders. These were simply to proceed straight to Malplaquet, and there bivouac for the night. Accordingly I continued my route independent as heretofore of my brigade. Nothing could be more horridly uninteresting than this country. Well cultivated, yet no habitations, or very few—no enclosures, or rather no hedges, there being banks to some of the fields; no trees, and hills just high enough to prevent an extended view, without adding one jot of beauty to the landscape. Most dismal country! To add to our wretchedness, the clouds which had been collecting all the morning began to drop their contents, so, snugging ourselves under our cloaks, on we jogged sulkily enough. We had left the great Chaussée de Maubeuge, and had been marching some time on a cross-road, occasionally confined between bare banks—not such ramparts as one sees in the county of Cork, but low clay banks about knee-high, with the ditch whence the material has been taken. In this way we had reached a point where a greater elevation of the ground allowed some scope of vision; and when emerging from between the banks, we came on something like a heath, bordered on one side by a large wood. Here an assemblage of rustics appeared waiting us. Their principal object, no doubt, was to gaze at the strangers; but they gave themselves infinite trouble to make us comprehend that we were about to cross the frontier and enter on the soil of France. Drawing a long line in the mud, right across the road, and vociferating altogether, "Ici, monsieur!" "Voila, monsieur!" "Regardez, monsieur!" "C'est ici, monsieur, que vous entrez en la France!" and when we crossed their line, they grinned and jumped about like so many monkeys. I could not divine what pleasure they derived from seeing strangers violate the sacred territory, nor what could induce the energetic "Voici, monsieur, la France, voila la Belgique!" which they roared in chorus. How different would have been the feelings and actions of Englishmen on a similar occasion! Frenchmen, however, draw amusement from everything—even misfortune.

But did they look upon our invasion as a misfortune? From what I have seen of these people, it appears very doubtful whether they care a farthing who reigns over them. Be that as it may, we undoubtedly entered France amidst cheers and greetings of the populace.

Soon after this we arrived at Malplaquet without being able to see it—the truth is, that it consists of a number of large farmhouses, etc., all standing isolated, and surrounded by thick orchards. In one of these we established our bivouac. A beggarly looking old house, built of wattles, plastered with clay (which in many places had fallen off), windows without glass, and doorways without doors, stood in one corner of our orchard, and as this was very cheerless from the heavy rain, we agreed to do comfortable and dine in the *house*. Accordingly, our grog and materials were conveyed thither, and the dame was desired to make a fire in her best salon; yet, after all, it was a matter of doubt whether we should not have been more comfortable under the apple-trees, barring the droppings. The place was a perfect picture of misery; rooms disgustingly filthy, and besides, blackened with smoke; floor of earth, broken into all sorts of holes and inequalities; ceiling of loose planks and full of large holes, as were the partitions; furniture— a rickety table, two or three as rickety chairs, and a sort of chest of walnut, serving the place of a chest of drawers, black as ebony from age and dirt. The mistress, a grown-up daughter, and three or four young children, were the only inmates of this wretched mansion we saw—filthy as their dwelling, their clothes all in rags, and without shoe or stocking. These poor creatures were so alarmed at us that they scarcely seemed to know what they were doing. Our dinner, of course, was none of the most comfortable; but some hot grog and cigars afterwards put us all in good humour, and we passed the evening admirably. In due time we retired to the nests our servants had provided for us in the orchard, and I was soon sound asleep, but was aroused about two o'clock by the sergeant-major, with a lantern in one hand and a paper in the other, which a dragoon had just brought from headquarters. This was an order to march at 4 a.m. Raining hard.

CHAPTER XV

22*d.*—Morning fine, and things look more cheerful. March, according to order, at four. Troop turned out of its wet bivouac; did not look very brilliant; moreover, there had been no time for cleaning. The village street such a perfect slough that even the riding-horses struggled through with difficulty, and our carriages stuck fast several times ere they could be brought to the hard ground beyond. Immediately on emerging from the orchards, we entered on the same cheerless uninteresting country as before: interminable fields of corn, without enclosures, only broken here and there by small patches of coppice or young timber. Through this sort of country marched to Bavay; and here we formed up in the fields by the roadside and dismounted, whilst an officer was sent to summon the garrison of Maubeuge—the first word of an enemy since quitting Waterloo. As the infantry continued moving on, we were somewhat at a loss to conjecture what was to be done should the answer to our summons be unfavourable. The whole army—cavalry, infantry, and artillery, English and allies, all appeared to be marching along this one line of road. We heard nothing of any columns moving parallel on our flanks, and for about three hours that we halted here this incessant passing afforded us some amusement. The crowd was endless, though varied—regiments of infantry or cavalry following each other in constant succession, intermingled with, and striving to pass, the as endless file of waggons, baggage-carts, baggage-animals, led horses, batteries of artillery, and convoys of stores. All struggled to get ahead to choose a bivouac, or get the first-fruits of any village or farm on or near the road, which was sure to be left quite bare the moment the first corps passed—I mean bare of provisions; for I believe our people did not otherwise plunder. It might truly be said that a torrent of men and animals rolled along the road. Even when we resumed our

march there was no cessation, no diminution of the crowd.
The numbers of servants, sutlers, stragglers, and women
were incredible, and added not a little to the general confusion.
As far back, too, as I could see, the same swarm covered the
road—the troops seemed to form the smallest part of the
crowd. What the answer was to our summons we have not
yet heard, but suppose all went on smoothly; for, after a wait
of three or four hours, we again got under way, and made an
attempt to penetrate the throng, but in vain—we got jammed
and stuck fast. Lord Edward, seeing our case hopeless,
abandoned us as soon as he could get his dragoons disengaged
from the crowd, and took across the fields, leaving me directions to make the best of my way to Cateau Cambresis, and
bivouac there if I did not find him and the brigade. In this
state we were obliged to give up all thoughts of pushing on,
and rest contended to swim with the stream. This swept us
in due time into one end of Bavay (pleasingly situated on a
rising ground) and out at the other, leaving just time to see
that the place had a clean and cheerful appearance, and that
the street we passed through was well built and had many
genteel-looking houses in it. Quitting the town by a steepish
hill, we entered the forest of Mormal; and the road was
bordered on both sides by a thick coppice of hazel, young ash,
etc., over which the larger timber-trees reared their heads.
Many corps of infantry had drawn off the road, and were busy
cutting down the coppice to prepare their bivouacs by constructing huts of leaves and branches. Fires were made, and
cooking already going on. Officers, divested of swords and
sashes, were strolling amongst the thickets, or listlessly lolling
under their leafy bowers. All this would have been very
pretty, but that a heavy shower, which fell as we struggled
through Bavay, had left everything dripping, consequently
deteriorated the scene much. Still the grouping of the
figures round the fires, or interspersed among the thickets,
was very good. Emerging from the woods, we again entered
on the ocean of corn; but here the features of the ground
were bolder, and the view more extensive, though not less
cheerless.

At some distance ahead, in a deep valley, of which the
heights all descended by fine bold slopes, stood the little
town of Cateau amidst flat alluvial meadows, the lively

verdure of which, and that of a few trees, contrasted strikingly with the golden hue of all the country around it. The road along the plateau on which we now travelled was hard and excellent, so that, by watching our opportunity and pushing in whenever an opening in the crowd permitted, we managed, with some considerable wrangling, to get ahead. This was rather a dangerous operation, for the Belgic, and particularly the Nassau troops, were so savage, and so constantly threatening us with their bayonets, that I feared every minute we should come to blows. In this manner we had struggled on to the crest of the hill descending toward Cateau, where, to lessen the descent, it had been cut down, consequently was confined between high banks. Now, as the devil would have it, we got into this gully at the same time with a battalion of Nassau, and as both parties pressed on to head the other, some jostling ensued. Our wheels were too formidable to be resisted when in motion; but at last we got completely entangled, and then they turned upon us, striking our horses, and even pricking them with their bayonets. Our men, of course, resented this, and a serious affray was likely to take place; but at last, assisted by their officers, we disengaged ourselves without any one being materially hurt, although many had bruises, scratches, and slight bayonet-stabs. In this affair one fellow was very deliberately going to give me a *coup de bayonette* in the side, but old Quartermaster Hall knocked up the point with his sabre, and could scarcely be prevented from splitting his skull. The English, with whom we also occasionally crossed and jostled, contented themselves with abusing us. For some days after, we were constantly falling in with these very people, and our so doing resembling the approach of two angry dogs. I was constantly alarmed lest some serious affray should take place. But they have led me ahead of my march. Somewhat more than a mile before we came to the descent above mentioned, we passed through Forêt, a pretty large village, surrounded as usual by orchards, with a few small woods scattered about the vicinity, which diversified agreeably the otherwise monotonous scenery. On approaching this village, a dirty sheet or tablecloth, attached to a pole, and projected from a window of the church-tower, attracted our attention. It was the first time we had seen the immaculate *pavillon blanc*

since entering the French territory; and one could not but
admire the wisdom and foresight which had established as a
national standard what could be readily furnished at any
moment by every, even the most humble, *ménage*. A tall,
thin, venerable-looking old man in the clerical habit stood by
the roadside amidst several peasants, male and female. His
countenance was radiant with joy, and he appeared quite elated
in contemplating the column as it passed along. Pinch after
pinch he took from a little tortoiseshell snuff-box in his left
hand, whilst with earnestness he pointed out to, or seemed
describing, something in our column. As I came up,
followed by my trumpeter, the old man, uncovering his
white head, made me a profound obeisance. This opened
the interview, and I was soon master of his history. He had
been driven from his *curé* by the Revolution; returned on
the abdication of Napoleon last year; but the return from
Elba had again nearly caused a second flight. He had, however, ventured to remain, upon the affectionate assurances of
his parishioners, and after suffering during the Hundred
Days most horrid anxiety and even indignities, had at last
been restored to security and tranquillity by the battle of
Waterloo. He was now come out not only to witness the
passage of the brave English, to whom his country and himself stood so much indebted, but also to meet and do homage
to his beloved monarch, who he understood would pass
through Forêt on his way to his capital. Nothing could
exceed the good man's joy; his spirits quite ran away with
him, and his tongue ran nineteen to the dozen. At parting
we cordially shook hands, and he tendered me the little
tortoiseshell box with the most amiable *bonhommie*. How
the rustics gazed. They seem a very ignorant, simple people,
the peasantry of this country. Hitherto, since passing the
frontier, we have found them everywhere pursuing their rural
labours with as much tranquillity as in the most profound
state of peace: quite undisturbed by, and exhibiting very
little curiosity about, the continued passage of foreign troops
along their roads and through their villages. The village of
Forêt presented a cheerful rustic aspect—such as a village
should. Thatched barns and farmhouse in the usual style
of such buildings in England, standing detached and retired
from the broad street, if so it might be termed, embosomed

in apple or cherry orchards;—quite unlike what one so often meets with in other parts of France, where the villages, of stone houses three or four stories high, with large windows, etc., appear more like pieces of towns cut out and popped down here than what is consonant to our ideas of villages.

From the place where our scuffle with the Nassau men took place we descended into the valley by a long winding hill, at the bottom of which the little village of Montay lay like an oasis in the desert; verdant meadows overshadowed by numerous pine-trees, a pretty rivulet winding along amongst them, here passed by a narrow stone bridge; the place itself consisting of one large farm, several cottages, and a small church;—altogether offering a refreshing variety in this ocean of corn. The heights rising abruptly above it on either side make this a sort of pass, which, had the retiring French thought fit to defend, would have cost us some trouble and many lives, no doubt. As it was, although we understood their outposts were not far, not a man was in sight; and we were allowed to pass as quietly as our own internal dissensions would allow, for the narrowness of the bridge produced here a fearful struggle. The road along which the army was marching, passing through Montay, immediately ascended the opposite heights. A road branching from this led to Cateau along the foot of these heights and through the meadows about a mile or rather more higher up the stream. We took this road, and thus, for the first time since leaving Nivelles, enjoyed the indescribable pleasure of having the road to ourselves. From the heights on this side of Forêt, whence the view was very extensive, I could distinguish nothing of the brigade; and now finding ourselves quite alone, and seeing no symptoms of troops about Cateau, I began to be rather uneasy. In this dilemma I was about to establish my bivouac on a piece of turf just without the town—for the evening was fast closing in—when our lieutenant-major-general of cavalry, Lord Greenock, rode hastily up, and demanded why we were here. "My orders were to march to Cateau, my lord, and bivouac, with which I am complying. I expect Lord Edward will join us here"; and I gave him an account of their taking to the fields, etc. "There is some mistake in this," replied Lord Greenock. "Your brigade has halted at Forêt, and you must return thither, for you are now in a very dangerous position, and at all events ought not to have crossed the river. The enemy's outposts are on the heights; and should they attempt anything during the night, which is probable, you could never recross the bridge. Return, therefore, without delay." This was comfortable, to have to grope our way to Forêt, and when there pick out a bivouac; and the alternative that of remaining and being caught in this *coupe gorge*. The idea was not a pleasant one. Disobeying orders, too! We countermarched, however; but on reaching Montay the stream of people and carriages sweeping over the narrow bridge made it evidently useless attempting to move in a contrary direction. I gave up the idea, and established my bivouac in the little churchyard close to the bridge. I felt less compunction at doing this, because several regiments of Hanoverian infantry had extended themselves in bivouac along the meadows, both up and down the stream, on the same side; and, moreover, I had learned from Lord Greenock that two or three troops of horse-artillery and a large corps of hussars were occupying the plateau in front, between us and the enemy. Under the impression of security, therefore, I laid myself down after our evening meal was finished, expecting a good sleep; but my eyes were scarcely closed ere the never-to-be-mistaken sound of a distant cannonade caused me to start up again. Everything around was perfectly still; the Hanoverians seemed to be all asleep; and no stir or bustle of any kind in our immediate neighbourhood indicated an alarm. The cannonade, too, though sometimes more distinctly heard than at others, did not, on the whole, seem to approach. After listening for a time, sleep got the better of me, and I sank down in spite of the distant cannonade and the more immediate concert of thousands of frogs in the adjoining ditch.

23*d*.—A fine day. Uneasy at hearing nothing of the brigade being in motion. The cannonade during the night proceeded from Sir Charles Colville and the 4th division attacking Cambray.

About noon Sir Augustus Frazer, with Sir Julius Hartman of the K.G. Legion horse-artillery, paid us a visit. From them I learned that headquarters are established in Cateau, and that the Duke intends halting in our present position for a day or two to give time for the rear of the army to close up, since, from the rapidity of our march, and from the whole marching in a single column, many corps are still a long way in the rear. At the same time, Cambray on our right and Landrecy on our left are to be secured before we advance farther. Moreover, we are likely, it seems, to have another battle immediately, for the French army has rallied in considerable force, and is in position not far in front of us. Upon this intelligence I decided on remaining at Montay until the brigade should come up; therefore, leaving my second captain to inspect ammunition, and forward cleaning, repairing, shoeing, etc., I set off with our two visitors on their return to Cateau. This place, which is very small, is situated in a rich alluvial bottom amongst fine, well-irrigated meadows. The only trees, however, in this bottom are at Montay. The town is surrounded by a simple wall, perhaps only for excise purposes; and I was at a loss to conjecture the use of a single battery of two or three pieces near the gate leading to Montay. On entering this gate I was struck by the dismal aspect of the street within—narrow, dirty, and composed of mean-looking houses built of sombre-coloured stone, and scarcely a human being visible; for although headquarters were here, none of the members of it were to be seen in the streets. Priests in their black cassocks and band strode solemnly along from time to time. The house in which the Duke lodged was the only decent-looking one in the place. It stood at the extremity of the street, crossing at right angles the one we entered by—large, and pierced with numerous windows, apparently new, and having the advantage of a row of three or four fine trees in front. Some pretensions there were, too, to architectural decorations in the façade, which was of stucco, painted buff. Cateau was soon seen, and I returned to Montay, where I found the poor farmer (the farm adjoined the church) in great distress. The Hanoverians were plundering barns, farmyard, and all. "Ah, monsieur, tout sera abimé!" cried the poor fellow, wringing his hands, and presenting the very picture of despair. Yesterday evening he complained to me, and I did what I could to prevent it, but without much effect. The bivouac of these marauders in the adjoining meadows was only separated from his garden by a sort of willow hedge; and although I planted sentries for the protection of it, everything disappeared.

This morning, becoming bolder, they have plundered his barns, etc., and even threatened the house itself. As we draw our own supplies of eggs, milk, etc., from the farm, I did what I could to save him from further plunder, and sent Breton to remonstrate with their commanding officer, and give him to understand that, unless he kept his men under better discipline, I would report him to the Duke. Got nothing by this, for he persisted in not understanding English. Thus we have been obliged to be constantly on the alert, and to keep them out by main force. The poor farmer is very grateful and loud in praise of *les bons Anglais*, whilst he *sacrés*, etc., their allies down to the bottomless pit—"aux enfers." He admits the truth of what I said about retaliation, and turned up his eyes in horror at the account I gave him of the ravages committed by French troops in other countries. "Mais, monsieur, je le crois bien, les soldats Français sont de vrais brigands; ils pillent partout même dans la patrie; oui, monsieur, ici même"; and he related how a detachment of cuirassiers had quartered on him for three days, having only departed the morning of that in which we arrived. They had treated him cruelly; and not content with living on him all that time, were on the point of destroying everything that was left and burning the premises, when the unexpected appearance of some of our advanced corps obliged them to make a precipitate retreat. In the evening, a general parade of the Germans. They have formed a sort of diminutive tents for the night by striking two ramrods into the ground, crossed, to form each end; I forget how they form the ridge. A blanket is laid over, and the other two serve to lie under and over the three men the tent just holds. The different bands, all good, continued playing until after dusk, which we enjoyed sitting in the willow hedge smoking our cigars. The scene was remarkably pretty. Groups of men scattered about amongst the little tents, some preparing supper, etc.; the bands, with officers in picturesque costumes hovering about them; the town of Cateau in the background; and on either hand the picture shut in by bold naked slopes of the neighbouring heights.

24*th*.—Fine warm morning, but day promises to be rather too hot. Not a gun to be heard to-day by the sharpest ear;

the business at Cambray must be settled somehow or other. Getting accustomed to our churchyard. To be sure, none of the graves are recent; it seems long since any one has been buried here. Hitchins and I have decided on breakfasting together; and as he is more at leisure than I am, he has undertaken the foraging department. This morning our repast consisted of bread (sour as vinegar), cheesy butter, and hard eggs, washed down with weak grog (Hollands)—table, a grave. Ever since we passed Mons good bread is not to be had—all is of this horrid sour description. To the eye it is well enough. The peasantry make their bread in large flat loaves, 2 or 2½ feet in diameter—no mistake!—nearly circular. Sometimes the loaves are annular, and of the above diameter. Enter Lieutenant and Adjutant Bell, R.H.A., and I can write no more, for he no doubt brings news.

9 *p.m.*—Here we are, then, back again in Forêt. Bell brought us the order to return forthwith, as the brigade was to march without delay on Landrecy, the commandant of which place refuses to surrender. We lost no time in obeying the order, and the road being now quite clear—indeed solitary—marched here in a very short time; and instead of finding the brigade ready to move, were surprised on reaching the village at seeing the Lifeguardsmen quietly grooming their horses in front of the barns and stables of their billets. The place being already full, we were directed to bivouac, and accordingly I pitched upon this orchard, which is high and dry; but the trees are too young and too far apart to afford us much shade, which we want just now. The arrival of strangers attracted a concourse of villagers to our bivouac, many old women and young girls bringing quantities of very fine cherries for sale. The former were remarkably coarse and ugly, the latter generally pretty, and all had sparkling, speaking eyes. These, of course, sold their cherries first; but the article was too grateful in such a roasting day as this has been not to insure the sale of all. The costume of these women—who, by the way, seemed quite at home with us—was rather picturesque. Lofty white caps, with long flaps hanging down to the shoulders, their naked stays sometimes not very closely laced, bosom covered with a coloured hand-kerchief put on with a degree of taste, coarse woollen petti-coats of a blue stuff striped with white or pink and reaching

only to the calf of the leg, coarse woollen stockings, and clumsy wooden shoes (*sabots*). Most of them wore large gold or silver rings in their ears, and many a little golden cross suspended from the neck by a black riband or a strip of black velvet. The Duke has published a manifesto from Cateau. Several copies are stuck up in the village, and the people here seem very much pleased with it; and well they may, for it assures them they shall be treated like gentlemen, and not get the punishment which France, as a nation, so richly deserves. It calls upon the people to remain quietly at home, as we make no war on them, but ought rather to be considered as their allies; further, it goes on to assure them that the strictest discipline will be maintained in the Allied army, and that everything required by the troops must be paid for at its full value. The Forêtiens, and particularly the Forêtiennes, actually express astonishment at our generosity.

Louis XVIII., etc., passed through the village this evening on his way to Cateau. Leathes and I rode a little way out to meet him, which we did about a quarter of a mile off. The cortège consisted of several Berlines, escorted by about two squadrons of the Royal Garde de Corps—fine young men (all gentlemen), dressed in a very becoming uniform, blue turned up with red, and silver lace tastefully disposed, with Grecian helmets, silver, with a golden sun on the front, the most elegant I ever saw. The King was in the last carriage, on each side of which rode the Duc de Berri and that General whose acquaintance I made on the drill-ground near Alost. We had drawn up on the roadside as the cortège passed. The moment the Duc de Berri and the General saw us, they came up, and, offering us their hands, poured forth such a torrent of compliments and congratulations as made even our horses blush. His Royal Highness could never sufficiently testify his gratitude to the English nation, etc. etc.; was impatient to see us in Paris, for then and there indeed, etc. etc. The General was equally profuse in compliments and promises, so that, forgetting the adage, "Put not your trust in princes," Leathes and I have ever since been feeling the Croix de St Louis dangling at our breasts—*nous verrons!* The monarch was detained from his dinner more than half an hour by my worthy friend Mons. le Curé, who, in full pontificals, and followed by his

congregation *en habits de Dimanches*, met him at the entrance
of the village, and, standing on a little bank at the coach-
door, delivered a long harangue, set off by mandarin-like
bobs of the head at the end of every period, and a most
profound bow at the conclusion, all which were received
and returned by his Majesty with exemplary patience and
punctuality.   At length the cortège moved on, and we
returned to our orchard.

   25th.—Here we are, another day's march in advance, not
only without the expected battle, but also without having
either seen or heard of an enemy.   Nor have we seen any
traces of one, having found the peasantry everywhere as
peaceably occupied as if no war existed.   Nothing more
have we heard of Landrecy, which, I suppose, must have
surrendered, since Lord Edward sent us orders this morning
to march on Sequehart, where the brigade halts to-night.
Accordingly I marched immediately towards Montay in a
thick drizzling rain, which made this dismal country appear
ten times more dismal.   The cavalry regiments marched
at the same time (about 5 a.m.?) and we kept company as
far as Montay; but there they left us, for we found the road
again so choked with baggage, etc., that although we succeeded in passing the bridge, yet the deep hollow road
(*encaissé* between very high steep banks), ascending to the
opposite heights, was so inextricably crammed with carriages,
and the unctuous soil so slippery, that I feared we should
bivouac in the churchyard again.   We attempted the ascent,
and being better horsed than the others, succeeded in getting ahead wherever an opening offered.   Our column was
broken into as many fractional parts as we had carriages.
At length, after a most arduous struggle, we mustered our
whole force on the plateau, and pushed forward in the old
way—sometimes getting along pretty smoothly by keeping
one side of the road; then a choke would stop us for a time,
until, an opportunity offering, the head of our column would
make a dash and break the file of waggons; but occasionally
in doing this, if the rear carriages did not keep close up, the
waggoners would dash in their turn, and cut them off.   Then
again we got foul of our Nassau friends, and the old quarrel
was revived; cursing, swearing, and bayoneting followed
as matter of course.   The road itself was execrable, and in

places a complete slough. It appears that our march has been so conducted as to avoid the main avenues, and thus turn the fortresses; consequently, with the exception of some little bits of chaussée, we have been travelling on the cross-roads—in France always execrable. On gaining the plateau we saw everywhere around us again those interminable fields of wheat—not a hedge nor a dividing wall; the only relief a few small woods here and there. A hamlet we occasionally met with, and sometimes a solitary cabaret of the meanest appearance—"Ici on loge à pied et à cheval," scrawled on a board in black letters, on a dirty-white ground, invited the traveller to enter. Sometimes a longer inscription set forth other inducements. I pity the luckless wight who trusts to their hospitality. A remarkable feature in the cheerless scenery of these oceans of corn is the row of apple-trees so frequently seen skirting the horizon. The by-roads here are frequently bordered by apple or pear trees, which accounts for this. As we advanced on the plateau, and still found no concentration of troops, or other indication of the neighbourhood of the enemy, our expectation of another battle vanished. Insensibly we had deviated from the general route, and found ourselves only accompanied by Major Bull's troop of horse-artillery. Bull had got the same discretionary orders from his general as myself, and was also making his way to Sequehart, where his brigade was to halt. The country had become prettier and more interesting, and the rain had ceased. Woods were more frequent and larger, and at last we marched through what might strictly be termed a wooded country. The ground, too, became more undulating, and pastures of green meadows occurred to relieve most agreeably the tiresome sameness of the corn crops. Occasionally, also, openings between the woods would give us glimpses of distant and pretty country. But where dwell the husbandmen who cultivate those lands? In this district we saw not a single habitation, and only here and there met a solitary peasant—not working, but in the road—moving from one place to another. Of these we incessantly demanded "Où se trouve Sequehart?" and the response was invariably "N'sais paw, Monsire," or a shake of the head. Bull and I began to be uneasy as the evening drew on, whilst we were surrounded by woods, and not the slightest appearance of a village to be seen. Our own people were now the only troops visible, and we began to suspect what proved to be true—we had lost ourselves!

We were so enclosed by woods that it was impossible to see to any distance; and cross-roads branching off right and left became very frequent, so that we were puzzled how to proceed. Every peasant we met persisted in knowing nothing of Sequehart, nor had met any other troops. We were evidently astray. At last an old man, to whom the usual questions were put, after puzzling over it for a few minutes, begged we would repeat the name. "Sequehart!— Sequehart!" said he, two or three times. "*Monsire, n'le connois paw*; mais, ma foi, ce sera sans doute Escars que vous cherchez." We stared in our turn, but the old man was positive, and insisted that we were leaving it behind us. After some little irresolution, Bull and I made up our minds to follow his directions; and accordingly, after a few miles threading our way between woods, arrived here a little before sunset. The village is already full of Life Guards, and therefore we are obliged to bivouac again; but that is of little moment, for we have an excellent spot on a rising ground, covered with short velvety turf, close to the chaussée leading to St Quentin, on the other side of which, about two or three hundred yards distant, is the village of Seque-hart, or Escars, so buried in the foliage of fine walnut-trees, and of the hedges enclosing the gardens and some fields, that scarcely a roof is to be seen; and it is only through the ascending columns of blue smoke from amongst the trees that the site of the village is to be detected. From the swelling hills up which the St Quentin road runs in front of us, the short clean turf, and the chalk (or gypsum) that appears in patches where this has been removed, we might fancy ourselves on the South Downs, in Sussex. It is a sweet rural spot, and, what is better, we see few signs of war about us; for except Walcott's troop (rocket), which has just come up, no other soldiers whatever are to be seen. Bull left us at the other side of the village, and our cavalry are, like it, buried in the foliage and invisible to us. We under-stand headquarters are at Joncour, a village not far off, and that Lord Hill's division is at Belleglise, somewhere in front, so that we may sleep securely to-night. Lovely evening.

26th.—Fine morning. Marched early, and, crossing the downs, traversed beyond them a pretty well-wooded country, diversified very agreeably by several large sheets of water, formed by embankments, and regained the route of our army, which we had deviated from yesterday at Belleglise, just as the bustle commenced. Plunged once more into the torrent, with all its *désagrémens* and vexations, and swam along with it as before. The wooded country gave place to the dismal sea of corn a little beyond Belleglise; but after travelling about four or five miles through this tiresome region, we once more came amongst trees, and crossed a deep ravine, or rather wooded valley, in which was situated a most respectable-looking country-house, brick, with stone angles, window-cases, etc., standing upon a terrace, with an old-fashioned garden divided into rectangular beds, with stone vases, etc., sheltered in the rear by the woods, and to the south looking upon a fine sheet of water—artificial, no doubt—most probably formed by damming up the stream which we crossed in the bottom. The country people told us this place belongs to Caulaincourt, Duc de Vicenza, which is no doubt the truth, since in my map I find it called Caulaincourt. The hanging woods and shady winding paths of this ravine appeared to us heavenly when contrasted with the dreary exposed plain above; and this, if possible, was more hideous than ever when we again debouched upon it—a dead flat, unrelieved by the slightest undulation—a sea of wheat extending to the horizon, with here and there a few clumps of beggarly pines, and the usual straggling lines of apple-trees fringing the horizon. I forget where, but it must have been just before crossing the valley at Caulaincourt that we left the direct route, together with Bull's and Whinyate's troops, as we were directed to halt for the night at Etreillers. After marching two or three miles more over this uninteresting plain, on passing one of these circular pine clumps we suddenly came in sight of fine trees bounding the horizon, intermixed with buildings, which, on approaching it, proved to be Etreillers. The village is a very large one, composed principally of large farms, with a few dwellings of an inferior description, all, however, standing back in gardens, or in their large straw-yards, which are separated from the broad avenues consti-

tuting the village street by high walls, with a great gateway
of entrance, and generally surrounded on three sides by
orchards. Such quarters are quite a luxury; for although we
are three troops in the village, yet all get under cover, man
and horse, in houses, barns, stables, etc. The appearance
of the place is not gay, and may truly be said to harmonise
in tone with the dreary but fruitful plain around. The
buildings are generally of a dark stone, with enormous
thatched roofs, which, if not lively, has at least an air of
substantial comfort that makes ample amends for everything else.

I have established myself in a most comfortable farmhouse
of the first class, and, to complete my good fortune, have
an exceedingly pretty and most obliging hostess. Instead
of the black looks an intruder like myself might have expected, I was received with smiles, and a welcome which
sounded sincere. I was shown into their best room (the
one which I now write in), my horses into the best stable,
and everything done to make me most comfortable. My
fair friend has let out one reason for all this, although I still
believe genuine hospitality has a great share in it—she is
delighted at having English instead of Prussians quartered
on her; all the country are in dread of the latter. As may
be supposed, we were soon quite at home—I say we, for
my second captain (Newland) was with me. In the stable,
men and boys have been at work helping our men to clean
their horses, whilst in the house the women busied themselves in arranging our room, cooking dinne·, and even
asking for our dirty linen, which they are in the act of
washing for us, so that to-day I can afford a clean shirt and
still start to-morrow with a clean kit. The room we occupy
is large and rather dark, for there are only two small windows
looking out to the farmyard, and these rather obscured with
the white draperies with which they are ornamented. The
furniture is coarse and clumsy, made of walnut, and is as
black as ebony. One side of the room is occupied by two
sleeping-places, let into the wall, exactly like the berths on
shipboard. The bedding in these, though coarse also, is
very good, and, like everything else, scrupulously clean;
the sheets have just been put in. Our servants have comfortable beds allotted to them, and have become as much

at home in the kitchen as if they were old acquaintances. Whilst dinner was preparing, I sallied forth to see how my people were put up, and had scarcely left the yard when I encountered an old peasant wearing an enormous cocked-hat, and having a drum suspended from his neck by a broad band, on which he occasionally gave a sort of roll or flourish. His grotesque figure, as well as his employment, attracted my attention, and I was somewhat mystified on observing that every flourish on the drum was responded to by an opening of doors and the sallying out of old ladies, each bearing under her arm one of those enormous loaves already mentioned. What can all this mean, thought I? Is it possible that in this most military of all nations even women are subject to regulations, and obliged to conduct the *ménage* by tap of drum or sound of bugle? One old lady, with a huge annular loaf, whom I questioned, soon solved the query. The commissary had ordered the inhabitants to feed the troops, and this drumming hero was the crier, who gave notice to that effect, and was likewise collecting all the ready-baked bread at the church for distribution. The thing seemed perfectly well understood, each roll of the drum producing precisely the same effect as the crier moved along the great rambling street. The old women, as they trotted towards the church, made a clatter with their sabots like so many horses. Many of the people I found had, on our first arrival, concealed everything; but the dread of being plundered was soon removed, and all is now confidence. As far as I can judge, these people seem to live well enough in their own way; and in every house one is sure to find good beds, very high, being raised upon an enormous palliasse. There is no want of silver spoons, and even forks, in many of them; and their stock of household linen (good) is really astonishing, many small *cultivateurs* possessing as much as would set up two or three of our middling farmers. I use the term "*cultivateur*" to designate a class quite common in France, but scarcely known in England. They are proprietors of small estates (perhaps only a few acres), fractions of large ones sold in lots during the Revolution. These, of course, they cultivate themselves, with the assistance of their families, and are thence styled "*cultivateurs*" by the Government, and are obliged to put this, coupled with their number (they are all numbered), upon their carts, etc.—for example, "Joachim Laroque, culti-vateur, No. 3755"; or "Jean Baptiste Amand," etc. etc. etc.

We find them a simple, obliging, but very ignorant race; and their patois is to me almost unintelligible. Some with whom I conversed this evening either were, or pretended to be, quite ignorant of what has been taking place in the great world. They had heard that France was at war with England, Russia, and Prussia, but that was all. They had never heard of Wellington, nor of Nelson, nor even Louis XVIII. They had, however, heard enough to inspire them with some dread of the Cossacks and Prussians. I asked them if they knew Buonaparte? "Non, monsieur—non y pas!" "Napoleon?—aw mais oui, monsieur, c'est l'Empereur que ça—n'est ce paw vrai, monsieur?" They had heard of him because he made them pay taxes; but of his wars they were as ignorant as all the rest, and did not speculate the least in the world as to how and why we are here.

Returned *home* (conceive being *at home* in a French farmhouse!) just as the good woman was placing a most inviting fricasseed fowl and *omelette aux herbes*, smoking hot, upon our table, to which, with a good bottle of *vin du pays*, we lost no time in doing justice. We have passed a most comfortable evening; and if we may judge by the laughing and chattering in the kitchen, our servants and the rustics have not passed it badly. As their door is opposite to ours, we have occasionally peeped in upon them, and been much amused at seeing the ploughmen equipped in our men's helmets, belts, etc.; but their chief source of amusement appeared to be reciprocally teaching each other English and French words—the attempt at pronouncing which causes infinite fun.

CHAPTER XVI

27th.—Fine warm morning. Started early after an excellent breakfast of coffee and et ceteras. Our orders were to rejoin the grand column at Ugny l'Equippée; but we had not gone far from Etreillers when two roads, branching off in different directions, brought us to a halt. Lord Greenock came up just at the moment, and blamed me for not bringing a guide from the village—"Better late than never." I took the hint, and sent Trumpeter Brown back with orders to bring the first person he could lay hands on, *nolens volens.* He went his way and brought back *a tailor*, escorting him like a prisoner with his drawn sabre. Not knowing why he was thus forcibly taken from his home, the poor tailor appeared terribly alarmed—imploring mercy even with tears. When told, however, what was expected of him, he soon became tranquil; so, sticking him at the head of the column, we jogged on again. At Ugny l'Equippée we rejoined the column and dismissed our tailor, slipping into the main stream as heretofore. We now learned that the army was about to cross the Somme, and soon felt that it was actually engaged in so doing from our long and tedious halts—there being but one ford, which made the operation a very slow one. As we drew near the river the country improved somewhat, became more undulating and more wooded, consequently prettier.

The Somme here is but a small stream; flat meadows extend some little way on each side, and are bordered by moderate hills, running out here and there into knolls. The point chosen for our passage was a ford just above a mill on the road to Nesle. Peronne having been taken yesterday by General Maitland's brigade of Guards, the only enemy we heard of in our vicinity was the garrison of Ham, and they could scarcely have opposed our passage even had they not been shut up by a brigade of light infantry and a troop of horse-artillery (Ross's), which had been sent to summon them. The different divisions of cavalry, infantry, and artillery, winding down the swelling knolls, some of which were prettily wooded, and the picturesque groups of staff and other officers on the points of these knolls, superintending the passage of their respective brigades, etc., formed altogether an animated and pleasing picture, although not much could be said for the beauty of the country on the opposite side of the river, which looked cheerless enough. It was in one of those groups, and the most picturesque of them—for they were German hussars—that I recognised and shook hands with my friend General Victor Alten, whom I had not seen for more than three years. An interesting meeting, for he was surrounded by a number of other old acquaintances of the 2d Hussars.

A foot-bridge at the mill enabled the infantry to file over; but we had to ford, and got a tolerable wetting, for the water was up to our saddle-skirts. On the other side, about a mile from the river, we reached Nesle, the intervening country enclosed but not wooded, consequently much more ugly and uninteresting than if it had been open. Nesle is a dismal, dirty town, situated on an eminence of no great elevation, and perfectly in character with the melancholy country around it.

This is the first town we have marched through in France. I think it must have been market-day, from the number of people in the streets; yet not the slightest apprehension or agitation appeared; and, as we passed along, the market-people merely turned up their heads, and the shopkeepers came to their doors to gaze on us, much as if we had been marching through Exeter, or any other English town accustomed to see troops.

Since crossing the Somme, the army has marched more cautiously than hitherto, consequently we have been all day with our brigade. At Nesle we got on a chaussée, bordered on each side by large elms, consequently forming a fine avenue; the country on either side without enclosures and not interesting, although better wooded than immediately about that town. Roye was ahead of us, but when within a few miles of it the head of our column led off the chaussée, crossing the fields by a by-road, and then another chaussée,

Peronne to Paris, until we gained the village of Goyencour, situated in a pretty, because well-wooded, country. This village, like most of those we have hitherto passed through, is composed of a number of farmhouses scattered over a large space, and embowered amongst orchards and some of the finest linden-trees I ever saw.

The Life Guards and my troop are all housed, so that we are fortunate again. For my part, I am quartered on a small shop, which, however, is very clean; and we have excellent beds, Newland and I. In front of the house an open space affords good room to draw up our guns, etc., adjoining which are the very pretty pleasure-grounds of a handsome villa, seen through a stately avenue of lindens. This place belongs to some lady, who it seems has taken to flight on hearing of our approach, leaving, however, her butler and some other servants behind; so that Lord Edward, who has taken up his quarters there, is as comfortable as he could wish to be. I have just returned from dining with him, and a better dinner, dessert, and wines,[1] it is impossible to have enjoyed. What a treat in the midst of a campaign to enjoy such a party. Besides his lordship's personal staff, there were the two colonels of the Life Guards. The front of the house, having part of the pleasure-ground (it might almost be called a park) in the fore, has the town of Roye in the distance; a pretty terrace with aloes in vases and other choice shrubs occupies the space immediately under the windows, which, opening to the ground, admit one into a suite of elegantly furnished rooms. Lord Edward was perfectly at home, and did the honours as if the house were his, and so did the butler and other servants. A quieter, better-ordered dinner, and more excellent, I repeat, could not be.

Lord Edward had heard that, after a little show of resistance, Ham had surrendered this morning; and we were speculating over our first glass of wine on the probability of reaching Paris without resistance, when an officer of the Life Guards came in to report that a strong corps of cavalry had been seen amongst the woods about a mile from the

---

[1] There was a species of Malmsey Madeira, the most delicious wine imaginable. The cellar seemed well stocked, and our table consequently was well supplied.

village. As his lordship knew positively that the main body of the French force was retreating before the Prussians, who had got a march ahead of us, he contented himself with ordering out a strong detachment to reconnoitre, and we continued at table. In the course of the evening the detachment returned, and a report was brought in that they had ascertained that the cavalry seen was a corps of about 600 men, composed of deserters from the French army; and these people, taking advantage of the present state of affairs, have been plundering and levying contributions in all the villages, and even towns, throughout this country—that the inhabitants of Amiens itself are greatly alarmed, and have been anxiously expecting our arrival as their only protection against these brigands—a French population actually hailing the arrival of their English invaders with joy! Not knowing what these desperadoes may attempt, we have doubled our guards. The division is ordered to be on the alert, and patrols are established for the night. I shall undress and enjoy my nice clean bed, nevertheless.

28th.—A fine morning, after a quiet night, notwithstanding the banditti. Marched early to Roye by a cross-road bordered by apple-trees. Here we rejoined the main column, and got upon the chaussée to Paris by Pont St Maxence, etc., a fine broad road as usual, the middle paved (rather roughly) with a summer or unpaved road on each side, the whole bordered by noble elms, and generally a perfectly straight direction: tiresome this from the long vistas which open on one from the summit of every elevation. The country on either hand flat and covered with corn as usual, but had nothing of the wearying sameness of that I so much complained of a day or two ago; for here it was prettily broken by woods and villages, and the distance, instead of terminating with the fringe of apple-trees, presents an interesting range of blue hills. This day's march, however, has not been marked by any occurrence, either of scenery or adventure, worthy of notice. Towards evening, when Lord Edward was about to establish his night-quarters, he directed me to leave the chaussée to take possession of a little place about a quarter of a mile off; and here I am in Mortemer, perhaps one of the most miserable hamlets in all the country. Its short straggling street of poor cottages

we found quite deserted, and they have taken away everything that could be useful to us, leaving only the walls and
roofs. These cottages are built of rough limestone, and the
interiors we have found so filthy and full of vermin, that,
one and all, we have preferred to bivouac in the orchards
ourselves, and have put our horses into the houses; straw
spread under guns and ammunition waggons, with the
painted covers closing them in to windward, forms no
despicable sleeping-place. One of my drivers, rummaging
about, has discovered a vast quantity of excellent household
linen buried under the floor. Several other discoveries of
this sort have been made; but I have strictly forbidden
anything being touched, only leaving these *caches* open that
the natives may know they have not deceived us, but are
beholden to us for our moderation. Had we depended on
Mortemer, we should have gone supperless to bed; but
Mr Coates has been so successful in foraging the neighbourhood, that both man and horse have fared sumptuously.

   29*th*.—Since yesterday the character of the country has
been insensibly changing: country-houses with extensive
gardens and pleasure-grounds, and a more careful style of
architecture, seem to indicate an approach to the capital.
The villages, too, alas! in my estimation, are changed for the
worse—the large thatched farmhouses, barns, etc., and
rural cottages, scattered amongst orchards and verdure,
have given place to regular streets of three-story houses.
Pieces of towns—surely not villages—these! Mortemer
was an exception. The scenery, too, has improved: features more bold and varied, better wooded, and habitations
more numerous. The chain of blue hills seen yesterday
continues to bound the southern horizon. The first village
we passed after leaving Mortemer was almost entirely
composed of respectable houses standing in gardens, and
having lofty iron railings (*grilles*) to the street. I think this
was Cuvilly. Hitchins and I breakfasted as usual, *en
chemin*. We find this a good plan, marching as we do so
early. Each of us has his cold salt-beef and biscuit in his
haversack, and weak grog in his canteen. The troop fairly
started, we drop astern a little, the Doctor produces the
profits of his evening's forage in the shape of hard-boiled
eggs, etc. I have seldom enjoyed anything more than these

ambulatory breakfasts in the cool refreshing air of a calm morning. A cigar always concludes my repast, and prolongs the pleasure of it.

After travelling some distance through the sort of country just spoken of, we again emerged upon a high and open tract of corn, and in a hollow some way in front saw the neat village of Gournay, forming a broad street of clean-looking buff cottages, all, I think, slated. Here we stumbled upon the first traces of our allies the Prussians, who bivouacked (at least some of their corps) last night upon these heights. Of all disgusting objects in the world, there is perhaps none more so than the deserted bivouac—the ground everywhere covered with half-extinguished fires, broken jugs, etc., bits of rags, shreds of uniforms, straw trampled in the miry soil, remnants of food of all sorts, etc. In histories of war and warlike operations, the pomp and glitter and excitement are all that present themselves to our mind's eye, whilst the bivouac, the battle-field encumbered with carnage and misery, the hospital with its heartrending scenes, the plundered cottage, the brutal outrage, and a thousand other disgusting and harrowing episodes, are carefully slurred over if touched upon, but more generally never produced. Up to this moment I have actually not known with what part of the army we have been marching. As far as I could see, we have had an apparently interminable column ahead and astern of us; now, however, I find we are with the advance.

A few paces from the highroad, and in the midst of the bivouac (at the point from whence we obtain sight of Gournay) stood a monument of Republican and Prussian revenge—pitiful revenge!—such as, having enacted, a schoolboy would blush at—the mausoleum of some illustrious lady, whom a long inscription, in the true French style of mawkish sentiment, told us "had been lovely in person and elegant in mind—that, soaring above superstition, she eschewed the folly of laying her bones in *consecrated* ground, choosing rather to lie overshadowed in death by those trees of which she had been so enamoured (*passionné*) whilst living," etc. The monument was a stone pyramid, standing in a small square space enclosed by an embankment, and planted round with acacias. The Prussians had cut down the trees, nearly levelled the embankment, and made a fruitless attempt at destroying the pyramid itself. Descending from this eminence by a long but gradual slope, we entered Gournay after crossing a little stream tumbling from the heights. This certainly is the neatest and cleanest place we have seen in France; pity it is, however, that it stands so bare—scarcely a bush to be seen. I don't know how it happened, but when we reached Gournay we were ahead of almost everybody. About the middle of the long village several well-dressed persons were standing at the door of an auberge, attentively watching our advance. As we approached they hurried forward to meet us, eagerly demanding when the Duke of Wellington would come up. Now I suspected the report which we heard yesterday—of Paris having surrendered to the Prussians, and that Buonaparte had fled—might be true, and that these people were deputies sent to avert the wrath of the conqueror; so, addressing myself to the principal person, a short, square-built, rather pursy man, wearing some decoration, I asked if it were so, and when we might arrive there. My friend, drawing himself up, and affecting an air of contempt, exclaimed aloud, "*Paris se rendre?*—non, monsieur, n'y contez pas! il faut passer sur les corps de 200,000 hommes, avant d'y arriver," at the same time coming close up, and tapping me on the knee, he whispered, "Mais si votre Duc de Vellintone traitera, il tient la bonté à ses pieds, et fera tout ce qui lui plaira." I thanked him for the confidence, told him I knew nothing about the Duke, which made him stare, and rode on.[1]

Leaving Gournay, the country became more pleasing, because more wooded, and the fields generally enclosed by hedges. This style of scenery continued until it brought us to the valley of the Oise, by far the most interesting part of France we had yet seen. How can I describe my feelings when it first opened out before me? How, alas! can I describe the scene itself? But to see and feel it aright one must first have passed over the monotonous melancholy country extending almost uninterruptedly from Nivelles

[1] These people were deputies sent from the Provisional Government to treat with the Duke, but I have never made out yet who he of the decoration might have been.

to the Oise—must have had the retina so imbued with the eternal brown and yellow of that ocean of corn as to see everything of a yellow or jaundiced hue—then he may imagine somewhat of the pleasurable relief with which the eye rested for the first time on the lovely scenery and refreshing verdure of this charming valley. The ground, descending by a gradual slope on our side, ran into a vast succession of most beautiful green meadows, everywhere adorned with magnificent elms, either standing detached, or in groups, or in rows. Beyond these, at about a mile from us, ran the Oise—a broad stream, sometimes exhibiting its sparkling surface nearly on a level with the meadows, at others encased between steep banks of some height. Immediately above the river rose a bold range of hills, thickly wooded from the river-banks to their summit. To the right and left this sort of scenery continued until farther view was shut out by the overlapping hills. The road by which we travelled ran straight as a line across the meadows; and at the point where it appeared to cross the river was a pretty-looking little town, Pont St Maxence, partly on one bank, partly on the other. If we were to be opposed, there I thought is the position in which the French await us, and tough work we shall have of it. These ideas occurred to me as we descended toward the meadows; and as the corps in advance of us approached the town, I momentarily expected to see flashes and smoke issuing from masked batteries in the opposite woods; and it now struck me for the first time as a singular circumstance that cavalry should be allowed to advance alone in the face of such a position, for we had considerably outmarched the infantry. Of course the Duke knew there would be no opposition; and yet it was difficult to imagine what then had become of the French force, which we knew was retiring before us—of the 200,000 men our friend at Gournay had spoken of. No opposition was there. Instead of finding the banks of the Oise garnished with cannon and bristling with bayonets—instead of broken-up roads and inundated fields, woods full of riflemen and the town of grenadiers—instead of all this, we found a peaceable population in a lovely country, labourers in their fields and fishermen on the rivers, whilst flocks and herds pastured in quiet security on the verdant carpet which overspread the plain. The little town of Pont St Maxence looked cheerful and pretty as we approached it, lying partly on one side of the river, partly on the other. The wooded hills rose abruptly over it, the lower part of their slopes interspersed with pretty villas, standing amongst vineyards and in gardens, with terraced walks overhanging the scenery below. After marching all day in a hot sun, what a feeling of coolness and enjoyment was conveyed in the appearance of the large open windows and shady balconies, draperied, with clematis and other elegant creepers, of these sylvan villas! It appears that the bridge had been broken down last year, and never repaired. To do this a detachment of the staff corps was pushed forward either yesterday or early this morning; but when we reached the end of the town they had not yet rendered it passable, and we were ordered to take post in the neighbouring splendid meadows, where, expecting to remain all night, we commenced at once establishing ourselves. Several troops of horse-artillery and some regiments of cavalry were already up, and others of all arms were continually arriving. The horses, un-harnessed and watered, were already feeding, fires were lighted, kettles on, and every one was congratulating himself on having halted on so charming a spot. Thus settled, I strayed into the garden of a neighbouring mill, full of fine currants and cherries, to which the pretty *meunière* not only bade me welcome, but even herself helped me to the best fruit. I was just in the height of enjoyment of the delicious coolness of the fruit, and the piquant badinage of my com-panion, when suddenly the "boot and saddle" re-echoed through the valley, and a confused hum of voices arose simultaneously from every bivouac. With hurried thanks I took leave of my "Maid of the Mill," and hastened back to my people, expecting every moment a fire would open upon us from the opposite woods, having no idea that so sudden an alert could proceed from any other cause than the approach of the enemy.

In a moment our horses were reharnessed, the nosebags with the unconsumed part of their feed attached again to the saddles, officers' baggage replaced on the mules, the kettles, with the half-cooked messes in them, suspended under the carriages, and all was ready to move. Corps after corps filed out of the meadows and took the road to the town; we followed the general movement, which we now learned was occasioned by the coming up of the infantry, who were to occupy the ground we left, whilst the cavalry was to push on beyond the river as long as daylight lasted. Still no word of an enemy.

The broken bridge had been repaired by the staff corps in so temporary a manner, that the very first detachment of hussars who passed deranged it so much as to render it quite unsafe, and we had to dismount at the entrance of the town and wait a full hour ere it was again rendered passable. This bridge, with its right-lined top, was to me an extraordinarily beautiful piece of architecture; and there is a charm in this right-line which I could not have imagined. The little town was all bustle, every auberge crammed with officers enjoying the luxuries of the French cuisine and vintage. At last the bridge was reported safe, and we recommenced our march, regretting the necessity which prevented our seeing more of this lovely place. Immediately on crossing, we turned to the right and pursued a tolerably good road winding about the foot of the wooded heights, which on the one hand rose immediately above us, whilst the silver Oise glided tranquilly along its course on the other. About a mile, or perhaps more, from Pont St Maxence, we quitted the river, and turning up a beautiful ravine, the slopes of which were partly covered with wood, partly with the rich foliage of the vineyards, we pushed into the bosom of the hills, quitting with regret this sweet river. It is impossible to imagine anything more beautiful than this evening's march. The picturesque scenery of the ravine; the clearness and serenity of the sky; the warm colouring thrown over the one side of the ravine by the declining sun opposed to the deep purply tones of the other; the various and varied picturesque military groups reposing on the turf by the wayside, or winding along amongst the vineyards, altogether formed a picture, or rather a succession of pictures, perfectly ravishing. Never shall I forget this evening!

The sun had set some time when we reached the village of Verneuil, which was to be the termination of this day's journey. Seated in the bosom of the hills, now veiled in a purply obscurity, intermingled with that yellowish hazy light always succeeding a warm sunset, the place looked beautiful. Several corps had already halted—some had taken possession of the houses, barns, etc., other bivouacked amongst the vineyards. Immediately about the village were large gardens enclosed by stone walls, and it was some time before I could make up my mind to invade these. There was no alternative, however. We could not remain in the road; the only fields I saw were covered with rich crops of wheat ready for the sickle, and even these could not be approached but through the gardens. The great gates of one of these were immediately forced open, and trampling under foot artichokes, asparagus, etc., and flowers, we reached the field after a struggle through the *eschalots* of an intervening vineyard, which, with the vines and their fruit, were miserably crushed beneath our gun-wheels and horses' feet. I could not but regret this devastation, though it could not be avoided. The wheat shared the fate of the artichokes, and we soon established ourselves on it, surrounded as with a wood by the tall stalks of what was still standing.

What a splendid Rembrandt-like picture presented itself from this spot: the valley buried in hazy obscurity; the whitened dwellings, just made out, scattered over the slopes of the hills, whose bold outlines, one of them crowned by a ruined castle, cut strongly against the glowing but gradually fading tints of the clearest sky. In the farm just by we have found stabling for our own horses and lodging for some of our people. But the evening is so fine that I infinitely prefer the field. Seated on the ground with a lantern by my side, I scribble my notes in comfort; but an attempt has just been made to turn us out even from this humble abode—an officer of hussars with an order from General Grant to quit the ground immediately, as he wants it for his hussars. Good man! he thinks a 9-pounder or its ammunition waggon as easily moved as a hussar and his horse. It proved, however, a mere bugbear—he wanted the house and stables: and his emissary having full power to treat, the affair is amicably arranged by our giving up the stable.

30th.—Fine morning again. Quitted with regret this

lovely country, and climbing the hills by a steep gravelly road, gained the plateau—covered with corn as usual, but here diversified by a pretty sprinkling of trees.   Lieutenant Breton, who slept at the farmhouse last night, gives a bad account of our hussars, who, not content with living at free quarters, completely sacked it this morning before they marched—one of their officers taking away a beautiful pony in spite of the old farmer's entreaties, who begged with tears in his eyes that it might be spared, since it was a pet of the whole family.   The pony, however, marched.

After marching some distance on this plateau by very good gravelly cross-roads, we rejoined the chaussée from Pont St Maxence to Senlis, and soon after began descending towards the latter place, which is separated from the former by this ridge of hills, covered in most parts by the forest of Balatte.   Though not to be compared to Pont St Maxence in point of situation, yet Senlis stands in a pretty country, well wooded, surrounded by fine meadows, watered by the little crystal Nonette.   Just beyond the town, on the Paris side, commences the forest of Pontarme, a continuation of that of Chantilly.   Senlis being the first place of any importance through which we have passed, was of course approached with much interest, and this was heightened by its picturesque appearance: antique walls, pierced by an arched gateway, the summit decayed and irregular, fringed with verdure.   Spires, and lofty houses showing themselves above it, appeared to advantage through the foliage of the trees, which ran scattering and in clumps up to the very gate, through which crowds of peasantry, with little carts and asses laden with the produce of their farms, were passing to the market.   When we passed in our turn, we found the street so thronged that it was with difficulty we could get along, for the market was held in it. The passage of our column, threading its way through the crowd of stalls and baskets of poultry, vegetables, etc., did not seem to excite any very lively emotion, or to interrupt the business of the day.   Some of the more idle, or more curious, left their stalls to get a nearer look at *les Anglais*. Nothing like apprehension was visible even among the women, and the boys were as bold and familiar as usual. Here and there I heard a shout of "Vive le Roi!" once or twice it looked in earnest.   To try the sincerity of this versatile people, I stooped in passing near some of the most vociferous, and in a subdued tone treated them to "Vive l'Empereur!" The result was always the same—staring first at me, then at each other, with a sly expression of countenance, some one of them, slapping me on the thigh, would reply in the same tone, "Mais oui, monsieur, vive l'Empereur—vive Napoleon! C'est bon, monsieur, c'est bon—vive l'Empereur!" seemingly delighted at being able to express their true sentiments. This might have been mere fun, certainly, but I thought them in earnest. I found this the case everywhere. To us they were never backward in avowing their attachment to Buonaparte or their hatred of the Bourbons, of *Louis le Cochon*. The animated scene in the streets prevented me paying much attention to the town. The impression I retain of it is, that it is gloomy and the streets narrow; but that there are many most respectable-looking houses, some of them very prettily situated amongst shrubbery, and particularly one just as we left the town and crossed the Nonette—the long open windows of which enabled us to peep into spacious and handsomely furnished apartments, looking most deliciously cool. Just beyond the town we overtook the rear of the Prussian baggage, escorted by a corps of lancers, whose simple and serviceable costume pleased me much: plain blue frocks, buttoned close up to the throat,[1] and drab trousers or overalls; not a particle of ornament, nor a superfluous article about their appointments. I think they are the most soldier-like looking fellows I have ever seen. This is our first meeting with any of their army since the 18th. Continuing our route through the forest of Pontarme, we soon came out on a more open but still well-wooded country —the chaussée constantly bordered and overshadowed by lofty elms, the cross-roads by apple, pear, and cherry trees, all now loaded with fruit. Here a sudden and disagreeable change took place in the aspect of the towns and villages. We had got on the route of the Prussian army, which was everywhere marked by havoc and desolation. What a

---

[1] The close Prussian collar, now so well known to the British Army, was a novelty to us then : our collars were low, and cut down in front. The cavalry and horse-artillery particularly affected very narrow sloping collars.

contrast! In Senlis, a few miles back, all was peace, plenty, and confidence,—here traces of war in its most horrid form, desolation and desertion. The inhabitants had everywhere fled, and we found naught but empty houses. Troops and their usual followers were the only human beings we saw now. The village of Loures,[1] where we arrived about noon, presented a horrid picture of devastation. A corps of Prussians halted there last night, and, excepting the walls of the houses, have utterly destroyed it. The doors and windows torn out and consumed at the bivouac-fire—a similar fate seems to have befallen furniture of every kind, except a few chairs, and even sofas, which the soldiers had reserved for their own use, and left standing about in the gardens and orchards, or, in some places, had given a parting kick to, for many had fallen forward on the embers of the bivouac-fires, and lay partially consumed. Clothes and household linen, beds, curtains, and carpets, torn to rags, or half-burned, lay scattered about in all directions. The very road was covered with rags, feathers, fragments of broken furniture, earthenware, glass, etc. Large chests of drawers, *armoires*, stood about broken or burned. The very floors had been pulled up and the walls disfigured in every possible way. It were needless to add that no human being was to be seen amidst this desolation. It was with no small pleasure I found we were not to halt amid this disgusting scene, as I expected, but to move on somewhat farther; and with still greater pleasure I received the order to quit the chaussée for the village of Chenevière,[2] about a mile to the left. This removing us out of the Prussian line of march, we hoped to find things somewhat better. The village, like most others we have seen, consisted of a number of farmhouses with their barns and outbuildings, etc., all standing amidst orchards and gardens—the whole surrounded by corn, corn, corn! The place, I should think,

---

[1] This must have been a mistake, for the Duke dates his despatches from Loures on the 30th June, and the headquarters would hardly have been established in a place so utterly destroyed as is here described. Perhaps the place was La Chapelle, which I find in the map. My recollection of the scene here portrayed is quite perfect even now, although not of the name.

[2] This makes it appear that my notes are right, answering with the map as they do.

has not been visited by the Prussians, for no pillage or destruction is to be seen; but it is deserted—not a soul except our soldiers to be seen. Besides our brigade of cavalry, two or three other troops of horse-artillery are here, so that the place is pretty full; and as we are among the latest arrivals, we have not got under cover, but are bivouacking in a very nice orchard, separated from the village street by some large open sheds; but as the weather is fine, and probably from habit, my people have *littered themselves down* as usual under their guns instead of profiting by these—this they are enabled to do very comfortably here, for there is no want of straw. The people, in their retreat, seem to have taken little with them, except their animals, so that we have all kinds of pots and pans, jugs, basins, etc., *ad libitum*. In short, we should be pretty comfortable but for one want, and that a most important one. The weather is dreadfully hot, and we have scarcely any water; there is but one good well in the place, and that has been surrounded by a crowd ever since we arrived. It is impossible to imagine what a gloom this throws over everything: were it not for the abundance of ripe cherries growing along the roadsides (not of the best flavour, but juicy), we must have suffered to-day terribly from thirst in this burnt-up plain. The corn (standing) is almost bleached—it should have been cut long ago.

CHAPTER XVII

July 1st.—Tiresome work this—very! Here we are in Chenevière with little to do but smoke and sleep, or saunter about the hundred yards of street, which is all the place can boast of; and that can hardly be called a street, being formed of stone enclosures or the backs of barns, etc., the dwellings being in the yards. A rivulet once enlivened one end of this street, but now, alas! when most needed, it is not there —the dry bed with a slimy pool or two, still unevaporated, are all that remain to tell the tale of its quondam existence. How melancholy! I scribble *pour passer le temps*. Some good, however, results from this tiresome halt. Marching at or before daybreak, and not halting until dusk, our shoeing was in a bad state, which Farrier Price and his myrmidons are now busy remedying. The forge is established on the bank of the *ci-devant* rivulet in the rear of our orchard, and under two or three spreading elms. As it is on the edge also of the corn, we have been on the eve of consummating the ruin of the poor fugitive *habitans*, for it has been once or twice on fire. Another piece of service the halt has rendered, is the allowing Hincks with the guns and carriages left at Waterloo to overtake us. He brings also a remount of tolerably good horses, though rather fatigued, since he has made tremendous marches to overtake us. These arrive most opportunely; for with all care we have a number of galled backs and shoulders, though in this respect we are not half so bad as the cavalry, amongst whole squadrons of whom there is scarcely a sound horse.

Another reinforcement has just joined us. That beautiful but unfortunate regiment the Cumberland hussars has been broken up for its retrograde movement on the 18th ultimo, and distributed amongst the different corps, to be employed as forage escorts, etc., for the commissaries. Being all gentlemen in Hanover, it is easy to imagine they are rather

irate at this degradation.   A corporal and four privates have
joined us.   They are all amazingly sulky and snappish with
every one, forgetting that neither I nor Mr Coates, nor any
of our people, have anything to do with their disgrace.   They
come, however, very opportunely, since for the last day or
two Mr Coates has been resisted by the peasantry, and only
this morning several shots were fired at him and his convoy
of forage from a wood near which he was obliged to pass.
In general, during the above period, he has been obliged
to help himself from the barns and granaries, having found
every place deserted.

Lord Edward ordered a sale to-day of the effects of the
slain.   This occasioned a little stir in the village, and passed
away an hour or two.   I have purchased a good large cloak,
erst the property of poor Colonel Fuller of the 1st Dragoon
Guards.   Things sold well in general.

From the front we heard (I don't know how) that the French
army are in position at Montmartre, where they intend to
fight us again.   If they are beaten—of which we entertain no
doubt—the fate of Paris is certain; every one fully expects
it will be plundered and burned, and thus my prediction
verified, the campaign ending with a *grand embrassement*, as
I have already written down!   There is some firing just
begun in front.   The Prussians commencing, no doubt!

July 2d.—Having no candles last night, could not write
up as usual, but was forced to sit in the dark smoking our
cigars and listening to the incessant firing in front.   This
morning is beautiful again, but terribly hot.   The latter
part of yesterday evening we passed on the tiptoe of expectation, for the firing became constantly heavier and more
distinct; that a battle was fighting could not be mistaken.
Lieutenant Bell, our adjutant, came to tell me my troop was
for the reserve.   He also told us that many messages had
passed between the Duke and the French authorities.
Anxiously we gazed across the top of the waving corn,
hoping every moment to see the messenger bringing orders
for our advance.   Twilight began to shorten our ken, and
still the cannonade continued without intermission.   At
last an orderly dragoon did come, but he brought an order
for the rocket troop only to advance, whilst we were to be
saddled and ready to move at a moment's notice.   The

rockets soon moved, and our bivouac became more gloomy than ever. Fatigued more from excitement than anything else, I lay down at a late hour to sleep; but though I slept I did not rest—feverish dreams of Paris in flames; of plundering, mutinous soldiers and all sorts of horrors; so that I could hardly believe my eyes and ears when I awoke this morning at three o'clock and looked round me. The orchard presented a scene of the most perfect tranquillity; the firing had ceased; my people, ensconced in the straw, their blankets drawn over them, lay quietly sleeping under their guns; no sound broke the silence of this most delicious summer morning save the jingling of our horses' collar-chains, and the sweet songs of birds, with which the trees were filled. I could scarcely credit the agitation of yesterday evening—it all seemed part of my dream. By degrees our village was all alive; and as the morning advanced, so has our excitement, for the cannonade in front has recommenced. Evening approaches again; the firing has lasted all day without intermission; and yet here we are, doing nothing, or worse, for both our horses and ourselves are drying up with thirst. We cannot stay here much longer, for our only well is almost exhausted.

July 3*d.*—Fine and hot morning. Yesterday morning I awoke and found myself under the trees of a thick orchard; this morning I am lying amongst artichokes, and the Lord knows what, upon a soil somewhat like that one sees about Hammersmith, and, instead of the warbling of birds, the air is filled with the hum of a multitude and the monotonous beating of a water-mill close at hand, which has never ceased its "thump, thump, thump, thump" all the livelong night, the quartermaster of some regiment having been placed in it with a detachment to grind corn for us all. Yesterday evening, near sunset, an order arrived for all the artillery at Chenevière to move to the front, but that the cavalry should remain, which puzzled us a little. Accordingly we marched forthwith in company with Major Bull's troop; but I saw nothing of the others, for we were all left to march independently. The order was scrawled out on a scrap of dirty paper and hardly legible, so that neither Bull nor I could make it out perfectly, and were consequently in some doubt as to the exact point to march upon, although in none about going forward in the direction of the cannonade. Instead of returning to the chaussée by the way we came,[1] as I believe the other troops did (they were not so quickly ready as we were), Bull and I took a road which appeared to lead straight to the front. The country we marched through, though perfectly flat, was still interesting:—one vast expanse of golden wheat, divided as it were into beautiful fields by the crossing of numerous roads, all bordered by two, or even four rows of most magnificent elms. A few vineyards, with here and there a village, diversified very agreeably this scenery. For a time we seemed to approach the field of battle—the firing became more distinct; and at times we saw, or thought we saw, the slate-coloured smoke rising over the tufted tops of the elms. By and by it drew off more to the right, and insensibly became less intense, though still kept up with great vigour. Notwithstanding some little anxiety as to the correctness of our route, and an impatience to arrive on the field of action, still I could not be insensible to the beauty of the noble avenues, umbrageous and cool, along which we marched. They are at all times superb, but became exquisite when seen as we saw them, illumined by the blaze of a cloudless sunset. At a place called Vauderlan we rejoined the chaussée, and had marched little beyond when I observed Bull's troop, which was ahead, suddenly come to a halt at a point where another chaussée came in from the left. What was my surprise, on riding forward, when Bull told me we had run in upon the French outposts: and sure enough, not far in front of us, a long line of vedettes extended across the fields to a village—Blanc Menil, with its white houses and white garden-walls—about a mile on our left; and to our right were lost behind the little woods with which that part of the country was covered. In rear of the vedettes, on the chaussée, was an intrenchment, with an abatis in front of it; beyond was another village;[2] and to the right the lofty spires of St Denis, towering above the woods, showed us that we were nearer that place than we had expected.

What was to be done in this dilemma? Two troops of

---

[1] We did this to be enabled to march more expeditiously and freely, observing this road to be quite clear of troops.

[2] Bourget.

horse-artillery, totally unsupported, within musket-shot of
the enemy's lines! During our march we had not fallen in
with a single corps, and every house was deserted, so that we
had no opportunity of gaining information. I had relied
on Bull's experience, which, however, in this instance, was
at fault. We both agreed as to the necessity of a retreat;
as also that we ought to betray no hurry and confusion in so
doing. The French pickets and those within the intrenchment were evidently watching us very attentively, but made
no move, nor did we for a short time. Whilst thus hesitating, a few of the staff corps made their appearance in the
fields on our right, and from them we were rejoiced to learn
our neighbourhood to the main body, which occupied all
the country in that direction; the staff corps being on the
extreme left in the village of Dugny, which, though close at
hand, was hid from us among the trees. This accounted
at once for the inactivity of the enemy; so, reversing, we
followed a miserable cross-road through some low swampy
ground to Dugny, where the officers of the staff corps succeeded in deciphering our ticket, and gave us directions
for finding Garges, the place mentioned. The infantry
must have advanced whilst we halted at Chenevière, for
these people appeared settled in their quarters. The route
pointed out led us for about half a mile between meadows
surrounded with high trees and intermingled with little
thickets; then, after crossing a small muddy rivulet, we
debouched upon more open ground, and a most interesting
scene burst upon us. On our left, and very near, the Abbey
of St Denis with its elegant spires reared its venerable form
above the intervening thick masses of foliage, formed by the
converging of several chaussées with their noble bordering
of elms, to a point near the town. Beyond, in the distance,
appeared the heights of Montmartre, with its telegraph and
numerous windmills and chalky cliffs; a narrow gap, through
which was seen the dome of St Genevieve, separated them
from the heights of Belleville, where a succession of the same
sort of white cliffs encouraged the idea of a gap having here
been broken through the range of heights, leaving Montmartre an isolated mass. Through this gap we obtained
the first view of Paris, and the heights were everywhere gay
with white buildings, gardens, shrubberies, etc.

To our right the ground ascended by a gentle slope to the village of Garges, whose numerous villas and summer-houses (kiosks), intermingled with shrubberies yet illuminated by the warm mellow light of the western sky, crowned the summit; whilst the intervening space presented one vast bivouac alive with men and animals, and all busy with preparations for passing the night. This ground a day or two ago was covered with the most luxuriant crops of flowers, fruits, vegetables, and some corn—now all trampled under foot; in like manner the chaussée descending from the village had been bordered with fine trees—now lying prostrate in the form of an abatis a little to our left. In our front the dense foliage and rounded summits of the trees in the Park of Stains cut strongly against the yellow sky of the west. It was certainly an animating, interesting scene. Here at length was assembled the advanced-guard of our victorious army, in full view of the devoted, fickle, guilty city—of that city which, in the days of her prosperity, arrogated to herself the empire of the world; that city which for years—nay, for our whole life—had been the great centre of our most intense interest; that city which both historical and romantic reading had rendered perfectly classical, and over which the long exclusion of Englishmen from the Continent had drawn a veil of mystery, rendering her doubly interesting. There she lay, as it were, prostrate at our feet, awaiting in breathless anxiety the fiat of her conqueror.

The firing had now become very indistinct, and ceased to occupy our attention, for here we found the troops quietly establishing themselves, and no appearance whatever of any fighting. There, to be sure, was the intrenchment and abatis similar to that we had seen near Bourget; and there were the French vedettes extending across the plain and those of our Rifles opposite them; but all remained peaceable and quiet. The troops in bivouac presented in the twilight many a picturesque group as we marched along, none more so than a corps of Brunswick lancers, with their sombre uniforms and drooping black plumes—the horses, all saddled, picketed in a line, and in rear of them the lances stuck upright in the ground. The dark mustachioed visages of these men completed the colouring of the picture. Amongst these I met some old acquaintances, who were lounging at the roadside to see us pass. They were all elated and eager for the morrow, which they confidently expected would see Paris delivered up to the punishment she deserved. Leaving them, we turned to the right up the treeless chaussée and soon reached Garges, which we found principally occupied by our artillery; but here the scene we passed through greatly cooled the excitement caused by our march through the bivouacs. The village, or town I should call it, is composed of one long and broad street of good houses— generally, I fancy, the country residences of the Parisian cockneys. These have all been gutted and disfigured in the same manner as at Loures: torn carpets and paperhangings, broken furniture and glass, and even pianofortes, encumbered the streets in all directions. Inhabitants there were none—not a cat remained in the place; and our soldiers and their horses were the only living animals to be seen. The sight of this devastation cast an inexpressible gloom over me; and I shall never forget the sickening sensation I experienced whilst traversing the street of Garges in search of some unoccupied garden in which we might establish ourselves for the night. All the best houses and gardens were already occupied; so, after marching through the whole place, on arriving at the end of it we were obliged to content ourselves with a great unsheltered market-garden, close to a muddy sluggish rivulet; and here we are, Hitchins and I, sitting amongst potatoes and artichokes. This fine rich soil does not make the most agreeable parlour-floor. In short, contrasting our position with that of our other troops, we think we have a right to grumble. Every one that I looked in upon on my search had a house and offices more or less convenient (shells, to be sure), and the troop-horses and men who could not be accommodated under cover found themselves almost equally well off amongst the *allées*, *berceaux*, and shrubberies of the gardens. On the contrary, we have a damp location; no shelter of any kind higher than an artichoke, or, much the same thing, a vine. There is a well on the premises, certainly, but the water is so brackish that it is not drinkable; and that of the neighbouring rivulet, naturally foul, is now so impregnated with soapsuds, from the multitudes of washermen and washerwomen at work in it, that we are at a loss how to water our horses, for they won't touch it. Bell (our adjutant) has just found us out, and communicated an order to remain harnessed and ready for an alert, as it is expected the enemy will attempt something during the night. The firing which we have heard these two days has proceeded from the Prussians having attempted to force the French lines; but they met with a more determined opposition than they expected, and kept fighting their way round to the right to a place called Argenteuil,[1] where, throwing a bridge over the Seine, they have crossed that river, and Bell says are at this moment in possession of St Cloud. So that Paris is, in a manner, invested.

July 4th.—Last night passed very tranquilly; and, *malgré* our position, I never enjoyed a sounder sleep or woke more refreshed. If the French intended an attack, they thought better of it, and let us sleep quietly. We have had some visitors already this morning from some of the neighbouring bivouacs. They tell us the Prussians are reported to have lost 15,000 men in the last three or four days' fighting, and, what is more interesting, that the Duke, *en grande tenue*, and followed by a numerous retinue, also in their smartest uniforms, has just galloped down toward St Denis—that a rumour of negotiations is afloat, and not a word about advancing. Pretty mess, then, we are in. If this be true, we may stay in this mud-hole for a week yet. Fortunately for us, Dynely, who occupies a very fine house and garden a little way up the street, has a most abundant well of excellent water, to which he has given my people free access, although he guards it most jealously from everybody else. My poor horses suffered last night in getting no drink after their hot march.

7 p.m.—I have already got some little confusion in my notes from not writing them at once, therefore must jot down to-day whilst daylight enough yet remains to do so. *Imprimis*, then: This has been a completely idle day; very fine, very hot, and very dusty. Having nothing else to do, I have amused myself with rambling about the place, smoking a cigar here and a cigar there, etc. etc. Bull was

---

[1] Mistake. They passed at St Germain on the 30th June, and were in position between Plessis Picquet and St Cloud, with reserve at Versailles, on 2d July.—See Duke's despatch.

more fortunate than we were last night—he stumbled upon a most excellent bivouac, which I paid my first visit to this morning, as it is not far up the street.   The place is said to belong to the Prince of Eckmuhl (Davoust), and must have been a delightful residence; it is now *tout à fait abîmé*.   The pleasure-grounds and gardens, laid out in the English style, are quite delicious, not only from the lovely shady walks and prettily disposed shrubberies, but also from the splendid terraces, and the views they command of Paris and the neighbourhood.   Bull's guns, etc., are parked amongst parterres of the choicest and rarest flowers: the *berceaux* and shady walks form excellent stables, and there his horses are picketed.   The officers occupy a charming kiosk, partly embosomed in wood, but open to the extensive view over the country toward Paris.   Here I found some of them sleeping on the floor, whilst the vacant blankets of others marked the spot they had chosen as their own.

The house itself, large and magnificent, had already been completely pillaged.   The doors and windows, where not torn from their frames, were all flying open; furniture of every kind, broken to pieces, and partly thrown out into the garden or courts, and partly littering the rooms; pier-glasses of immense size shivered to atoms; the very walls defaced and smeared with every species of filth.   A few of the rooms had escaped this species of pollution, and, except the destruction of their furniture, remained in pretty good order.   One of these (which I wondered at) was very handsome, of fine proportions, well lighted, and the walls exquisitely painted (*not stamped*), to represent an Oriental landscape through the open sides of the room, the roof being supported on pillars, which stood so strongly forward that, at the first *coup d'œil*, the illusion was complete.   Unless this were saved by the interposition of some officer—a man of taste— I much marvel at the barbarians leaving it untouched; perhaps whilst I write the destruction is accomplished, for I left numbers of Dutch, Nassau, and Belgian gentry wandering about on the hunt for plunder.[1]   A large room adjoining

---

[1] Several regiments from America marched through Garges this evening, and took up their station in front—fine corps of veterans, all having served in the Peninsula, and subsequently in America.   Many a cheer from old comrades greeted their arrival.   It was a soul-stirring sight, the proud march of these well-tried troops into our camp.

was hung round with very fine prints from Vernet's paintings of the French ports, all in rich frames. These, by some miracle, had all escaped destruction, though not one article of furniture was left. My friend Hitchins, an amateur, thought it a pity they should be left for destruction, and appropriated the whole of them, and not only them, but some fine paintings which he found elsewhere, and cut out of their frames with his penknife. This certainly is not justifiable, but his argument is a specious one—better save them at any rate than leave them to be destroyed by the Belgians. At the back of the house, on the same floor, had been a handsome library, but here as elsewhere the genius of destruction had been busy. The furniture was broken to pieces, the books pulled from their shelves, scattered over the floor, many of them torn to pieces, and many, thrown out of the windows, lying in heaps on the pavement of the court below. The foreigners were not the only busy people in Garges—our own troops were not idle. Leathes' servant in this very house has found a magnificent work in three folio volumes, splendidly bound—a series of views of the principal buildings and scenery in France, in the best style of line-engraving. This appears to have been considered the greatest treasure in the library, being the only work attempted to be hidden. He found it under a cask in the wine-cellar, where he had no business. In the gardens and shrubberies the foreign troops were searching for plunder very systematically. Armed with watering-pots, they proceeded regularly over the ground, watering as they went, and whenever the moisture was quickly absorbed, dug. In this manner I understand they have already found many valuable things—certes, whilst I was at this chateau they found a batch of very fine wine buried under a flower-bed. Our men are not so indefatigable; they certainly take what they want when it presents itself, but do not give themselves much trouble in hunting things up. A party of Dutch (Protestants) broke into the church this morning, and after amusing themselves for a time with dressing themselves in the priests' garments, etc., and turning into ridicule the Roman Catholic ceremonies, finished by breaking to pieces the altar and destroying everything they found in the church or vestry. Our allies are by no means an amiable set, nor very cordial with us. If an English corps (as Bull's troop) occupy a chateau and its grounds, still they leave free ingress and egress to any others so long as they do not interfere with them. On the contrary, a single Dutch, Nassau, or Belge, will sometimes (if a commanding officer) occupy a whole place himself: sentinels are placed at every gate, and the place strictly tabooed. They are a brutal set. The Dutch appear the best. They are all uncommonly insolent to us.

July 5th.—Our conjectures as to the business which took the Duke to St Denis yesterday prove to be correct. It is rumoured this morning that the preliminaries of peace are signed, and that the *war is at an end !* So terminates, then, our campaign—short, but active, brilliant, and honourable to all concerned. Another fine but hot day.

This morning rode to Gonesse, the headquarters, through a country no doubt pretty enough before our arrival, but in which armed men now occupy the place of vines and fig-trees, etc.—in short, one continued bivouac. Arnouvilles, through which I passed, is a pretty village, and, although the houses were filled with soldiers, did not seem to have suffered like many other places, especially that unfortunate Garges. Four short but well-built and clean streets branch off from a pretty circus, the area of which is a nice smooth turf planted round with young elms. The shrubberies and pleasure-grounds of the Archbishop of ———— (I forget who), all untouched and in good order, added to the pleasing appearance of the place, forming, as it did, such a contrast with the desolate state of the surrounding country. Louis XVIII. occupies the palace, and his Suisses, Gardes du Corps, etc., the village. Gonesse is a nasty, dirty, gloomy place, and I made little stay there after getting my English letters. My garden begins already to be *home*, spite of its *dés-agrémens.*

July 6th.—All quiet; not a word about moving. Hitchins and I were both very ill last night after drinking some coffee. This we had brought with us, and therefore it was good : the horrible water here must have caused our illness. Passed the whole morning in idling about the street. There is a very pretty house with (apparently) delicious gardens at the upper end of the town; but some Dutch colonel has got possession, and his sentry turned me from the gate rather

rudely. This evening the Doctor and I rode down to St
Denis to see the lions. The French outposts had been withdrawn and their barricade removed, so that nothing impeded
our progress until we arrived at the entrance of the town,
and had a glimpse of the long dusky perspective of its
principal street; but here we found an English guard, whose
orders were to permit no one (officer or soldier) to enter the
place. This was somewhat of a disappointment, but we
must see it soon. Just at the entrance to the town is a very
fine barrack of grey stone, with a spacious parade, separated
from the road by a handsome *grille* or iron railing. The
little muddy rivulet which runs through Garges and Dugny
crosses the road, just by the entrance, into St Denis, and
then falls into the Seine. This feature had been taken
advantage of in the intended military defence: the bridge
removed and a battery constructed with earth and casks
quite across the road. The approach to St Denis on this
side is very fine; for at a short distance from this battery
three chaussées converge to a point, and a more magnificent
coup d'œil cannot be conceived than that which presents itself
to a person placing himself at the point of union, which at
once commands three splendid avenues of the finest elms
joining overhead and forming so many lofty arches. From
Garges to this point our bivouacs extend; and the rich
harvest of wheat which had covered the adjacent fields is
completely trodden down. Just by the *etoile* formed by
the meeting of the roads, we found Dick Jones encamped
with his corps (about 500) of Flemish waggoners with their
horses and waggons—a motley and not unpicturesque crew,
with their blue smock-frocks and *bonnets de nuit*, wooden
shoes, etc., as they sat in groups cooking, or smoking their
short pipes. As it was yet early, we did not relish returning
immediately to Garges and therefore made a detour to the
left through the vineyards, plantations of artichokes, rose-
bushes, etc. It was quite refreshing to find this part of
the country untouched, everything uninjured and thriving.
But there were no vine-dressers, no inhabitants of any kind
—not a soul; field and houses all alike deserted. Philoso-
phising as we went on the horrors of war and the beauty
of the scenery we were passing through, which contrasted
so strongly with that about Garges and every other place

where the army halted, we rather unexpectedly entered a pretty village—that is, it had been once so; now devastation had visited it, and the forlorn deserted street was everywhere encumbered as usual with broken glass and fragments of furniture, etc.; every window in the place was destroyed. In front of the church was a small open space, whence a handsome lodge and *grille* gave a view of a long avenue terminated by a chateau. In this place about twenty or thirty hussar horses were standing linked together under charge of one hussar. I believe these people were Prussians, but I can't say. From this man we learned that his comrades were at the chateau, and thither we went, curious to ascertain what they did there. We were certainly not quite so much shocked at the scene of ruin and havoc which presented itself as we went down the avenue as we should have been a week ago; they are becoming familiar now. The fragments of sofas, chairs, tables, etc., lying about the grass, bespoke a richly furnished house, and the nearer we drew to the house the thicker became these signs of vengeance. Large pieces of painted paper torn from the walls, remnants of superb silk window-curtains, with their deep rich fringe, hung amongst the bushes; broken mirrors and costly lustres covered the ground in such a manner as to render it difficult to avoid hurting our horses' feet—the brilliant drops of these last, scattered amongst the grass, might, with a little stretch of imagination, have induced us to believe ourselves traversing Sinbad's valley of diamonds; slabs of the rarest marble, torn from the chimney-pieces, lay shattered to atoms; even the beds had been ripped open, and the contents given to the winds, and conveyed by them to all parts of the park, covering in some places the ground like newly fallen snow. The trees of the avenue were cut and hacked, and large patches of bark torn off—many were blackened and scorched by fires made at the foot of them, with the mahogany furniture for fuel; the shrubs cut down or torn up by the roots; the very turf itself turned up or trampled into mud by the feet of men and horses. Hitchins and I dismounted at the grand entrance into the house; and, by way of securing our horses, shut them up in a little room to which a door was still left, and proceeded to inspect the interior of this once splendid mansion. Shouts and laughter resounded through

the building. The hussars were busy completing the work
of destruction; and as we passed the magnificent stairs
leading up from the hall, we narrowly escaped being crushed
under a large mirror which these gentlemen at that very
moment launched over the banisters above with loud cheers.
The ground-floor on the side fronting the park consisted
of a suite of magnificent rooms, lofty, finely proportioned,
and lighted by a profusion (as we should deem it) of windows
down to the floor. These had been most luxuriously and
richly furnished; now they were empty, the papering
hanging in rags from the walls, and even the cornices
destroyed more or less. Every kind of abuse of France and
the French was written on the walls. In one room was the
remnant of a grand piano. The sad reflections awakened
by this sight may be more easily conceived than described,
and I turned from it with a sickening and overwhelming
sensation of disgust, in which I am sure Hitchins fully
participated. The next room seemed to have been chosen
as the place of execution of all the porcelain in the house,
which had there been collected for a grand smash. The
handsomest Sèvres and Dresden vases, tea and dinner
services, formed heaps of fragments all over the floor, and
a large porcelain stove had shared the same fate. Another
room had been lined with mirrors from the ceiling to the
floor; it appeared these had been made targets of, for many
were the marks of pistol-balls on the walls they had covered;
little remained of these except some parts of their rich gilt
frames. The last room of the suite had the end farthest
from the windows semicircular, and this end had been fitted
up with benches, *en amphithéatre*. The whole of this room
was painted to represent the interior of a forest, and on one
side was a pool of water, in which several naked nymphs
were amusing themselves. The plaster was torn down in
large patches, and the nymphs stabbed all over with bayonets.
The upper floor consisted of bedrooms, dressing-rooms, and
baths, and exhibited the same melancholy destruction as
those below; even the leaden lining of the baths, the leaden
water-pipes, etc., were cut to pieces. On inquiring of one
hussar why they so particularly wreaked their vengeance
on this house, he said because it belonged to Jerome Buonaparte, whom every German detested. Having seen enough

here, we looked into another chateau somewhat smaller, but which had also been something very fine; it was precisely in the same state. A very fine library had been here, but the books had been thrown out of window; a small pond below had received multitudes of them, and the rest were scattered all over the park. In the pond I saw several beautiful Oriental MSS., and I fished out a pretty little edition of Seneca, which I pocketed. Disgusted, we returned to our garden, which, by the by, begins to look rather the worse for wear, and I hope if we stay any longer we may be able to get into some house.

July 7th.—Fine hot day. Since early morning the road from Paris has been crowded with people of all ages, sexes, and conditions flocking to Arnouvilles to greet their *beloved monarch.* The whole population seems to have turned out, so continuous is the stream. Berlines, caleches, equestrians, and pedestrians, flow along without cessation or diminution of numbers. All are in their *habits de Dimanche*, and all gay and merry. It is a perfect holiday, which all seem to enjoy without alloy. I could scarcely persuade myself that the gay throng passing before me was the same that, after being accustomed for a quarter of a century to look upon themselves as invincible, then twice within a twelvemonth saw themselves humbled to the dust, and those whom they had so long been accustomed to trample on in military possession of their capital, who now were hastening to do homage to the family twice driven from their throne—and who, in traversing the bivouac of their conquerors, saw on all sides the wreck and ruin of their own houses, fields, and gardens;—yet, nothing daunted, on they went, laughing, chatting, and even singing, in the gayest of all possible moods. For them it was a *jour de fête*, which they seemed determined to enjoy, no matter what its origin. The smart dresses and lively colour contrasted strongly with the dingy clothing, hardy embrowned visages, and apathetic demeanour of our soldiery, who lounged at the roadside, amused by the passing crowd. There were the members of the Legislative Assembly in their embroidered uniforms, some in carriages, some on horseback, others walking and looking dignified; near them, perhaps, a group of pretty brunettes, with brilliant black eyes and coquettishly arranged *cornetts.* Then comes a

National Guardsman with his blue and red uniform, with white breeches and *brown-topped boots*, strutting along most consequentially, a handkerchief in hand, which ever and anon he applies to wipe away the dust from his fair face. High and low, rich and poor, jostle along together; and not the least remarkable amongst them is the *limonadier*, in his light cotton jacket and cocked-hat. On his back is suspended a tall machine of lustrous tin or some such metal, picked out with brass. Its shape is that of a Chinese pagoda, and from the lower part of it two long slender leaden pipes, terminating in brass cocks, lead round under his right arm. *Chemin faisant*, the tumblers which he carries in his left hand are filled from one or other cock as may be called for, and handed to his fellow-travellers. One cock furnishes lemonade, but of the produce of the other I am ignorant— perhaps a light beer, for the French seem fond of such thin drinks, although the constant repetition of the words "*Eau de vie*" (sometimes "*Au de vis*") indicates that they are not altogether averse to something more stimulating. In the afternoon I mounted Cossack and joined the throng. There was no choice but to go at their pace, so completely filled was the road. The easy, natural, good humoured manner in which my companions, right and left, chatted and laughed with me, left no room to feel one's self a foreigner, much less an enemy. We were all "*hail fellow well met.*" Occasional openings allowed me from time to time to push on, and thus change my company. There was, however, no difference between them in one respect—I always found my new friends just as chatty and good-humoured as those left behind.

At Arnouvilles, still following the stream, I was swept into the palace gardens, and found myself in the midst of a most gay *fête-champêtre*. All had come provided with a little basket, or something of the sort, and now, seated round a clean white cloth spread on the grass, numerous parties were enjoying at once the coolness and fragrance under the shade of fine trees or thickets of acacias, laburnums, syringas, etc. etc. Merry laughter, and an occasional "Vive le Roi!" resounded on all sides, and was from time to time responded to more loudly by the crowd assembled without, all anxious to get a sight of their *new old* King. I longed to try the same experiment as at Senlis, but did not dare.[1] Handsome young men of the Garde de Corps, in their classical helmets and brilliant uniforms, were strolling along the gravel-walk, their countenances radiant with joy.   I could not but sympathise with them in thus returning into the bosom of their country, and again meeting with those dearest to them after an absence which, though short, had at its commencement promised a most hopeless duration.   Indeed, I did witness more than one tender recognition and affectionate embrace.   In the palace his majesty was holding a levee, which, judging from the numbers crowding in, must have been very fatiguing work.   Whilst strolling about amidst this scene of festivity, the sharp notes of a trumpet recalled me to the palace, where I found all bustle.   It was the *boutselle* that had sounded, and the Garde de Corps was already formed on parade to accompany the advance of the royal cortège.   As I wished to see this, and had as yet not dined, I returned forthwith to Garges, which a diminution of the throng fortunately allowed me to do speedily, and having got my dinner, regained the highroad (which crosses at the higher end of our village) just as the cortège and crowd came up.   First marched the Garde de Corps, resplendent with steel and silver; then came the Garde Suisse, about two hundred as handsome young men as can well be imagined, and such as I never before saw in one body—tall, straight, even genteel figures.   They owed nothing to their dress, which was shabby in the extreme—old threadbare frock-coats, once blue, now of any colour, and sufficiently ragged; trousers to match, and mean misshapen forage-caps; arms and accoutrements all wanting—to be sure, some of them carried sticks; knapsacks of long-haired goatskins, once white, but now of a reddish-yellow hue.   To these succeeded five or six 4-pounders, in style and equipment a fitting match for such soldiers, who, I should have added, marched along very dejectedly, as if ashamed of their mean appearance. The guns were drawn by little ragged farmers' horses with their own common harness, driven by the *cultivateur* himself

---

[1] Amongst these parties some were of the *haut-ton*, and I saw many very elegant women.   Indeed, amongst the bourgeoise there was no lack of beauty, and in manner much to admire, since they infinitely surpass our countrywomen of the same class in gracefulness of carriage and gentility of address.

in his smock-frock, nightcap, and sabots; carriages, deplor-
ably in want of paint, and further disguised by Belgic mud
still adhering to them, were loaded (limbers, trails, and all)
with women, children, and bundles; a few old cannoneers,
quite in keeping with all the rest, walked beside the wheels;
—the whole corps more fit to march through Coventry than
to accompany the triumphal entry of a monarch into his
capital, and that eminently military. The royal carriages,
drawn by post-horses, came next, and in outward appearance
were little better than those of his majesty's guns. Louis
was in the last carriage, and a dense cloud of pedestrians,
with a plentiful admixture of British officers on horseback,
closed the procession. I accompanied the throng as far as
St Denis, which took up a considerable time, since its movements were necessarily slow. No complimentary movement was made by our troops, although his majesty passed
through the midst of us. The more curious crowded to the
roadside, which was lined by them, but all in their fatigue-
jackets, or even without any—but numbers remained at their
occupations, or sitting smoking at a distance. The brigade of
Highlanders alone cheered as the King passed through their
bivouac. Why was this? Is there any connection between
this and the protection afforded the Stuarts by the Bourbon
family? Certain it is that the Highlanders alone cheered!
The entrance to St Denis was almost impossible, such was the
multitude choking up the street, peasantry as well as citizens;
and, as the royal carriages approached, they made the air ring
with their shouts of "Vive le Roi!" "Vivent les Bourbons!"
Only a short month ago, perhaps, these same people, and on
this very spot, had shouted as lustily, "Vive l'Empereur!"
"Vive Napoleon!" "A bas les Bourbons!" etc. etc. I never
felt prouder of being an Englishman! From Garges to St
Denis I kept close to the royal carriage, watching the countenance of his majesty in order to detect any emotion. He
betrayed none. It was calm, serious, and unvarying in general,
occasionally illumined by a faint smile as he returned saluta-
tions, but the smile was evanescent—very—and the features
immediately resumed their calmness. Our troops seemed to
attract considerable interest, particularly the Highlanders;
and to every English officer he paid most marked attention,
returning their salutes with eagerness and punctilio.

CHAPTER XVIII

July 8th.—Here I am in heaven, as it were—in *Colombes*!—in a *perfect paradise!* More of that hereafter. I am sitting scribbling at last in a handsome room, all to myself! But to begin at the beginning. This morning was (as usual of late) very fine and very hot. At an early hour we received orders to hold ourselves in readiness to march, and understood that we were about to move on the Loire, where the French army had mustered in force and refused to acknowledge the capitulation. Hitchins and I had just found a very pretty little house vacant near our bivouac, and little damaged. Into this we proposed getting to-day, and were rather disappointed when the order for moving came. It was no small comfort, however, to escape from Garges and all its horrors of plundered houses and bad water. The filth of the bivouac, from such long occupation, was becoming intolerable, and the water, bad as it was, was failing fast.

Being sufficiently occupied, I did not notice at what hour we marched, but it must not have been late; for, notwithstanding delays, we arrived here early in the afternoon—the distance probably six or seven English miles. A column of cavalry, composed of our brigade and some other regiments of heavy dragoons, preceded us, and all together took the road to St Denis. Arrived at the point of junction of the three chaussées, instead of marching through the town we struck off to the right. This was not the road to the Loire, and we were puzzled. Wherever we were going the road was beautiful, and the cool shade of the green vault under which we marched peculiarly agreeable in so hot a day. All the country right and left was like a garden; laid out in little square plots of vegetables or roses, an astonishing quantity of which flower is grown in this neighbourhood. Passing through the pretty village of Epinay on the banks of the Seine, we soon after came to a singular ridge of chalky hills separating the road on which we marched from the river. Here then we quitted the chaussée for a cross-road skirting those hills on the side next the river, which we now understood was to be crossed by a pontoon bridge thrown across a little lower down.

Quitting the delicious shade of the elms for the open fields, and these lying on a southern slope, the heat was intense, and when, getting between vines and fig-trees (of which we found whole fields here), the little air there was became shut out from us, it was quite suffocating. The ripe, cool, juicy figs with which the trees were loaded, relieved us, however; the poor fellows placed to watch these looked on rather piteously, but we committed no waste nor destruction beyond eating a few as we went along. These were the first peasantry we had found in the fields since passing Senlis. All along our route dead horses in abundance poisoned the air, and marked the line of operations of Blucher's army. The bridge was at Argenteuil, another pretty village; but on arriving there we found so many corps to pass before us, that, having got into a shady spot, we dismounted and disposed ourselves to rest. The Seine here appeared to me such another river as the Thames at Vauxhall Bridge. The ground on our side sloped rapidly down to it; on the other the banks were low and rushy, an extent of flat meadow-land lay beyond, and thence arose gently swelling hills, covered with shrubberies, villages, villas, etc. The scenery was animated by the masses of our troops and the novelty of the pontoon bridge, together with the interest excited by a number of women and pretty girls who brought us in abundance (for sale) flowers and very fine cherries.

What a change from the sickening, desolated, deserted country we have left, where everything breathed war! Suddenly we enter a land of peace, plenty, and happiness, fields covered with luxuriant crops of various kinds of vegetables, amongst which the large, dark-tinted leaves of the artichoke predominate; vines, figs, and myriads of roses are extended over the face of the hills; whilst the meadows beyond the river exhibit a vast tract of the richest pasture. Innumerable villages, all full of people; their dwellings comfortable and in good order. No desertion here; no sign of military exaction or plundering; no apprehension betrayed at our approach. We are received as countrymen might be. The people are confiding and happy; nor would one imagine that the blast of war had passed so near and left them scathless.

At length our turn to pass arrived, and we crossed the Seine. It seems there were not pontoons enough by half for this bridge, consequently what they had were placed at double distance; the bridge was therefore so weak that the utmost precaution was necessary in passing it, and our guns and detachments (the latter dismounted and leading their horses in file) were obliged to go over separately; but it was also necessary to take the three pair of leaders (eight horses to a gun) off, and let the wheel horses alone take over the guns. Even then, each pontoon sank until its gunwale was within two or three inches of the water as the gun passed over it.

My tutelary genius, Major M'Donald, met me in the meadows, and, as we rode along together, pointed out a village on a rising ground peeping through the trees as my destination—the village of Colombes. "Are we to halt there to-night?" I asked. "Yes, a good many nights"; and then, for the first time, I learned that our army was going into cantonments. On entering the village I found we were not to have it all to ourselves. Bull's and M'Donald's troops were here before me; but as it is very large, and there are plenty of good houses, we have all got abundance of rooms and capital quarters. The place consists principally of two long streets, with a good many detached country-houses of citizens; and as the houses of these streets are generally two or three stories, it holds us well. We have divided the village into three districts: Bull has all the upper end towards Courbevoie; M'Donald has a fine chateau and park at the bottom of the hill, in the meadows, with the adjacent parts; I have the end where the two streets join on the road to Nanterre—by far the pleasantest.

The peasantry all remain here quietly; but whether fled in alarm, or that it is not the fashion to be seen in the country at this season, I know not; but, certes, all the villas and better description of houses are either entirely empty or only a few servants left in them. Such is the case with this house I now write in. My men and horses are all well put up with *cultivateurs*, and the officers are superbly lodged in the different *quintas*. My own is charming; and no one can imagine the delight of such a residence, nor the pleasure I enjoy at again having a place to myself, and that, too, such a paradise. One drawback there is; I have been obliged to park my guns in my own pleasure-grounds—a sad invasion of my privacy this; but I have made it as little annoyance as possible by forming the park close to the farther gate, with orders to the sentry to allow no one to pass beyond; and as there is a thick shrubbery between that part of the grounds and the house, it is completely excluded. Another very sad one was the loss of my poor old dog Bal, who had been my companion day and night about eleven years, always sleeping under my bed or by my side. In 1807 he accompanied us to South America. On arriving at Colombes he was first missed. I sent Milward back to Garges, but never heard more of him. *My establishment* appears to be small; I have only seen one old man-servant as yet, though I know there are more. He is extremely obsequious and attentive to my wants, apparently somewhat alarmed, and not quite certain whether I mean to eat him up alive or not. He gave me an excellent dinner to-day and delicious wine— so that he hopes his fate is deferred. A most luxurious-looking bed tempts me, and as I am somewhat tired, and more lazy just now, I shall consign myself to it without delay, and describe my house, etc., to-morrow, when I shall have had time to examine it more leisurely.

July 9th.—Hot, beautiful day. A haziness in the atmo-sphere—the effect of this great heat—makes the distance quite *dreamy*. After so many bivouacs and cottage-beds, the delicious sensation with which I took possession of my voluptuous couch last night is not to be set forth in words, any more than the puzzled astonishment with which I gazed around on awaking this morning. It was some time ere I could clearly recollect where I was—surrounded by every-thing rich, beautiful, and luxurious. From my bed, too, I could see the meadows below, the silver current of the Seine, and the vine-clad hills beyond. It was impossible to jump up in my usual abrupt manner immediately on waking. I was loath to bring so much pleasure to a conclusion, convinced as I was that it must be less keen to-morrow; so I lay on until hunger reminded me that there were other duties to attend to—other pleasures to be enjoyed.

I have now completed the inspection of my domain, and a right lovely one it is. Let me try and preserve a *souvenir* of it. Architectural pretension the house has none—its charm consisting in the elegant and luxurious fitting up of its interior, together with the exterior accessories by which it is surrounded. A neat (not small) house of two stories, with dormitories under the usual very high roof character-ising most French houses, seated on the very brink of the rather steep *coteau*, and thus overlooking the meadows, the Seine, the country beyond; and having in the foreground, and immediately below it, the fine massed foliage of the noble trees in the park occupied by Major M'Donald's troops. From the village you enter by a *grande porte cochère* into a neat gravelled courtyard—having the house in front, offices on the left, and a range of excellent light airy stables, and one or two coach-houses on the right. The lower floor of the *corps de logis* consists of a suite of handsomely furnished saloons, in one of which is a billiard-table—a most delightful solace in such a situation. The end room, having a large window opening to the floor upon a flight of steps leading down to a pretty terrace, is ornamented with some good statues. The corresponding rooms upstairs are all fitted up as bedrooms. The opposite side of the house from the court looks upon a charming garden presenting every variety of parterre and shrubbery, among which wind cool and shady walks; whilst the innumerable flowers of the parterres fill the air with their perfume; and the sparkling waters of a fountain continually playing under the windows impart a refreshing coolness and throw an air of romance over the whole. A broad terrace, overshadowed by linden-trees and acacias, runs along the edge of the *coteau* from the end of the house, as above mentioned, to the extremity of the grounds, commanding a charming prospect through its whole length, but particularly from its termination, where, from a picturesque little kiosk seated on an artificial tumulus-shaped mound, the eye wanders down the sweet scenery of the valley until in the extreme distance it rests on the palace and park of St Germain-en-Laye. Masses of roses, carnations, lavender, geraniums, and a multitude of other flowers, planted in beds along the upper side of the terrace, contribute their fragrance to enhance the delight of this lovely walk. Immediately beneath the terrace, enclosed by a wall covered with vines, and roofed or coved with large picturesque tiles, is a spacious kitchen and fruit garden, covered just now by its luxuriant crop of all kinds. The more distant part of the grounds is laid out in lawns of smooth turf, interspersed with a variety of shrubs and forest-trees, scattered about singly, in clumps, or sometimes in close thickets or open groves. A lofty stone wall encloses three sides of this domain, the terrace forming a fourth, and a gateway in the farther part permits access to my park without trespassing on my *homestead*. The house is elegantly furnished with articles of the most costly and luxurious description, and exquisite statues of white marble decorate the corridors, staircases, and the large saloon before mentioned. The apartment I have chosen for myself is immediately over and corresponding to this, and is a perfect *bijou*; it is fitted up with a taste and splendour that bespeak the inhabitant at once voluptuous and refined. Separated from the other apartments by a small antechamber, it occupies the whole extremity of the house, overlooking the Seine, etc. In this end, like the saloon below, one large window opening to the floor, but into an iron balcony, commands a most delicious view. Immediately below is my well-stocked rich-looking garden; beyond that, yet still, as it were, under me, the finely rounded luxuriant masses of foliage of the stately elms in the park; then stretch out, like a verdant carpet, the spacious meadows, the sameness of their level expanse diversified and rendered interesting by thickets of underwood, bushes, and occasional clumps of trees. These are bounded by the silvery waters of the Seine, above which rises rather abruptly a curious chain of hills, round-topped, and broken in places by gypsum cliffs, their slopes clothed with vineyards, and separated from a similar isolated hill,[1] evidently a continuation, by a singular gap, through which

[1] Three windmills and an obelisk stand upon the summit next the gap, and a single mill on the isolated hill beyond it. The neighbourhood of Paris may be said to be characterised by the windmills which occupy every height, and thus testify to the sluggish nature of the streams watering the plains by the want of water-power.

is seen a rich country extending far back, and in the extreme distance the chateau and park of the Montmorenci. The contrast between the purply haze enveloping this country, and the more vivid colouring of the nearer landscape, gives it a dreamy and indescribably mysterious appearance. At the foot of the hills on the river-bank, and immediately opposite my window, the white buildings of Argenteuil, mingled with foliage, form a pleasing object, its church-tower decorated by the sacred *pavillon blanc*, which waves continually from its upper window. To the left the picturesque little village of Bezons and its ruined bridge, and beyond a wide extent of open, not picturesque, though rich country, covered with wheat, vines, and fig-trees, extends to St Germain—the sombre trees of whose park terminates the view in that direction. The other windows look over the garden, and the bubbling, sparkling fountain throws its glittering drops quite up to them, if not actually cooling the air, at least refreshing to the imagination. Here the view is bounded by the thick foliage of the shrubbery; but the contrast between this and the extended view from the balcony only serves to enhance the one and the other. The balmy fragrance arising from the parterres, the splashing of the water, and the cheerful songs of innumerable birds, with which the trees are filled, make this a most luscious apartment. But for the interior!—the walls are nearly covered with large mirrors, reaching from the floor to the ceiling, encased in frames richly carved and gilt. The compartments between these are filled up with fine engravings or drawings. In a recess (as the French fashion is) stands a spacious and sumptuous bed, which may be concealed at pleasure by curtains of green silk with deep rich yellow fringe. The bedstead is of mahogany, highly varnished, sculptured, and enriched with gilt ornaments, but looks unfinished to an English eye not yet accustomed to the absence of posts and curtains. The bed itself the most luxurious and fastidious must be content with; the silk counterpane matches the curtains of the recess; the enormous pillows, encased in the finest and most delicately white linen, are edged with rich lace; the sheets are as the pillow-cases, and in texture rival cambric. An elegant little table, standing between the two side windows, serves as a stand for beautiful vases of

Sèvres porcelain, holding large bouquets of the choicest productions of the garden; a large round table of mahogany, covered with oilcloth and edged with gilt bronze, occupies the middle of the floor;—the rest of the furniture, in short, is of a piece, and the accessories of a bedroom are of porcelain or fine crystal. A little door beside the recess opens into a narrow passage leading round to the rear of the house, where a small cabinet, lined with mahogany and lighted by an *œil de bœuf*, leaves no want on the score of conveniences unsupplied. At the other end of the room a small closet, fitted as a library, contains a collection of the most splendid editions of the best French authors. Here, however, the voluptuary was conspicuous; the licentiousness of Voltaire, Louvet, and others, is innocence itself compared to many works in this collection. My establishment consists of the old butler (Monsieur Ferdinand), the gardener, the cook, and, I believe, a girl as a scrub. These, with the addition of William and my two grooms, make up a snug little family. M. Ferdinand is attentive, and seems solicitous to please. Cook sent me up yesterday a remarkably nice dinner; and the gardener brought a fine fresh bouquet this morning for my vases, which he promises to do daily, also fruit for my dessert. My larder seems well stocked, and so does my cellar, for I had a bottle of excellent wine yesterday; therefore I have every reason to be satisfied with my good fortune.

The houses in which my officers lodge are all either entirely or nearly deserted; so that, having the only convenience for the purpose, I have acceded to their request, and allowed our mess to be established here, though it is hardly fair upon the proprietor, on whose resources we shall draw largely; however, I have given orders for the dinner to be prepared to-day, and M. Ferdinand has made no scruples.

July 10th.—Splendid morning, but heat excessive. Sorry to say that at the parade this morning I found we had no less than thirty horses with sore backs. This is terrible! but I know others are worse. Yesterday we dined together, and a capital dinner and excellent wine we had. After dinner, the evening being so fine, Hitchins, Breton, and I, mounted our horses for an exploration. We first crossed the meadows to the river, and rode a little way along the banks; at the ferry we found the ferryman asleep in his boat, and I could not prevent Breton from launching him into the stream—how far he went down we have not yet heard. This was childish, certainly. Quitting the river-bank we made for a high hill, whence we expected a view of Paris. *Chemin faisant*, we stumbled on some singular quarries, immense caverns cut in the soft calcareous stone, and going farther in than we thought it prudent to follow. These were in the middle of the fields, in the low ground between Colombes and Nanterre. As we enjoy the privilege of travelling over fields, etc., and are therefore quite independent of roads, we made straight for the hill, and gained its summit just as the sun was setting in all the glory of a fine summer's evening. We had judged rightly, for Mont Valerien (so it is called in my map) commands a most lovely view. Before us all Paris lay extended as in a plan; we could see every part of it, and even the far-away country beyond. Here was no dingy, orange-coloured smoke, like that which obscures the London atmosphere, and blackens the country for miles round. *Au contraire*, the clearness of the Parisian atmosphere was scarcely deteriorated by the very light transparent vapour floating over the city, which rather increased the interest and beauty of the scene by the softened outlines, and by the rich purply tint communicated to all parts of the landscape seen through it. The country immediately around, and the slopes of the hill itself on which we stood, had the appearance of one vast and productive garden, being divided into rectangular patches planted with rose-bushes, cherry-trees, vines, fig-trees, artichokes and several other sorts of culinary vegetables, all growing in the greatest luxuriance, and presenting a most extraordinary mass of verdure. Amongst all this, the white walls and red-tiled roofs of several neat villages and picturesque villas harmonised charmingly. The foot of the hill towards Paris was washed by the gently flowing waters of the Seine, on whose placid bosom a few boats occasionally appeared.

The lively verdure of a long narrow strip of meadow-land lying on the opposite bank of the river, and the white walls of several large-windowed Italian-like houses bordering on them, contrasted strongly with the sombre tones of the

Bois de Boulogne behind them, amongst whose thickets several columns of blue smoke, and a line of white tents seen here and there on the lawns, attested the presence of some part of our army. Along the line of the river were the villages of St Cloud, with its bridge; Suresnes, Puteaux, and Neuilly, from the end of whose bridge a most superb avenue of elms stretched away toward the city. Beyond could clearly be discerned the column of Austerlitz, the dome of the Pantheon, Nôtre Dame, with its high-pointed façade, circular window, and two flanking Gothic towers. A little to our right the elegant dome of the Invalides, its gilded decorations glittering in the last rays of the setting sun; the cream-coloured portico of the Hôtel de Bourbon; and the more deep-toned architecture of the Hôtel des Monnaies and its dome. Still farther to the right the scene was closed by the wooded heights of Bellevue, which appeared continuous with the Park of St Cloud. These, wrapped in deep shadow, formed a mass of sombre verdure, balancing well the other parts of this brilliant picture. In the distance beyond the city were the smiling heights of Belleville, covered with villages and country-houses, gradually descending into the vale of the Seine, of whose waters an occasional glimpse might be caught winding their tortuous way like silver threads through the rich plain. To the left the buildings of the city spread up the steep slopes of Montmartre, the summit of which presented a formidable appearance with its lines of fortifications. Windmills and a telegraph occupied the higher end of its ridge, whilst that next us terminated in a perpendicular precipice, the white face of which overhung the tufted groves of Monceaux and Clichy. Still farther to the left extended the plains of St Denis, yellow with the golden harvest, beyond which arose the town and abbey. The horizon on this side was bounded by a low range of blue hills, of pleasing though not very varied outline. The balmy softness of the evening air— the varied noises, softened by distance, arising from the village below—the sounds of music, mirth, and revelry coming up more distinctly,—all contributed to heighten the interest of this charming panorama. Long did we linger on Mont Valerien, until the coming shades of night reminded us that we were strangers to the intricate maze of vineyards, etc., which we must traverse to regain Colombes, and we turned our backs on the lovely scene.

July 13th.—This is our first wet day. Hitchins and I went to Paris this morning; but the rain set in so much in earnest that we returned forthwith, and I have devoted the remainder of the day to bringing up my leeway; for, between much occupation and much idleness, I have let my journal drop astern, and now I hardly know how to begin what I have to record, which, though trifling for others, is to me worth its weight in gold—at least will be so years hence.

Imprimis, then, I have discovered my landlord to be a M. L'Eguillon, who is an old bachelor (seventy-four years of age), and resides in a handsome town-house, Rue des Enfans Rouges. He is said to be very rich, but I cannot find out whether he has or had any employment under Government. I find that I can in some measure repay him for my good living here by sending his hay, oats, or anything else he may want, under an escort, as otherwise it would not be allowed to pass the *barrière*.[1] I suppose Ferdinand has reported us as good people, for I have received a most polite and obliging note asking this favour, and at the same time assuring me that Ferdinand has orders to pay us every attention. I sent Bombardier Ross up the other day, as he speaks French, with a load of hay, and he reported that nothing could exceed the kindness with which he was treated, and that the old gentleman's town residence is a magnificent one. A very pretty girl of sixteen (Mademoiselle Ernestine), whom the servants call his niece, lives with him. There seems a mystery, however, in the matter, for the gossips of the village declare she is not his niece. It is Mademoiselle Ernestine's apartment which I have taken possession of, it seems.

Up to the present moment nothing could have been more delightful than my residence here—so much so, that it was some time before I could tear myself away from it to go to Paris, though only about six English miles distant, and then with reluctance. To me the country at all times has so many charms, and the city so few, that it is never without

[1] The Prussians seize all forage not under escort and for our own use. Had they known this last was not the case, our non-commissioned officer would have availed little.

regret that I exchange the one for the other. Situated as I
am here, during this fine season, and surrounded by luxuries,
it is a hard task to think of sacrificing even a single day to the
close, disagreeable streets of a large town. Rinaldo in the
gardens of Armida was not more completely enthralled than
I am in this little paradise. On first awaking in the morning,
my delighted ear is saluted by the melodious warble of innumerable pretty songsters in the shrubbery, which comes
accompanied by the soft murmurs and splash of the fountain.
My toilette occupies a much longer time here than it ever
did anywhere else, so great is the luxury of wandering about
in a dressing-gown: finished, however, it must be, and then
I descend to my stable, talk nonsense to my horses, examine
poor Cossack's wounds, which were not improved by our
lengthened march, and then stroll into my garden, cool my
palate with some of the delicious fruit, take a turn or two on
the terrace under the linden-trees, look at St Germain, think
of the unfortunate James who died there in exile, then at
Argenteuil, where Heloise pined for her mutilated lover,
return to my *penteralia* and find that William has arranged
a delicious little breakfast. A parade of the troop in the
village street follows; a visit to the quarters, stables, etc.;
an inspection of carriages; concluding with a little peroration
with Farrier Price and Wheeler Rockliff. All this occupies
the first part of the morning; the remainder is passed in
lounging about the village, visiting the other troops, or
wandering about my own delightful grounds; sometimes
a game at billiards, sometimes a little scribbling. So pass
my mornings. Five o'clock usually finds us all assembled
in the *salle de compagnie* awaiting M. Ferdinand's annuncia-
tion, "On vient de servir, M. le Commandant," throwing
open the *battants* with a bow and an air worthy a groom of
the chambers. Dinner consists of a *potage* and several other
dishes, always excellent; it is followed by a dessert of fine
fruit from my *own* garden. Our wines, too, are not only
of the best quality, but we have an astonishing variety—in
short, we live like fighting-cocks. After passing a reasonable
time at table, and drinking a reasonable allowance of M.
Eguillon's wine we break up for the evening. Some resort
to the billiard-room, some to the neighbouring troops, and
I either take a ride or saunter about my terrace as I did in

the avenue at Strytem, smoking some of the few remaining excellent cigars I have brought all the way from Brussels—doubly precious now, since I find there are none such to be got in Paris. Cigars are, I think, a government monopoly here as in Spain—at least there is some mystery which I don't understand further than that the French Government has been concerned in forcing the lieges to smoke bad cigars or none at all. Only two kinds are procurable here: the one, a little black thing made of the commonest tobacco, they call Dutch, *des cigars Hollandais*; the other, a large cigar of very common bad tobacco also, has a wheaten straw stuck into it to suck the smoke through; and this, besides the villanous taste of the tobacco, burns your palate horribly.

The other evening I had retired after dinner to the terrace to enjoy, as usual, the charms of a fine sky and fine landscape. Twilight crept gradually over the valley, and, by obscuring the distant parts, allowed play to imagination, and gave additional interest to the scenery. Light airs from time to time sighed amongst the overhanging foliage; the joyous laugh of the villagers comes softened on the breeze, united with the monotonous splash of the fountain. I had seated myself in the little kiosk at the end of the terrace; the smoke of my cigar arose lazily in the air; my eyes were fixed on the silver Seine, and my mind travelling over again the events of the last three or four weeks, drawing comparisons between the feverish excitement prevailing through the former but greater part of that time, and the delicious tranquillity of the present, when suddenly the grating sound of angry voices wounded my ear and dissipated my reverie. I listened; the speakers appeared to be at our park, or near it. There were English voices and foreign of some sort. A quarrel between my men and the natives, no doubt. But how came the latter in the grounds? The voices became louder and fiercer; there was a rattling of sabres, too. Good heavens! are the French renewing the Sicilian Vespers? Whilst asking myself this question, I was already hurrying along the tortuous path leading to that part of the grounds, and soon came upon the scene of action. Here I found Quartermaster Hall and several gunners struggling with our hussars of Brunswick, whose horses, bridled and saddled, seemed the objects of contention from the way in which they were alternately seized by one or the other and most unceremoniously dragged about by both.

High words and threatening gestures, pulling and scuffling, seemed the order of the day, but no blows were interchanged. Both parties seemed equally enraged, but neither understood the other,—for one swore in German, the other in English; the gestures, however, spoke a sort of universal language which all parties comprehended perfectly. At the moment of my arrival one of the hussars, having rescued his horse from the grip of his opponent, had raised his foot to the stirrup, and was in the act of mounting, when an athletic gunner, seizing him by the waist, swung him to some distance, rolling on the turf. The fellow, springing up again, had half drawn his sabre as I emerged from the shrubbery with an authoritative *"Halt da!"* which was instantly obeyed by all; whilst old Hall, the moment he saw me, cried, "They are off, sir—they are going off." The hint was sufficient. I despatched a gunner with orders to the guard to shut the iron gates and allow none to pass, then proceeded to investigate the origin of this quarrel. I had placed these people in the grounds from the first, that they might be more under surveillance. They have a tent for themselves, and their horses are picketed near our guns. This I have found necessary, from the sulky mutinous spirit they have always evinced since the first day of joining us. They have always been a source of considerable worry to me, and have been getting worse lately. According to their own account, they are all *volunteers* and *gentlemen*; therefore they feel very severely the degradation of their present position, particularly being put under a vile commissary, whom they affect to treat with the utmost contempt. Their present complaint was about their bread, which they said "was not even fit for *common soldiers*"; and they accused Mr Coates of having purposely given them this bread as an insult. In their rage they had saddled their horses with the intention of returning home, or the Lord knows where, when Hall interfered, and the scuffle took place. The corporal (a fine young man) was particularly indignant, and held forth most vehemently on what was due to a gentleman, partly in German, partly in French. Hall's insolence he spoke of with great bitterness, giving me to understand that he expected my men should pay him somewhat of the same deference as to their own officers. My answer to all this was short: "The bread is of the same quality as that served out to our own men; therefore, if the *gentlemen* disliked it, they might leave it. As to their rank in civil society, I know nothing about it; they were put under my orders as any other soldiers, and as such should do their duty." Two or three of the most refractory I made prisoners of, and if they still remained discontented, they at least remained quiet. This disturbance, however, spoilt my evening; so, having consumed my cigar whilst lecturing the gentlemen, I retired to my room and spent an hour or two over Voltaire's *Philosophical Dictionary*.

Notwithstanding the raptures in which our people spoke of Paris, which some of them visited the very first evening of our coming here, yet it was only a day or two ago that I could tear myself from the country and go thither. The village and *les villageois* had not yet lost the freshness of novelty. Strolling about the street gossiping with the people has been a source of infinite amusement to me, and I have been much interested in observing their peculiar manners and habits. The harvest, which has just commenced, causes considerable stir in the village, as all the produce of the fields is brought to be stored in their granaries here. The villages round Paris have anything but a rural aspect: houses of stone, roofed either with tiles or slates, from two to three and even four stories high; large windows, like those of town houses; the attics are their granaries, hay-lofts, etc., and a window or door, furnished with a crane and tackle similar to those of our merchants' stores, furnishes the means of hoisting in the sheaves, bundles of hay, etc. The consequence of this is, that our streets are all in a bustle—loaded carts continually arriving from the fields, and drawing up under the entrance-window of their respective houses. Bundles and sheaves are mounting into the air, and various gossiping groups are formed below. The peasantry in this neighbourhood are almost all of them proprietors of the lands they cultivate. As with us, the law obliges every man to put his name, etc., on his cart; so we see continually "Jacques Bonnemain, cultivateur," "Jean le Mery, proprietaire," etc. The figures composing these street-groups are sturdy well-made men; much more active and springy than our clowns, although sufficiently rustic. Their costume, too, widely differs from everything we are accustomed to associate with rusticity. The bronzed visage, surrounded by its setting of black locks, surmounted by the *bonnet de nuit*, usually white, or having once been so, round jackets of blue-striped cotton stuff, and trousers of the same—bare feet, thrust into a pair of clumsy sabots, complete the costume. Amongst the young men and boys I have remarked a much greater proportion of handsome intelligent faces than one usually sees in any English village; our rustics are generally coarse-featured, and have a most unintellectual expression of face. The French peasant not only has the advantage in point of person and carriage, but infinitely so in his address. The women partake of the labours of the field, and enter largely into the composition of our village-groups. Their general costume is not unpicturesque. They are always without gowns, the exposed stays (not always very clean) sometimes laced up, sometimes quite loose and open; blue and white, or pink-striped petticoats; neck partially covered by a coloured handkerchief (*fichu* [1]); the head by another, gracefully turned round it, something in the shape of a turban; [2] large gold or silver hoops in the ears, and a small cross of the same suspended by a black ribbon from the neck; stockings of grey or blue thread, or bare legs; large sabots, the insteps frequently garnished with a strip of rabbit skin. Such are our village belles. At a superficial glance one does not see amongst them such gradations from youth to age as among our own women. All are either old or young, hideously ugly, or pretty, or very pretty. About the age of puberty (which seems to be earlier than with us), they become masculine and coarse, though still handsome. But about thirty (or earlier, if they have children) they lose all pretensions to good looks, and immediately assume the appearance of old age—wrinkled, skinny, with sunken cheeks, hollow eyes—and such necks! Like the men, these women are vastly superior to our female peasantry in carriage of person and in manners. The former is invariably erect and commanding, giving to the ugliest old woman an air

[1] In English we have no word which will translate.
[2] The *cornette*.

of dignity never or very rarely to be met with among our working classes, and not always amongst our ladies. Some of the young ones, well made and tall, with their firm determined step, are really majestic creatures.

The ordinary diet of these people seems little calculated to enable them to go through the portion of hard labour that falls to their lot. Bread, black, coarse, dry, and diabolically sour, a bit of hard tasteless cheese, compose the usual breakfast and dinner, with the occasional addition of haricots, or some other vegetables; for supper, broth (*potage aux herbes*), in which a bit of lard or some kind of grease is melted to give it richness and perhaps flavour. Their beverage is a poor sort of *vin du pays*, very sour, and very inferior to the sound rough cider used in our apple-counties, Hereford and Devon. In the cabarets beer is to be had of a pleasant quality, although not strong. The *bonne double bierre de Mars* is of a superior caste, and, when bottled (as it is sold), a refreshing, agreeable drink in hot weather.

March is to their brewers what October is to ours. This *bierre de Mars* (from the month, I presume) one would suppose exclusively military, from the numerous coloured prints stuck on the window-shutters of most cabarets, representing officers and soldiers in the acts of drawing, pouring out, or drinking this favourite tipple. The most common of these represents two officers in *grande tenue*, plumed hats, swords by their sides, spurs on the heel, etc., seated at a small round table. Each holds in the right hand an uncorked bottle, in the left a tumbler, the *bierre* rising in a jet from the bottles, forming two intersecting arches, terminating precisely in the opposite and apposite tumblers. The shutters frequently bear both pictorial and scriptorial annunciations not a little amusing. I have seen numbers on our march, but thought no more of them; and it was only the other day, at Courbevoie, that "*audevie à vandre*" upon a shutter gave rise to the idea of making a collection of them. The universal "*Ici on loge à pied et à cheval*" is parallel to our entertainment for man and horse.

I have before noticed that on arriving here we found all the gentry fled. That was not quite the truth. A few days since I discovered that a certain handsome house, in Bull's quarter of the village, is still inhabited by the proprietor, an old lady of seventy (la Marquise de * * *), very partial to, because somehow connected with, the English, and therefore remaining at home in full confidence of good treatment. She has judged rightly; not a soul has trespassed upon her except as visitors, of which she is very proud, and holds a sort of daily levee, which we sometimes find a convenient lounge. Brought up in the Court of Louis XVI., Madame la Marquise is a strict observer of all the etiquette of the old *régime*. A light active figure, and a natural (or perhaps assumed) sprightliness of manner, added to a very juvenile costume, give her at a little distance quite the appearance of a girl. A nearer approach, however, spite of rouge, etc., most liberally applied, betrays the *septuagénaire*. At my first visit I found this extraordinary old woman alone, dressed, and evidently expecting visitors. I introduced myself, and was received with almost affectionate kindness. Our *tête-à-tête* was a long one, for she would make me listen to the whole of her family history, and how one of her ancestors, having married some English lady of rank, she considers herself *à moitié Anglaise*. She was not content with telling me her history, but showed me her whole house and gardens (both very handsome and in excellent order), even her own boudoir, *chambre à coucher*, etc. On taking leave she exacted a promise of being a good neighbour, which I have endeavoured to perform by devoting to her a small portion of my leisure time. It is to her that I am obliged for breaking the spell that bound me to the village, and at last *visiting Paris*. The other morning she expressed such unfeigned astonishment at my want of curiosity that I resolved to see the place forthwith, if only for a few minutes. Accordingly, after dinner I mounted Nelly, and set off by what I guessed must be the road thither. The day had been exceedingly hot, the roads were very dusty, and, half irresolute, I rode slowly over the uninteresting parched-up plain between Colombes and Courbevoie, made disgusting, moreover, by the trodden-down corn and carcasses of horses, etc., which marked the old bivouacs. The handsome cavalry barracks for the Imperial Guard at the entrance of Courbevoie detained me a moment, and then I descended the winding shabby street, and came suddenly on the beautiful Pont de Neuilly. The lovely scenery here, above and below the bridge, and the magnificent avenue beyond it, put an end to my Paris trip.   For the life of me I could not resolve to exchange such scenery, and pass such an evening in the streets of a city, however fine they might be. This bridge, and the one at St Maxence, are elegant things, certainly; but the straight line, which is one of their great beauties, must not be claimed by the architects as an original idea.   The Roman bridges at Alcantra and elsewhere no doubt have been their prototypes.   I found here defences similar to those at St Denis—the road to the bridge broken up and obstructed by carts, and a sort of abatis; this was commanded by a 2-gun battery, built across the road on the Paris side, secured at each flank by a stockade.   These mementos of war were unpleasing objects certainly, yet they could not divert the mind from the sweet scenery on every side.   The Seine came gliding tranquilly along through green meadows, fringed with willows, bordered on each side by villages and villas; several verdant islands, also, decorated with large umbrageous willows, divided its stream into different channels, on which floated boats of various descriptions—some plain and of coarse construction, laden with goods; others of a more elegant construction, gaily painted, and filled with joyous light-hearted people, already forgetful of the downfall of their idolised Emperor—of their national glory tarnished—even that, in these their moments of mirth and recreation, they were in the presence of their conquerors—of their ancient enemy.   British soldiers stood on the river-bank as they passed along—British soldiers occupied the barracks of the late Imperial Guard, under which lay their course, and yet the laugh was as joyous, the countenances as bright, as they could have been after the bulletins of Austerlitz or Jena.   Not so, I ween, on the slimy Thames had England fallen as low, were London the cantonment of French legions.

A most superb avenue is the road which gradually ascends from the Pont de Neuilly to the Barrière de l'Etoile, the unfinished works of which terminate this unrivalled perspective.   I forget whether there are two or four rows of elms on either side—and such trees!   This splendid road was alive with carriages, equestrians, and pedestrians, as I rode up it to the *barrière*; and here another magnificent scene burst upon me. Hence the road descended gradually towards the city, handsome houses, and even rows of houses, intermingling with the masses of foliage on either side; and far away, in hazy, dreamy distance, this avenue was terminated by the heavy but imposing mass of the Tuileries, with the spotless banner of ancient France waving gracefully in the evening breeze from the elevated central mass. I returned from this interesting excursion just as the fading tints of the western sky began to sober down into the greys of twilight. My curiosity was excited by this peep of Paris, and the next morning actually found me riding slowly down from the Barrière de l'Etoile towards the Place Louis Quinze, delighted with the novelty of the scene by which I was surrounded. On either side of the road, among the noble trees, were handsome houses, the large open windows and balconies of which were filled with green shrubs and brilliant flowers. Beyond these I came to a wide open space everywhere covered with trees, but poor ones compared to the giants forming the avenue. Under these a regiment of English hussars, and a band of Cossacks, were in bivouac together—a novel and amusing scene. The soldiers and their horses were objects of curiosity (English as well as Cossacks) to a crowd of idle Parisians who stood by, not in silent contemplation of the *strange animals*, but chattering like a pack of monkeys, and explaining what they saw to those of their neighbours less gifted with the powers of conception. Carriages, too, as they passed, and groups of young men on horseback (looking half-military, half-bourgeois, from their mustachioed upper lips, erect carriage, holstered saddles, and cavalry bridles), paused to contemplate the foreign bivouac. If these last were amused with my countrymen and their friends, I was no less so with them. There was something irresistibly comic in their self-satisfied air as they paraded their managed cats of steeds before the fair ones in the carriages, and the affected, contemptuous looks they cast on the hardy fellows who had so recently chased their own braves (perhaps some of themselves) from Brussels to Paris. The equipages, too, were worthy of notice: they reminded me of Ireland—"*Nothing of a piece.*" Handsome carriage, well-dressed servants, dog-horses and shabby harness; or shabby servant and beautiful horse, new harness, and an old jarvey of a carriage—the fair dames within invariably smart. No comparison can be instituted between French and English equipages. The neatness and perfect completeness, beauty, finish, lightness, and goodness—all are on the side of the latter. Their cabriolet, however, is something *sui generis*, and worthy of admiration. They are generally drawn by one horse, some-times a postilion on a second horse attached as an outrigger. It was one of these that captivated my fancy near the *barrière*. Such a turn-out! The carriage was just like other cabriolets, only a very smart one; and here I must acknowledge an exception to what I have just written—the whole *was* of a piece—good, smart, and respectable; but, *mon Dieu*! what a spectacle! The heavy harness under which the horses were almost buried was covered with plated buckles, bosses, etc. On the outrigger sat a fine, well-made fellow, six feet if an inch, erect as a grenadier. On his head an enormous cocked-hat, bound with broad silver lace and loop, stuck square on; a blue coat, collar, skirts, and sleeves, all covered with silver lace; the clothing of his nether limbs hid in a tremendous pair of boots, sticking six inches above his slightly bent knee, and armed with a most formidable pair of spurs; like all the rest of them, riding exceedingly long, consequently bumping along at a moderate trot with most imperturbable gravity. How I should have liked to see this equipage trotting down St James's Street! A passer-by, of whom I asked the question, informed me that this was Les Champs Elysées. I could hardly credit him. What! the far-famed, much-vaunted, much-bescribbled Champs Elysées! Impossible!—or, if true, what a disappointment! I hardly know what sort of an idea I had formed of the Champs Elysées—certainly nothing like the reality. No turf, no verdure, in short, no fields, but a gravelly dusty space, surrounded nearly by buildings, and barely shaded from the scorching sun by a parcel of miserable-looking half-grown trees, sufficiently powdered to conceal whatever verdure they might have. If ever the grass had grown here, every trace was now obliterated. Bivouacs are sadly destructive of nature's beauties. "Thus, then," said I, "here is one illusion dissipated. Let us see farther, perhaps all will equally vanish in smoke and dust." A certain feeling

of exultation, a tumultuous rising of spirits came over me
as I rode into the Place Louis Quinze, and pulling up,
regardless of the moving throng of people, contemplated
at my leisure the scene around me. I have now got a map
and a *Guide de Paris*, both of which I have since had
opportunities of elucidating or confirming by inquiry and
viva voce evidence. Then, I knew not that I stood precisely
on the same spot where the martyrdom of Louis Seize and
the fair Marie Antoinette had been consummated. I knew
that the walls in front of me as I entered the Place from the
Champs Elysées were the ramparts of the Tuileries; that
the bowery trees which overtopped them were in the gardens;
and that the immense pile seen again over these was the
chateau itself: but I did not know that the magnificent
ranges of buildings, with their rich sculptures and Corinthian
colonnades on my left, were those of the Garde Meuble;
nor that the fine but short perspective by which they were
separated was the Rue de la Concorde; nor that the handsome bridge on my right was the Pont de la Concorde, and
the imposing portico which reared its lofty Corinthian
columns beyond was the entrance to the Salle des Repre-
sentatifs. Although ignorant of the names and destinations
of the noble objects, I could not but be sensible of their
effect individually and as an *ensemble*; and I did acknowledge that nothing could be more imposing, more strikingly
magnificent, than this entrance to the city of Paris.

Every faculty absorbed in the contemplation of the various
and varied novelties around me, I progressed mechanically,
and without knowing or seeking to know where I was going,
found my way down the Rue de Rivoli, and so into the Place
Vendôme, where the column of Austerlitz, by its beautiful
workmanship, and the historical recollections associated
with it, arrested my course for some time. Strange, however, that a nation like France should borrow from Rome—
that she could not produce an original idea to commemorate
a great national triumph. It is nevertheless a superb
monument; and at least the idea of using the guns taken
in the battle to decorate the city—was not *that* an original
idea? The Place itself I do not like. Its houses are
certainly fine, and uniformly built, but the style is heavy,
the material dismal, and the want of *trottoirs* gives the whole

the air of a "mews." In approaching the Place Vendôme by the Rue Castiglione, I crossed the Rue St Honoré, the busy stream flowing along which would have induced me to follow it, but the column in front drew me forward like a magnet. The streets of Paris are infinitely more amusing than those of London, inasmuch as they everywhere teem with animation, from the pavements to the roofs. Nowhere do we meet such long, tiresome, dull avenues of brick and mortar as Baker Street, Gore Street, Gloucester Place, etc. In London, "home's home," etc.—and when people are at home, they like quietude and retirement. In Paris, *au contraire*, people cannot exist in quietude, and solitude is abominated. To see and be seen seems the universal maxim. The varied forms of the houses, too, and the still more varied styles of ornament, render the streets much more picturesque and interesting in Paris than in London. There is something very picturesque and interesting, I think, in the immense long perspectives between the tall houses of such streets as the Rue de Richelieu, into which I was led by the Rue Neuve des Petits Champs. This is the Bond Street of Paris, and is a most amusing one. Here everything savoured of the fashionable world. Shops of a more respectable description richly decorated; goods of the most costly kind arranged for display with a very superior degree of taste and even elegance. Numerous equipages with liveried attendants driving about or waiting at the doors. Numberless loungers sauntering up and down, or philandering in the shops, a striking feature among these the foreign officers, particularly English, all indicating the Rue de Richelieu as the focus of fashionable resort. After all, however, there is something about this as well as all the other streets of Paris, with a few exceptions—such as the Rue de Rivoli, de la Concorde, de la Paix, and some part of the Boulevard—that displeases an Englishman's eye and nose. The buildings in general have a worn and shabby appearance; their great height, and the narrowness of the thoroughfare, throws a degree of darkness and gloom over everything; but, above all, the olfactory nerves are continually offended by a certain pervading odour, difficult to be accounted for, since it is everywhere the same—not arising from any visible cause, but omnipresent and unvarying.

In the Rue de Richelieu not all the fragrant odours issuing from that *magazin* of odours, the Cloche d'Or, and fifty others, were sufficient to overpower this most unsavoury of smells. It may be said to characterise Paris—to stamp it as the sulphureous city. My attention was attracted by a broad avenue crossing one end of it, and along which flowed a dense and continuous stream of passengers and carriages. I directed my horse's head thither, and in a few minutes found myself in the Boulevard des Italiens. The excitement and interest of that moment will not soon be forgotten. The breadth of the street, the mixture of trees and houses, the number and variety of the immense multitude moving on, all contributed for a moment to electrify me, and I should have forgotten Colombes and the lateness of the hour had not Hitchins at that moment rode up and asked me if I was not going home to dinner. Colombes and M. Ferdinando's good cheer regained their sway, and we trotted off together, vowing an early return to explore the wonders of this mine of novelty and excitement.

CHAPTER XIX

July 17*th.*—Alas! how transient is all earthly happiness! To-morrow I quit Colombes and my delightful residence for ever; except, indeed, I pay it a casual visit, and that I shall hardly have heart to do. A few short days passed in this elysium have endeared it to me beyond expression, and, spite of certain little differences, M. Ferdinand and I have become quite friends. The old man's manner is always so kind that I really believe he likes me; but then these French are consummate *blagueurs*. Our principal quarrel has been invariably about wine. At first he always produced such as would have done honour to any table, but by degrees he began from time to time to introduce a bottle of inferior quality. It was, however, too late; our palates were formed, and could bear nothing but the best, which we insisted on having, spite of his equivocations and harangues to prove to us that we were no judges of wine. Some droll scenes have arisen out of this; for we discovered that M. Ferdinand has the greatest horror of our invading his territory, and availed ourselves of the discovery whenever he tried to play us a trick. Nothing could be more comical than the expression which his countenance assumed on these occasions. "Ferdinand!" "Monsieur!" "Ce vin ci n'est pas bon!" "Ce vin n'est pas bon, monsieur?" arching his grey eyebrows. "Non, il est exécrable, vilain." "Mais, monsieur," with emphasis, "c'est du meilleur vin de la cave, je vous assure"; and then, with an "Excusez, monsieur!" he takes the bottle, pours a little wine into the palm of his hand, tastes it, makes a grimace indicative of pleasure, rubs down his stomach with feigned ecstasy, and exclaims, "Dieu merci, comme il est excellent!" "Eh bien, M. Ferdinand, vous ne savez plus plaire à notre gout; allez vous en, cherchez une chandelle et la clef de la cave, j'y descendrai choisir moi-même," etc. etc. This always

produced the desired effect—the comic expression of his
countenance would give place to one of extreme anxiety.
"Tenez, monsieur!—tenez! cela ne sera pas bon; la cave
est si obscure, si humide. Ah, je ne le permettrai jamais.
Si monsieur le trouve bon, je descendrai chercher d'autre
vin, et peut-être je serais plus heureux." Without waiting
for a reply he would rush off with the activity of a man
twenty years younger. In due time, allowing for the
supposed search, re-enter M. Ferdinand with a joyous
countenance and bottle in hand, from which, the long cork
duly extracted, he would deliberately fill a *large* glass, look
exultingly around, and, making a most profound bow
(without, however, spilling one drop), drink "au bonheur
de Monsieur le Commandant et des braves Anglais," then
triumphantly plant the bottle on the table with renewed
assurances of the excellence of its contents, which we
invariably found to be perfectly true. On the whole, however, as I before said, we were excellent friends, and Monsieur
le Commandant a special favourite with honest Ferdinand,
whose attentions were unremitting. It grieves me, certainly,
leaving Colombes—but go I must.

Yesterday Sir George Wood received despatches from
Lord Mulgrave appointing Sir John May and Major William
Lloyd to the two troops vacant by the deaths of Ramsay and
Bean. This is a disappointment, for I had fully expected
one of them; however, it is somewhat softened by the handsome manner in which his lordship directs that I be retained
as a supernumerary captain of horse-artillery until a vacancy
may occur, which it is known must be soon, for poor Lloyd
is too severely wounded to survive. But the worst part of
the story is, that my old troop, in which I have now been
nine years, is to be taken from me and given to Major
Wilmot, who has just arrived from England, and I am to
go to D Troop, late Bean's, now Lloyd's, and no doubt soon
to be mine. This morning Sir Augustus Frazer inspected
G Troop, previously to my giving it up to Wilmot, in the
field by the side of the road from Neuilly Bridge to l'Etoile.
I took the opportunity of complaining that certain malicious
reports had been circulated by persons unknown, to the
injury of my character. These set forth that the great loss
sustained by G Troop on the 18th arose from my culpable

stupidity in having unnecessarily exposed my detachment, gun-horses, etc. Sir Augustus acknowledged having heard such a report, which he had taken every pains to contradict, and added, "I have told everybody that the imputation is false; and, moreover, that if blame attach to any one, it must be to myself and Major M'Donald, for I placed you in your position, and both of us visited you repeatedly during the action, and ought to have corrected anything that was wrong." This has been some ill-natured, jealous person, who envies us the little credit we got on that occasion.

After our inspection I sent Newland home with the troop, and accompanied Sir Augustus to La Chapelle under Montmartre, on the road to St Denis, where he inspected the D Troop, now commanded by Major D., previously to his giving it up to me to-morrow. It is a wretched troop, and very badly officered; the state of discipline such as I never thought could have existed in such a perfect service as the horse-artillery. Frazer flattered me by saying, in answer to my complaint, "Never mind; I am sure you will soon have it in a very different state." I hope so. To-morrow, then, I depart hence—give up my elysium, and exchange one of the very finest troops in the service for the *very worst*. But I must try and bring down my journal, if possible, to the present day, so as to begin a new score at my new station, wherever that may be. The 13th was the wet day on which I last wrote, and then did not finish up to the date, I think the 12th. Hitchins and I breakfasted at seven, and set off together immediately after for Paris. The road thither, with the exception of the naked plain between this and Courbevoie, is most interesting. At the Place Louis Quinze we dismounted, and Milward brought the horses back, whilst we continued on towards the Louvre by the Rue de Rivoli, etc. The Louvre is now in all its glory—nothing has been touched, although restoration is talked of. The Place du Carrousel we found occupied by Prussian infantry in bivouac. Not far off, near the Boulevard de la Madeleine, are several large timber-yards. Blucher, less scrupulous than Wellington, has emptied the contents of one of these on the Place du Carrousel, where his people have constructed a little town of sheds or shanties with the planks. A singular spectacle is this bivouac. The sheds form regular streets parallel to the Grille; along the centre of these are lines of fires, with camp-kettles suspended over them, and soldiers in most slovenly (even beggarly) *déshabillé* sitting round, peeling potatoes, turnips, onions, etc., or cutting up very carrion-like meat for their messes. A chain of sentries kept back the crowd, which was immense—all eager to see the warriors so often beaten by their own troops, now in their turn conquerors, and enjoying the fruits of their victory on the very ground where the mighty Emperor of the West had passed in review those *soi-disant* invincible legions, and whence they had successively departed for Madrid, Vienna, Jena, and Moscow.

Except a scowling ex-*militaire* here and there, nothing could exceed the *bonhommie* apparent in every countenance. Curiosity—pure curiosity—had drawn them thither, and their staring physiognomies did not betray an idea beyond the gratification of it. What a holiday for the Parisians this is, after all! The city seems in a continued state of festivity, and at the same time of fever. Amidst such a crowd and such excitement it was not possible to indulge reflections; yet, spite of these, a confused jumble of very curious ones flashed across my mind as, *en passant*, I contemplated this host of foreigners, domesticated, as it were, on the *sacred territory*; beyond them, and overtopping their temporary dwellings, the celebrated triumphal arch, surmounted by the four Venetian horses; and beyond these again, the immense façade (dark and gloomy) of the Tuileries, scene of such strange and startling events. Struggling through the crowd, our approach to the Gallery of the Louvre was announced by a host of boys and women, "A bill of the play, sir?" "Please to buy a bill of the play?" which was soon exchanged for "Catalogue du musée, monsieur? un franc, monsieur." "Voulez-vous un catalogue du musée, monsieur?" etc. etc. These people are more persevering than our vendors of these articles; however, the purchase of one was a mouth-stopper, and we were then suffered to proceed unmolested to the great doors, where two servants, most respectably dressed in blue and silver, with white waistcoat and breeches, received us, and pointed out the way to the first *salon*. A perfect stream, almost all foreigners, was setting in, and the *salons* were already pretty full, although so early in the day.   I cannot set up for a connoisseur either in painting or sculpture, therefore have little to record of this celebrated collection beyond my unfeigned admiration of what I there saw.   My emotions in each individual rencontre with the different *chefs-d'œuvre* here assembled might be a source of amusement to myself at some future period had I faithfully noted them down at the moment, but that was impossible in such a crowd; moreover, I had a companion, the most complete hindrance imaginable in my estimation to the enjoyment of anything admirable either in art or nature.   Now they are nearly obliterated, and I can only say that I was delighted, though in some cases disappointed.   This was particularly the case with the Venus de Medici.   I scarcely know what I expected to see; but when a statue, patched and cracked, the marble discoloured and disfigured with greenish stains, such as one sees in our garden Neptunes, Tritons, etc., was pointed out by the number in our catalogue as the Venus, I could scarcely believe but that it must be a mistake.   Such was the effect of the first *coup d'œil*.   Upon a more attentive examination, however, I could not but admit the thing to be a most beautiful piece of workmanship as such; and the lady represented a very pretty woman, but I felt no raptures. The colossal group of the Laocoon, occupying like an altar-piece, the whole extremity of the same apartment, hence called the Salle de Laocoon, had no charms for me.   In the first place, I dislike colossal statues as much as I dislike allegorical paintings; both are a departure from nature, which I am not poetical enough to appreciate.   Secondly, I hate such subjects—I hate a gratuitous contemplation of horrors and suffering—and to me there is something exquisitely disgusting in this subject.   Thirdly, I dislike all attempts at representing violent action either in painting or sculpture, except for a momentary glance; they cannot deceive the senses—there is no illusion.   Specimens of either should be subjects to dwell upon, to contemplate, to study. But who can dwell upon action that *stands still*?   What can be more tiresome than the continually uplifted arm of the Laocoon, or the immovable struggles of the two little (by comparison) men (for they are not boys), with formal curly wigs, on each side of him ?   In short, I hate this so far-famed

group. Occupying the extremity of the next *salle*, is the
Apollo. Here I was not disappointed. The action has
just ceased—the figure is in a sufficient state of repose to
keep up the illusion and bear continued looking at. And
who could ever tire of this? Such grace and ease, such
lightness and activity—activity written in broad characters
upon a figure not in movement—such an elegant and perfect
form, and such a divine head! How often I have returned
to gaze upon this most perfect conception of the human
mind—this most perfect execution of the human hand!
How often have I turned into the *musée*, and, heedless of
the Venus, the Laocoon, and all the other celebrated statues
in my way, have passed along, seeing nothing and heeding
nothing, until I stood once more before this most exquisite
piece of statuary! In collections of this kind too many
choice *morceaux* in juxtaposition, or in immediate neighbourhood, injure each other—they distract the attention;
and it is only after repeated visits that we become cool
enough to attach ourselves to particular pieces. It was thus
with me at my first visit both to these and the *galerie*;
and I have left the same effect in passing through a wild
and picturesque country exhibiting beautiful features and
pictures at every turn. I have been cloyed, even fatigued;
and looked with pleasure on, and found relief in, a landscape
of a tamer description.

From the *salons* we ascended to the Galerie du Louvre
by a most superb staircase. English riflemen were posted,
not only on the landing-place, but also distributed at intervals
through the whole length of the gallery—whether to preserve
order or the pictures, I know not; but I do know that the
appearance of their green uniforms, as they stood leaning
on their rifles all along this magnificent perspective, was
another of those sights calculated to excite in our minds
such strange tumultuous feelings. What must have been
those of the Parisians, of whom a part of the immense crowd
that thronged the *galerie* and anteroom was composed?
They apprehend that the spoliation will commence directly,
and are therefore assiduous in their worship of those treasures
about to quit them for ever, and with them, they think, their
national glory. The only record I make of the *galerie* is,
that Poussin's "Deluge" fascinated me. Never did I see

a picture inspiring so much awe. Paul Potter's "Bull" pleased me as an inimitable copy from nature, but as a picture it struck me as wanting in poetry. Some beggar-boy, by Murillo, perfectly ravished me, *malgré* the disgusting subject: here was nature and the most delicious colouring imaginable.

As both Hitchins and I proposed paying many more visits to the *musée*, we did little more than walk to the end of the *galerie* and back, and then departed, crossed the Prussian bivouac, and wandered into the palace of the Tuileries. We went as we listed, no one offering us the slightest obstruction; and the sentinels (I think they were of the National Guard), although they did not salute us, yet drew up respectfully at their posts as we passed them. Ascending a magnificent staircase, we found our way into a large handsome saloon, over the fireplace in which was a very fine painting of a battle. I think this was the Salle des Maréchaux. There was not a living soul to answer our questions; but I have since learned that what I took for a painting was a piece of Gobelins tapestry. Unheeded, we rambled on from one large room to another; indeed we met but few anywhere, until at last we walked most unceremoniously into one where a number of servants in the royal livery were laying a dinner-table, which, to our astonishment, we found was for his Majesty. They hardly noticed us, and answered all our questions in a most good-natured but most respectful manner. There was a beautiful service of Worcester ware, and, for a private gentleman, a decent display of plate, but nothing more—so far all was respectable; but what a tablecloth! I doubt whether most of our gentry of even the second table wouldn't turn up their insolent noses at such a one. Sure I am that no gentleman in England ever sits down to so coarse a thing. As dinner was just coming up, the butler (I suppose) very civilly begged us to retire, as his Majesty would be in immediately. We descended to the gardens. I had heard and read so much of the gardens of the Tuileries, that here I experienced a disappointment similar to that inflicted by the Champs Elysées. Nevertheless they certainly form a very agreeable promenade. That part immediately under the windows of the palace is laid out in parterres of flower-beds of different geometrical figure. I should say that the garden is a dead-level.[1] Between the parterres are broad walks, well rolled and well swept. The farther part is a grove, forming a cool and pleasant promenade or lounge, much taken advantage of by the Parisians, who may be seen lounging in one or two chairs, as may be, in all directions. These chairs are the property of individuals who bring them there, and make a livelihood by letting them out at two or three sous the chair. Similar accommodation, it appears, is to be found in every public place, even in the Boulevards. The ramparts (rather grandiloquent, when speaking of a mere terrace), which surround the garden on three sides, are planted also, and afford a most interesting promenade from the views they command; yet, strange to say, people appear to prefer the more confined one below. Although I do not like the formal laying out of these gardens, yet can I not but confess there is something very lordly (or kingly) in them. The broad, well-kept gravel-walks, the play of the fountains, the numerous orange-trees in boxes, which fill the air with their delicious but rather overpowering perfume, the multitude of statues, the view down the centre *allée*, which is prolonged into an immense perspective by being on the same line with that of the Champs Elysées, and on the other hand the ancient and venerable pile, with its numerous windows, long covered verandas, etc., overlooking the whole. The gaily dressed crowd, too, by which the garden is almost always filled, gives it a holiday air very pleasing. Passing once more through the palace and traversing the Place du Carrousel, we soon reached the southern entrance of the Palais Royal. It was "change time," and the place in front of the gate was filled with business-like people, exactly as in our Royal Exchange. What a strange propensity the French have for misnomers! On entering the so-called "*garden*"[2] of the Palais Royal, I was for the third time disappointed. Instead of a garden I found myself in an immense arid esplanade, surrounded (at least on three sides) by lofty uniform buildings, the façade of which was decorated by Corinthian pilasters, and surmounted by vases, etc. An

---

[1] Le Nôtre had five feet (French) difference of level between one side and the other to remove. There is no accounting for taste.
[2] It once was a garden, but was destroyed by the great fire.

arcade ran all round the base.   The side by which we entered was disfigured by a shabby wooden erection, under which were numerous stalls of petty dealers in every sort of articles, but apparently all of inferior quality.   Under the arcades were shops of a better description, intermingled with cafés, restaurants, etc., and here was certainly a splendid display of goods of the richest kind.   Watchmakers exhibited the most elegant little toys, enriched with pearls and chased-work; jewellers the most splendid articles in precious stone, gold, silver, etc.; shops of *gourmandise* (if I may be allowed the term)—everything that could stimulate or pamper the appetite.   Many were entirely filled with knick-knackery or articles of *vertu*; others with steel or cutlery; in others, again, were tastefully displayed the finest cashmere or merino shawls and *fichus* of the most brilliant colours.   In short, I cannot remember the tenth part of the rich display under these arcades.

In the esplanade were a few shabby trees, some benches, and piles of chairs.   The crowd of loungers, etc. (for I presume most there were so), under the arcades, was very great, principally, I think, military.   Prussian and Russian officers in blue or green uniforms, waists drawn in like a wasp's, breasts sticking out like a pigeon's; long sashes, with huge tassels of gold or silver, hanging half-way down their legs—pretty red and white boyish faces, with an enormous bush of hair over each ear; lancers in square-topped caps and waving plumes; hussars in various rich uniforms, one more remarkable, sky-blue, curiously laced with a sort of chain-lace, very ugly to my taste; Austrian officers in plain white uniforms, turned up with red—very neat, very soldier-like, very becoming, and the men who wore them more gentlemanly in their appearance than any of the others; English officers in all sorts of dresses, fancy, half-military, and quite so.   To say that women abounded amongst these would be almost superfluous—some very handsome, some quite the contrary—all wearing looks of the boldest and most meretricious character.   Boys, too, abounded, as in the Pays Bas, following and pestering you with their odious propositions.   The cafés and restaurants were principally filled with officers smoking, drinking, playing chess, etc. etc.   A few turns in the promenade, and then it was so late that we returned to the Place Louis Quinze, whence a cabriolet in due time brought us to our quiet peaceable village.

The next day (13th), although it looked black and threatening, we went to Paris; but the rain set in so heavily that we returned forthwith, most completely drenched, to Colombes, having seen nothing.

The 14th was fine again, and I resolved on an expedition to Malmaison and Versailles if possible. The road lay through Nanterre, on the *coteau*, but a little elevated above the meadows through which the Seine holds its course. The scenery, without being very striking, was very pleasing and pretty. On my right at some little distance ran the river, beyond which rose a ridge of vine-clad hills, a continuation of those behind Argenteuil; on the left, the vine-yard, corn-fields, and rose-gardens terminated in a range of high ground, wooded, continuing from Mont Valerien towards Marly, where the waterworks, projecting from the there steep acclivity, formed rather a picturesque object —following the windings of the Seine through a less interesting country (because all corn). In the distance one sees the chateau of St Germain, with its long white terrace, backed by the dark foliage of the park; beneath, the waters of the river glitter like silver in the bright light. Malmaison is on the higher ground; and on ascending to the park-gates, I was pleased to find two neat little lodges, and an entrance perfectly English, which was the style all around. The house had nothing extraordinary in its appearance, but the little lawn in front was redolent of the perfume of the orange-flower, numerous trees being ranged around all in full blossom. I found but few servants in the house; on asking to see which, a ladylike person was called, who acted as cicerone with the easy and graceful manner so characteristic of French women. Had it not been for the interest one attaches to whatever is connected with great or extraordinary people, the houses at Malmaison perhaps were not so much worth seeing as many houses even of our commoners. There was only one room remarkable for its fitting up, and it was in other respects the most interesting. It was Josephine's bedroom. A little scene took place here. My companion idolised her former mistress; the recollections of past times and of her beloved Empress, renewed by my questions, overpowered her. I believe she was sincere. The furniture of this room (which was, I think, an octagon) was certainly splendid. Scarlet cloth (very fine) with trimmings of broad gold lace, and deep gold fringe of bullions. The bed-curtains and coverlet were of the same, and the walls were covered with it instead of paper, the gold lace serving as a border to the panels, etc. I did not admire the taste of Josephine in this. Here it was she expired. Running at right angles to the front of the house is the *galerie*—a beautiful *salon*, full of exquisite morsels of sculpture, all modern, but in my estimation many of them rivalling the antique. Taking leave of my amiable conductress, I set off to pick my way without a guide through a woody, intricate, wild country, where the openings were of no extent, so that no view could be obtained. After riding up one avenue and down another for some time, I began to fancy I was lost, when suddenly riding out upon an open I saw several peasants, male and female, at work near a *bergerie*,[1] which occupied the centre of the place. I rode forward to inquire my way, when lo! down went hoes, and away went men, women, and dogs as fast as their legs could carry them into the neighbouring woods, leaving me as much at a loss to account for their fright, as to which of the many roads (*forest*) diverging hence I should take to extricate myself from my dilemma. As the English nowhere inspire terror, these people must have taken me for a Prussian hussar, from my pelisse and enormous mustache. As no information was to be procured, I had nothing left but to push on and take my chance. I had not ridden far when the ground began to descend (I had been travelling on an elevated plateau), the thickets and wood became thinner and more scattered, and below me I saw several farmhouses. From subsequent inspection of the map, this must have been La Selle de St Cloud. I rode up to the first substantial-

---

[1] These *bergeries* are very numerous in the neighbourhood of Paris, where it seems the fashion among the great proprietors to keep flocks of merinos. Almost every chateau has its *bergerie* and *vacherie*. We have one here in Stain belonging to M. le Marquis de Livry, as I know to my cost. The *bergerie* consists of low sheds, forming a square. Within, they are fitted up with low racks for hay. The sheep are kept in these all the winter, and at night during the summer.

locking house, tied my horse up in a shed, and without ceremony marched into the kitchen, where the mistress and her maids were busily employed in their household concerns. My entrance did not in the least disconcert them, or even occasion them any apparent surprise: they entered gaily into conversation without for a minute interrupting their work. No running away here. I was very hungry, but, *malgré* the opulent appearance of the house, the good lady could give me nothing but bread (sour, as usual), some very fine cherries, and delicious milk. For this she would accept no remuneration, but her maids thankfully accepted the trifle I offered them for their trouble. I found that my deviation from the direct road to Versailles had not been great; and having received instructions for my future progress, and taken leave of my kind hostess, I once more plunged into a forest, from which, however, I soon emerged upon a cultivated country sprinkled with farms and villages, and very agreeably diversified with hill, dale, and woodland. At last the palace of Versailles, overtopping the trees and buildings in its neighbourhood, burst upon me with imposing grandeur, and I soon after entered the town.

In front of the palace is a large, almost triangular, esplanade, narrowing from the palace until it terminates in the road to Paris. A clumsy thing enough, for when building the palace they might as well have laid out a handsome square in front of it. The place looked dull and lifeless, few people, except some Prussian soldiers, being visible. The number of hotels, taverns, etc. etc., announced it as the resort of strangers and idlers. The palace itself, from all its window-shutters being closed, looked as dismal as the rest. Having secured my horse, I sounded the bell at the palace gate, which brought out the *Suisse*, who sounded another bell, which brought a most gentlemanly, but very melancholy looking, young man in the royal livery, who, upon being informed of my wish to see the palace, made a very polite bow, and requested me to follow him. It were needless repeating the history he gave of each splendid apartment, and they appeared innumerable. Solitary and silent, an overpowering sensation of melancholy came over me in comparing their present deserted state with that which had for ever passed, and I no longer wondered at the pensive manner of my interesting young companion,

though he was too young to have known Versailles in the
days of its splendour. I believe, with the exception of ourselves and the *Suisse*, whom we had left at the gate, this
immense fabric did not contain another living soul. So long
did we continue wandering from room to room, that at last,
on returning to the vestibule—no time was left to visit the
Trianon as I had intended, or even the gardens—all that I
saw of them was from a terrace upon which we were admitted
from one of the central *salons*—unless I remained all night.
It became necessary to depart forthwith, or find my way in
the dark back to Colombes.

The great road to Paris is a superb avenue, but it was disfigured by dust, which, spite of yesterday's rain, I found a
real nuisance.

Numerous were the villas along the road, but, like those
in the neighbourhood of London, the shrubberies in which
they were embowered, and everything about them, was grey
and dingy with the dust with which they were powdered.
A great part of this line seemed inhabited only by washerwomen. The foul linen of all Paris seemed assembled here.
The abundance of fine water, perhaps, is the cause of this.
Pity that some portion of it were not employed in making
this otherwise beautiful ride somewhat more enjoyable. It
was growing so late as I passed Sèvres, that I merely can say
I saw the exterior of the celebrated manufactory of porcelain.
A thick dark avenue of trees, turning to the left, here seemed
to promise a short cut to St Cloud; so up it I turned, but had
not proceeded far ere I stumbled on a guard of Prussian
jägers in an old summer-house. The sentry stopped and
ordered me back. The corporal coming out, and finding
that I was an English officer, very civilly informed me that,
as Prince Blucher had his headquarters in the palace of St
Cloud, no one was allowed to cross the park. Back, then,
I went, and descending to the Seine found a good road, by
which, passing through St Cloud, Suresnes, etc., I returned
hither just as it got so dark that I was obliged to my horse
for bringing me safe home. The latter part of my ride along
the charming banks of the river, and in the cool of a fine
evening, was truly delightful.

15*th*.—I went to Paris again, wandered about the streets
without any fixed plan, and quite by accident stumbled upon

the Hôtel Dieu. I like this random mode of proceeding much better than following any fixed plan of sightseeing: it is more independent. I walked into the hospital and through its wards. Nothing could be cleaner or better arranged; but the whole place, especially about the main entrance, had such an overpowering smell, that I was glad to make my escape and find my way to the Cathedral of Nôtre Dame. There is something exceedingly impressive in the interior of a Gothic cathedral at any time. Mass was performing as I entered the church, the solemnity of which, from the little light and rather heavy style of the architecture, was increased by the fine bass voices of the canons who assisted in the service, every one in his stall. From Nôtre Dame, after taking an omelet in a neighbouring restaurant, I had a long stroll by the quays to the Invalides. The old soldiers lounging or walking about the approaches to this fine establishment, although perfectly respectful, I thought looked displeased at seeing me. There were even some who did not attempt to conceal looks and gestures of hatred and contempt. They are to be pitied more than blamed for this feeling, since these were the men who fought and *always* conquered in Italy and Germany. Notwithstanding their scowling looks, I could not help regarding these fine veterans with the most profound veneration. I found no difficulty, however, in procuring a cicerone to show the lions, and under his guidance walked through the halls, where the tables were already laid for dinner; through the dormitories, where the beds were all clean and neatly made up, and looking comfortable, etc. etc. In the officers' dining-rooms the tables were also laid—round ones for four or six persons each—not as with us, all at one long table. A bottle of wine was here placed by the side of each man's plate. Nothing could be more comfortable or more respectable. We then visited the church under the dome where are the tombs of Turenne and Vauban.[1] All this was not very amusing, but my guide, leading the way up several staircases, at last ushered me into a large but low room, immediately under the roof, filled with beautifully finished models of almost all the frontier fortresses

---

[1] I cannot FEEL in public, especially when a *showman* is telling me in a garbled manner that which would spontaneously flash across the memory if left to one's self. When we do not *feel*, we *can't write*.

in France. Here I passed the remainder of the day most delightfully. The most interesting of these models were Château Trompette; Brest, with its harbours and the adjacent country for three or four miles round; Strasbourg and neighbourhood; but one of the most amusing was an exquisitely finished model of the battle of Lodi, under a glass bell. A fine boy of about fifteen or sixteen, to whom my quondam guide had delivered me over on entering the model-room, excited my surprise not only by the clearness with which he explained everything to me, but also by the shrewdness of his remarks, and the great knowledge he evinced of military affairs in general; quite an incipient Buonaparte, I should say—only Buonaparte was never half so handsome. I could have lingered for a week over these interesting models, but the diminution of light obliged me at last reluctantly to leave them. Whilst we were wandering from loft to loft, for there were several, we came accidentally into one where two or three Prussian officers were super-intending the dismemberment and packing up of all such as had any relation to the possessions of their monarch; and my young companion told me he suspected they meant to take away Strasbourg, and that they had already packed up several which could not come under that denomination. The poor boy spoke very feelingly on the subject, and seemed heart-broken at losing his favourite models. I shall fre-quently visit the Invalides, unless the Prussians quite strip it of the models. It will be a delightful lounge, those lofts.

Yesterday, being Sunday, our three troops assembled, under Major M'Donald, in the park, where Captain M'Donald's troop is quartered, and had divine service. Passed the afternoon in riding about the neighbourhood, and the evening in the enjoyment of my beautiful terrace, etc. etc.

To-morrow I go in search of my new troop, somewhere about St Denis.

CHAPTER XX

Sunday, July 22d.—This is the first time I have been sufficiently settled and quiet to sit down to write since the evening of the 17th, my last at Colombes—dear Colombes! The intervening space has not been passed in idleness. On the morning of the 18th I was fully occupied in giving over my troop and stores to Major Wilmot, who takes possession also of my charming apartment, and Mademoiselle Ernestine gets a new neighbour. After an earlier dinner than usual, Hitchins accompanied me to St Denis; my servants and horses started in the morning. At St Denis I could gain no immediate and distinct information. Some of Ross's non-commissioned officers whom I met with said they thought the troop must have halted in Stain. I shuddered at the very name of the place; it was the worst I had anticipated. As Hitchins knew the desolation of Stain, and the utter impossibility of my giving him a bed, even if I could get one myself, he took his leave, and I proceeded thitherward alone. It was with a heavy heart that I traversed the once rich crops of grain, now trodden into mud by having been the bivouac of our troops, and still heavier that I rode through the dismal street of the ruined village. I soon met some of the gunners, who confirmed my worst fears—viz. that the troop actually was stationed here. The officers were living and messing in a house close to the church, and opposite the *grille* of the great chateau; and thither I repaired, and found them accordingly sitting at their wine. My servants had been here some time, and had taken possession of the Petit chateau, already mentioned. The house I found my officers in belongs to the Sœurs de la Charité. I was sensibly struck on entering it at the contrast with my villa at Colombes; mean, gloomy, dirty, and scarce an article of furniture in it, and what there was, of the poorest description. To counterbalance all this, it is the only house in the place (at least so they thought then) that has any glass in the windows, and how it escaped is extraordinary. They were seated in a dismal room, very low, and having a very disagreeable odour, overpowering even that of the dinner, in which the flavour of onions predominated. After introducing myself, and drinking a glass or two of wine, as the daylight began to fail I set off to inspect my new quarters. The appearance of this in its best days would not have been pleasing after Colombes; but now, forlorn, deserted, plundered! The handsome furniture which had once adorned it, mutilated and torn to pieces, was yet fresh when last I saw it; the fragments retained their paint or gilding, the mahogany its varnish; the tatters of silk fringe and curtains, scattered over the lawns and walks, or hanging from the branches in the shrubberies, yet retained their colour in all its freshness: now, after having been drenched by rain, and bleached in the sun and wind, all remains of former beauty were gone—all associations with splendour and magnificence vanished; they conveyed to the mind no feeling but that of squalidness and wretchedness. Amidst all this I entered the house. There things looked even worse. The winds of heaven had freely coursed through the paneless windows, the rain had inundated the floors, decay had already commenced, and the place looked as if it had been years deserted. Chilly, comfortless, and wretched, the floors still covered with fragments of glass, which, crunching under one's feet, added not a little to the misery of the scene, still further enhanced by a most gloomy evening, and the dismal sound of the wind through the branches foretelling a stormy night. At length, after wandering from room to room, always finding one worse than the last, the approaching darkness obliged me to decide quickly, so I pitched upon a large one, with a recess for a bed, where I could at least be at some distance from the windows. My men had already made themselves tolerably comfortable in the stable, and I now summoned all hands to make me so too. Brooms were speedily made by stripping the branches from some acacias or laburnums in the court-yard, and all the rubbish and broken glass swept out of the window; candles were procured from the mess, my bed made in the recess upon a bedstead, nearly sound—the place began to look a little better, and I a little more cheerful.

Though not so luxuriously, yet I slept as soundly as ever at Colombes, *malgré* the forlorn feeling that crept over me as I fell into unconsciousness at the idea of being the only person in the great rambling mansion, with doors and windows all open, and admittance free to whomsoever might come.

My gloominess had construed the sighing of the wind among the foliage into a presage of rain and storm. Neither came; and the next morning I was awakened by the sun streaming full in my face, the carol of birds innumerable, and the soft, balmy, yet fresh air of a most lovely morning. As our mess-breakfast was not very early, I jumped up determined on a thorough examination of the whole village, in hopes of finding something better than the Petit chateau. After looking into several, all equally miserable, I found the one where I ought to have begun, the only one habitable. It was only across the road, shut in by high walls, overtopped by acacias. This house had escaped the observation of others as it had mine; and, strange to say, had scarcely been visited by the spoiler. All the windows were perfect, and the only injury visible on the premises was the breaking to pieces of a number of paltry plaster Cupidons and their pedestals, that had erst disfigured the garden. I took possession immediately, and here I sit in my cabinet about to give a description of it. The house is tall and narrow— four stories counting the ground-floor to the front, and three towards the garden, which is higher than the court. The ground-floor consists of stables, wood-houses, etc., opening on this court, which is planted with acacias and shut in from the village by a high wall with great close gates. On the next (or garden ground-floor), is the only decent-sized room in the whole house: all the rest are divided into those useless little cabinets of which the French seem so fond, many of them with glass doors. All the rooms have the abominable brick or tile floors so common here: however, all the windows are sound, which is the grand object. I have chosen the floor above the garden—that is, third from the court—where I have a narrow slip, with glass door at one end and window at the other, the view from which certainly does not rival that at Colombes, for it is bounded by the four high walls of my garden; another piece, with a recess in it, serves me for a bedroom, and into these two I have collected all the furniture remaining in the house, which is but little, and that of the meanest description—a few clumsy, old-fashioned chairs, and a table or two.   One of the former is a curious article: the seat lifts up, and behold a *bidet*; the top of the thick back has two or three little boxes in it for holding soap or what not.   My three domestics occupy the floor below me, and are next the animals.   The garden, which rises in a gentle slope from the house, is a long narrow strip, neatly laid out and abundantly stocked with flowers, vegetables, and fine fruit—particularly grapes, plums, and peaches, etc.   The whole is the property of two old maids, Les Demoiselles Delcambre, Marchandes des Modes, who, on the approach of the Allies, removed all the furniture worth removal, and left the place in charge of an old Flemish servant—a virgin, like themselves.   Mademoiselle Rose, as she is called in the village (and I should have mentioned that most, if not all, the peasantry have returned, and that only the chateaux and country-seats of the citizens remain unoccupied)—Mademoiselle Rose is a character.   Strong in the confidence of her want of charms, she is said to have remained faithful to her charge,[1] even when the Prussians entered and plundered the village, and thereby, the villagers assure me, saved her mistress's property when all else was destroyed.   A short, squat figure, clad in coarse black frieze, a face of the ugliest, set off by a pair of black mustaches fit for a hussar, which gives her a fierce and masculine aspect, like the dragon of the Hesperides, for she performs the part of watching the fruit most unremittingly.   The moment I enter the garden she skulks after me; and on looking about I am sure to detect her ugly phiz watching my movements from behind some bush, not presuming, however, to interfere. More than once I have noticed the sudden disappearance of fruit from some particular tree; and William tells me that Mademoiselle Rose strips the trees at night and sends the fruit to Paris.   I should suspect my own people, only that they would not take it in such quantities.   This, however, is not of any great consequence, since we have several other well-stocked gardens in the village from whence to

---

[1] Angélique told me since that Mademoiselle Rose fled to the woods with the rest of the villagers, and only returned when they did.

help one's self without trespassing on those attached to the officers' houses, which are, of course, considered as private property. There are, *par exemple*, the chateau belonging to Jerome Buonaparte; the Petit chateau to M. Domer, who, I believe, is something in the Admiralty; another large handsome chateau, with very extensive, well-kept gardens, to Admiral le Comte Rosily; a very pretty villa, garden, etc., the property of some rich shopkeeper; and several little boxes of minor importance. The village itself may be said to consist of two streets, short, and neither of them continuous. It is situated on a dead flat, consequently has no other beauty to boast of than what it derives from the foliage of the trees in the grounds of the chateaux, etc. The fields about it are corn and vines—principally the latter, I think.

It was at first certainly rather a nuisance changing from Colombes, though I have already got pretty well accustomed to the new situation. The difference was only not in the style of my lodging, beauty of the surrounding country, etc. etc., but also most particularly in our living. Instead of the comfortable, well-served table, and excellent wine of M. Ferdinand, and the new milk, nice fresh butter, and new-laid eggs—produce of my dairy and poultry-yard—here we daily sit down to miserably cooked soup and *bouilli*, made of ration-beef, and a bad steak of the same, served in ill-cleaned tin (canteen) dishes. Vegetables, to be sure, we have in abundance. Then for wine, we have some very poor stuff, which Ambrose (my surgeon) bought somewhere in Paris, and, from not understanding French, got cheated. At home here I have managed to get up a breakfast, though a poor one; the bread is so abominably sour, and the butter so cheesy. Nor have I been able to dispose of my time in the same agreeable manner as at Colombes; for between the constant attention my wretched troop requires, and the plague of the villagers, I have but little left for amusement. The former of these, the troop, I have quieted a little, by giving one of them a severe flogging; but its disorganised state may be guessed at, when it is known that the payment (contrary to our regulations) is in the hands of the sergeant-major, and that my predecessor, poor Bean, died in debt to this man at least £300. Of course everything was winked at.

The villagers (unlike those of Colombes, who have never been disturbed), after being scared from their dwellings by our advance, have returned to them, only to find everything ruined and destroyed. Of course they are not in charity with us, and full of complaining. This is all brought to me by the Maire, who pays me a regular visit every morning, and frequently in the evening also, waylaying me, besides, whenever I go from home. The Duke's system of discipline is well known, and these people seem disposed to take every advantage of it, fair and unfair. One complains of our occupying his house and stables, another of his field being mowed, another of something else, and so on. It is inconceivable that a conquered people, and a people whose armies have shown no forbearance in foreign countries, should thus dare lift up their voice and complain that the conqueror disturbs them, and puts them to some inconvenience. So it is! If I attended to one-half the complaints brought before me, we should soon be turned out of the place altogether. The very morning after my arrival, M. Bonnemain (Maire, etc.) called, and was introduced—a dry, thin, old man, rather above the middle height, in a suit of rusty-brown clothes, snuff-box in one hand eternally, and the other gesticulating in aid of his drawling voice and interminable oratory. After the introductory bow, he commenced by welcoming me to Stain, eulogised the village and villagers, expressed his satisfaction at my appointment, having already heard of my high character as an officer; under the command *d'un tel* Monsieur, everything must go on in the happiest manner possible. Then followed butter, thickly laid on, after which he cautiously and dexterously introduced his business, no doubt guessing that, having placed me on so elevated a pinnacle, I should be more cautious of a fall. "Mais, Monsieur le Commandant," he continued, "nous sommes des pauvres malheureux, pour nous tout est perdu —tout abimé, etc."; and so he went on expressing his confidence in the justice of M. le Commandant, and that he would not oppress the poor. Then followed a long—very long—story about a worthy industrious man, with a large family, whose house was occupied by our men, and stables by our horses, and a request that I might have the goodness to relieve this unfortunate family from so oppressive a burden.

He had not reckoned without his host: Monsieur le Commandant swallowed some, at least, of the dose; was softened; the quartermaster is called, and orders given that the detachment should be removed from the farm in question. Monsieur le Maire is still more profuse in bows and compliments, amidst which he retired, to my great satisfaction, for I was tired of him. The next day Monsieur le Maire again appeared, and in similar manner pleaded the cause of another excellent *malheureux*, whose crop of oats our people were cutting. Again he was successful; but as Monsieur le Commissary-General had begged us to supply ourselves in this manner from the fields, I requested Monsieur le Maire to point out how we might do so with the least possible injury to the inhabitants. He did so, and I gave the necessary orders for confining our foraging parties to the fields indicated, and to avoid unnecessary waste. Again Monsieur Bonnemain is announced; but this time he came accompanied by a genteel but rather important-looking personage, just arrived in a handsome cabriolet, whom Monsieur le Maire introduces as the postmaster of St Denis. They are somebody these postmasters. An exordium of a most complimentary character ushered in, as usual, a complaint, or rather a protest, against our cutting this gentleman's oats. Monsieur le Maître des Postes condescended (and he made the condescension evident) to inform me that he farmed the land in question at an exorbitant rent; that the produce was absolutely requisite to enable him to fulfil his contract with Government; that he should suffer much inconvenience from our depredations; and that, the public business of the Government being thus obstructed (with a most ominous shrug and extension of both hands), it was impossible to answer for the consequences. Hereupon the great man, with an air of perfect indifference, turned his back on me, and began asking trifling questions of some villagers who had flocked in to witness the negotiation. My answer was very brief: "Monsieur le Maire had himself designated the fields we were to cut." (Here a most portentous glance was shot by Monsieur le Maître at Monsieur le Maire.) "That if the public suffered in the business of posting, it was of infinitely less consequence than that any part of the British Army should become inefficient for want of forage.

As, in the present case, somebody must suffer, it were better
that the burden should fall on those best able to afford it."
Monsieur le Maître then shifted his ground somewhat,
complaining of the waste committed by our foragers, who,
he said, trampled down more than they cut.   I promised
this, if found to be the case, should be remedied, for
our own sakes; and, at his request, that one particular
non-commissioned officer should superintend the foraging.
Monsieur, finding he could get no more, bade me adieu
with more politeness than he had condescended to use on
our first meeting, mounted his cabriolet amidst bows of the
assembled peasantry, and drove off.   This fellow's opposition
has not been without consequences.   My villagers have
become more bold, and even begin to draw up petitions to
the Duke.   Some of these have already been sent to me,
with an intimation that I must not oppress the inhabitants
unless it be unavoidable.   This happens to be the case—
therefore I have taken no notice of them.

July 25th.—Yesterday our army (British only) was reviewed by their Imperial and Royal Majesties.   I marched
early, as the line was to be formed by nine o'clock.   After
passing through St Denis, we took the great road to the right
by St Ouen, and came on the Neuilly road just above the
village, where we formed, being on the left of the whole,
except the 18-pounder brigades.   Ross and Bull's troops
were on my right.   We had a long and tedious wait;   and
as the day was very hot, it was no small treat to discover that
an apothecary hard by had some excellent raspberry vinegar,
which, I think, we exhausted.   At length the approach of the
sovereigns was announced, and they came preceded and
followed by a most numerous and brilliant cortège, in which
figured, perhaps, some of almost every arm of every army
in Europe.   It was a splendid and most interesting sight.
First came the Emperor Alexander and the King of Prussia,
in their respective green and blue uniforms, riding together
—the former, as usual, all smiles;   the latter taciturn and
melancholy.   A little in their rear followed the Austrian
Emperor, in a white uniform, turned up with red, but quite
plain—a thin, dried-up, thread-paper of a man, not of the
most distinguished bearing;   his lean brown visage, however,
bore an expression of kindness and *bonhommie*, which folk

say his true character in no way belies. They passed along, scanning our people with evident interest and curiosity; and in passing me (as they did to every commanding officer), pulled off their hats, and saluted me with most gracious smiles. I wonder if they do the same to their own. Until yesterday I had not seen any British infantry under arms since the evening the troops from America arrived at Garges, and, in the meantime, have constantly seen corps of foreign infantry. These are all uncommonly well dressed in new clothes, smartly made, setting the men off to the greatest advantage—add to which their *coiffure* of high broad-topped shakos, or enormous caps of bear-skin. Our infantry— indeed, our whole army—appeared at the review in the same clothes in which they had marched, slept, and fought for months. The colour had faded to a dusky brick-dust hue; their coats, originally not very smartly made, had acquired by constant wearing that loose easy set so characteristic of old clothes, comfortable to the wearer, but not calculated to add grace to his appearance. *Pour surcroît de laideur*, their cap is perhaps the meanest, ugliest thing ever invented. From all these causes it arose that our infantry appeared to the utmost disadvantage—dirty, shabby, mean, and very small. Some such impression was, I fear, made on the sovereigns, for a report has reached us this morning, that they remarked to the Duke what very small men the English were. "Ay," replied our noble chief, "they are small; but your Majesties will find none who fight so well." I wonder if this is true. However small our men and mean their appearance, yet it was evident that they were objects of intense interest, from the immense time and close scrutiny of the inspection. At length they finished, and, taking their stand in the Place Louis Quinze, we marched past in column of division. The crowd assembled to witness this exceeded anything I had ever before seen. Not only were the people packed as thick as they could stand in the area itself, but the buildings of the Garde Meuble, the ramparts of the Tuileries, even the roof of the Hôtel Bourbon over the river, were all crowded—windows, roofs, and every cornice that could hold human beings. After passing, we took our route along the Rue Royale, Boulevard and Rue Poissonnière, starting off at a good trot, and got home about six o'clock. In St Denis

I met Captain Gaffon and the little doctor of the Brunswick hussars, neither of whom I had seen since we were in barracks together at Woodbridge. The meeting really seemed to please them, as they had heard I was killed at Waterloo. It seems somebody is determined I did or ought to have died. One of our people told me the other day, that the day after the battle a staff-officer had shown him my name in a list as dangerously wounded. And during the retreat of the 17th, whilst I was with the cavalry at Jemappes, one of the Blues who overtook my troop on the road told them that I was killed, for he had himself seen me cut down by a French dragoon—*Cependant me voici !*

July 30th.—More trouble, more complaints. Another memorial to the Duke from my subjects, complaining of cutting their oats. This I have very easily disposed of; but lo! here is a more formidable adversary to deal with—no less than M. le Marquis de Livry, *rentier* or *propriétaire* of the gambling *salons* in the Palais Royal, and, as such, a man of immense influence. He has property in this commune, and a *bergerie* in the village, where he keeps a flock of merinos. The sheep being absent when the troop arrived, the *bergerie* was converted into a stable; but having lately returned, under their shepherd, part of the building has been appropriated to their use. The shepherd, a perfect Sancho Panza in person, not content with this, has ever since been intriguing to obtain entire possession. I have been fairly pestered to death about this *bergerie.* Almost daily M. le Maire and M. le Berger de M. le Marquis de Livry make their appearance at my quarters, or intercept me in the street to tell me the same story over again, and to get the same answer. Finding his perseverance useless, M. le Berger (no doubt assisted by M. le Maire) draws up a very moving petition to the Duke, which M. de Livry takes care shall be presented under proper auspices, and behold the consequence: A positive order from his Grace to evacuate forthwith the premises of the Marquis de Livry, and *to put up our horses elsewhere in the best manner we can; that is, respect the rich man's property and oppress doubly the poor*—for we must divide the forty horses hitherto stabled in the *bergerie* among the poor villagers, who already have more than is good for them. The Duke of Wellington's ideas of discipline, etc., are rigid—his mode of administering it summary; but he is frequently led into acts of the grossest injustice. A notorious instance of this I am now suffering under, and one that makes the *bergerie* business a mere flea-bite. Only a few days ago, whilst sitting after dinner at our little mess, an officer of the mounted staff-corps (*gendarmerie Anglaise*) was announced. He regretted being the bearer of disagreeable orders, etc. etc., but Colonel Scovell, commandant of the mounted staff-corps, had directed him to show me the paper, which he produced, and to inform me that his Grace had ordered it should be immediately complied with. Further, that the Duke was excessively angry, and had expressed himself very harshly on the subject; therefore Colonel Scovell recommended me to make no remonstrance, as he could not foresee what might be the consequence. The paper was a petition from a certain M. Fauigny (an Italian), setting forth, I think, that he is proprietor of the Grand chateau which has been miserably plundered; but more particularly that the English troops now quartered in the village have stripped the lead off the roofs, from the baths, water-pipes, etc. etc., and sold it. This is, as nearly as I remember, the petition. A note written with a pencil by the Duke himself on the margin was too brief and pithy not to be remembered, and here it is, verbatim : " Colonel Scovell will find out whose troop this is, and they shall pay.—W." I was thunderstruck at the complaint and the decision— the one so unfounded, the other so cruelly unjust. I signed an acknowledgment of having seen the order ; and the officer took his leave, recommending me to try and compromise with M. Fauigny, who stated the damage at about 7000 or 8000 francs. Upon inquiry of M. Bonnemain, he asserts that this M. Fauigny is the agent of Jerome Buonaparte, to whom the chateau actually belongs, as we were told by the Prussians who plundered it.

The next morning I had just ordered my horse, and was about to set off for Paris, when William announced a gentleman who wished to see me; and a rather genteel-looking man sailed into my little parlour with an air of *nonchalance* and easy familiarity quite amusing. My friend seated himself with the utmost coolness, and drawing out his snuffy pocket-handkerchief, displaying it—whilst he spat all about the floor, to my utter disgust, for I had been in the act of finishing my breakfast—informed me with a slight inclination that he was M. Fauigny, and had called to know when it would be convenient to settle this *leaden accompt*. Finding him already acquainted with the Duke's order, I was obliged to make the best of it and put him off with excuses, which he did not seem to relish, having evidently counted on touching the cash forthwith. However, the man behaved like a gentleman, kept his disappointment to himself, and turning the conversation on general subjects, proved himself a man of very general information and a most agreeable companion. Although he would not partake of my breakfast, he paid a very long visit; and the moment he was gone, I set off also for Paris, and went straight to Sir George Wood's quarters in the Rue de Richelieu. From Sir George I learned that the affair was much more serious than I had imagined. The Duke is furious about it, and Sir George says my only chance is by evading payment as long as I can, in hopes some favourable opportunity may offer of inducing the Duke to think more leniently on the subject; in the meantime, to make every inquiry into the truth of the statement. Accordingly, we have been at work, and the result is a discovery that M. Fauigny is a villain—has made a false statement to the Duke in hopes of gaining payment from us for what has been actually done by others, but from whom he knew nothing could be recovered. The villagers themselves have informed me how the thing happened, and have denounced one of their own body as the robber, for the lead has in reality been stolen, as set forth in the petition, only not by us.[1] M. Plé is *couvreur* by trade, and did precisely the same thing last year when the village was occupied by a Russian corps, against which a charge similar to the one against us was brought, but not with the same success. Their General did not condemn his people unheard like the Duke of Wellington. However, having gained this piece of intelligence, I set off to St Denis, and stated the whole affair to the chief of the police, who smiled, and

[1] I suspect a fact I have since remembered must have suggested the idea of charging us with the lead. Finding the horses very ragged when I first joined the troop, I ordered all their manes to be plaited and loaded with lead, of which a sufficiency could have been picked up about the chateau or lawn, or off the ends or remnants of the *already* cut pipes.

anticipated me by himself mentioning M. Plé as a culprit and an old acquaintance, adding that he would lose no time in sifting the business thoroughly. A *procès verbal* was drawn up, and I took my departure, well pleased with the politeness and urbanity of the French civil authorities.

Two *gens d'armes* were despatched to arrest M. Plé and search his premises. A day or two afterwards, I received a note requesting my attendance at the police the next morning at eleven o'clock. Thither I went, and was met at the door by M. le Chef, who addressed me with a smile and an assurance that the lead was secured. Accordingly in the office stood M. Plé between two sentinels, and on the floor lay several enormous rolls of lead. This was only a part of the plunder, the rest having already been sold. In short, with admirable dexterity and perseverance, they followed up the business, and finally ascertained beyond a doubt that M. Plé was the thief, both now and last year; but although there is some suspicion of collusion between him and M. Fauigny, nothing has been brought out that throws any light on it. I don't think he seems known to our villagers, as one would suppose the agent ought to be. M. Plé is lodged in some prison in Paris, but I have no idea what eventually will become of him. The exposure of the affair has not in the least altered my position with the Duke of Wellington, for none dare tell him the story; and even Sir Edward Barnes, who kindly undertook it, met with a most ungracious rebuff, as he himself told Sir G. Wood. Meanwhile M. Fauigny continues to pay me an occasional visit. Sometimes I see the scoundrel *par nécessité*, but always keep out of his way if I can. Knowing, as he does, the Duke's humour, he continues dunning me with most unblushing effrontery for payment.

Were it not for these complaints, and most particularly this horrible affair of the lead, I could be happy enough here. I am getting quite reconciled to my house and to the village, and getting acquainted with the people, who have pretty well put things to rights again. Old Bonnemain I find quite manageable and very useful. Another ally has turned up in the person of the *garde champêtre*, who has at last ventured back and resumed the insignia of office. A very different character this from Petit Jean of Strytem; fat, pursy, stupid, dressed in shabby plain clothes, with a broad embroidered belt over his shoulder, altogether looking like a rat-catcher, for which I at first mistook him.

Moreover, to be completely on a peace-establishment, our village church has been reopened, and mass is now regularly celebrated there. The *curé* fled with the rest at our approach; but, unlike them, has never returned to his lair, and for some time the church remained closed. The other morning, shaving with the windows open towards the garden, I was astonished at hearing a most stentorian voice chanting in the church, which is not far from my garden-wall; and as nothing does or ought to take place without my knowledge, William was forthwith despatched to ascertain what was going on. In a few minutes he returned accompanied by M. Bonnemain, who, with his usual profusion of bows, commenced a most humble apology for the step he had taken without first obtaining my permission, which, however, he trusted would not on that account be withheld. He had sent to Pierrefitte (a neighbouring village) and engaged M. le Curé, a most worthy and exemplary man, to come over and "faire la messe"; and further, provided it met the approbation of M. le Commandant, and was no disturbance to him, he had engaged M. le Curé to come over every morning. So we have had mass ever since, and my morning shave is regularly accompanied by the bass, nasal chant of M. le Curé performing *l'office* to about a dozen old women; for, sometimes when I have been earlier and gone in, I have never found any other congregation. Yesterday (Sunday) it was more numerous, for then the girls go; but I am uncharitable enough to believe only to exhibit their finery. Even on that day very few men attended; indeed, throughout, since we entered France, we have found religion at a very low ebb: the churches always thinly attended, and principally by women; the Sabbath observed, if at all, only as a holiday, apparently totally unconnected with any religious idea; shops everywhere open; and agricultural labours, as well as every other kind, going on as usual, unless people choose to rest and make a holiday of it.

In looking back at this journal (if so we may term what is written by fits and starts, as an otherwise idle day occurs), I find omitted altogether the review of the Prussian army,

which took place some days ago in the Place Louis Quinze
as usual, only in this case the line was formed along the
Boulevard, and the column entered the place by the Rue
Royale. I have neglected this so long, that I remember
few particulars of the review. The troops looked well,
their equipment appeared good, the men young, active, and
well drilled, countenances full of animation, and apparently
proud of being soldiers; cavalry well mounted, and the
cuirassiers wore black cuirasses, instead of polished ones
like the French. The crowd was as great as when we were
reviewed, and the ground was kept by a parcel of wild-
looking Cossacks in blue frocks and very shabby-looking
horses and appointments—*voilà tout!* But there was one
occurrence at that review that I shall never forget. The
Cossacks were under an old chieftain, evidently of high
rank, whom I understood to be no less a person than their
Hetman Platoff, besides whom several Russian general
officers rode about giving directions to the Cossacks.

It was with some difficulty that I made my way through
the crowd and gained a front place, not far from the *débouche-
ment* of the Rue Royale. The only military man near me
was a proud-looking Russian officer, who, from his large
epaulettes and numerous decorations, I took to be a man of
some consequence, and, from the sidelong glances at my
plain and rather shabby pelisse, somewhat annoyed at my
near neighbourhood. We were, however, knee to knee,
and, *bongré malgré*, destined to keep company, for the throng
was too dense to admit of changing place; and so, as it
fluctuated backward and forward, we were forced to advance
or retire like files of the same squadron. The Cossacks
were very actively employed with their long lances keeping
us all back, but still the crowd continually pushed us forward
until we were sometimes almost in the ranks of the advancing column. At length, tired of his ineffectual attempts
at restraining us within bounds, the Cossack who was our
immediate sentry made an angry complaint to one of the
general officers, and, from pointing our way, evidently
particularised me and my neighbour. The general, flying
into a passion, first looked thunder and lightning at us, and
then, cane in air, rushed to the charge. It will readily be
imagined that the ferocious gestures meant to drive us from

the field only roused my John Bullism, and caused me to assume an air of defiance. Not so my superb neighbour; on him it had full effect. He looked intimidated, reined back his horse, and, turning, endeavoured to push through the crowd and make his escape, leaving me to bear the brunt of the attack. The general, however, knew his game; so, passing me with a scowl which I smiled at, and a grumble which I did not understand, he pursued my friend with uplifted cane, which every moment I expected to see descend on his back. The scene was the most degrading I had ever witnessed—an officer in full uniform, his breast covered with decorations, actually bending low on his horse's neck and making a back to receive a caning, whilst with upturned face his looks seemed abjectly craving mercy. I wonder what the French thought of it. I blushed for the cloth, and most sincerely congratulated myself on being an Englishman. The chase continued until the discomfited hero was fairly driven from the field, when his bully returned fuming and chafing and looking very fierce, and apparently very much vexed at the insolent indifference with which I purposely surveyed him.

Being on the subject of reviews, I may as well note here one that took place yesterday, which I have just heard of, but did not see. It seems that we have been the *raræ aves* of the day ever since our review. The rapidity of our movements, close-wheeling, perfection of our equipment, etc. etc., excited universal astonishment and admiration. The consequence of this was an application to the Duke for a closer inspection, which he most magnanimously granted, and ordered Ross's troop out for that purpose. They paraded in the fields near Clichy. The reviewers, I understand, were *maréchaux de France*; but there was also a great concourse of officers of all nations. After the manœuvres the troop was dismounted, and a most deliberate inspection of ammunition, and even of the men's kits, appointments, shoeing, construction of carriages, etc. etc., took place. I believe they were equally astonished and pleased with what they saw, and, as there were several among them taking notes, have no doubt that we shall soon see improvements introduced into the Continental artillery.

Paris, and the country for leagues round, form one immense garrison. The Prussians have their headquarters at St Cloud, where Prince Blucher occupies the palace. Their army occupies all the country west of Paris—Versailles, Sèvres, Bellevue, etc., and round to the southward as far as Charenton. In Paris they occupy the arsenal, and at first had a bivouac of infantry in the Place du Carrousel, and of light cavalry in the Champs Elysées, both of which have since been withdrawn and sent somewhere into quarters. They also had infantry in bivouac in the Jardin du Luxembourg, Place Royale. I do not know whether they are withdrawn yet or not. Our headquarters are at the Elysée Bourbon; and our cantonments, commencing at Suresnes, extend along both banks of the Seine to Argenteuil and St Germain en Laye, all round the north side of Paris to the heights of Belleville. The greater part of our cavalry is, I believe, on the left bank of the Seine. The Life Guards, Blues, etc., are at Nanterre, Rueil, etc.; hussars at Suresnes, Puteaux, etc., and Gardiner's (Sir Robert) troop of horse-artillery. This last is, I think, quartered on the Duc de Feltre (Clerk). The 12th, and another light dragoon regiment, at Courbevoie, in the fine barracks. Infantry at Anières, Villeneuve, and Genevilliers. Colombes— my old troop, Bull's, and M'Donald's. Bezons—the rocket troop. Neuilly—two troops of Hanoverian horse-artillery. St Ouen—Brunswick cavalry and infantry; some in the village, some in bivouac. Epinay—pontoon-train. Pierrefitte—waggon-train. St Denis—commissariat magazines, etc., two regiments of English infantry (64th one of them), a brigade of 18-pounders, and Sir H. Ross's troop [1] of horse-artillery. Malmaison—cavalry headquarters. I think there are cavalry at Marly, St Germain en Laye, etc. etc. Stain —my troop; [1] communication kept open by the bridge of Neuilly, and pontoon-bridges at Argenteuil and Anières. Clichy, Courcelles, and Villiers—the fifth division, partly in camp, partly in quarters. Bois de Boulogne—infantry, encamped. Passy—English artillery. Rue Poissonnière— a regiment of English infantry in the barrack. La Chapelle —Hanoverian dragoons and a brigade of 18-pounders. Montmartre—English infantry. Clignancour—21st Regiment of do. Faubourg de Montmartre—English infantry.

[1] The two reserve troops.

Faubourg de Clichy—Rifles. Chaussée d'Antin—Foot Guards. Vertus, or Aubervilliers—English infantry and Major Morrison's 9-pounder brigade. Gonesse—English infantry and artillery. Chenevrière—do. do. do. Luzarches, and along the line of road to Chantilly—Belgic contingent. Dugny—Staff-corps. Garges, Arnonville, etc. —Nassau troops. Headquarters of our artillery, Rue de Richelieu. Belleville and the neighbourhood is occupied by Russian infantry. Abattoirs de Montmartre (the barrack at)—a regiment of cuirassiers, in white, with black cuirasses; I think they are Russian—not sure. Faubourg St Denis— Austrian or Hungarian infantry. The Emperor of Austria lives on the Boulevard (I think des Italiens). The Emperor of Russia and King of Prussia I know not where; but the Hetman Platoff (as well as our Colonel Sir A. Frazer) lives at the Hôtel du Nord, Rue de Richelieu, where his guard of wild-looking Cossacks, with their little shabby horses picketed in the court, furnish gape-seed for the *badauds*, a crowd of whom are continually at the gate. It is a singular spectacle to see the public places in town all doubly guarded —a French and an English or Prussian sentry. When I ride into Paris by the Barrière de Clichy, as I generally do (that way being so much pleasanter than passing through La Chapelle and Faubourg St Denis), I am at once amused and interested at seeing the two sentries soberly pacing backward and forward, opposite each other, one on each side of the street. As I draw near they simultaneously front and pay the usual compliment (there is something piquant in receiving a salute from a French soldier), each after his own fashion. There they stand; on the one side a tall handsome fellow, with a fair face and prim shopkeeper-like air, with his high fur cap and trim uniform, almost spick-and-span new; the other, a shorter but more sturdy figure, bronzed visage, and jacket of brick-dust red, marked in various places with bivouac stains, and faded from exposure to sun and rain, but with arms and accoutrements in far better order than those of his smart neighbour. On first taking possession of Paris, the Prussians posted one or two field-pieces at each of the bridges, with a guard of infantry. These guns were kept constantly loaded, and slow-match lighted. Latterly they have been withdrawn; but we still have guards at every public building—such as the Louvre, Palais Royal, etc. These are generally English.

Yesterday I made a most interesting excursion over all the scene of last year's battles,—the plain of St Denis, Vertus, the heights of Belleville, Montmartre, etc. Independent of historical associations, these heights are extremely interesting, from the fine commanding views they afford; but particularly in a geological point of view. Rising abruptly to the height of some hundred feet from the (almost level) Plain de St Denis, their appearance is very remarkable as we approach by the great northern road to La Chapelle, almost everywhere terminating in lofty white precipices of gypsum (or sulphate of lime)—hence called plaster of Paris. Montmartre appears once to have been a continuation of the heights of Belleville, from the similarity of the gypsum cliffs opposite to each other. It is now isolated, and, with its precipitous terminations and crest covered with windmills, forms a very remarkable object from the plain below. These windmills are principally on the end over Clichy; towards the other is the celebrated telegraph—known by fame to all Europe—whence were transmitted at various periods orders for the invasion of Italy, Austria, Russia, Prussia, and Belgium, and by which Paris was so often roused to the boiling-point of vanity when it brought intelligence of Jena, Wagram, etc. But *revenons à nos moutons*. The heights are separated by a narrow gorge, in which, under the cliffs of Montmartre, is a small hillock [1] (Mamelon), crowned by three windmills, which appears to have been formed by detritus from above. The dome of St Geneviève seen through this gorge gave us the first notice of the French capital the evening we arrived at Garges.

The intermediate part of Montmartre, though not precipitous, descends by a very rapid slope towards the plain. About midway of the descent is the pretty village of Clignancour, the houses of which, having their first floor on a level with the ground behind, command from their windows and balconies a most extensive and pleasing view over the country below, and are delightfully intermingled with shrubberies

[1] Under the cliffs at the other extremity, near the Barrière de Clichy, is a similar mound, originating, no doubt, in the same way. It is now covered with fine trees, and forms an agreeable object as one approaches the Barrière. Its name (*Monceau*) perhaps points to its origin.

and gardens.   The descent towards Paris is less steep, and is covered all the way with the suburb of Montmartre.   The whole summit is enclosed by Buonaparte's celebrated, but, as it has turned out, useless lines, erected last year for the defence of the metropolis.   Of these I need say little, as I know they are surveying by our engineers, who will no doubt give us a detailed account of them—a piece of slavery which I am not at all disposed to engage in.   All I can say of them is that, considering the hurried manner in which the work has been done, they are very creditable—that they cover all the ground in front with their fire—and that a tremendous concentration of fire, direct and flanking, commands every important point.   They are continued partially across the gorge, the bank of the Canal de l'Ourcq, and fully up the opposite heights of Belleville.   They may, however, be easily turned on either flank.   The gorge is occupied by the humble and uninteresting suburb of La Chapelle.   The heights of Belleville are extremely pretty, being almost covered with a succession of cheerful and sometimes elegant villas, gardens, shrubberies, vineyards, and the village. I envied the Russians such pretty quarters; yet they would be just as well pleased here as there, perhaps.   From these heights I got a peep at Vincennes, with its park, chateau, and tower, on which the Lilies of France have at last replaced the Tricolor.   The governor (*un vieux moustache*, with one leg) refused for a long time to surrender; and the sovereigns, out of respect for the old man, did not insist; but after a time he grew insolent, and I understand either did or threatened to fire at some officers who went too near his stronghold.   This was too much, and preparations were making to reduce him when he was fortunately persuaded to surrender.   Having rambled about until I had seen all worth seeing, and got an omelet in one of the *ginguettes*, or whatever they call them, I descended from the heights of Belleville, and crossing the fields (all without hedges here), and the great road to Soissons, made straight for Vertus. As far as the road to Soissons, the number of gardens, with summer-houses perched on one angle of the enclosing wall, thick shrubberies, and the fine umbrageous avenue which the road itself with its quadruple rows of elms presents, made the country interesting in spite of its flatness; but beyond,

when one comes on what may more strictly be termed the
plain of St Denis, there is no redeeming point—it is a
vast extent of monotonous corn-field, unrelieved by tree or
shrub, and only broken by the buildings of the village of
Vertus and the elevated bank of the Canal de l'Ourcq. The
great road to Compiègne, which crosses this plain from La
Chapelle to St Denis, once had its trees also; but they were
cut down, I think, last year; and the only objects one now
sees along this dreary line are a mile (or a league) stone on
the left going to town, and a cross or Bon Dieu on the right.
Young trees have been planted along part of the line, but
at present they are mere sticks. Met Major Morrison in
Vertus; his 9-pounder brigade is stationed there, together
with a regiment of infantry. By the way, the name of that
place is Aubervilliers, or Nôtre Dame des Vertus, but one
never hears any more of its name than the last word—so
that it is Vertus *par excellence*, and all the rest is superfluity.

I have had a long scribble this morning; so now, having
jotted down nearly everything to the present date, I have
a right to go and idle a bit with the girls. This is a lounge
of which I have as yet said nothing, because I thought it
commonplace; hereafter, however, it will be interesting to
look back and see as in a picture all that is now transacting
—*allons donc !* Through the middle of our village runs a
little sluggish rivulet, very like that at Garges. On the banks
of this, every fine day, may be seen assembled the scraggy-
necked dames and black-eyed nymphs of the village, all
pretty much alike in costume—that is, arms bare, stays
loosely laced, and petticoat of *siamoise*, with the eternal blue
stockings and wooden shoes; each has her bundle of linen,
her heavy bat, and generally a bit of board to kneel on.
Here, then, kneeling in a line along the banks of soapy waters,
they laugh, chatter, and sing; whilst the bat incessantly
goes slap, slap, slap. Just where the street leading to St
Denis joins ours, in the centre of the village, a bridge of very
humble dimensions spans the stream, on the parapet of
which I have established my divan; and thither I repair
to smoke my weed and enjoy a little badinage with the fair
daughters of Stain—to gain a little information from their
wrinkled mothers. Amongst our village maidens there are
several exceedingly pretty—some one or two would be

beautiful, were not their feminine *delicacy* (perhaps the word may be used morally as well as physically) much injured by their being constantly employed in the fields, which cannot but make their persons coarse. There is one exception to this, however, in Josephine Chamont, who is really a beautifully delicate, ladylike girl; but then she does not go to the fields. Angélique, on the contrary, is as fine a woman as ever I saw; she is about twenty—a perfect Juno—tall, erect, with a beautiful countenance and splendid black eyes; she walks like a queen. When our invasion was expected, the women of the commune formed themselves into an Amazonian regiment, and Angélique was their sergeant-major.—But I must to the bridge.

M. Fauigny paid me a visit this morning: I did not see him.

CHAPTER XXI

August 1st.—Our fine weather still continues—with the exception of one or two days, we have scarcely had any rain since we arrived here. Our army is breaking up from hence and going into Normandy. Some of our troops of horse-artillery marched the day before yesterday, and yesterday some regiments of cavalry. The infantry are also preparing for their departure. Ross's troop and mine, belonging to the reserve, are to remain in the neighbourhood of Paris. This appearance of peace has, I suppose, induced the Beguines, or Sœurs de la Charité, to return to the village, much to our annoyance; for their house is the one in which we mess, and where Ambrose and Maunsell live. Five of the sisterhood called on me this morning for the purpose of obtaining the restoration of their house, and permission to return and inhabit it. I was at breakfast, but these good dames would take no refusal, and William was obliged to show them up. My little room was crammed.

I have always up to this date associated most inseparably in my mind youth and beauty with the term nun. It was, therefore, not without some trifling emotion that I awaited the five nuns whom William had announced, and heard them bustling along the narrow bricked passage leading from the head of the stairs to my room. Such being the case, it may easily be imagined that it was not without disappointment I saw entering, one after another, five ugly old women, in shabby black dresses, and at the same time became sensible of a very unpleasant odour accompanying the ladies. All this was enough; and, in the politest manner possible, I hastened to meet their wishes as soon as known, in order to get rid of them. Here I reckoned without my host. The good dames found my politeness so winning, that they were in no hurry to move, nor did they until they had inflicted on me the whole history of their adventures and sufferings from the first invasion by the Allies last year down to last night. When, at length, they did depart, I thought I could never sufficiently inhale the fresh air of heaven.

Having got rid of the ladies, after visiting the parade (which we hold in the park of the great chateau), I rode to St Ouen and Clichy. In the last and neighbourhood our fifth division is quartered, and I was astonished to see the Prussian-like manner in which the place is occupied. One very handsome villa I visited had its pretty pleasure-ground trampled and spoiled as much as the chateau at Stain; and, to my surprise, in the house I found two formerly splendid *salons* converted into stables, and actually occupied by officers' horses. I don't know what the Duke will say when he comes to know this. The neighbourhood of Clichy is pretty—all villas and gardens, etc.

August 2d.—Another beautiful day. More regiments marching towards Normandy. In consequence of the return of our nuns, we moved our mess establishment to-day into the Petit chateau, having prepared and made as comfortable as circumstances would admit the grand *salon* in the centre of the front. This is a very fine room with a boarded floor in little squares (*parquet*), which looks very well, but is very creaky, as all these floors are. We collected what chairs were still serviceable as seats, and as they were few, the wheeler patched up others; a table was a more difficult article to procure; the floor served as a sideboard. There being no glass in the window, we are obliged to make the venetians (which fortunately are unbroken) answer, lowering those to windward when the air is too much. We are raised about six feet above the lawn, and two winding flights of steps afford the means of descending from the windows of the bowed front to the turf below. Fatigue-parties have been employed all yesterday and this morning clearing the lawn of the fragments of furniture, rags of curtains, torn books, and broken glass, that encumbered and disfigured it—so that now our domain looks decent, and we have actually wondered we could stay so long in the gloomy old house we have left. By way of a house-warming I gave my champagne on promotion, and we have had a merry evening, without excess, or I should not be able to write this.

3*d*.—No headache this morning; our champagne was excellent and very cheap. In England we should pay from 10s. to 15s. per bottle. This cost me precisely 5 francs, or 4s. 2d., a bottle—some little difference. But to my journal. Rode to Paris, and as usual put up Cossack at a stable I have discovered in Rue de Malle, just by the Place du Carrousel, consequently very convenient. When I arrived, there were several people in the stable, who gathered round me and Cossack, asking with apparent curiosity if he was in the battle of Mont St Jean. I told them Yes, and all about his eight wounds—the scars of which were visible enough. This seemed to excite great interest; and I walked off, leaving them assembled round the fellow's stall, having first, however, warned them of his heels. The Palais Royal, Rue Vivienne, and Boulevard were the scenes of my promenade. The first I have spoken of before, and hope to do so again; the second is a kind of Bond Street, leading straight away from the northern entrance of the Palais Royal. Like Bond Street, it is narrow—so narrow, indeed, that the London street becomes broad by comparison, and is infinitely its superior in the convenient *trottoir* which the Rue Vivienne totally wants. In short, in London this narrow, badly paved avenue, with its gutter down the centre, would only rank as a lane. Here is to be seen all the beauty and fashion of Paris; for here, as in Bond Street, are all the fashionable shops. If some of those under the arcades of the Palais Royal are more splendid, the articles in these are more substantially rich and good. But the Boulevard is the great point of attraction for me, and there I passed this morning, until it was time to return here before dark, lounging from the Rue Royale to the Boulevard du Temple and back again, with an occasional turn down the Rue de Richelieu, or the Passage des Panorama and Feydeau, into the Rue Vivienne and Palais Royal. The Boulevards (for there are many, every few hundred yards having a different designation) form a sort of circular road round what once was Paris, separating it from the Faubourgs, now forming part of the great whole; and these Boulevards form a street about as broad as Oxford Street, perhaps broader. This, without excepting the Palais Royal, is the most amusing part of Paris. The houses along this immense avenue are neither regular nor uniformly handsome, but high and low, rich and poor, wood and stone—from the cottage to the palace. A broad footway (not a paved *trottoir*) next the houses is in many parts shaded by rows of lime-trees, and separated from the road by a shabby wooden railing. The road is incessantly thronged with carts, fiacres, cabriolets, private equipages, and horsemen; every now and then a detachment of *gens d'armes* is seen urging their way soberly through the crowd. This forms a lively and amusing scene enough, particularly just now, from the contrast between numerous well-appointed English equipages and the clumsy vehicles and tinsel finery of the native. But it is in the footway one finds the greatest source of amusement, and most food for philosophical contemplation. Here one meets promenaders or passengers in every variety of European, and even some Asiatic, costumes. Some, you may know by their lounging gait, are employed only in killing time and dispelling *ennui*; others, bustling from shop to shop and from table to table, are people whose money burns in their pockets, and their amusement consists in getting rid of it as quickly as possible for articles utterly useless to them, and which, laid aside to-morrow, will quickly be forgotten. Again, a third, and by far the most numerous class one sees here, have a directly contrary employment to the last—they are people whose pockets burn to have money in them; and accordingly here, in this great thoroughfare, we find them resorting to all sorts, even the most ludicrous, the vilest, and the most degrading means of obtaining their end. Here tables innumerable are set out under the trees covered with all sorts of cheap articles—toys, perfumery, cutlery, combs, and articles in horn, bone, wood, metal, glass—everything and every article upon each table of the same price. In passing along, one is deafened by the incessant and rapid vociferations of these dealers enumerating the various articles upon their tables, eulogising them in the most ridiculous terms, and announcing their price: "Dix sols pour chacun!— dix sols, dix sols—dix sols seulement, messieurs!" Then there are jugglers, mountebanks, and importunate beggars. My great torment in the Boulevard is a little wretch of a girl, about ten or twelve years old, whose ostensible business is the sale of toothpicks, but in reality is begging. This little

animal fixes herself on one with the tenacity of a leech—
running by one's side, occasionally holding up the articles
of her pretended trade, and unceasingly plying her song:
"Ah, monsieur! curedents, monsieur? En voulez-vous,
monsieur? deux sols, monsieur! Ah, monsieur! le pauvre
père, monsieur; il est malade, monsieur!" and then, when
she becomes convinced of the inutility of perseverance,
suddenly stopping and entering into an indifferent, perhaps
merry, confab with some chum, and again starting after
some other likely looking customer. She frequently follows
me from her stand, which is at the end of the Rue de Richelieu
to the Rue de la Paix. Other characters there are of different
descriptions, and many of them forming a feature in this
motley and daily crowd. Amongst these I have particularly
noticed an old man, with long grey locks flowing in a most
picturesque style over his back and shoulders, strumming
a cracked guitar; and a female, somewhat advanced in years,
dressed in shabby old finery, her faded charms partially
concealed under a rusty-black veil, who attempts to excite
interest in and extract metal from the passengers by warbling
a pathetic love-song in a most ominously husky voice. A
little farther, a proud and stately Mohammedan, in full
Turkish costume, offers for sale I know not what, and
evinces much indignation at the itinerant sausage-vendor,
who pushes steadily through the crowd, the fiery brasier
suspended before him by a strap passing round his neck,
everywhere opening for him a free passage. Over the
brasier a square pan contains the savoury-smelling, hissing
sausages, which as they fry he is able, from having his hands
at liberty, to keep turning, or to serve out to customers and
receive their sols in return. The steaming pan has frequently made my mouth water, and I give no credit to the
fierce and angry look of our stately Turk when startled by
his near and unexpected approach. I'd wager a sol did they
but encounter in some obscure passage he would himself
become a customer to the Giaour's polluted pan.

At the angle formed by the Boulevards du Temple and
St Martin, and opposite to the beautiful Fontaine de Boudi
or des Lions, in a snug recess formed by a break in the line
of building, may daily be seen a table, covered with a cloth
scrupulously white, on which are arranged sundry piles of a

peculiarly inviting *gâteau*. This table is constantly surrounded by a certain description of young men, whose
bronzed features, mustachioed lips, and confident, insolent
stare, denote the *militaire en retraite*, or half-pay officer.
Here the presiding goddess is a comely dame of some forty
years' standing, a little inclined to *embonpoint*, with a bold
masculine countenance embrowned by constant exposure,
but yet having strong claim to a certain description of beauty,
which she understood how to enhance by the tasteful and
coquettish arrangement of her blue *cornette* and a studied
neatness in every other part of her dress. With her customers
this fair dame carries on a conversation animated and somewhat free, if she likes them; but Englishmen are by no means
favourites. This portrait will be readily recognised by
those to whom the Boulevard St Martin is familiar. The
immense number of tables spread with books, as well as
little sheds for the sale of the same—and their cheapness,
are quite astonishing. I may say the same of engravings,
many of them really good. Equally astonishing is the open
and barefaced display, in these stalls, etc., of the most
licentious works, and pictures of the most indecent kind.
Although the best shops are certainly in the Rue Vivienne,
etc., yet are there many very splendid ones along the Boulevards, particularly the Boulevard des Italiens. Here are
also some good restaurants and cafés; and, amongst other
ornamental buildings, the Bains Chinois. Amid all these,
however, there is a characteristic eyesore which strikes one
as quite incongruous: I allude to the intervention of shabby
wooden sheds amongst goodly shops and houses. Besides
the book-stalls just spoken of, one sees every here and there
a long, low, mean-looking shed, its front almost all window.
This is a news-room, where, for a few sols, you may read
all the daily journals published in Paris, if you have patience
to wait until they be disengaged, for these places are generally full; and I often amuse myself by stopping before the
broad windows, always open just now, and contemplating
the line of odd figures—some spectacled, others (from the
manner of holding the little—after our own—minikin *feuille*
at arm's length) who evidently ought to be; and all absorbed
in the meagre nonsense which every one of these papers I
have looked into contains: a number of people may com-

monly be seen in attendance awaiting their turn. The fellows who keep these sheds must make a mint of money. Another feature not confined to the Boulevards, but common to all the public gardens and places of general resort, is the numbers of well-dressed and often dandified loungers on chairs, and the piles of these against the trees. To us at first it was a novelty seeing groups of people seated on chairs in the open street; but I have now got accustomed to it, and even to appreciate the luxury myself. These chairs, which are of the plainest kind, form the stock-in-trade, and furnish the livelihood, of many a poor old man or woman, who otherwise could do nothing to support themselves; and, *en passant*, I should note the admirable address with which I have seen these people turn the wants of human nature to account. On a rainy day some sally out with a common oilskin umbrella, which is offered to the first unfortunate wight caught out in a hat or coat likely to suffer. Others, providing themselves with a thick plank, repair to some great thoroughfare where they know there is an insufficient gutter that will overflow—and this may be everywhere. The plank, laid over the rushing stream of black water, is paid for by those who are generous by a sol or two, thus verifying the saying, It is an ill wind that blows nobody good.

The hire of a chair per hour is a mere trifle—a sol or two; and thence it is, I suppose, that a Parisian exquisite seems to think it degrading to occupy only one. Two or three is the common run; but I saw one gentleman this morning who actually occupied five whole chairs. He had chosen an excellent position to be seen, on the Boulevard des Italiens, just by Hardi's, whither I was bound to get some dinner. One chair sustained the main body, another the right leg, a third the left, a fourth afforded a rest for the left arm, whilst the fifth, bearing gloves, *mouchoir*, and *canne à pomme d'or*, stood conveniently by his right. The self-satisfied air with which this exquisite scrutinised with his *lorgnette* the passers-by, was not the least amusing part of this entertaining microcosm. Cogitating on the various means used by mankind to court or win admiration from their fellow-men, I mounted the steps in front of Hardi's, and entered the airy, nicely furnished *salle à manger*. "Garçon! la carte!" I cried, throwing myself into a seat near the window, the table by which appeared unoccupied. There is about as much difference between one of our dark close coffee-rooms in London and the *salle à manger* of a Parisian restaurateur (at least Hardi's or Very's), as there is between a tallow-chandler's back parlour in St Martin's Lane and Lady B.'s beautiful drawing-room in Park Lane.   Here are no closely shut-up boxes, with their green curtains, etc.; all is open, airy, and cheerful.   Small tables (just sufficiently large to dine four people) stand about the room covered with snow-white tablecloths, napkins, and silver forks; and instead of the dingy smoked walls of a London coffee-house, and windows so covered with dust that the panes of glass, although translucent, are not transparent, here the walls, covered with a gay painted paper, have an air of cheerfulness quite indescribable, especially when connected with the moving, lively scene without, of which the constantly open door and windows afford an uninterrupted view.   In looking on the scene below, the continuous lines of trees give such a rustic appearance to the whole, that it is difficult to imagine one's self in the very heart of a great capital.   To me the Boulevard had more the style of Lewisham or Clapham, or some of those *"rus in urbe"* sort of places so numerous in the vicinity of London.   It seems bells are not in use at these places, and calling out or making a noise is vulgar. Therefore, instead of the constantly reiterated "Waiter! waiter!" a sort of masonic signal has been invented to call the attention of the attendants.   I began at my first visit to Hardi's as I would have done in England, and summoned the *garçon viva voce*; but I soon discovered by the glances shot from the tables, and the quick turning of heads, that there was something wrong, at least something unusual. I observed there was no calling, and yet tables were served; and by the occasionally sudden turning and going up to some particular one, I became aware that some other mode of communication must be established.   I watched.   The *garçon* was standing near the door looking at an English regiment at that moment passing along the Boulevard.   An elderly gentleman, in a sad-coloured suit, who had hitherto been busily employed at the next table discussing his *potage*, stopping suddenly, looked sharply about the room as if in search of some one.   His inquisitive glance settled at once on the *garçon*, and taking up the sharp-pointed knife that lay beside his plate (the knives here are all of one pattern, very common, and apparently made to be used as stilettos instead of for cutting beef or mutton), gently touched with it the side of his wine-glass, producing a slight jingling sound that scarcely reached my ear, close as we were to each other. It proved sufficient though, for the *garçon* started and was at his side in an instant. "Ma foi!" thought I, "this is a 'wrinkle to my horn.'" I shall be quite an *habitué*. I tried the experiment again and again:—it never failed; and being now up to the thing, I soon observed that everybody used the same signal. It reminds me of the Spanish call, "Hist!" uttered from the tongue alone, without any sound from the chest. Things are uncommonly well cooked at Hardi's, and served in most comfortable and respectable style. The napkins at a public table are quite new to us Englishmen. I had a *potage*, and one or two *petit-plats*, that I selected at random from the *carte*; for amongst the numbers figuring there, I knew not one by name, and most probably as little by nature. One thing I dislike in French cookery is the abominable fashion of disguising vegetables; one cannot even get a potato plain and unsophisticated. *Gâteau de pommes de terre*, or some such mixture of potatoes, butter, etc. etc., is the only way they are eaten here. Having finished my plate of strawberries and a bottle of very excellent Lafitte, I set off for the Rue de Malte; but instead of going directly thither down the Rue de Richelieu, I made another little promenade on the Boulevard, and finally down the Passage des Panoramas and Feydeau, Rue Vivienne, Palais Royal, etc. The lamps were already lighted, doors open, sentinels posted, and crowds rushing into the Théâtre des Variétés as I passed. The passages looked brilliant by the light of multitudes of lamps, and the arcades of the Palais Royal, where the illumination was only beginning, already swarmed with depravity, and proposals rung in my ears from my entrance to my sortie from this sink of iniquity. The decreasing light warned me not to loiter; so, mounting Cossack, I made the best of my way over the abominable pavement of the Faubourg St Denis, until, gaining the end of La Chapelle, the road became better adapted for rapid movement. Daylight closed, however, just as I got through

St Denis, having just enough to save me from the wheels of the numerous chariots and other vehicles with which its long narrow street is always crowded. Having only open fields to traverse afterwards, I cared less; and trusting myself to Cossack's sagacity, he soon brought me safe home—and thus ends one of the many pleasant days I have passed in this most interesting place. I find M. Fauigny has been here to-day. He gets hot after his money. I doubt, however, if he will ever finger any of it.

August 4th.—Beautiful day again. Every pleasure in this life has some drawback—as if this were necessary to prevent our thinking we have already arrived in paradise. That, then, which in a measure neutralises our enjoyment of this fine warm weather, is the incessant torment of swarms of flies (common house-flies) which infest us within and without doors. From these wretches there is no respite, except it be at night, or may be in a darkened room. The mosquitoes cannot be worse, though they may be as bad. It is not as in England—merely the buzzing about and tickling caused by their alighting on and walking about one. No; here the brutes bite, and so sharply as to bring blood. My greatest suffering from these plagues is in the morning, when I may wish to lie in bed later than usual, which is not often. I am generally up too early for them;[1] for it is only after the sun acquires strength that they begin to be troublesome: then, unless the room be well darkened, there is no possibility of sleeping; and in my naked house there are not the means of doing this—window-shutters, to be sure, but they fit so badly that there is little difference as to light whether they be closed or open. In the village the road is quite black every day in front of our butcher's with the dead flies thrown out. He poisons them with an infusion of quassia sweetened with sugar. In my garden there is abundance of the finest fruit—peaches, nectarines, figs, plums, and splendid grapes, now all quite ripe; but such swarms of the detestable brutes infest the trees that they spoil everything. It is impossible to eat any of the fruit without first washing it: this spoils it. Half the battle is picking it off the tree and eating it.

[1] Early riser as I am, my neighbour here beat me considerably, for I always used to hear him harnessing his horses for work before daylight, which he did with a pretty annoying quantity of noise and chattering.

What strange things we live to see and hear! I do think that during the period I have been in the world, more strange, wonderful, improbable (and what once would have been deemed impossible) events have occurred than the whole history of the world, since Noah landed on Mount Ararat down to 1789, could furnish altogether. Not the least strange amongst these is the general order just published to the British Army by Wellington, calling upon commanding officers to give every assistance required by the French farmers or *cultivateurs* in getting in the harvest! In consequence, English soldiers and French peasants are seen everywhere side by side, sickle in hand, or binding sheaves, etc.—the invader and the invaded alike peaceably occupied, and reciprocating kind offices one with the other. 'Tis a goodly sight, truly. Further good consequences are very perceptible in our village. All mistrust and dislike of each other are at an end; and our people are now quite on an intimate and friendly footing with the peasantry. Many an amicable little knot may be seen of an evening sitting at their doors enjoying at once the cool air, their pipes, and the pleasures of conversation, or rather of trying to understand each other. Some of the villagers have already picked up a little English, and our men a little French. The gayest of the latter occasionally mix in the rustic dance; and although rather rough and bearish in their manner of swinging the girls about, yet are they sought after as partners, the pretty *paysanne* who has for her partner *un canonier* evincing in her look and manner a degree of satisfaction not to be mistaken. Already symptoms of jealousy have made their appearance among the young *paysans*, and I have consulted M. Bonnemain on the subject, expressing my fears lest it might disturb the harmony already subsisting. "A bah! n'y a pas de danger!—n'importe, n'importe," is always his answer; and accordingly neither I nor my officers have observed anything like a diminution of friendship among the males. These French girls are clever creatures. They have hearts and flattering tongues for all. It is a pleasing sight of an evening to see our people returning frolicking home from the fields, with the loaded carts, the cargoes of which all are busily assisting in stowing away in the *grenier* —soldiers, *paysans*, and *paysannes*.

Generally speaking, these latter (male and female) are very respectable, well-mannered, and well-spoken people in their way. There is, however, one, the most perfect Caliban I ever met with in my life. Bonnemain says he is not an inhabitant of Stain, but comes from some part of Normandy—I forget where. Short, thick-set, and powerfully built; covered with hair—head shaggy as that of a savage; long beard and naked breast, like a bear's; broad squat face and enormous features;—indeed, when standing close to, and trying to converse with him, I feel a sensation as if looking at his face through a powerful magnifier. Of his language (he speaks very fast and very loud) I cannot succeed in catching a single French word, and I observe that the inhabitants themselves seem to have some difficulty in comprehending his meaning. I have christened him Caliban!—beautiful monster!

But it is almost time to go to bed, and as yet I have not mentioned my ride to Paris to-day—I should say *usual*, for few days elapse without my going thither. In general I prefer the road by St Ouen, Clichy, and Monceaux, etc., because it has trees, the scenery is better, the line is not so tediously straight, and by the Barrière de Clichy one enters at once on a decent part of the town, the Rue de Clichy and du Mont Blanc, instead of having to pass through the long blackguard suburbs of La Chapelle and St Denis. To-day, however, I took this road. How unlike the neighbourhood of London, where, for twenty miles (certainly ten) from town, the country is covered with villas, and the roads with carriages, equestrians—indeed, travellers of every kind and in every way! Here we have a long straight road stretching away with an almost imperceptible ascent for about three miles—not a tree nor a bush lends its shade or breaks its painful monotony (if I may so apply the word)—nor house, nor fence. In the middle reigns a horrible pavement, and on each side of this an unpaved road for summer use; after rain these become sloughs, and then, sooner than travel on the pavement, I take to the fields. These, as I have before said, extend to a considerable distance right and left, naked and cheerless, forming the plain of St Denis. There is another by-road leading off near St Denis, which, keeping about midway between the chaussée just mentioned and that by St Ouen, ascends Montmartre by Clignancour, etc. This may be travelled *in dry weather*. In my progress from St Denis to La Chapelle, as usual, instead of the bustle of a London road, a solitary cabriolet now and then passed me; and from time to time I overtook a long-bodied cart, with what we should call half a load—the horses with their broad painted hames, and the waggoner in his white nightcap (or mayhap a cocked-hat), blue frock and white stockings, sabots, etc. These things have now lost their novelty—I am too much at home to be amused by them; so I was pacing along thoughtfully when the wildest thing in the shape of an equipage whisked past in a twinkling. It was Russian— a sort of low clumsily built barouche, with the head thrown back. In this were seated two officers in full uniform, cocked-hats, and long drooping black or bottle-green plumes; four or five (for I did not exactly ascertain which) little, long-tailed, long-maned, wild-looking horses were driven at a gallop by two boys as wild in their appearance, seated on the off-horses, and using the end of the reins as a whip, in the manner of our hussar bridles. I was delighted; but the thing came up so suddenly, and passed me so rapidly, that I had but half a look at it. *En revanche*, standing at the northern entrance of the Palais Royal, I saw to-day again a regular Russian equipage. This was a low carriage also, but of a peculiar construction, drawn by four little rough horses harnessed with rope. On the driving-box sat one of the most picturesque figures I ever saw in my life. Conceive a head of Jupiter as to features, and the splendid beard that fell in thick masses over his ample chest, eyes shooting thunderbolts, overhung by the brow of majesty itself; the support of this head a neck—such a neck!—such a muscular column!—such a bust altogether! His costume, too, was piquant from its novelty. Nothing European was there except the hat, if one might admit this as such, which differed from anything else of the sort I had ever seen; crown exceedingly low, and about twice the diameter at top as at bottom, encircled by an amazingly broad band; brim very broad, and turned up in a peculiar way at the sides—body wrapped in a kind of caftan with loose sleeves, and girt round the waist by a broad sash. On the off-leader sat one of the most beautiful and wildest urchins it is possible to conceive, wrapped in a caftan of similar colour and make to that of the coachman's, grey forage-cap, and neck quite bare. He was about fourteen this boy, and a more animated, lovely face could scarcely be imagined. In repose it would be lovely; but when lighted up by the quick play of two brilliant eyes, partially overshadowed by long elf-locks, the beauty and wildness of expression almost exceeds belief. Whilst I stood wrapt in admiration of these two figures, a Russian officer in a plain undress came out of the Palais Royal, and stepped into the conveniently low vehicle. The coachman shook his reins, the boy, who had been looking back, turned sharply to the front, uttering a loud, shrill, but musical cry, the little wild horses tossed up their noses with a snort, burst at once into a gallop, and away they went like a whirlwind down the Rue Neuve des Petits Champs. For the rest of this day I have never been able to get them out of my head, and everything Russian has borne with me a double interest. Strange that, going as I do every day to Paris, it should never have fallen to my lot before to see a Russian equipage; and yet every day, at least every time I pass through La Chapelle, I see hundreds of their soldiers (infantry) without bestowing on them the slightest attention. These, smart as they are on the parade, are the dirtiest slovens in the world off it: the usual costume in which one sees them running about La Chapelle is a dirty forage-cap, as dirty a grey greatcoat, generally gathered back by the waist-strap, so as to be out of the way, dirty linen trousers, shoved up at bottom by the projection of the unlaced half-boot. Such is the figure I generally see slipping from house to house, or going across the fields at a sort of Highland trot. Curiosity they have none, or it is restrained by their discipline, for I do not recollect once having met a Russian soldier dressed and walking the streets, as if to see the place. Sometimes, in passing their quarters, I have heard them sing in their squalling, drawling style, in a voice as if mocking some one; there is, however, something wild and plaintive in their ditties. Karl's "Imitations," which I always fancied a caricature, is, I find, most excellent. The Prussians, by the by, show themselves as little about the streets as the Russians; but Austrians or Hungarians I meet constantly, generally walking two together—staring into the shop-windows, etc. etc. Tall, heavily built, boorish-looking fellows, but apparently good-natured and orderly in their behaviour. Happening to go into a shop on the Boulevard a few days ago, one of these came in, and making some observation on my purchase, was surprised at my answering him in German, and immediately became quite friendly. Whether he knew I was an officer or not, it is impossible to say, but he followed me out of the shop, and walked some way along the Boulevard with me, and it was not without difficulty I at last succeeded in shaking him off. They are a heavy people altogether, these Austrians. I frequently pass the hotel where the Emperor lodges, and in this hot weather all the windows being open, see from the Boulevard the whole interior of the waiting-room, where the stiff formality of the Garde du Corps on duty, in their ugly, old-fashioned uniforms of grey and silver lace, with ill-shaped cocked-hats stuck square on, is not a little ridiculous. However, they are, as I said before, a good, quiet people.

CHAPTER XXII

August 5th.—I had intended seeing some of the sights to-day —so accordingly, after breakfast, mounted on Nelly, cigar in mouth, and followed by my smart orderly, Fitzgerald, paraded slowly through the village, crossed the fields to St Denis, having passed which I had already got over half the dreary road to La Chapelle, when Nelly suddenly fell dead lame. Upon examination we found a great nail which had run into her foot (off hind), between the frog and bars. This put an end to my day. So I returned quietly, put the mule into the stable with Cossack and the brown horse, Nelly into the mule's box, sent to St Denis for Mr Coward, who is veterinary surgeon to our division, made Farrier Price meantime pare her sole almost to the quick, put on a bran poultice, and have at last sat down to amuse myself by scribbling something about Paris—observations, description, or what else it may be. To proceed, then. I shall not soon forget my first ride to Paris from Colombes. Although already noticed in its place, I like to dwell on a subject to me of so much pleasure, and shall ever recall with emotion my feelings on first passing the Barrière de l'Etoile and gaining a *coup d'œil* of the magnificent avenue beyond, terminated by the venerable palace of the French monarch—its noble trees, its crowds of carriages, horsemen and footmen, and all the et ceteras of such a scene. Arriving by this side, the head filled with preconceived ideas of filthy narrow streets without *trottoirs*, what was my surprise on passing through the Place Louis Quinze and entering the magnificent Rue Royale. My previous knowledge of Paris, picked up in books of travel, etc., has all proved erroneous. Some travellers are extravagant in its praise; but I think the greater part have dwelt too much on the dark side of the picture, otherwise why these unfavourable impressions that occupied my brain? The natives, on the contrary, are too extravagant in its praise; and knowing their gasconading style, one is slow to believe their highly coloured descriptions, and particularly their saying, "Qui n'a vû Paris, n'a rien vû"—a sentiment now become a proverb with them. But this same, or something very similar, is said of many other cities, if I mistake not—Vienna, Rome, Naples, Florence, Madrid, Lisbon, etc. However, like everything else, this has two sides—both parties are right, both are wrong. In the same manner as any other city, Paris has its clean and its dirty quarters, its St Giles and its Grosvenor Street, its fine and its mean buildings, its poverty and its opulence—in short, its *agrémens* and its *désagrémens*. I can't translate these words. Agreeables and disagreeables won't quite do. Everything depends on the good or bad humour of the traveller, or the reception he meets with in the country he undertakes to describe. It generally, therefore, is either a Pays de Cocagne or a Tierra del Fuego.

Divided into twelve *arrondissements* or *mairies*, and every *arrondissement* into several *quartiers*, one finds such a difference between these divisions—in the manners, habitudes, and physiognomy of their inhabitants—as scarcely to believe they form part of the same community. Thus les Quartiers des Tuileries, des Roule, des Champs Elysées, etc. etc.—in which are situated the court, the hotels of all the *grand seigneurs*, etc., consequently the richest, smartest, and best shops—distinguished for elegance, cheerfulness, and cleanliness. Le Quartier de la Chaussée d'Antin is the residence of the rich bankers, as in like manner that of the Palais Royal is of merchants, brokers, etc. The Marais is inhabited principally by people of moderate incomes, fond of quiet and tranquillity; and among these are to be found the principal remaining specimens of the *bon vieux temps*—good, easy, old-fashioned people. The Pays Latin—as the neighbourhood of the Rues St Jacques, de la Harpe, etc., is called, from containing the College de la Sorbonne, the schools of the University, etc. etc.—is the cradle of science, and the residence of almost all the bookbinders, parchment-makers, etc., of Paris. Here reside professors and students of theology, medicine, law, natural history, etc. etc. All is here quiet gloom, and some small degree of filth. Les Halles present the singular spectacle of a rural population in the heart of a great city. The other parts of Paris, inhabited by various classes of artisans, are not only different from all those already spoken of, but differ even amongst themselves, according to the business pursued in them. Thus the Rue de Clery is one complete magazine of furniture and cabinet-work, etc.; and most of the work in silk, such as curtain-fringe, etc., is done in la Rue de la Feronnerie and Marché des Innocens, etc.—but of the more distant quarters of this description I only speak from hearsay, the temper of their population being such as to render it dangerous for an Englishman to appear there as an idler; therefore have I never yet seen the Quartier de St Antoine, nor the Place Royale—the very focus of this spirit.   It is clear, therefore, that Paris cannot be characterised by a *trait de plûme*—as clean or dirty, grand or mean, etc.   Handsome, and what we should call fine, streets there are, and others which, without any pretension to these names, are yet striking from their extent and bustle of business, etc. etc.   Of the former are the Rues de la Paix, Royale, de Rivoli, de Mont Blanc, de la Place Vendôme, du Faubourg St Honoré, etc. etc.   All these are scrupulously clean and very cheerful, full of fine hotels (*not inns*), fine shops, and for the most part have good and spacious *trottoirs*.   The first two in particular are very handsome streets.   Of the latter description are the Rues de St Denis, de St Martin, de l'Université, du Faubourg St Denis, Neuve des Petits Champs, and many others. These are generally long streets, some of them very wide, but almost all of them without *trottoirs*.   Beyond these the streets are generally very narrow, dirty, and dark,   This obscurity is caused by the enormous height of the houses in the old parts of the town, and their sombre hue—I was going to say *their being blackened by smoke*, but that can scarcely be possible, since from using so much wood one never sees that thick canopy of smoke hanging over Paris that usually shuts out the feeble rays of the winter's sun from the citizens of our metropolis.   The close confined streets, indeed all the older streets of Paris, are redolent at all times of a most disagreeable odour.   Evelyn, 160 years ago, said the streets of Paris smelt of sulphur.   The innumerable lamps swinging from ropes over the centre of these streets give them, in my eyes, a very mean appearance.   I don't know why, but they seem, too, in the way.   These ropes lead down the wall on one side of the street in a sort of wooden case, the key of which being kept by the lamplighter, mischievous people are unable to get at the lamps without breaking open these cases—an operation requiring time, and not performed without noise, therefore almost impossible with such a vigilant police. But the greatest ornament of the town, and no doubt that which contributes most to its salubrity, is the great avenue which, under various names, is called generally the Boulevards, from occupying the site of the ancient ramparts of Paris. Since the increase of the faubourgs has placed these in the midst of the town as it were, a second concentric circle, called the New Boulevard, has been formed; but this seems a mere circular road, not much frequented: and along it is the only enclosure Paris now possesses—a simple stone wall, connecting the barriers, and thereby insuring the fiscal duties. Of the old Boulevards I spoke some days ago; it were needless, therefore, to fill my journal with repetition. They must be acknowledged as a most agreeable and amusing lounge. After the streets, the quays of Paris naturally attract our attention—a feature so ornamental, so commodious, so salubrious, that we wonder our own metropolis should be destitute in this respect. What a noble thing it would be were our fine river bordered by such quays as those de Buonaparte, des Tuileries, de Voltaire, de la Conference, etc., instead of being enclosed as it is between such a set of shabby wooden or brick warehouses!

But if London is inferior to Paris in this respect, how superior she is in public squares! The costly iron railings, the masterly statues that decorate some, and the pleasant shrubberies, smooth, well-kept turf, and well-rolled walks which characterise most of them, are nowhere to be seen in Paris. The Place Louis Quinze is not what we should call a square in London; it is a sort of esplanade, separating the ramparts and gardens of the Tuileries from the Champs Elysées; the third side is closed by the river, and the fourth is the only side having buildings—those of the Garde Meuble. It is an agreeable esplanade, but is no square. The Place Royale is, I believe, the largest square in Paris; but, for the reasons before mentioned, I have as yet never seen it. From all that I have heard, it is surrounded by very lofty, and perhaps once handsome houses, which then were the habitations of the principal *noblesse*, though now of a numerous population of artisans. In the middle of it, I understand, is a fountain, some trees, etc., in the manner of our squares.

The Place Vendôme is the next in size to the former; it is octagonal, and the houses, all uniformly built, are of a respectable class, but the style of them is heavy and dull: the want of a *trottoir*, the houses standing as they do with their ground-floors unscreened or unprotected from the carriage-way, spite of the splendid column springing from its centre, gives this place a mean, *triste* appearance. I could not divest myself of the idea of its being a mews. The Place des Victoires, meant to be circular, is only a small concern, neither handsome nor ornamental, and perhaps only useful as admitting light and air into a very thick and closely built part of the town. These are, strictly speaking, the only real public squares; for the Parvis Nôtre Dame, Place du Carrousel, etc. etc., are only esplanades in front of the Cathedral and Tuileries. On the whole, however, Paris is a much more cheerful place than London. In this respect there is no comparison between them.

8 *p.m.*—Rambled up the road to Garges, which is still nearly as deserted as ever; but the rags and tatters, and broken glass, etc., with which the street was strewed, have in a great measure disappeared. After dinner, Nelly being still rather lame, I rode Mula through the vineyards to Pierrefitte. The country is much prettier on that side than with us, being hilly, whereas we are on a dead-level. Our waggon-train officers are doing cavalry with a vengeance, and making a great swagger among the natives. Took a round by Villetaneuse—through vineyards, plantations of artichokes, etc.—and passing along the enclosure of a very handsome domain, with a fine house of brick, let Mula find her own road home, which she did very cleverly and very directly. I think (at least on smooth ground) mules are not so surefooted as is usually believed and asserted—perhaps amongst rocks and mountains they may be. 6*th*.—Sunday.

7*th*.—To town as usual this morning for sightseeing. From the Rue de Malte took my course through the court of the Louvre and the Place de Jena, still boarded up, crossed the Pont Neuf, "where it always blows," and accordingly did blow there to-day certainly, more than elsewhere. Henri IV., with his manly countenance and pointed beard, smiled on me as I made my way through the crowd and plunged into the gloomy and shabby streets of the Pays Latin. Stopped at a mean, rather dirty restaurant in the

Rue St Jacques, where I got a bad lunch, of course, and a bottle of sour wine; but for this there was no remedy, as I did not know of any better in the neighbourhood, to which I am a stranger. After doubling and threading my way through a number of dirty obscure streets, which no stranger could have done in London, I at last came out on the Quai St Bernard, where suddenly I found myself among hundreds, if not thousands, of pipes of wine ranged in tiers. It is the Marché aux Vins; and whilst seated upon one of these pipes enjoying the busy scene around, I mentally bless the ingenious system of numbering the houses and naming the streets that has enabled me to steer through such a labyrinth as I have just passed, and which might so well and so easily be applied in London. All streets running to the Seine are numbered in *black*; all those parallel, or nearly so, to the river in *red*. Starting from the river, the numbers commence in a double series in these transverse streets; and in the longitudinal streets the series of numbers follow the course of the stream,—equal numbers always on the right, unequal on the left. In the same manner the names at the corners of the streets are of a similar colour to the numbers; and moreover, some remarkable object, giving a designation to the quarter, is painted at the corners. The Jardin des Plantes, or du Roi, is adjoining the Marché aux Vins, and thither I went, walking in amongst other company without let or hindrance of any kind. In this garden, the Menagerie, and the Cabinet d'Histoire Naturelle, I passed nearly the whole afternoon in the most agreeable manner possible. Much as I had heard of this establishment, the reality rather surpassed than fell short of it—and sorry I am to say we can boast of nothing at all equal to it in England; nor, if we did, could our populace be admitted to it with the same freedom as the more volatile yet more considerate *badauds* are to this. Everything would soon be ruined. The men would trample over the beds, the boys would break down the hedges and fences; knives would operate in all directions; even the women would find some means of doing mischief;—in short, it would never do. Here, on the contrary, it was with pleasure that I observed people of all classes of society, even beggars, conducting themselves with a modesty and decency of manner not to be surpassed. The choice of ground has been very judicious, as the plan presents a pleasing undu-

lation of surface that gives infinite interest to a promenade.
The botanical part is flat and even, divided by walks into
compartments, each forming a small distinct garden by
itself.   These are either enclosed by well-kept hedges, or
by rails and rustic fences of every possible useful fashion—
which may serve as models for those in want of such things.

These little gardens each contains some family of shrubs
or plants, and are all arranged according to their respective
climates.   The dividing walks form most agreeable prom-
enades, as was evinced by the number of people I found
lounging in them, many evidently not taking any interest in
the botanical treasures around.   This flat space is bounded
on one side by a magnificent avenue of elms, under the shade
of which are numerous *vendeurs de boissons* and *de pâtisserie*,
as well as one or two regular restaurateurs.   On the other
side, the ground, swelling gently into hill and dale as it were,
is fitted by enclosures of simple rail or strong stockade, as
occasion may require, for the confinement of an elephant or
a deer.   Here in little paddocks, with room to move about
and a house to shelter them, we find a number of animals,
who, perhaps, well fed as they are, little regret the loss of
liberty.   The elephant even has a pond to wallow in, to the
great amusement of the *badauds* who constantly throng the
stockade.   The more savage beasts (genus *Felis*, etc.) are
confined as with us, in dens.   It was only in looking over
the catalogue of the menagerie, and finding the beasts enclosed in the paddocks classed as ruminant and *fauve*, that
I remembered we have no term to translate the latter word.
This part of the establishment is very entertaining, and I
lounged away a great part of my time in wandering about the
winding walks between the enclosures, amused by the curiosity and *naïveté* of many of the visitors.   The menagerie is
separated from the gardens by a rampart and ditch.   In the
latter are the bears, great favourites with the public, particularly the boys, of whom numbers are always hanging on
the wall, watching the heavy animals climbing a high pole set
for the purpose.   The hothouses contain all sorts of things;
but what interested me were the palms—some of these I saw
out of doors.   Just by the hothouses is a high mount, ascended by a spiral path, bearing a sort of temple on the top,
whence there is an extensive and much-vaunted view over
the city and neighbourhood; but not half so extensive as,

nor in any way comparable to, those from Belleville, Mont-martre,[1] and, above all, from Mont Aurelian. The School of Comparative Anatomy is very interesting: it contains perfect skeletons of almost every species of animal, bird, or fish, from the most diminutive to the largest—from the minnow to the whale, from the shrew-mouse to the mastodon, from the humming-bird to the condor.

Evening was drawing on, and I ran hastily through the two floors of the Cabinet of Natural History, that I might get home before dark. The entrance to the Jardin des Plantes, by a handsome *grille* from the quay opposite the Pont d'Austerlitz, is very good, but I could not stop to admire it; and hurrying along the *quais*, instead of blunder-ing amongst the streets, succeeded again in just getting home in time.

August 8th.—It seems as if I were destined always to fall under the Duke's displeasure, and to be the victim of his injustice. When I called on Sir Augustus Frazer this morning at the Hôtel du Nord, the first greeting I got on entering the room was, "*Mercer, you are released from arrest!*" At first I thought this a joke, but Sir Augustus assured me seriously that I had not only been in arrest, but *that*, too, ever since our review on the 24th ultimo. He then told me that I had not been the only unfortunate. Himself and Major M'Donald had been supposed under arrest at the same time and for the same *crime*; and what was this?—this very grave crime for which two field officers and a captain had actually been under ignominious punishment for a whole fortnight? In the column of review on the 24th ultimo, my troop was on the extreme left (or rear), except the two brigades of 18-pounders. Our order of marching past was in column of divisions (we have three divisions), and my post for saluting was considerably in front of the leading one, to leave room for the division officers at open order, consequently I was fully a hundred yards distant from my rear division when passing the Duke. Now it so fell out that, at that very moment, a horse of one of the rear-division carriages got his leg over a trace. The limber gunners, with their wonted activity, were off, cleared the leg, remounted, all in sufficient

---

[1] To me the most interesting part of this mound was its history, rising abruptly as it does so much above the surrounding ground. Is it an enormous barrow, like Silbury, or is it a natural accumulation of alluvium?

time for the division to pass his Grace steadily and in good order. But this little halt, momentary as it was, checked the 18-pounders; and Ilbert, or whoever commanded them, ignorant of the saluting-point, trotted up to regain his distance, until suddenly, seeing the sovereigns and their suite, he resumed his walk too late, and passed them in confusion. The Duke fell into one of his furious passions, asked how this happened, and (what he did with the foot-artillery I know not) immediately despatched the Adjutant-General to put Sir Augustus Frazer, Major M'Donald, and myself under arrest. The two former, however, had departed; and whilst the Adjutant-General was struggling through the crowd after me, I had cleared the Rue Royale, and setting off at a trot down the Boulevard, had turned down the Rue de Clichy, consequently was out of sight ere he reached the Boulevard, where he gave up the pursuit and said no more about it. Whether the Duke forgot us, or whether he purposely kept us in arrest, we are left to conjecture—certain it is, that we three actually appear by name in the General's orders of yesterday as released from our arrest. *Mens conscia recti*—I snap my fingers at the disgrace.

Leaving Sir Augustus, I accompanied Bell to his pretty lodging in the Rue Mont Blanc. I don't know who the people are, but it is an uncommonly genteel, well-furnished, well-appointed house. A young gentleman there is who visits Bell occasionally, and a young lady who serenades him (if I may so apply the term) continually. She touches the piano well, has a musical voice, and sings with taste. "L'Exile" is the favourite just now, a pretty song, which, from so often hearing there, I shall always henceforward associate with Bell's nicely furnished apartment, and the little pleasure-ground, of some thirty or forty feet square, with one or two acacias in it. Frazer, too, has very handsome rooms in the Hôtel du Nord, richly furnished, with green silk window-curtains, etc. etc. Sir Edward Kerrison and old Platoff also live there. Passed the remainder of this morning lounging about the Boulevard, as much amused as on the first day. All the fun, crowd, etc., I observe, is confined to the right side going up from the Rue Royale; on the left there is comparatively nobody, except, perhaps, at the Porte St Denis and St Martin, through which (or rather by which) a crowd is continually setting, and one is deafened by the importunate clamours of fifty cabriolet-drivers, all calling at once, "Voiture, Monsieur—Voiture?" "St Denis, Monsieur?" "Memorency, Monsieur?" "Garges, Monsieur?" "Arnouville?" etc. etc. These fellows are most active rogues, and their carriages very convenient, and far more agreeable than the fiacres; and that is the opinion of the public in general, I presume, from seeing one fiacre plying for ten cabriolets or coucous, or whatever name they go by. The coachmen of the former are so well aware of this, that they generally are dozing on their boxes, giving themselves no trouble in looking for customers. Perhaps, however, this may arise from their being only servants, whilst the others are themselves the proprietors of the vehicles they drive. Although conscious that these *portes* are in reality triumphal arches, yet I never pass them without experiencing something of the same feeling with which one would view the magnificent bridge built by Philip II. over the dry bed of the Manzanares if ignorant of the impetuous floods to which that river is liable. The Boulevard presented if anything a more busy, noisy scene than usual. The Turk I found with an attentive and apparently much-interested audience, whom he was haranguing with vociferations and gesticulations truly astounding. In vain I tried to catch the purport of his harangue—the curious *badauds* were packed so close, and so firmly maintained their ground, that it was impossible to approach one inch into the circle. I lounged on and admired the beautiful Fontaine de Bondy, or de Lions, I know not which it is called, but its sheets of falling water are singular, and I think it a beautiful fountain. What a magnificent air these fountains give to the town! How refreshing and delightful is the splashing of their waters in warm weather! and oh! the contrast presented to them by our conduits, etc.—shapeless masses of masonry or brickwork, with a brass cock stuck in each side, or mayhap the said brass cock protruding from a common wall.

The French are an ingenious people, and contrive a thousand curious, uncommon, and often admirable devices for opening people's purses, instead of sticking to the unvaried, dismal chant of our beggars—although "*Pour l'amour de Dieu*" is not uncommon here. Our wretches drive one away, but the gentlemen of whom I speak grasp, retain, and even squeeze their auditors as one would a lemon.

Nor do they always assume the repulsive rags, etc., which our beggars think so essential to obtain their end. An instance of this I frequently meet on the Boulevard St Martin—an elderly man, of a grave physiognomy, well featured, and of rather a genteel appearance, clad in garments somewhat seedy, though fashionably cut. This man I stumbled on to-day at the corner of the Rue du Temple lecturing on moral philosophy. Like the Turk, he had a numerous and attentive audience, but, generally speaking, composed of a better description of people. To a clear, sonorous voice, he added a manner demonstrative without being dogmatic, and persuasive without betraying doubt of his own powers. He defined the motives and rules of human actions, and showed that these rules are immutable—that we cannot violate them with impunity. He then went at some length into the morals of the ancients, touched on the doctrine of expediency, on the desire of distinction, ambition, etc., and very naturally, though cautiously, introduced as an illustration Napoleon. No one could mistake the sensation produced by this magic name—a sensation which, having produced, he proceeded to neutralise by gradually slipping into the connection between religion and morality. I left him explaining the insufficiency of natural religion, etc. Although this man does not beg, there is no doubt he makes a good trade of preaching; numerous were the offerings silently put into his hand and quietly pocketed without once interrupting the thread of his discourse. Another actor of the same description is a man who usually frequents the northern entrance of the Passage Feydeau: an immense power of grimace, and amazing execution on the violin, are the means by which he gains his daily bread. Clad in an old threadbare frock, that once was brown, with a pair of enormous spectacles riding astride on his prominent nose, he takes his stand on the steps at the entrance of the passage. Heels close together, body drawn up at attention, and with his gaze directed upwards at the window of the fourth story of the opposite house, he appears perfectly unconscious of the presence of the admiring crowd assembled round him, whilst he executes with astonishing justness, feeling, and rapidity, the most difficult passages from some of the favourite composers of the day—distorting his face all the time in a manner so wonderfully ludicrous that his really excellent

music is almost drowned by the uncontrollable laughter of
the surrounding multitude. These are some of the many
means employed in this gay metropolis for extracting coin
out of the pockets of their fellow-men. Gay, however, as
it is, misery exists here as well as elsewhere, and I shudder
even now at the harrowing tale Bell told me this morning
of suicide, to which he was witness a day or two ago. Passing
through the Place Vendôme, he observed several people
looking anxiously up at the Column of Austerlitz, and
naturally turning his eyes in the same direction, beheld a
man in the act of climbing over the rails of the gallery, having
effected which, he deliberately lowered himself down until
he hung suspended by the arms over the frightful depth
below. In this position he remained a few seconds, perhaps
as if repenting him of the rash act he was about to perpetrate;
but, unable to recover the gallery, he eventually let go his
hold, and was dashed to pieces on the pavement at the foot
of the column: the very idea is harrowing!

A trait of the times, and a very striking one too, which a
person meets with at almost every step in walking about
Paris, is the announcement of the change of dynasty—from
an empire to a kingdom—exhibited in the titles of shops,
lycées, and every other establishment; the old word *imperiale*
slightly painted over to make way for the more humble *royale*
—*lycée royale*, etc.—which is sometimes painted over it,
but more frequently by the side of it, leaving the former
word quite legible through the thin daub of paint laid over
it. The postilions, too, are changing their imperial green
livery for the royal blue; yet this change goes on but slowly,
for we still see many of the numerous English equipages
daily arriving brought in by postilions in green livery jackets.
In the palaces and other public buildings, the letter N was
abundantly introduced into all the architectural decorations,
besides the armorial bearings of the Emperor: workmen
have been some time employed effacing or altering all these.
Wherever it is possible, the obnoxious letter is removed
altogether; but where that is not the case, which happens
frequently, it is changed into an H and the numeral IV.
added. These and many other changes incident to the
present state give a curious aspect to the nation, and afford
much food for speculation and contemplation. Met my
old schoolfellow Courtnay Ilbert coming out of town, and

we rode together to St Denis, where his 18-pounder brigade is stationed. On reaching home found that M. Fauigny has been here. Poor man! he is not likely to get much from me.

August 9th.—Not quite well this morning, but I went to town to meet Hitchins, and make a sightseeing day of it. Accordingly we have done pretty well, galloping through the Luxembourg, Les Monumens, and wandering over almost the whole southern part of Paris. I can't say, however, that this has been to me a day of much interest; I prefer a thousand times wandering about the town by myself —observing the habits, manners, etc., of the people—to all the sightseeing; but I allowed Hitchins to shame me out of the idea of leaving Paris without seeing everything. Much, however, I fear I shall have to blush for, if that be necessary, and amongst others the theatres, not one of which have I ever entered yet. The Luxembourg is a fine palace, and I like its style of architecture much better than that of the Tuileries, though it is vilely situated. The gardens are much the same —parterres, ponds, ramparts—*voilà tout*. The great attractions here are the Chamber of Peers, and the Galleries of Rubens, Vernet, and of the French Raphael Le Sueur. The first I cannot bear, spite of his beautiful colouring and well-managed *chiaro-oscuro*—allegory is my abomination; the pictures of the second are more to my taste; but the blue works of the French Raphael I could not appreciate. Besides these, we saw a multitude of other masterpieces; and I was particularly pleased at having an opportunity of seeing some by David, of whom I have heard so much. Here disappointment awaited me, and a glance at the "Judgment of Brutus" satisfied me—all yellow and glare, and extravagant attitudes. Surely the human spine would never admit of being doubled in the manner of the fainting female introduced in the foreground of this picture—a perfect parabola. To reach the Chamber of Peers, we passed through a grove of orange-trees in boxes, and then mounted a very fine staircase ornamented with statues of great men, among which two were very spirited—those of Condorcet and of General Dessaix, said to be likenesses; I had no idea the latter was so young. The Chamber itself is a very handsome semicircular hall, having the President's desk in the centre of the chord, and those of the members round the curve. Beyond this is the

Salle de la Paix, a very handsome room, the walls of which are covered with paintings by David, representing the victories of Napoleon, weakly enough hid with green baize, and not allowed to be seen.

Of the monuments I have little worth recording. Interesting specimens there are of French sculpture of every age—all preserved by M. Lenoir from revolutionary vandalism. The only thing, however, that I remember worth noticing, is the tomb of Louis XII. (I think), on which the corpses of himself and queen soon after death are laid out: the countenance of the king is expressive of great suffering. The horrid truth of this sculpture, aided by the colour of the marble—so completely that of a corpse—leads one to believe that it must by some means have been actually copied from nature. In a little yard, about twenty feet square, and surrounded by the high walls of the neighbouring houses, stands the Paraclete. Its situation is a sad drawback to the interest one might otherwise take in this specimen of ancient architecture, for in the history of the Castrato and his love I can take none. In wandering about the town, amongst other places we stumbled upon were the poultry or game market, and that of flowers—two opposite extremes. The first is a very handsome building on the Quai des Grand Augustins, and this being one of the days on which the game, etc., arrives, the quantity was prodigious; but the smell was more than we could stand, and obliged us to a very precipitate retreat; so, crossing to the Cité, we rambled on, and quite by accident found ourselves in the empire of Flora, redolent of mignonette and a thousand other odoriferous plants, and presenting a *coup d'œil* not to be excelled: hortensias and camellias appeared quite common. The Parisian flower-sellers are adepts in making up nosegays, and, I believe, understand using them as the language of love like the Turks. Tired with our walk, we returned to Hardi's, where, having made an excellent dinner, we separated; and here I am half asleep recording the day.

Sunday, 13th.—I have been idle as to writing since Wednesday, but not so otherwise, having been every day in town; in the meantime, domestic transactions require some notice. Our vineyards are blessed this year with a most extraordinary crop of grapes, to secure which from marauders I have acceded to M. Bonnemain's petition in

behalf of the villagers, and established a regular patrol of
our men—a precaution certainly most necessary, seeing what
neighbours we have: at Pierrefitte the waggon-train; on
the other side, bivouacking along the chaussée from Garges
to St Denis, Jones's corps of Belgian waggoners, five hundred
in number, men totally unacquainted with the restraints
of military discipline, with full leisure to meditate mischief,
and most persevering foragers for their horses, which are
their own private property; in our rear, at Garges, etc.,
are our savage and lawless friends of Nassau, and some
Belgians. So surrounded, vigilance becomes absolutely necessary, not only for the sake of our villagers, but also for our
own; and nothing has gained their affections, or united
us more, than the establishment of this patrol, especially
since it has taken some prisoners. The other day the *garde
champêtre* detected soldiers stealing along amongst the vines,
but not daring to go near them himself, hurried into the
village and reported it to the sergeant-major, Oliphant, who
lost no time in despatching a corporal and four mounted
gunners in pursuit. The fellows were soon taken and
brought in triumph to my house, the *garde champêtre* stalking
at the head of the procession in his cocked-hat and broad
bandoulière, prisoners between the escort—M. le Maire
and some twenty peasants, making more noise with their
sabots than the iron hoofs of the horses, bringing up the rear.
The unfortunates were Belgians, quite lads, so I held a sort
of court-baron in my yard, and upon their expressing great
contrition, and begging a thousand pardons, at M. Bonnemain's request I forgave them, but sent the escort to see
them home to Garges, whence they came. The effect on
the villagers has been very good—they have all become the
most kindly obliging creatures possible, and our men are
as thick as brothers with them; I trust this harmony may
continue. I have likewise another source of amusement,
which makes my residence here more agreeable—I have
hired a very good violin, and bought some music. The
off-handed liberal manner in which Madame Duhan informed
me of the hire, and allowed me to take away the instrument,
stranger as I was to her, without any security, surprised me
much. I rather think none of our musicsellers in London
would lend even their worst instrument to a Frenchman in
the same manner. On Thursday last I went to see the

Bibliothèque Royale, a magnificent establishment, and where I passed a most delightful morning; it is in the Hôtel de Colbert, Rue de Richelieu, from which street the main entrance opens into a square court surrounded by the building, and having in its centre a naked statue of Diana in bronze, of fine execution, but in my opinion misplaced here.

The library occupies two entire and part of a third side of the quadrangle (about 300,000 volumes), and is on the most liberal footing. Any well-dressed person is freely admitted, and may range about unobstructed; but he must touch nothing. Chairs, tables, pens, and ink, are there for those who wish to write, and servants, in rich liveries of blue and silver lace, are in attendance to furnish the books required. These people are positively forbidden to accept anything from the visitors; and yet no one can be more obligingly attentive. In the Cabinet des Medailles are many curiosities; amongst the most interesting, I thought, were the iron chair of King Dagobert, and a silver disc found in the Rhone, and supposed to have been the shield of Scipio —I don't know why. Two enormous globes, more than 12 feet in diameter, are mounted on the ground-floor, and circular apertures have been opened in the floor above to admit part of their circumference through it. The fourth side of the quadrangle is a most delightful lounge; it is the Cabinet des Gravures. In this are preserved specimens of the works of every artist of every nation—from the most ancient period down to the present. The collection is immense, and is the constant resort of all the artists of the capital, and a crowd of picture-loving people. I could pass whole days there, so interesting is the collection, and so great the facility of using it. This place occupied my morning so completely that I had barely time to get my *potage à la julienne*, etc., and come home before dark.

Friday.—It sounds oddly to an English ear, smuggling into a town from the country; but the free circulation that exists throughout our country is unknown here. Everything is examined at the *barrière*. What would our farmers and their wives say if they were liable to be stopped at the gate of every principal town, and their loads of hay, or baskets of eggs, etc., submitted to the scrutiny of excisemen? Several loads of hay preceded me this morning as I rode through the Faubourg St Denis. At the *barrière* the column was

halted, and as the passage was blocked up, I was obliged
to wait patiently and see every load as it passed in succession
probed through and through by the officers with long iron
skewers, to ascertain that nothing was concealed amongst
the hay.   The signs exhibited by the various shops in Paris
are often quaint and amusing.   A description of them would
fill a volume.   The one which calls forth this remark struck
me as I entered the Palais Royal this morning from the Rue
Vivienne.   I don't well know how to designate the sort of
shop which exhibits the sign of the "Gourmand"; they
are numerous in this part of the town, and I think more
nearly resemble our Italian warehouse than any other.
Here is to be procured every dainty that can stimulate the
palate—pickles, preserves, hams, tongues, hung-beef, cheese,
dried fruits, nuts of all sorts, sauces, dried and cured fish,—
in short, everything.   The *enseigne* of this shop represents
a fat greedy-looking fellow seated at a table, under which,
his legs are spread out.   The table is covered with every
kind of dainty, which, whilst discussing a large salmon, he
is eagerly devouring with the eyes.   If the Boulevard is
amusing for the life and movement it exhibits, so is the
Palais Royal in a high degree, and to the charms of the
former it adds that of an endless variety of rich and beautiful articles of dress, *vertu*, and a number of others, which
employ me incessantly at the windows.   The display of
elegant little toys in Bobon's window is scarcely to be surpassed—such little beauties of watches,[1] not larger than
half-a-crown, cases most tastefully chased and set in rich
pearls; in other shops rich and elegant shawls, *fichus*, and
silks, of the most splendid colours; then jewellery, so much
taste combined with costliness; then cutlery and works in
steel, etc. etc.; and not the least amusing, the numerous
cafés or restaurants.   The crowd under the arcades is as
varied as it is immense.   If, on entering from Rue Vivienne,
one turns to the right, not many paces in that direction will
bring him in front of the favourite haunt of Austrian and
Prussian officers.   It resembles a great conservatory, being all
glass, and is in the garden, not in the house, whence every re-
freshment has to be brought across the piazza.   About two or
three every afternoon this is crowded, and it then reminds me

---

[1] It must be remembered that in those days these, as well as many other
things quite common in France, were novelties to Englishmen.

of a glass beehive, from the busy stir within, and the facility
of observing this from without. The celebrated Café aux
Milles Colonnes is not far off, upstairs about half-way
down the next branch. I lounged up to it and was disappointed. A decent *salle* enough, which, being everywhere
panelled with mirrors, the green marble columns are reflected so repeatedly as to give some colour to the appellation
assumed by the establishment. There are several rooms;
but whether the place is only frequented at night on certain
days, or that something *fâcheux* had occurred, I know not—
certain it was not in a state to receive company, wherefore
I made no further advance than to the door, and having
peeped in, wheeled downstairs again. Among other curiosities of Paris I have often stood and contemplated the air
of importance and grave bustle of an establishment unknown
to us in London, where the operation in question is performed
in a very modest manner in the public streets. This morning I walked into the shop of a fashionable *décrotteur*, that I
might see more perfectly all the detail of this most useful
business. The *salon*, a large room, was lighted by numerous
windows near the ceiling (these, like other artists, affecting
a preference for light coming from above: thus I have seen
many receiving it through skylights). The handsomest
establishment of this kind is in the Passage des Panoramas.
A certain degree of taste, too, was visible in the decorations
and arrangement of several large mirrors (mirrors are in-
dispensable to a Frenchman). A sort of divan, a few feet
broad, extended nearly round the apartment, on which were
many gentlemen seated on chairs, gravely reading the daily
papers; whilst one foot, raised on a sort of iron resembling
the scraper at a door, was being operated on by a journeyman
décrotteur, who rubbed and polished away with most admirable despatch and dexterity. In the middle of the room
stood the master-spirit, superintending the active operations
of his myrmidons, receiving the acknowledgment for services
performed, ushering the one out of the shop and the other
up to the divans, conversing with the newly arrived aspirants,
and doing the amiable everywhere. A good-looking, well-
dressed man this master-shoeblack, who might easily be
mistaken for a minister.

Disappointment awaits the man who, having read or
heard the French account of any place in France or the

French dominions, expects to find it realised, or even nearly
so. With them all is exaggeration and bombast; even the
accounts of their most respectable and veracious writers,
in all matters relating to France or the French, must be received *cum grano salis*. Disappointment certainly was mine
after reading and hearing so much of the several gardens
(as Frascatin, Tivoli, the Jardins Turc and du Prince) when
I turned into the latter of these two celebrated places in the
Boulevard du Temple. Certes, I took it *en déshabillé*, for
the evening and by lamplight is its hour of triumph, and
then I am here always. The guide-book speaks of "un
jardin agréable." What did I find? Certainly no garden
—a yard (gravelled) divided by hedges (such ones as may
be expected in a town) into several compartments, in which
are a few boxes; one side bounded by the *salle*, with its
usual accompaniments—the others, by gables or back walls
of the neighbouring houses; figure irregular, and space
very confined. Having nothing fixed for Friday, I made a
wandering day of it. Up one gloomy street, down another;
at last found myself in the Place des Innocens, in which is
held the principal vegetable-market of Paris. The Place
is large but gloomy; houses very high, of a dark-coloured
stone, and in the usual French style, windows open, and
exhibiting all the variety of clothes hanging to dry, flowers,
rich curtains and common ones, etc. etc., incident to buildings
inhabited by so many different families. The area presented
a varied, characteristic, and moreover an interesting picture.
The whole space was covered with large umbrellas, fixed
upright over the different tables, etc., the convex surfaces
of which, of all the hues of the rainbow (pink predominating),
reminded me strongly of the *testudo* of the ancients. Amidst
these arose, to the height of some forty or fifty feet, the
noble Fontaine des Innocens, with its fine *nappes d'eau*.
Not only the Marché itself, but the Rue de la Ferronnerie,
and several adjacent ones, seem quite the focus of business,
such stir and bustle do they present. The profusion of
fruits and vegetables in this market is remarkable, more
particularly when it is remembered that not only Paris itself,
but also the whole neighbouring country, is occupied by
countless hosts of foreigners. The old ladies, seated under
their immense umbrellas (formed generally of alternate pink
and white breadths), or stumping about in their sabots, give

a very animated air to this scene, which, however, is rendered less pleasing from the overpowering smell of decayed and decaying vegetable matter profusely strewed over the pavement. It is an amusing place this Marché, and although only now mentioned, I have visited it more than once. Besides this, there are numerous other markets in different parts of the town, the neatest of which, and one that I always have pleasure in passing through, because always clean, is the Marché des Jacobins, off the Rue St Honoré, and not far from the Place Vendôme. Speaking of these markets reminds me of the Abattoir de Montmartre, which I frequently pass in my way in or out of town, one of several buildings in different quarters destined for the slaughter of cattle—a most excellent arrangement, since the blood and filth which usually pollute the kennels in the neighbourhood of our slaughterhouses, the disgusting stench arising from them, and the consequent deterioration and unhealthiness of the surrounding atmosphere, are completely obviated.

Yesterday (Saturday) I devoted to another visit to the Louvre, and its interesting collections. What crowds of English and other foreigners! The gallery of pictures exhibits just now a new feature—French and other artists, with their easels, etc., busily employed copying many of the pictures of which they are soon to be deprived. Among them, working with the utmost composure, were two or three women. But women mix themselves up in every transaction in this country—even in war, as has been illustrated in the formation of our Amazonian battalion at Stain. Somehow or another the statues have more attraction for me than the pictures. The *salles* are less crowded than the gallery, consequently one is quieter and more at liberty to contemplate these admirable sculptures at leisure. The naming of these, however, appears to me very gratuitous, and I much doubt whether one-half of those in the catalogues are properly designated. Faun is a very vague term. What absorbing reflections arise in the mind whilst wandering amongst this collection of cold marble stones! Even when, as has happened occasionally, I have been the only individual in the vast apartment, it has been hard to fancy myself alone, so surrounded by beauteous forms, amongst which such perfect harmony of expression reigns—not an attitude or gesture amongst them but what is ease and elegance; nothing constrained, nothing proud, forced, or unnatural; in all, passion, emotion, repose and tranquillity, love, anger, joy, sorrow—all, all expressed by these marble stones in language not to be misunderstood. How powerful is the imagination! These forms address themselves peculiarly to it. Some excite a train of thought associated intimately, I might say inseparably, with historical recollections; others, again, are associated with sensations of voluptuousness, which, however repressed, cannot be excluded entirely—beautiful rounded forms associated with our sense of feeling, and conveying to the too ready imagination ideas of softness and elasticity. How much more we should appreciate these splendid specimens of human skill and conception, could we contemplate them separately and alone, instead of thus jumbled together and in public. In the Salle d'Apollon, however, I think this inimitable statue rather favoured by his company, amongst which are several Egyptian statues, the constrained positions of which—knees pressed together, arms hanging straight down by the side, stiff draperies, and angular ornaments—contrast strikingly with the elegant contour and graceful attitude of this masterpiece by an unknown hand. In this same *salle* are two chairs in beautiful *rouge* antique, both of them found in the Roman baths, and said to have been used in the Middle Ages at the inauguration of the Popes. Pius VI. restored them to the Museum of the Vatican as antiques, and thence they came here.

I cannot admire the coloured walls of these *salles*: there is something in them that does not accord with the severity of statuary, and it struck me that one uniform tint, perhaps maroon, would considerably enhance the *éclat* of these fine statues. Nor do I admire these imitations of nature being perched upon pedestals: were the Venus, for instance, placed on the floor, or on a low platform as the Apollo is, I think it would add considerably to her interest. Every visit to this splendid collection adds to my wonder and admiration, and I returned yesterday evening with my mind full of enthusiasm for the science which could so nobly conceive, and the art which could so skilfully execute, these exquisite productions of the chisel.

CHAPTER XXIII

I BELIEVE in a former part of this journal I noticed a chateau belonging to an Admiral Rosily. It is situated quite at the extremity, or rather beyond the village, on the road to Garges, and therefore so far out of the way that, except to visit the stables (for we have a detachment in it), I never have paid any attention to it, and suffered the people to do as they please. On my return yesterday evening from Paris I found the following letter:—

"*Ce* 11 *Août* 1815.

"MONSIEUR LE COMMANDANT,—J'apprends que vous faites mettre des chevaux chez moi. Le Duc de Wellington connoit les destructions qu'on a causé dans ma maison, il avoit bien voulu même me donner une sauve garde, qui n'a plus en lieu depuis que le regiment de Lord Portarlington est parti pour Amiens.

"Je vous prie seulement, que les hommes qui ont soin des chevaux n'entrent point dans mon jardin, et respectent ma propriété.—J'ai l'honneur d'être, Monsieur le Commandant, votre serviteur,

"L'AMIRAL COMTE DE ROSILY."

The Admiral has taken a much more efficacious way of preserving his property in thus committing it to my care instead of making a complaint to the Duke, and certainly a more gentlemanly one. I walked down to it this afternoon, and was surprised to find a spacious, well-kept, and most productive garden, enclosed by a high wall, one side of which runs along the side of the road to Garges, and the other along the lane leading up to the village. The house is large, but its exterior not handsome; some fine rooms within, but every scrap of furniture had been removed before our arrival. In the rear, all the offices carefully numbered, and

their names and uses painted in large letters on the doors,
"*vacherie*," "*laitérie*," etc. etc. Our men have behaved
well and destroyed nothing, and the produce of the garden
has suffered little, the officer of the division having preserved
it for himself. I have given directions which no doubt will
leave the Admiral no room to repent of the step he has taken,
although it is not possible to remove the men and horses.

The Duke, it seems, continues to bear malice. I cantered
up this morning to Paris, and called on Sir G. Wood to beg
him to forward my application for two months' leave of
absence, which he declined doing, as he said it would not be
prudent just now "*to remind the Duke of me in any way.*"
Rather hard and unjust this!

In the anteroom at the Rue de Richelieu (Sir George's
quarter) I met Captain Light (Bull-dog, as he was called
at the academy). He is just returning from Egypt, where
he has been travelling, and tells me that he ascended the
Nile farther than any one yet. All the honour and glory
attending his expedition he would have gladly exchanged
for that of having served the campaign with us. He much
blamed himself for not having done so. Sir George wanted
me to stay and dine, but I begged off.

16th.—The vengeance of the Duke has at last fallen on
the 5th Division, and it must be confessed they deserve it,
having ruined one of the prettiest villages and some of the
most charming villas in the neighbourhood of Paris. It is
said that damages are laid at £5000, and that the Duke has
ordered it to be paid. There is, however, no depending
on reports, everything is sure to be so much exaggerated.
Nothing else to-day, except that I took my usual ride into
Paris, where I lounged away the time principally in shopping,
etc.

20th.—I can hardly tell how, but true it is that my time
for writing is wonderfully curtailed, although in reality I have
so little to do. The journeys to and from town occupy much
time; and now that we are, as it were, settled, people have
taken to visiting, so that we have frequently dinner company,
which forbids all attempts at nocturnal writing. Sunday is
my quietest day in general, although not always. To-day I
passed my morning in strolling about the park of the chateau,
the village, etc. Our scenery is too flat to be very pretty,

although the chaussées on either side of us, with their fine
elms, are noble avenues. These are the roads from Pierrefitte and Garges, which unite near St Denis. There are
several spots in the Park affording interesting peeps in the
direction of Paris. Having a clump of picturesque trees in
the immediate foreground, the level verdant carpet stretches
away until bounded by the rich masses of foliage of elms
bordering the chaussée, above which tower the light spires
of the Abbey of St Denis; farther on, an opening in the
avenue allows the eye to range over the naked plain of St
Denis, bounded in the extreme distance by the heights of
Montmartre and Belleville, with the dome of St Geneviève
rearing itself in the gap between. Except such peeps, our
view is everywhere confined by the foliage and the rising
ground extending all round our rear from Garges to Pierrefitte. Water, or the want of it rather, is a great drawback on
the scenery about the district: true, there are two or three
muddy rivulets, such as the Rouillon, La Vieille Mer, Crouy,
etc., but they are too insignificant and too much encased to
aid in any way the scenery.

Yesterday, when I called at the Hôtel du Nord, I was
surprised at meeting Lady Frazer, her brother, and two
sisters (Dr James and the Misses Lind).

The festival of our patron saint was celebrated last Thursday with much merriment and conviviality, and it was very
pleasing to see the familiar and confident manner in which
our people mingled in the amusements of the day, and the
cordiality with which they were treated by the villagers.

The favourite (indeed, the principal) game played by the
young men was one resembling our trap-ball, with this
difference, that instead of a trap, the ball was made to
rebound from a large sieve placed on the ground, and propped
upon one side so as to present an inclined surface. In the
evening a most animated dance was kept up in the park until
a comparatively late hour.

Angélique was the distinguished belle of the evening, and
by far the best (as she was the stoutest) *danseuse*, although
thay all dance well. As I saw her swinging through the
figure, "Cutty-sark" came forcibly to my recollection, and
mentally I exclaimed "weel done," etc. We were at mess
when M. Bonnemain called to announce that all was ready,

but that he had forbidden the commencing until the sanction of M. le Commandant was obtained.

This is of a piece with his whole conduct now: everything that passes in the village I am made acquainted with; he has even confided to me several important family secrets; —in short, on every affair, even of the slightest moment, M. le Commandant is consulted. Moreover, M. Bonnemain pays me a regular visit at ten every morning to know my pleasure for the day. Several ridiculous petitions to the Duke (all of which he attends to) have been suppressed, and the complainants brought before me. But this is out of fashion; at present nobody thinks of complaining; we are all too good friends for that. Nor is this all: I begin to have hopes that my Fauigny affair has at last obtained a proper hearing, since an officer sent by Sir Edward Barnes came down to inquire how matters stand, and whether I have as yet paid any of the money.

August 21st.—Called at Rue de Richelieu this morning to learn from Sir George Wood what is in the wind, but he knew nothing about it.[1]

August 26th.—I find an undoubted communication from Sir George Wood's major of brigade (Captain Baynes, R.A.), informing me that the Fauigny (or lead) affair had assumed a more favourable appearance, and that Sir George desired I would take no further steps in it until I heard again from him. This is established; but then follow contradictions which I cannot reconcile, and must therefore note them down as they are, rather than lose them altogether. M. Fauigny, quite elated at the attention paid to his first complaint, had employed an appraiser, or some such person, to draw up a complete estimate of furniture destroyed, and every sort of damage done to the chateau, with which he

---

[1] The rough journal from which I have with much trouble compiled this copy is here so confused and imperfect as to be of little or no use ; and my great auxiliaries—letters to my wife, from which I was enabled to correct or confirm dates, and to make more circumstantial many subjects only mentioned in the journal—I have unwittingly destroyed. During my stay at Stain, too, I wrote by fits and starts. Amongst new scenes of every kind, and new people, the excitement was too great to admit of shutting one's self up for study or writing. Thus, from the period I have now reached, my means are so few, that it is quite impossible to bring my journal (as I wished) down to our final departure from France —as complete as it might have been.

again waited on the Duke, in the hope that all would be
ordered to be paid as before. This time, however, he was
unfortunate in arriving just as the Duke dismounted, in
a very ill-humour, at his residence in the Elysée Bourbon.
With true French effrontery, M. Fauigny followed his
Grace up the grand staircase. Arrived at the landing, the
Duke, probably observing him for the first time, turned
sharply, demanding, "What the devil do you want, sir?"
Nothing daunted by this rough address, M. Fauigny mentioned his subject in a few words, presenting at the same time
his *bill*, instead of taking which, the Duke, turning hastily
away, in his usual rough manner, exclaimed to his aide-de-
camp, "Pooh!—kick the rascal downstairs!" Such is the
story as I got it—whether exactly true or not is more than I
can now decide; but this much is certain, that Sir Edward
Barnes immediately communicated to Sir George Wood
M. Fauigny's discomfiture, adding, "Send word of this to
your friend Captain Mercer, and let him do as he pleases
about the lead."

As I had been anxious for some time to get leave and go
to England, I find by the same memorandum that I went
that same day to ask Sir George to make an application for
me, which, however, he would not do, telling me that the
Duke had refused leave (and very angrily) to Captain Cleeve
of the German Legion Artillery, though summoned to his
father's deathbed. That I eventually escaped paying a
heavy sum of money for depredations committed by others,
is not attributable to the Duke of Wellington's sense of
justice, but to the irritability of his temper. An officer
holding a command in his army (particularly of cavalry or
artillery) was in constant jeopardy—constantly struggling to
reconcile two contradictions: 1st, to conciliate the natives,
and thus prevent complaints; and 2nd, to keep his men comfortable and horses *fat* (that is the word), which could only
be done at the expense of the natives. These, encouraged
by the Duke's orders, proclamations, etc., were never backward in complaining—indeed, they soon became insufferably
insolent: and whilst affecting to admire and praise the
grand Vellangton, and draw comparisons between him and
Blucher and his Prussian *thieves* (for so they invariably
termed them)—"*voleurs Prussiens*"—they in reality laughed

at us; whilst even the private soldiers of the Prussian army were (to their face, at least) treated with the most reverential deference. A sad contrast there was between our relative situations. As for gratitude, the wretches have not one grain of it. Many actually imagine that motives of fear have induced the Duke to adopt this (to them) strange line of conduct.

However severe his Grace may be in this respect, he is easy and indulgent in another which materially concerns our comfort—I mean dress. Every one pleases his fancy in the selection of his costume—some wear plain clothes; others, though in uniform (I speak of visiting and walking about Paris), choose to be unencumbered with sword or sash. Many cavalry men, etc., like, in this hot weather, to go with jackets open, with white or fancy waistcoats, etc. Some wear mustaches, others beards; others, again, both beard and mustaches. A neglect of military uniformity so striking, and so much in contrast with the precision and strictness of costume observed by all the other armies, could not but be noticed. Accordingly, it is said, one of the monarchs (Emperor Alexander, I have heard) made an observation on the subject to the Duke, who, feeling himself called on to do something, gave out a general order on the subject, in which he directed that all officers of the British Army appearing in the streets of Paris should be dressed either wholly in plain clothes or in the strict uniform of their corps. No doubt which was chosen. There is another general order of the Duke's quoted, and the cause of it—for which, however, I do not vouch, having never seen it. The story is this: An English officer, walking on the Boulevard, was rudely pushed off the path by a French gentleman, whom the Englishman immediately knocked down. The person so treated happened to be a marshal; and he, without loss of time, complained to the Duke, though unable to identify his man. His Grace in consequence issued a general order commenting on the outrage offered to a person of such high distinction, and winding up with desiring that British officers would in future abstain from beating marshals of France, etc. But I have digressed from the thread of my discourse, to which I must return, and endeavour to render it as connected as my disjointed records, aided by memory, will admit of.

After leaving Sir G. Wood's, I find no notice of further transactions until the evening, when, accompanied by Ambrose (our troop surgeon), I set off to ride home by the Rue de St Denis and La Chapelle. Returning through La Chapelle accompanied by Ambrose, a fellow sitting on his cart drove against him. Ambrose's temper is rather peppery, and he repaid the affront by a cut across the shoulders with his horsewhip. The carter, standing up in his cart, fell furiously on Ambrose in return with his whip, and a regular battle ensued, Ambrose trying to mount the cart, the other keeping him down and flogging him. In a twinkling a crowd assembled, and from reviling soon came to active operations; but I rode round the cart and prevented interference. At last they began to throw stones. This was too much. I drew my sword and charged in all directions, everywhere scattering the wretches like chaff, and thus kept the cowardly herd at bay until Ambrose succeeded in mounting the cart and breaking the fellow's whip over his own back, when, the crowd becoming very serious, he jumped on his horse, and we made our retreat, not, however, without showers of stones, none of which touched us, and being obliged two or three times to turn on our persecutors, who followed us some distance. At last we effected our retreat.

31st.—Review of the Russian Guards, etc. They were formed as usual along the Neuilly road, and had the saluting-point in the Place Louis Quinze. A finer body of men can scarcely be imagined; but to me their padded breasts and waspish waists appeared preposterous. The cuirassiers were also very fine men, well mounted, and neatly and serviceably equipped. I was fortunate enough to wedge myself into the very middle of the Imperial cortège. The Emperor of Austria received the salutes, and I was immediately behind his Imperial Majesty—on whose right was our Duke with his blue ribbon on, and all round about were princes, marshals, generals—all the mighty and distinguished of Europe. The Emperor of Russia himself gave the word of command, marched past at the head of the column, and saluted. The Prussian monarch took the command of a regiment of which he is colonel, and likewise marched past. When Alexander wheeled round after passing, and joined our group, he saluted Prince Schwartzenberg with a slap on the thigh, his countenance lighted up by his customary good-humoured smile. The proud Austrian bowed in acknowledgment of the honour done him; but as he cast his eye over his shoulder and met mine fixed on him, a frown soon chased away the forced unmeaning smile still lingering round his mouth, and it required no conjuror to see that he did not admire being treated so familiarly. The greatest good humour and cheerfulness seemed to reign amongst this group of sovereigns, sovereign princes, and renowned chiefs; and that intuitive awe which little people always experience in such company, began to give way to confidence and a feeling of delight at mingling thus intimately, as it were, with those hitherto to me historical characters, on whose faith depend the destinies of Europe. My next neighbour, a man of high rank—general, or what not— might have been a Czernicheff, Wittgenstein, or some other celebrated man; he wore a Russian uniform, and was covered with decorations. As he spoke French fluently (what Russian does not?), and seemed an honest-hearted man, free from vanity, we soon got into conversation, spite of my shabby old pelisse. Never was I more astonished than when, in answer to my question who the smart-looking lancers were who kept the ground, he replied "Cossacks." A very fine set of tall, handsome, genteel-looking young men, faces exhibiting a delicate pink and white complexion fit for a lady, quite undefiled by beard or mustache; dressed in scarlet jackets without any lace, fitting like stays; large blue-green overalls, with a broad red stripe, and, as usual, the waist drawn into the capacity of a decent grasp; their arms a sabre, brace of pistols stuck in their waist-belt, and a long red-shafted lance without the pennon; small rough horses— not of a piece with the delicate man and the quality of his equipment. The cuirassiers wore black-varnished cuirasses; and one regiment was entirely mounted on beautiful isabels, or cream-coloured horses. But the horse-artillery, as *en régle*, attracted my most particular attention. These, as far as men and horses went, appeared most efficient: the men stout, of active make, and not too tall; their dress smart, though exceedingly plain—dark green; their equipment, arms, and horse appointments all of the same description—plain, substantially good, and sufficiently neat, without anything superfluous. The gunners' horses were stoutly made serviceable animals; but the draught-horses (which seemed an anomaly, though they know best) were much smaller—and such little wild-looking beauties as one would be proud to show off in Hyde Park, or down Bond Street. The worst part of the whole were the guns and carriages—the former of very light calibre, and polished like brass candlesticks (not above 3-pounders, I should think); the latter very low, light, and painted bright green, looking more like toys than service articles. To these the horses were harnessed three abreast; the outer one on the off side, more for show than use, prancing along with the neck bent outward in the true classical position, to which it was confined by a side rein. The effect of this, as far as appearance goes, is certainly good. My friend the general, pointing out these pretty horses with an air of triumph that led me to suspect him of being in the corps, assured me that they had been almost incessantly on the march ever since the retreat of the French from Moscow. They were with the pursuing force, took their share of the campaign in Saxony 1813, advanced to Paris in '14. When the Russians retired, these little animals had drawn the guns back again, and had actually arrived on the banks of the Vistula (I think he said), when they were countermanded, and had now arrived a second time in Paris. Is not this quite astonishing? I could well enter into the feeling of satisfaction and complacency with which he begged my opinion as to their appearance, and unhesitatingly gratified him with my unqualified admiration of them. How could it be otherwise! They were round as barrels, sleek-coated, and full of life and spirit—in short, they were so beautiful that the thing looked more like a showy toy than what had for two years been incessantly in the field. The review over, I called on Sir Edward Barnes and asked his intercession with the Duke to obtain my leave, which he readily promised; so I adjourned to No. 36 Rue Mont Blanc, had some chat with Bell, heard his fair young hostess play the "Exile" again, and returned to my dominions.

September 2d.—Care less about Paris than I did, and stay more at home. The parapet of the bridge becomes again my smoking lounge.

7th.—This morning I received the long-wished-for leave of absence for two months; and wishing to start immediately, Ambrose and I rode up to town to take my place in the diligence for Calais. The Bureau des Diligence is in the Cour des Messageries, Rue Nôtre Dame de la Victoire—an establishment of which I had before no conception. The court is very large; there are several offices for different coaches; but what surprised me most was the parade of those heavy dismal-looking machines—I think there must have been fifty drawn up round the court. For Calais there was no room, therefore I have taken my places—one inside for self, one in the cabriolet for William—in the Amiens diligence, which starts to-morrow morning at five o'clock. The seats inside, etc., are not left as with us to the first comer, etc. On paying my fare I received a ticket with the number of my seat on it, which will be respected until I am taken up at St Denis, where they expect to be by six o'clock.

I know not whether the feeling be common to others, but I never leave a place where I have tarried ever so short a time without regret; accordingly my approaching departure has imparted a tinge of melancholy that I cannot shake off. Latterly I have been tolerably comfortable here; have got reconciled to my house; acquainted with the inhabitants; into a certain routine of amusements and occupations. The weather had been generally fine, though hot; and everything had begun to assume a hue *couleur de rose*: no wonder, then, that a slight cloud should interfere to alloy in some degree the joy at returning to all most dear to me.

White Horse Cellar, Piccadilly, September 13th.—Here I arrived last night, and having neither time nor inclination to write during my journey, must note down occurrences now as well as I can recollect them before I start for Farringdon; the which done, adieu to pens, ink, and paper—at least for a time.

On the morning of the 8th inst. I was punctually standing on the *trottoir* in front of a villanous *tabagie* in St Denis at six o'clock, William and my portmanteau beside me. The house was full of drunken, and therefore insolent, Flemish waggoners, and I had no inclination to enter. Our Noah's Ark did not keep me long waiting for its arrival, although it tarried sufficiently when it did come.

M. le Conducteur, a little man, but a most important one, wrapped in a brown greatcoat, a silk handkerchief round his throat, and his head covered by one of those grey linen forage-caps, descended from his airy perch on the roof with great gravity, and pulling out his way-bill, demanded of the *cabaretier* where was the English Monsieur who was to be taken up at St Denis. I presented myself. The little man, scrutinising me from head to foot, "Vous avez un port-manteau, monsieur?" "Oui, monsieur." "Où se trouvé-t-il donc?" "Le voilà, monsieur." "*Le voilà?—quoi ceci?*" "Oui." "Et vous appelez ceci un portmanteau? Sacre Dieu! mais c'est une malle que ça! Elle ne montera pas sur la diligence!" looking up at the insides, who had thrust their heads out of the window on hearing the row. "Sacre Dieu! cela *un portmanteau!*" and he began to swagger and fume and pester among the saboted, greasy nightcapped gentry who stood by, enjoying exceedingly having a John Bull on the horns of a dilemma.

According to our English acceptation of the term, my baggage was literally a large portmanteau; but the passengers within gave me to understand that Monsieur le Conducteur was perfectly right, and that I had better try to conciliate him instead of insisting. I took their advice, and my *malle* became a portmanteau, under which title alone it was admissible on the diligence, according to the laws and ordinances of La Cour des Messageries. I got inside, William mounted the cabriolet, and I bade adieu to St Denis —at all events for two months. I was agreeably surprised at finding the diligence such a comfortable conveyance; well padded and well hung, we rolled along most agreeably, though only at the rate of six miles per hour. My com-panions inside were—an elderly lady, very taciturn but very amiable; a young one about five-and-twenty, handsome, lively, chatty, and very shrewd—she talked for both; a good, honest, little man, who kept some sort of magazine in Paris; a young lad, clerk in some counting-house; and an officer of our own Rifles. We had not reached Pierrefitte ere Mademoiselle had managed to introduce us all to each other in such a manner that formality was banished, and we were the best friends possible—laughing, joking, quizzing each other or the *paysans*; nothing could be happier.

At Luzarches, a capital breakfast, and as much time as we pleased to take it in—M. le Conducteur all suavity and amiability. Our lively little friend kept up such an animated conversation that I saw only just enough of the country we were passing through to remark that it became much prettier and more picturesque as we approached Clermont, where the diligence stopped for dinner. M. le Conducteur took the head of the table, and our party was increased by a *soi-disant*, or *soi-pensant*, humorist of the *gendarmerie*, who, seating himself *sans cérémonie*, fell to, tooth and nail, as if he had not touched food for a week. This, however, did not much interrupt the display of wit, which principally was aimed at the cookery and dishes served up. A fricassee of rabbit he vowed he would on no account touch unless Madame produced *les pattes*, since, as he solemnly assured us, they frequently served fricasseed cats instead. Madame did not, however, produce *les pattes*, and although none of us touched it, the dish in a few minutes was cleared of its contents. This fellow reminded me strongly of the parasite in Gil Blas, and, his adulations being entirely addressed to our little vain conducteur, I set him down as the "Antorcha de la Filosofia!"—maybe our hero always dined with the passengers *par ordre et pour l'espionage*. Here, as at Luzarches, no *empressement* was betrayed: the diligence stood passively at the door without horse, without even an hostler visible; the ladies retired to a *chambre*; so the Rifleman and I agreed to walk on, which resolve we communicated to M. le Conducteur, who assented, and off we set. At the end of the town two roads appeared, one running straight along the valley, the other crossing the bridge to the right, then ran rump-fashion up the other side of the valley, divergingly from the former—and this road was our proper one; but, without condescending to ask a question, we very sagaciously chose the other, and had already proceeded some hundred yards along it, when fortunately (no hedges intervened—the valley was all grass, a rivulet running through the middle of it) we saw our lumbering vehicle slowly ascending the opposite hill. The distance that separated us from it was not great, and we shouted to M. le Conducteur to wait for us; but neither he nor the coachman heard us, and, being ignorant of the nature of the rivulet, after a moment's hesitation we decided our most prudent plan was to run back to the bridge, etc. This we immediately did; but although both of us were pretty active runners, we should have been left behind at last had we not luckily met a miller coming down on horseback. Him and his sacks we dismounted *sans cérémonie,* for the diligence, having now arrived at the summit, had commenced its jogtrot. Mounting the animal, I pursued as fast as the end of the halter could persuade my beast to move, and after a long chase succeeded at length in bringing the vehicle to. Our companions, especially the young dame, or demoiselle, had a hearty laugh at our expense, and so had our miller, for he grinned from ear to ear when the silver recompense (never expected) touched his palm, and he was still grinning and bowing when we looked back as the diligence drove on. It was about eleven at night when we reached the *barrière* of Amiens, and I had been some time asleep. A bright light presented to my eyes caused me to start up in surprise, and at first it was difficult to imagine where I was, until I perceived the uniform of a *gendarmerie,* who, after reconnoitring us by holding the lantern to our faces, very quietly demanded something for his trouble. Angry at such a humiliating operation, the Rifleman and I sent him to the devil; but our companions, whilst opening their own purses, made it so clear to us that the fellow had been extremely civil where he might have been extremely troublesome, that we concluded by doing in Rome, etc. etc.; and away we rumbled over the jolting pavement, and through a series of dark narrow streets, until at last we drove into the yard of the Hôtel d'Angleterre, as dark and deserted as the streets themselves. Hostlers, however, were soon forthcoming, the horses changed, my *malle* handed down, and William and myself left standing in the middle of the yard wondering what was to become of us. After a little hesitation, one of the hostlers condescended to direct us to the door of the house ere he retired, and after a good deal of knocking at that we succeeded in rousing an old fellow—whose duty I suppose it was to sit up for the diligence—who showed me into a large room, with a bed in one corner; and at my request for supper brought me a couple of cold widgeons, which I soon discussed, and jumped into an excellent bed.

9th.—In a dilemma; no conveyance forward but posting. Did not exactly believe this, and therefore inquired from *auberge* to *auberge*, until at last I discovered that a sort of caravan started every morning at nine o'clock from the * * * for Abbeville. This would be getting on, therefore I lost no time in securing my places. Having risen early, I passed the intervening time in visiting some of our people stationed here—younger M'Donald's troop, also 1st Regiment of Dragoons, K.G.L. Him I found in an excellent lodging. Our caravan was a curious machine, very much down by the stern, otherwise resembling a small house on wheels. William and a woman got into the *fond de la voiture*, whilst I occupied the front seat, in company with a neat, dapper, little, big-bellied man, wearing a very smart forage-cap, and speaking a very little English. We travelled very slowly, and made a long halt at Flixcourt (pronounced *Fleeshcour*)—nevertheless, to my great joy, we reached Abbeville by two o'clock. I found here the 13th Light Dragoons and my old troop G; called on Lieutenant Leathes; dined at the Hôtel de Londres, a very inferior house. Here I hired a cabriolet to take us forward to Calais for five napoleons. From the first I set my *voiturier* down as a scoundrel, from his physiognomy, and the event proved me a sound judge. The bargain struck, he tried all sorts of shifts and excuses, in the hope, as I discovered, of associating some other traveller with me. As soon as I made the discovery, I insisted on his starting instantly, and after some difficulty at last got him fairly on the road. It proved a very tedious mode of travelling this; he did not choose to hurry his horse, was continually stopping, and more uncivil in his manner than I thought a true Frenchman could be. The motion of the carriage was very disagreeable—sometimes too heavy before, sometimes behind; and at times it became necessary to put a great stone behind to relieve the poor horse of the weight. A sort of commercial traveller (bagman), who overtook us as we slowly crept up hill near Montreuil thus loaded, facetiously remarked, "Ah, monsieur, vous chargez des pierres, donc!" Our driver's villanous countenance became black as thunder, but he answered a dry "Oui"; and the other, seeing it was no joke, passed on. It was dusk ere we reached Montreuil, and then our poor

beast was so completely done up that I was obliged to
subscribe to the necessity of halting; and accordingly our
friend drew up at the door of a mean-looking cabaret, just
without the town, and we alighted, expecting but sorry
accommodation in such a place. If, however, La Renard
continue what it was, I shall have no objection whatever to
pass another night there when I return. A pretty little
airy parlour, well though plainly furnished, the windows
opening on a garden; as neat a little bedroom adjoining, bed
the very type of cleanliness; add an excellent supper and a
bottle of very fair wine, and it may be imagined that the
evening and night passed in the Renard will always be a
bright spot in the memory. It must not be concealed,
though, that a pair of very brilliant black eyes certainly
threw rather a witching light on my apartments. In the
morning, whilst Lisette was busy preparing my breakfast, I
was taking a stroll up and down the pretty rural garden,
when, to my astonishment, the apparition of a true John-
Bull farmer stood before me. At first it appeared an illusion, but the voice soon dispelled that—brown frock-coat,
breeches and gaiters, with good thick shoes. Out of these,
with the real country twang, issued "Marning, zir; queer
chaps here, zir; I doant onderstand one word as ony on um
says—not I." My friend then proceeded to ask my assistance as his interpreter, and explained his being there. His
son, it seems, is the saddler of the 13th Light Dragoons,
stationed just now in Abbeville, whither he had been on a
visit, and was now making his way back again to Calais, but
being short of coin (French—he had plenty of English) and
words, found himself here in a dilemma. Sorry I am that
I had not time to preserve the history of his adventures and
mishaps since arriving in France; they were most amusing
and laughable, but I have now forgotten more than odds and
ends. As he passed the evening in company with William,
probably that worthy may assist me in recollecting somewhat
of it.

My bill was extremely moderate for all the comfort I had
enjoyed, and I parted best friends imaginable with my
attentive hostess and her pretty daughter—*Au revoir!*

It is a curious town Montreuil, with its steep narrow
streets and high walls; but I only saw it *en passant*, for we

did not stop.   Beyond it, after ascending from the valley of
the Canch, we traversed a dreary open country for some way,
and then came to wood and very pretty ground, which
continued until a long descent brought us at length creepingly
to Samer, where we stopped to breakfast at the Tête de
Bœuf (William Mallet—a Frenchman, spite of the name).
A Cockney party of three ladies and two gentlemen had just
arrived from Boulogne—evidently the first time any of them
had been out of England.   They were all flutter and
curiosity, quite childishly so—chattering away bad school
French with a regular English enunciation, and giggling when
successful in making themselves understood.   Had they but
guessed that the brown-visaged, mustachioed, befurred hero
who stood before them and watched all their movements
was English, perhaps they would have been a little more
discreet.

One of the gentlemen drew, and had brought a camera
lucida, which he adjusted at the door of the Tête de Bœuf,
and disposed himself to take a view of Samer, surrounded
by some eight or ten gaping clowns in their blue frocks and
clumsy sabots, too picturesque objects to be missed; and
my man stuck two or three of them in positions to enter into
his picture—the only feature in it, for the point of view he
had chosen was a most unfortunate one.   As I leaned from
my window, right over the artist's head, and at no great
distance above him (for the Tête de Bœuf boasts but a very
moderate elevation), many an ogle did I get from the young
ladies, who kept running out incessantly in order to persuade
our hero that eating his breakfast was better than sketching.
But he was stanch to the backbone, and when my *voiturier*
summoned me to start, I left him in the same position,
indefatigably occupied upon his insipid picture.   Before
reaching Samer, my rogue had begun expressing doubts of
the soundness of one of his wheels; and true enough—for
just as we gained sight of Boulogne (beyond which, I believe,
he never from the first meant to go), smash it went all to
pieces, and down we came gently enough.   The vagabond
acted his part well—pretended astonishment, *au désespoir*,
etc. etc.—but I saw through him.   Under the circumstances,
only one thing remained to be done, as no assistance was at
hand: William shouldered my *malle*, I carried the et ceteras,

and on we trudged; and after a pretty hot walk we arrived at Boulogne, and entered the first decent-looking house that presented itself, and ordered dinner. Here I learned that a packet was about to sail in the evening for Dover, and decided on cutting connection with my rascally *voiturier*, who managed to bring in his vehicle shortly after us.

Accordingly in the evening we repaired to the pier and embarked at 2 p.m. My fellow-passengers were—Lord Charles Fitzroy; another officer, his friend; and a very pretty Frenchwoman. We had hardly made any offing, when the breeze falling, left us at the mercy of a long swell— the surface as smooth as a mirror. The rolling was terrible, and the poor Frenchwoman, dreadfully sick, cursing the ship, cursing England, and cursing herself for venturing on the sea. Early [1] the following morning we reached Dover, where, to the unspeakable horror of our poor friend, she was informed that she could not leave the vessel until her passport had been sent to London to be verified. O England! what naughty things did not she say of you then! A coach, starting within an hour after our landing, was very convenient, and in company of an officer of the 13th Light Dragoons, I took my seat for London, and here I am.

[1] At three in the morning, when Lord Charles and his companion immediately landed and tried to persuade me to do the same, but I remained on board until daylight.

CHAPTER XXIV

Two months I rusticated in Berkshire, and then, my leave of absence having nearly expired, set off in the beginning of November, taking with me my wife, whose determination not to be again separated, united to an eager curiosity to see Paris, overcame all the difficulties I threw in the way of such a winter campaign, and rendered her deaf to all my representations of hardships and privations which she would inevitably have to bear and put up with. My journal of this second residence was hurried, meagre, and very irregularly kept. She kept likewise a few memoranda, so that from the two, and what memory and collating will supply, I am enabled to complete this journal to the return of my troop to Canterbury in February 1816.

Sunday, November 5th.—Slept at the York Hotel last night, and embarked this morning on board the packet for Calais—forget her name—Captain Keys. All bustle and confusion when we went on board. Deck encumbered with a carriage and heaps of baggage, amongst which the complete, well-appointed baggage of Hamilton Hamilton, Esq., secretary of legation, or some such thing, was most conspicuous. In time carriage was stowed and baggage sent below, porters, leave-takers, etc., went ashore, and we quitted the pier. Passengers numerous: H. Hamilton does exclusive, and even betrays impatience and vexation at being shut up with such a *canaille*; then an old gentleman, with a broad-brimmed hat, assumes mighty airs of consequence, and even looks a little contemptuously at Hamilton Hamilton himself, who speaks to none but his *own man*; a Scottish gentleman and his spouse, who makes a terrible sputter about her dear little dog Rose, which is somehow or another left behind at Dover; a mean-looking man in a foraging-cap, a melancholy sergeant of dragoons, and his wife; a Russian dressed in forage-cap and green jacket, like a servant's morning one, wearing no gloves, and looking for all the world like a *courrier*, but F. insisting that such a white hand decidedly constitutes him a gentleman; besides a crowd, *gentium minorum*, of whom we make no record. As we left, the guns on Dover Castle announced Guy Faux by a royal salute. A fresh breeze and rather dark day—the one operating on the *physique*, the other on the *morale*, made all the passengers except very few, exceedingly sick. More than half-way over, our breeze gradually subsided into a calm, and left us bobbing about at a most tantalising distance from our port. To amuse the tedium of the calm, our Russian (by no means a handsome man), who had been ogling F. from the very beginning, managed to pick up a conversation; and in a very short time from ogling began to make love, which, however, was cut short by her getting squeamish, and being obliged to lie down. He then transferred his attentions to me, and I really found him a most gentlemanly, well-informed man, in spite of his exterior. After being tantalised for some time looking at Calais without being able to reach it, at length a breeze sprang up and carried us in. Crowds of Sunday people were on the pier, all anxious to see the arrivals. The usual squabble about baggage and forcing through the surrounding multitude took place, and we went to Quillacq's Hotel without the baggage—which, after all, was detained on board until it could be inspected at the custom-house on Monday morning, a most inconvenient arrangement, as we found ourselves without an article except what we stood in—a great rambling house, with large dreary (at this season of the year) rooms and long corridors. Amused with F.'s surprise at the number of little dishes served up at dinner—all, however, excellent. Obliged to borrow nightcaps of M. and Madame Quillacq.

6th.—Up at seven in the morning, and went to the custom-house for our baggage. *Douaniers*, a set of insolent scoundrels, gave themselves amazing airs, and tumbled everything out on the floor; particularly severe with Ham. Hamilton's baggage, who had sent his servant for it. At last I got mine out of their clutches; hired a cabriolet to take us to Paris, where we give it up to the correspondent. Well stuffed and comfortable, with innumerable little pockets. F. amused again with our set out: started at half-past ten a.m., preceded by the little gentleman in the broad-brimmed hat in one *calèche*, and the two Russians in another. At Marquise we passed them. Nothing extraordinary in our drive except Buonaparte's pillar near Boulogne, and the house he lived in at Pont de Bricq when he visited the army of England. Arrived at M. Mallet, Samer, by half-past four p.m. Found the house comfortable, except that our room smoked somewhat. Girls most merry; gave us an excellent dinner, but so-so wine. Amused ourselves with arrivals and departures. F. looked in vain, however, for her Russian lover—he came not.

But another character of more importance came not: Mr William should have joined us at Dover or Calais; but when at the latter we learned that he remained at Dover waiting for his trunk, which had been left behind in London.

November 7th.—Sophie gave us an excellent breakfast, after which we set off. Our postilion a character, in the Imperial green jacket; and from under his leathern hat, instead of the usual thick queue, flowed a mass of locks unrestrained. His beasts were a couple of long-tailed cart-horses, harnessed principally with rope. The long ascent, after leaving Samer, brought us on the plateau occupied by the dreaded forest—dreaded because we had heard reports of banditti and plundering; but we passed through it without interruption, and soon after saw the ramparts of Montreuil crowning the isolated hill, frowning like an acropolis over the lower town—the whole, standing as it does in a country destitute of the smallest feature of the picturesque, presenting a most sombre and forbidding aspect. Nor did the interior belie its exterior aspect which we entered by a long, squalid, straggling street, and ascended to the upper town by a very steep hill. Whilst the horses were changing we got an omelet. Scotch officer and his wife, who had come on *en voiturier*, we overtook here. As elsewhere, a crowd of beggars assailed us on alighting and re-entering our carriage. In this country they spoil their own trade, for they are too numerous. I hurry over all this, for my notes are very meagre.

Approaching Abbeville by a long descent, its cathedral, proudly elevating its beautiful Gothic front above the other buildings (dingy in colour, and unpicturesque in form) was the only redeeming point in the view; but that *was* an interesting one. The town, however, pleased us, though its streets are rather narrow and dirty. Found our old friends the hussars of the Brunswick auxiliaries and my old troop (G) quartered here.

8th.—Started at a little after seven a.m. Our postilion was the first one we had had, who astonished F. by wearing jackboots. Breakfasted at Flixcourt: little slop-basins instead of cups, with large spoons; as usual, sour bread and soapy butter—for all which the charge was exorbitant. During breakfast the beautiful band of the 1st Hussars, K.G.L., was playing on an open space near the house, where the regiment had its morning parade.

At Pecquigny met a bridal—all in their best; men and boys firing guns, and the bride carrying a little flag. A young rogue who stood by our carriage whilst changing horses begging in a most piteous accent, observing me start when the first gun was fired, just before the procession came in sight, could not resist the desire of amusing himself at my expense, whom he no doubt took for some Cockney, and shouted, in a voice of affected alarm, "C'est l'ennemi, monsieur!" and seeing that his *coup* had *manqué*, burst into laughter.

Beyond Pecquigny came on the valley of the Somme; and the scenery became somewhat interesting. Amiens we found full of Prussians, and only stopped to change horses—Maître de Poste quite a gentlemanly man, riding a managed horse. Fine old town and splended cathedral. Stopped for the night at Breteuil. Inn an immense old-fashioned house, like an old convent; great rambling wainscoted corridor; and our room large, lofty, and the walls hung with old faded tapestry, and two old-fashioned beds with curtains of yellow damask; sitting-room quite on a par with it. Our attendant Josephine (a very pretty girl) told us our teeth must be bad, because we complained of our fowl being tough; and to our complaint of knives, she said they were too sharp, for that she had just cut her finger with one of them. Apropos of knives, there seems but one pattern all over France, and that a very coarse one, which, however costly the table-service in other respects, appears everywhere to spoil the whole. Its sharp point one sees constantly used as a toothpick; and over and over again I have seen it taken from that employment and plunged unhesitatingly into some dish, etc. Soup served in a regular white jorden; however, we find fine Sèvres porcelain coffee-services everywhere. Wine here all out of one cask, though Josephine protested that the fifty different kinds she enumerated were literally and truly each from the place named. F. astonished at the immense long loaves. An English family had arrived in a smart barouche, with servants in a cabriolet. Forced to sit in their bedroom, ours being the only *salle*, such as it is.

November 9th.—Early this morning a large detachment of Prussian infantry marched into Breteuil, and the officers, as soon as their parade was over, came tramping *sans cérémonie* through every room in the house. F., whom I had left alone whilst I strolled out to see the place, was terribly frightened by three or four of them walking into the room, and standing there with the door open jabbering for some time, as if no one had been present, one of them ogling most furiously. Spite of our exertions, the family in the barouche got their horses and set off before us, to our great annoyance, as of course they would absorb all the attention and occupy all the accommodation to our exclusion. Josephine gave us a miserable breakfast, no doubt owing to that accursed barouche; and, after all, our bill was most exorbitant. Thought our postilion was mad—for never saw French postilion dash along so recklessly and at such a pace: the cabriolet rolled from side to side, and jerked and jumped so that I expected we should plunge through the windows. Still it was pleasant to get on. At last we overtook the barouche, and the mystery was explained, for our gentleman relapsed at once into the tamest of postilions, sticking himself close up to the other carriage, with his horses' noses under its very dicky. Occupant of this a gentleman's gentleman of the very first water, who sadly annoyed F. by his impudent staring. Urged our hero of the jackboots and sheep-skin pelisse to pass ahead, for the heavy barouche, although drawn by four horses, could only get on at a jog-trot pace. Urged long in vain. At last, just as he was about to push on, the gentleman in the dicky dropped his glove, and our most polite postilion actually stopped, dismounted, picked it up, and again driving up in the wake of the barouche, presented it with the utmost deference of manner to the supercilious scoundrel. Got furious now, and commenced such a volley that I at last actually succeeded in driving him ahead of the barouche just as we approached Clermont. Another marriage at St Juste: bride very pretty, and guns fired in abundance as before. Clermont uncommonly prettily situated. Did not alight, but enjoyed some delicious grapes which women and girls brought and sold for a song. Hence to Creil; a great improvement in the scenery, which became rich, diversified, and well wooded, until near that place we descended into the beautiful bottom of the Oise, with its wooded hill and white cliffs. Found here a garrison of Belges. Our postilion still more mad. As we had foreseen, there was some difficulty in getting rooms at the Hôtel de Bourbon at Chantilly, and we had scarcely secured them ere the barouche drove up, but could not find accommodation. Visited the chateau of the Prince de Condé. Stables magnificent; an immense lofty hall, as big as a church, with a fine cupola—around are the stalls, etc.—splendid idea! Our dinner even more than usually ridiculous by the number of little *plats*—a regular doll's; liqueurs of sorts, all very bad, in cruet-bottles—aniseed the only one drinkable. In the evening entertained by the singing of the Nassau troops stationed here. Bad news from Paris. In the next room a party of London shop-boys, or some such thing. One of these, pretty drunk, wanted to be called in the morning, and as our doors were open, we had the full benefit and advantage of the fine language propounded to the waiter: "Garçon! mon domestique à cinq heure et demie." Garçon does not comprehend; tries over and over again. "Je ne vous comprends pas, monsieur, se fait entendre toujours." At last impatient, "Well, dammee, 'tis simply this, my man: tell my servant to call me at half-past five o'clock." We went to our bedroom ere the matter was settled. The French seem to think nothing of damp sheets—ours were actually wet.

10th.—Our host gave us a most comfortable breakfast, after which we set off in high spirits for Paris; the day fine and scenery lovely. Whilst changing horses at Luzarches, some non-commissioned officers of the Belgic or Nassau troops stationed there were exceedingly impertinent to F., but I had no time to obtain redress, so left them.

After passing Pierrefitte, made our postilion turn off the

chaussée spite of his objections, and attempt to reach Stain; but we soon found the cross-road so bad, nearly smashing our wheels, that we were glad to regain the chaussée. Whilst stopping at the posthouse at St Denis, Frazer and Ambrose rode up. From them we learned that old Webber had made my house very comfortable; so determined not to stay in Paris, but to give up our cabriolet, and return forthwith to Stain. This we accordingly did, driving straight to the Remise, Rue Faubourg St Denis, where we hired a fiacre, and reached Stain about dusk. It was a cold gloomy evening. The story of comfort was exaggerated. Webber had hired some little, shabby, old furniture; but the place looked wretched, and when F. became fully aware of its discomforts, her enthusiasm gave way like snow before the sun; she burst into tears. The heroics vanished, and she confessed she wished herself again in England. The room had indeed a most forlorn appearance: a handful of fire flickered in the grateless, gaping chimney; the little furniture was of the coarsest kind; the uncarpeted floor of brick;— desolation everywhere! We had had no dinner, and, except some ration-beef, nothing could be procured. Some of this, however, was cooked and despatched; and as the best thing we could do, we set to work putting to rights, and making the most of it. Nothing could equal the surprise of Madlle. Rose at finding that the smooth-faced bourgeois was indeed the identical mustachioed commandant she had been accustomed to months ago. Next morning found a poultry-yard—rabbits, etc., all provided by the attentions of old Robertson, my quartermaster-sergeant. Things looked better; F. was refreshed, consequently in better spirits. The visits of congratulation and kind attentions of our villagers delighted her; but M. le Maire stood like one thunderstruck when introduced to his old friend with a new face. My cow dead, but another was negotiating for. The history of the defunct was, that she was a commissariat issue to me as so many rations; but, instead of putting her to death, I kept her for her milk.

Here, again, I am without a guide, or nearly so—my diary ends; and, to continue our residence at Stain, I am reduced to a few brief notices preserved in my general journal.

That residence was uncomfortable enough, for the winter

set in with a degree of severity unknown in England; and our house, both from its construction and furnishing, was ill calculated, under such circumstances, to afford comfort, or indeed at times to prevent suffering. However, we were in paradise compared to the situation of the little farmers (*cultivateurs*) and still poorer people amongst whom we were thus domiciliated. With them we found that it was no uncommon practice to live in the stable, etc., among the cattle, for the sake of sparing fuel—the animals helping to keep them warm.

Sometimes I took F. to Paris to see the lions; but it was sad, cold, dirty work. The streets were ankle-deep in mud; even the walks of the Palais Royal, the Passage des Panoramas, etc., were covered with mud, carried in on people's feet. Sometimes I took a walk; but the country, now stripped of its verdure, presented an aspect hideously cheerless. What could be more so than the extensive, dreary, snow-covered plain, extending from St Denis to the foot of Montmartre without a redeeming tree? Like other highroads, the one crossing this plain to La Chapelle, we were told, had once been bordered by trees, but they were cut down on the approach of the Allied armies, I think, last year.

Soon after arriving, having published through the commune our want of a female servant, Mademoiselle Rose introduced Angélique. My wife took a liking to her immediately; so, having exchanged written contracts with M. l'Ecuyer (her father), engaging to take care of, and send her back from England free of expense, she was engaged, and forthwith entered on her functions, as cook, lady's-maid, etc. M. l'Ecuyer is (like most of our neighbours) a *cultivateur*—works his own little bit of land, and is independent, except of poverty; for these little *cultivateurs* work hard and fare harder, as far as I can learn.

Sometimes our *séjour* was enlivened by visits from our own officers, or from some of those stationed in St Denis, La Vertu, and even from Paris: and occasionally more genial weather allowed F. to ride Cossack; but these rides were necessarily confined to the park. With the villagers we had become as much at home as Frenchmen could be. As for our *ménage*, it got on pretty well; and once we even ventured on giving a dinner to Wells and Ambrose, which went off pretty well; and once we went and passed a day with Sir A. Frazer at the Hôtel du Nord.

Again, one bitter cold black day, we visited the Abbey of St Denis, and went shivering through its vaults, and were shown the last home prepared by Napoleon for himself. The town was crowded with troops on their march northwards. Once or twice F. was able to ride to Paris; but it was hard work. Amongst other amusements in Stain, we had one not very agreeable, and which kept us in a continual state of excitement. Our men were continually setting fire to their quarters, particularly the chateau of Admiral Rosily. The villagers said this arose from their removing the ashes, and making their fires on the bare hearth, which thus became so hot as to set fire to the beams beneath. They therefore advised the men to leave the ashes and make their new fire on them. This they did; but Admiral Rosily wrote to tell me that no fires ought to be lighted upstairs in his house, as the chimneys were only intended as ventilators, and therefore begged us to confine the fires to the ground floor. At the stables of the chateau, over which a detachment was lodged, a fire occurred, and continued smouldering in the beams for a fortnight, the centre remaining on fire when we thought it extinguished.

At length the period of our departure drew nigh, and arrangements were made at headquarters which totally disorganised my troop at the moment when a perfect organisation was most necessary. During the campaign, a detachment of the driver-corps had been attached to each troop of horse-artillery, our own establishment being insufficient for the additional carriages. These were now to be withdrawn and sent home; and accordingly, all this rabble from Bull's and other troops still in the neighbourhood of Paris were sent to mine as destined for England. Secondly, all my officers were allowed to desert me. Captain Webber protested he was too weak to undertake such a journey, and obtained leave to remain in Paris; my surgeon (Ambrose) was permitted to remain in charge of him; Lieutenant Bruce neither liked the winter-march nor quitting Paris, where he was doing aide-de-camp to his cousin, Lady Castlereagh; two lieutenants (Maunsell and Wells) remained to march with the troop; but the former had resolved on leaving the service, and the latter had obtained an exchange to a troop forming part of the Army of Occupation, consequently he accompanies us only a part of the way to Calais —and thus no very great zeal could be expected from either of these. Thirdly, we were ordered to give up our white cross-belts to G troop, in exchange for their waist-belts— exhibiting thus our old worn jackets in all their nakedness. Fourthly, our overalls were in rags—new ones had been ordered, and were on the road from Brussels, but we were not allowed to wait for them. Add to all this the casualties of a long winter-march, bad lodging, and worse weather, and the condition of the troop on reaching Calais may be imagined. The defection of Ambrose, however, was counterbalanced by my old friend Hitchins getting leave to accompany us to England. He, too, intended quitting the service.

December 16*th.*—Hitchins joined us at Stain; and as he brought his own bed, I gave him a room in my chateau. The knotty question of how F. and Angélique were to travel was settled between them and Hitchins; and, overruling my scruples, it was arranged that a cabriolet should be hired for Calais, to be drawn by a pair of troop-horses, with the driver for postilion. Accordingly, on the 18th Hitchins went to Paris and procured the vehicle, whilst we continued our preparations.

19*th.*—The troop under Maunsell marched at an early hour for Beaumont, our first halting-place. One would have fancied that the village militia was about to quit home. No one thought of work: the whole population of the commune assembled in the park; endless the leave-takings, and I believe sincere the expressions of friendship and regrets at separation. Many of the *cultivateurs,* whose carts we had taken for the baggage, cheerfully volunteered accompanying us all the way to Calais.

Our own baggage delayed us so much that it was eleven a.m. before we were under way—F. and Angélique (whose relations to the twentieth degree had thronged our house all the morning) in the *calèche,* Hitchins and myself on horseback, followed by Gunner Fitzgerald, my orderly, and my groom Milward, in uniform and carrying my Waterloo lance. The day was fine, and the country pretty enough for the season; so that, after getting on the chaussée at Pierrefitte, we moved on merrily and agreeably until evening, when the sky clouded over, it became very cold, and soon a heavy fall of snow came on, in the midst of which we arrived at Beaumont, and found our people just forming the park, and those of Major Dyas already snug in their quarters. His battery had been ordered to march with us; but he had also orders not to interfere in any way with me or mine.

Our billet was on an iron merchant, and thither we proceeded, whilst Hitchins went in search of his own. Our house was a respectable-looking one outside; inside it was much like a great foundry or some such place—almost the whole of it being one vast hall, lighted from above, and full of bar-iron standing against the walls. An open staircase conducted us to a small gallery; up one more step and into a neat little room—but, from the scarcity of furniture and badness of the fire, looking sufficiently cheerless: a table, covered as usual with oilcloth, two or three plain chairs, a bed without curtains, and windows without shutters;—such was the domicile into which we were ushered by a hideously ugly and most sulky maid-servant. Assistance from the house we soon found we must not expect, and sent out for something to eat; but the answer was *nil*, and we were forced to content ourselves with some bad tea and bread and butter. The evening was wretchedly cold, and our fire so insufficient, that we were glad to get to bed; but here, again, were *wet* sheets, and we were obliged to get between the blankets. Miserable evening!

20th.—Weather improved. Started about eleven, and, traversing a beautiful and fertile country, arrived in the afternoon at the pretty village of Noailles, where we found ourselves billeted on a rich old gentleman, who did not ask us to his table, but in every other respect did his utmost to make us comfortable; and so in reality we were, for our apartment was delightfully so; our fare good; and our host furnished us liberally with good wine and cider. Passed the evening playing dominoes, and wishing we could stay in such nice quarters. Began to find Angélique [1] very useful in communicating with the people, whose ways she understood better than we. Noailles is but a poor village, although prettily situated; however, there is a manufactory here of those pretty bands which Frenchwomen wear below *the knee*.

21st.—A short march to Beauvais, where we arrived early; and whilst I parked the guns and saw my people put up,

[1] She cooked for us here.

Hitchins accompanied F. in search of my quarters. My duty finished, I followed to a handsome house, where I understood they were. Whilst making inquiries under the gateway, Madame herself came out and told me rather angrily that I could have no quarters there, as the colonel (my travelling title) and his lady already occupied all she was bound to furnish. I endeavoured to explain that the gentleman upstairs was my friend, that I was M. le Colonel, and had sent him to escort my wife, etc. etc. At the word *femme*, the *insolente* with a sneer turned from me with, "Ah! soi-disante." A scene occurred; Monsieur himself came out, who I insisted should be responsible for his wife's tongue. At last they begged pardon, and I mounted the staircase according to direction, and found a most comfortable lodging—two well-furnished rooms and a small cabinet. The people sent up soon after to invite us to dinner, they being ordered to feed us; but we would not go, and made them send dinner up to us. Our rooms had only one drawback—they were rather gloomy, the windows opening upon a courtyard. Stayed three days in Beauvais, during which we lived well at the expense of our host; and having bought some cards, Hitchins came every evening to coffee, and we had a game at casino. Our mornings were passed in visiting the beautiful Gothic cathedral and other churches; the manufactory of tapestry, equalling that of the Gobelins, of which this is a branch; in shopping, and in riding about the neighbouring country, which is pretty—somewhat resembling that about Bath. One evening we went to the play—a dark dismal house, and quite a second-rate set of actors. Don't know what the piece was, but the humour consisted in the patois of an old Picard servant, who was continually repeating, "Ya! ya! ya! Munsincur!" There were a good many of us—all the officers of Ross's troop and Dyas's battery, *par excellence*. The pit was full of French soldiers; yet all went off cheerfully, until our people called for "Vive Henri Quatre," which these Napoleonists fiercely opposed, and a row ensued, which terminated at last amicably. The ramparts of Beauvais form a delicious promenade, which I enjoyed; whilst F. and Hitchins were gadding about from shop to shop, buying lace, cambric, etc.

22d.—I intended marching forward to-morrow, but

Quartermaster Robertson, who was sent on to take up our quarters, returned at midnight with the intelligence that all the villages ahead of us were still full of troops. Relinquished the idea.

Major Dyas came to coffee. When he heard of the insult offered to F. he insisted upon going immediately to pull my host by the nose. "*Bloody D.*" was one of those jewels we received at the Union from the Irish artillery—tall, gaunt, and muscular, with a most truculent physiognomy. His cognomen was received on account of the ferocity he had displayed in the Irish Rebellion. Now he had become a gallant Lothario (not a gay one), and, if report spoke true, had already two wives, and had nearly succeeded in picking up a third in Paris—daughter of a gentleman of very good property, at whose house he had been billeted. Strange how insinuating these Irishmen are. To look at D. one would never suppose that a girl, young enough to be his daughter, handsome, and rich withal, could ever have fallen in love with such a man; and yet those best acquainted with the affair assured me that it was indubitably true.

23*d.*—Great market or fair—immense quantity of woollen cloth, manufacture of the town and neighbourhood. Preparations making for a grand procession in honour of Jeanne Hachette, who distinguished herself in the defence of the place against the Duc de Bourgogne in 1740. Until I looked into the history, I thought it had been, as some of the people informed me, in honour of Joan of Arc. Beauvais is a gloomy, old-fashioned town; the streets very narrow, and, during our stay, very dirty. What they might be in summer I can't guess, but they look as if they must be then redolent of the same sulphurous odour as those of Paris.

24*th.*—Marched to Grandvilliers; everything looking wretched, for the day was dark and excessively cold: in France, on such occasions, there are no redeeming features. The country is in most cases without enclosures, and the few trees, stripped of their verdure present most cheerless pictures, unrelieved by any appearance of warmth or comfort about the mean and wretched-looking dwellings of the peasantry. These, when we entered the village, presented rather a better appearance than usual, for all were *en habits de Dimanche*, which was the day. Lodged F. in the post-

house (here an inn), and then went round our billets.
Village very large, two broad streets crossing each other, but
the houses all farms or cottages, most of them of mud, like
the Devonshire cobbe, and all thatched; the site of the
place a dead flat, but pretty well clothed with trees. At
our posthouse we procured a tolerably decent though very
small parlour, the chimney of which, however, smoked so
terribly that, spite of the weather, we were obliged to sit
constantly with the door open; upstairs (this was a sort
of addition to the original house projecting into the yard) a
bedroom of the same size, in which were two beds; and
nothing could exceed the astonishment of our friend the
chambermaid at our arrangement of sleeping together. The
inhabitants here were ordered by beat of drum to feed us.
We now came under the command of Sir Denis Park, who
commands at Calais and up the road as far as this place, he
having the arrangement of the embarkations.

We lived well at our inn, and remedied the open door by
a large screen. Every evening we saw company—*i.e.* our
officers—and, although the weather was very cold, passed
our time pleasantly enough. One day an immense market
or fair afforded us ample amusement; another, our attention
and curiosity were excited by the arrival of a troop of the
National Guard, *à cheval*, from Beauvais; but, after stay-
ing the whole afternoon and night, they departed the next
morning without our being a bit the wiser. One day the
Earl of Westmeath arrived, and stopped all night; his lordship was obliged to put up with the rooms we had rejected.

January 1, 1816.—At last the order for our advance
having arrived, we marched this morning from Grandvilliers, several *paysannes* of the village following the troop as
volunteers for l'Angleterre, betraying the effects of idleness
in country quarters. Whilst preparing to set off, our host
presented a bill for our living, etc., amounting to nine
napoleons, which I was about to pay, when Hitchins and F.
interfered, asking the good man whether he would have
dared appear before a Prussian officer with such a thing,
and telling him after the manner his countrymen had treated
all other countries that he ought to think himself well off
in being treated so leniently. He did not subscribe to this,
and an argument ensued which I was sorry for, but was weak

enough to allow my better intentions to be overruled; and
at last, when Monsieur begged I would at least certify that
he had not been paid, I did so on the bill, stating as reason
that the inhabitants had been ordered to feed us. Our
march to Poix, the next halting-place, was through a country
that never could be very interesting, still less so in its wintry
garb, until, from the summit of a high hill, we looked down
upon the lovely valley in which that village is situated. On
arriving we found all the world *en habit de Dimanche*
celebrating the opening of the new year. The principal
features in this celebration were the kisses exchanging in all
directions, the enormous stiffly starched caps of the women,
and the music that paraded continually through the streets.
The *auberge* we found so noisy, smoky, dirty, and the
landlord such an uncivil brute, that we immediately commenced a search for a better billet. For a time success
seemed uncertain; the houses of the peasantry were too
filthy to be thought of. Not far from the *auberge* we found
a good house, but shut-up doors and windows. In vain
Hitchins and I knocked and threatened, or asked information of its inhabitants from the neighbours; nobody would
answer from within, and nobody would answer without—
at least more than "Je n'en sais rien, monsieur." At last we
found a respectable sort of old-fashioned farmhouse, the
mistress of which (a widow) was factotum to the Prince de
Poix, proprietor of the village, and much of the neighbouring
country,—and hither we immediately removed, bag and
baggage. A labyrinth of dark passages led to a large,
gloomy, wainscoted room, in one corner of which was a
great old-fashioned bed, with yellow damask curtains, like
the one we slept in at Breteuil. Here we established ourselves, and Angélique had a small cabinet hard by, whilst
the men were put up in the more distant part of the house
occupied by the family. Although there was a large fireplace, in which we kept up capital fires, the place was very
cold; but a couple of old screens in some measure remedied
this, and at last we thought ourselves tolerably comfortable.
Our park was formed on the site of the ancient castle of
the princes, now almost entirely gone, except a few mounds
marking out the ground-plan. The village of Poix, though
covering a great deal of ground, is not large; for, except

the few houses standing contiguous to the *auberge*, the others
are scattered up and down, widely apart from each other.
The situation is extremely pretty in summer, probably
beautiful: a deep and rather narrow valley, with a small
stream running through it; partly below the village covered
with woods, which also ran over and clothed all the surrounding hills—not close thick copse, but composed of trees
and thickets of coppice, through which one might ride in all
directions on a carpet of turf.   On a steep bank, immediately
opposite our dwelling, was the little church, unpretending,
but having a beautiful Gothic western doorway, over which,
as a record of revolutionary folly, was painted in large
letters, "*Temple de la Raison*"; these had been either
whitewashed or painted over, but insufficiently, for they
were still distinctly legible.   The weather during our stay
at Poix (seven days) was gloomy and very cold, yet we
managed to have many interesting rides amongst the woods.
Hitchins dined with us always, and came provided with
some excellent wine, which he procured from his own
hostess.   In one of our walks, at the fork of the roads to
Amiens and Abbeville, we found a diminutive chapel with a
figure of the Virgin in it, and as diminutive a priest, hump-
backed.   He showed us his chapel, and we put some money
into his box, and so parted mutually satisfied.   It was at
this corner that I met an elderly French veteran trudging
towards the village in his capote and forage-cap, with the
usual goatskin knapsack: he was minus an arm, and upon
questioning him I found that he had left it at Waterloo.
Something interesting in this interview.

In the village we found a corporal and four privates of the
18th Hussars, stationed here for despatches.   The corporal
fell in love with Angélique, and proposed for her, but was
rejected.   Her lover gave us an alert one night to deliver
a despatch (these hussars always come in the night!), and I
made sure we were off.   It was an order to have divine
service every Sunday.

8th.—At length on the 7th the order did come, and this
day we marched to Airaines through a sufficiently dismal
country, and weather very cold and gloomy, still followed
by the girls from Grandvilliers.   Some part of the country,
from its hilliness and numerous orchards, in some measure

resembled Devonshire; but as we approached the town these cease, and we saw again only extensive and treeless plains.

Airaines at first sight was not calculated to remove the unpleasant feeling excited by its neighbourhood: rather large for a country town, and lying on a gentle slope; its streets irregular, and buildings mean, dirty, and ruinous-looking;—altogether very gloomy. Our billet was on the *auberge* where the diligences stopped, a house of very inferior description, in which we did not establish ourselves without difficulty, and then wretchedly enough. For ourselves we got a room with two dirty beds in it, and only the coarsest kind of furniture; floor inch-thick in dirt, and having chinks between the planks, so gaping that we could see everything going on below—and being over the gateway, the great lounge of the postilions, *gens d'armes*, etc., we had not only the advantage of all their conversation, but also of their eternal tobacco-pipes; also the full benefit of a most cooling breeze continually blowing through the gateway. The only room we could procure for Angélique was occupied by a postilion, and he was unwilling to evacuate, so that a little tyranny became necessary to gain possession. We turned him out *vi et armis*. In this wretched place we remained a fortnight, during which the weather, always gloomy, was at times bitterly cold, or heavy rain. As the whole troop could not be lodged here, it was necessary to detach Maunsell with one division to a village at least five miles off; and Wells, pretending there was no lodging to be procured here, asked leave to accompany him—notwithstanding which, our surgeon, Ambrose, who overtook us here, immediately obtained very comfortable quarters. Hitchins also was uncommonly well lodged in the house of an old smuggler. Our park was formed on an open space by the road to Abbeville, just without the town, where, as the weather was too cold for our guard to remain in a tent, I asked the mayor to procure them accommodation in a house hard by. This he refused, until I made preparations to bring our park into the market-place, which alarmed him so much that he immediately complied. The market-place, by the way, was precisely similar to the old buildings one sees in English country towns; and here the two Sundays during our stay I performed divine service. To pass our time here we sometimes rode about the dreary neighbourhood, where we discovered a ruined castle; and in another part a rather pretty village, with a fine manor-house and park; but the people soon drove us away from this last, not only by their abuse, but even pelting us with stones. In bad weather we resorted to a wretched billiard-table opposite our inn, where I taught F. the game, and drank bitter coffee to my cigars. There was nothing extraordinary in her frequenting this table, as it is customary for females to do so; and there were seldom any other people present than our own.

In addition to our other occupations, the diligence afforded a daily and short amusement as it stopped at our inn door. I can see now the great lumbering machine just drawn up, a clown in a blue smock-frock, linen forage-cap with a huge peak sticking straight out, and a long coach-whip in hand, seated on the near wheeler, guiding by cord-reins the three cart-horses harnessed abreast as leaders; and two tall soldier-like *gens d'armes*, in their neat blue uniforms and cocked-hats, stepping up to the door, and whilst one examined the way-bill, the other mounts the step of the vehicle and scrutinises the passengers. They were fine fellows these, and we got tolerably intimate with them. Every evening Hitchins came to us and played a rubber of casino. One evening standing at our window, we saw some sheep come down the opposite street; two or three went into the passage of a house, the door of which was instantly closed by an old woman, and we both exclaimed, "Ah, the wretch! she steals the sheep." Our servants who stood by laughed, and explained that the old shepherd (who now appeared sauntering slowly along) was the guardian of the town flock, which he conducted to pasture daily.

Accordingly the next morning the old man again marched under our window towards the fields, blowing his horn, at which sound the door opposite again opened, and out sallied the same sheep following the old man, and forming with others assembling from all quarters a large flock, which we found him with in the fields when we went to ride.

22d.—Marched to Abbeville. Billeted on a velvet manufacturer with a pretty wife; excellent house, comfortable living. Visit the cathedral and walk about the town.

Forgot that I tried one of my men by a court-martial at
Airaines upon a charge of stealing bacon, brought against
him by a peasant of the village where Maunsell was quartered.
Sent on to Abbeville for a captain, and Close came over for the
purpose. The patois of the witnesses was so mixed up with
English as to astonish us; one in particular we shrewdly
suspected of being an English deserter. It was, however,
only the patois of Picardy. "Yes" was much oftener used
than "oui" by them. On our way here from Airaines,
descending to the Somme at Point de Remy, I saw a very
large Roman encampment on a neighbouring hill: country
about the river pretty as usual. Here most of my horses
were put up in the riding-school of the cavalry barrack.
Our host's family consisted of himself, a grown-up son, a
female cousin, and his pretty wife, who was very civil, and
went shopping with F., but disgusted me at breakfast by
holding up a beastly pocket-handkerchief and spitting at it.

23d.—Much pleased at marching to Montreuil, as we had
expected Rue and Nampont would have been our destination. Comfortable inn—the same Sterne was at; and our
salle the identical room in which La Fleur slept—so said our
host. Excellent dinner: Hitchins dined with us, and we drank
two bottles of prime champagne. Wells left us here to join my
old troop at St Pol. As we were tired, we slept so soundly
that we never knew until morning that the house had been
set on fire during the night by a drunken officer of infantry.

24th.—Wretched morning, snowing heavily, and very cold.
Hitchins suffered much from our ride, and got sulky because
F. and Angélique laughed at him. Stopped at Samer to see
our friend the Demoiselles Mallet, and get some hot wine.

At Boulogne our billet was on a capital house; but our
host, an old officer (I think colonel), extremely sulky and
disobliging—obliged to send to a restaurateur's for our
dinner. Walked about the town and on the ramparts. No
snow here, though the weather was excessively raw and
windy. Ramparts pretty; the only trees in the neighbourhood are on them.

At night had gone to bed, expecting to remain a day or
two, and were not yet asleep when some one tapped at our
window, which opened into a little flagged court. I got up
and found a hussar (as usual), who brought me a note,

which I could not read until he went and got a light. It was an order to march to-morrow to Guines.

25th.—As our landlord (commandant of the National Guard) had been anything but civil, we set off without taking leave of him. Other cavalry besides ourselves had halted in Boulogne, and we found the roads covered with troops, stragglers, and baggage. Amidst these we struggled on as far as Marquise, where we left the chaussée for a villanous cross-road, by which, about noon, we arrived at Guines, a very pretty little town, and the day being fine, a very cheerful-looking one. Our billet (if billet it were) was a capital one —the Château de Beauscite; the owner, M. le Baron de Guesclin, with Madame and his daughters, received us most kindly. The family consisted of M. le Baron, a good-natured, but ugly, and not very genteel-looking man, about sixty; Madame la Baronne, a jolly good-looking woman of forty; one very sickly looking daughter about twenty-two; another a year or so older, hideously marked with smallpox, but extremely obliging and good-natured; and a tall awkward son of about twenty. The house comfortable and well furnished. We were treated quite on the footing of guests, and even welcome ones. Style of living much the same as that of an English country gentleman of easy fortune. After dinner the Baron proposed showing us our room and the house. Passing through his own bedroom, with a knowing wink he gave me to understand that he did not follow modern fashions in sleeping separate from his wife; for, pointing to the ample and handsome bed, he exclaimed loud enough to be heard by all, "M., voila là fabrique des enfans!" Madame looked archly over her shoulder at me and burst out laughing.

26th.—Fine day. Breakfast of tea, etc., got up expressly for us, as when alone they have no such regular meal, but merely take a cup of coffee. Afterwards the son showed me the stables, stud, farm, etc., and then, mounted on a long-tailed Norman horse, with military saddle and bridle, took us to see the obelisk erected on the spot where Blanchard descended after crossing the Channel in his balloon. The country pretty, because well wooded; and from the hill I once more saw the white cliffs of England, although I will not pretend to have experienced any very great delight in so doing, as the future promised nothing good, and I would rather have remained in France.

Reduction, Woolwich duties, and insipidity from the total absence of excitement—such was the prospect before me.

In the afternoon a very handsome young man (an officer in some cavalry corps) came in and dined with us. His father, an old gentleman of good fortune in the neighbour-hood, had served many years in the hussars, and was (I believe) Madame's brother. In the evening came in the family confessor—a fat, greasy priest—who made himself quite at home; but they did not seem over well pleased with his company. Servants singing in the kitchen: opened a little trap in the wall of a cupboard which communicated with the kitchen to hear a young girl from St Omer sing "Brulant d'Amour" and "Partant pour la Guerre," which she did with great sweetness. Our hopes of enjoying this pleasant billet for some days disappointed by the order to march to-morrow into Calais, only eight miles off.

27th.—Gloomy cold day. A mass to be celebrated for the soul of Louis XVI. I had promised M. le Baron to allow my men to assist in the procession, but instead was obliged to take leave as they were about to begin. Early in the morn-ing all the front of the chateau was hung with black cloth. Nothing could be kinder or even more affectionate than our leave-taking, and Madame obliged F. to wrap up in a rich *pelerin* of her own, which we were to leave at Quillacq's. The distance being so short, we were not long on the road, which for the most part lay along the canal as far as St Pierre, a great straggling suburb of Calais, in which we were to halt. Nothing could be worse than our accommodations here—horses and men scattered about by twos and threes, far and wide; some of them were sent back almost to Guines—so near at least as to hear distinctly the church-bells. As for us, we were put into a farmhouse, where they gave us a room without a fireplace, insufferable in such a season; therefore, being obliged to go into Calais to report our arrival to Webber Smith, I left F. and Hitchins hunting for another quarter. After some trouble I got a billet from the Quartermaster-General on the Lion d'Argent, in Calais, kept by an impudent English scoundrel named Oakshot, who was not at all well pleased at our being put on him. Rode back to St Pierre, where I found F. and Hitchins in a bedroom they had procured at a dirty smoky *brasserie*; so we all adjourned together to the Silver Lion.

Here we were detained some time, which, however, was of less consequence, as we were lodged well and fed well. In other respects, however, the detention was anything but pleasant. Calais at the best of times must be a dismal stupid hole; at this season of storms, cold, rain, mud, etc. etc., it was scarcely endurable. Great part of my day was passed at or about the pier, whence, from time to time as vessels arrived, we shipped off some of our people.

Nothing can be imagined more harassing and destructive than this process of embarkation. For example, my people, as before mentioned, were dispersed in all directions round the neighbourhood, even to the distance of six or eight miles, by twos and threes, etc., so that they were under no control whatever. Meantime the guns, ammunition waggons, etc., all dismounted and ready to put on board, remained exposed to all the weather on the pier. At daylight in the morning, according to orders, men and horses assembled there also, and remained—rain, hail, wind or snow (of all which we had plenty)—until dusk in the evening, when they were permitted to return to their billets for the night. Nothing could be more subversive of discipline and harassing to the men, or more ruinous to the horses; yet, from the system adopted by those who ruled the transport service, it could not well be avoided, since the vessels engaged were all schooners, sloops, etc.; and it was necessary, when any of these returned for a fresh cargo, that the embarkation should be as prompt as possible, not only for the more expeditiously getting the troops across, but because they were obliged to leave the harbour with the same tide, or remain twelve hours. These vessels did not go all to one place; thus my troop was landed by sixes and sevens at Dover, Sandwich, Deal, Ramsgate, etc., and then assembled at Canterbury. Webber Smith was our immediate commanding officer here; and Sir Denis Park, who commanded, occasionally rode down to see how things were going on, so that there was no getting out of the way, and our only relief was an occasional stroll about the muddy, dismal streets, lounging in some of the shops, etc. Thus time hung heavily on our hands. Hitchins had left us on the very first evening of our arrival at the Silver Lion, and we sadly missed his kind attentions—especially F., who, whilst I was at the pier, had no one to escort her about, and of course in such a place going alone was out of the question. I found a pleasing companion to while away time at the pier in the harbour-master, an old captain of the French navy, and a well-informed, gentlemanly person, from whom I picked up a good deal of information. I cannot omit noting the fact that a female bookseller here, whose *magazin* we sometimes frequented, one day let out that she implicitly believed every one of the absurd lies respecting England contained in General Pelet's book, and would hardly credit our contradiction of them.

At last our tedious detention came, like all things else, to a conclusion. Two sloops, capable of containing all the remainder of my troop, came in one evening too late to sail before next morning, and with this last party I decided on embarking. When Angélique heard this she came and begged I would lend her a suit of my plain clothes, as the prefect had prohibited French women going with the English, and had already stopped many. Here was a dilemma. My old Scotch quartermaster, however, got us out of it. I don't know how he passed the gates, but he did manage on the morning of the 25th January 1816 to smuggle Angélique on board before daylight, and conceal her below, without the necessity of changing her female for male attire.

After breakfast we embarked and immediately sailed. Webber Smith went with us, as we were the very last of the Royal Horse Artillery. The weather was gloomy, cold, and stormy, but the wind was fair, and we were off Dover early in the afternoon. The tide would not admit even our little sloop into this miserable harbour before midnight, and she was hove to almost within speaking distance of the pier-head. Not relishing this position, we were glad to avail ourselves of a pilot-gig that came off and go ashore—although these fellows charged us a guinea a-head for thus carrying us about 200 yards.

After an early dinner at the York Hotel, Smith set off post for Blackheath, where his family was residing.

26th.—To Canterbury. F. and Angélique in a post-chaise, to which I and Milward (carrying his lance) served as an escort, for I had no men to march with.

So ended the memorable campaign of 1815.

AFTERWORD

JOURNAL of the Waterloo Campaign was first published in 1870, some two years after the death of its author, but was written in its present form some forty years earlier, from notes made at the time. It remains one of the most famous personal accounts of the climactic three days which brought to an end the military career of Napoleon Bonaparte, and is the more interesting because it is one of the comparatively few accounts of the Napoleonic Wars written by an officer of artillery. Having been a talented amateur artist, its author possessed a keen eye for nature and was a fine observer of the civilian and military scene, writing in an easy, humorous style which must have contributed to the success of the publication.

Alexander Cavalié Mercer was born in 1783, second son of General Mercer of the Royal Engineers. Although Alexander was his first name—he appears simply as A. Mercer in the official *Army List*—and although he signed his name A. C. Mercer, it was apparently his second name which he preferred: His son, Cavalié A. Mercer, who wrote the preface to the first publication, presumably was responsible for General Cavalié Mercer appearing on the title page.

Alexander Cavalié Mercer followed his father into that branch of the British armed forces controlled by the Board of Ordnance; from the Military Academy at Woolwich he was commissioned as a 2nd lieutenant in the Royal Regiment of Artillery on 20 December 1799, rising to the rank of captain on 3 December 1806. After serving in the disastrous South American operations of 1807, he missed the Peninsular War entirely, and was still a captain at the time of the Waterloo campaign, in which he commanded G Troop, Royal Horse Artillery.

Formed in 1793, the Royal Horse Artillery was intended to provide the mobile guns capable of keeping pace with the cavalry formations to which they were affiliated, but at Waterloo, a battle comparatively static as far as the British Army was concerned, the horse artillery was deployed as field batteries, not acting in direct concert with the cavalry brigades.

There were eight troops of Royal Horse Artillery at Waterloo, each of six guns, and each identified either by a letter or by the name of its commander. They included: A Troop, commanded by Lt. Col. Sir Hew Dalrymple Ross; D Troop, Major George Beane; E Troop, Lt. Col. Sir Robert Gardiner; F Troop, Lt. Col. James Webber Smith; G Troop, Capt. Alexander Cavalié Mercer; H Troop, Major William Norman Ramsay (an officer immortalized by Napier's *History of the War in the Peninsula* for his exploit in saving his guns at Fuentes de Oñoro); I Troop, Major Robert Bull; and the Rocket Troop, Capt. Edward Whinyates. Of these, Ramsay and Beane were killed and Bull and Whinyates wounded during the battle. Four of these Troops (A, D, G, and H) had been reequipped shortly before the battle with 9-pounder guns, at the request of the commander of the horse artillery in Wellington's army, Sir Augustus Frazer; two (E and F) retained their original 6-pounders; I Troop was equipped exclusively with $5\frac{1}{2}$-inch howitzers (of which all the other Troops maintained one, along with their five cannon); and at Wellington's insistence the Rocket Troop was equipped with five 6-pounders and one $5\frac{1}{2}$-inch howitzer in addition to its rockets.

Mercer's own troop originally had six officers: Mercer himself, in command; Capt. William Pakenham as second-in-command; and four lieutenants, Bell, Leathes, Hincks, and Ingilby. In the days before the battle there occurred a number of changes of personnel. Most significantly, Pakenham left G Troop to take up a staff appointment as adjutant of the Royal Artillery; he was replaced as Mercer's deputy by the newly-promoted Robert Newland, a 2nd captain since 20 December 1814. Mercer was not too impressed with Newland's conduct at Waterloo: Almost 44 years after the battle he still recalled how Newland had asked leave to go in search of ammunition and had not returned until two days after the battle, claiming, when asked, that he had joined his old Troop (Gardiner's), which, Mercer stated, had hardly been engaged. Evidently Mercer regarded Newland's actions as a rather too convenient absence from the hottest part of the action. Newland retired in April 1831.

Lieutenant William Bell also left G Troop for a staff appointment as Sir Augustus Frazer's adjutant. Bell's distinguished career had an unusual beginning: The son of a surgeon in Ripon, Yorkshire, he came to the notice of Colonel C. A. Quist, the septuagenarian Riding Master of the Ordnance Department, on a visit to Ripon to buy horses; he used his influence to obtain young Bell a cadetship to the Woolwich academy, from where he was commissioned. After service in the West Indies, Bell was posted to the Peninsular War, receiving a slight wound at Toulouse, and was awarded the Military General Service Medal with clasps for Martinique, Guadeloupe, Nivelle, Nive, and Toulouse. He progressed to become a general, Knight Commander of the Order of the Bath, and colonel-commandant of the Royal Horse Artillery. Upon his retirement he returned to Ripon, where he died in March 1873. Despite the many actions in which he served, his narrowest escape came at home, when he fell off his horse in front of a galloping battery, the drag-shoe of one of the guns removing his ear!

Next senior of Mercer's lieutenants was Henry Mussenden Leathes, third son and eventual heir of Major George Leathes. Commissioned as a 1st Lieutenant on 1 June 1806, Henry served in the Peninsula (receiving the Military General Service Medal with clasp for Corunna) and resigned his commission in 1819. Residing at Herringfleet Hall, Suffolk and known for the remainder of his life as a kindly philanthropist, Leathes reestablished contact with his old commanding officer in 1859, the resulting correspondence being published subsequently by Leathes' son, Hill Mussenden Leathes, as *Reminiscences of Waterloo*. Henry Leathes died at Lowestoft in December 1864.

John Hincks was the next senior lieutenant, his commission dating from 1 February 1808. The second son of Capt. Thomas Hincks of Marfield, Leicestershire, he attained the rank of captain himself and retired on half-pay in 1826. The most junior of Mercer's original lieutenants was William Bates Ingilby, whose commission dated from 9 April 1812, but who was an experienced Peninsular veteran (he received the Military General Service Medal with clasps for Busaco, Fuentes de Oñoro, Ciudad Rodrigo, and Salamanca, where he was wounded). Mercer refers to him as "old Lieutenant Ingleby" (sic: Mercer's spelling was in error) evidently out of deference for his campaign service or facetiously because of Ingilby's comments that the Peninsula was worse than anything experienced in the Netherlands. Ingilby was, in fact, just 24 at the time of the battle, born 30 April 1791, second son of the Rev. Henry Ingilby of Ripley, Yorkshire; his brother Ralph Mitford Preston Ingilby also followed a military career, rising to a captaincy in the 84th Foot. First commissioned on 1 April 1809, William Ingilby rose to the rank of general, Knight Commander of the Order of the Bath, and colonel-commandant of the Royal Artillery. Before Waterloo, however, he was exchanged with Lieutenant John F. Breton of Gardiner's Troop, with which Ingilby served at Waterloo. Breton, senior to Ingilby but the most junior of Mercer's lieutenants, was commissioned as a 1st lieutenant on 15 March 1811; he retired on half-pay on 1 October 1820 and died in March 1852. The last of Mercer's officers was the Troop's assistant-surgeon, Richard Hichins (or "Hitchins"), whose commission dated from 11 November 1811; he retired on half-pay in April 1816 and died in January 1866.

A number of distinguished artillery officers are mentioned by Mercer, including Sir Alexander Dickson. This renowned officer had commanded Wellington's artillery with great distinction in the later Peninsular War and proved to be one of the Duke's most capable subordinates. He was nominal commander of Mercer's G Troop, which perhaps explains why he paid Mercer a brief visit during the battle. Sir George Adam Wood, commanding the Royal Artillery in the campaign, had fulfilled the same position in Holland in 1814 and had led one of the columns at the storm of Bergen-op-Zoom. Commander of the horse artillery was Lieut. Colonel Sir Augustus Frazer (or "Fraser"), who had held the same position in the later Peninsular War and whose connection with the mounted branch of the Royal Artillery went back to 1795. He was given much of the credit for the effectiveness of the horse artillery in the Peninsular War and later, and had also commanded G Troop. Commander of the six Troops attached to the cavalry was Lieut. Colonel A. Macdonald, to whom Mercer refers as "Major M'Donald." Officers of the "foot" branch of the Royal Artillery to whom Mercer recollected speaking at Waterloo included Captain Samuel Bolton, commander of his own battery (who was killed towards the end of the day, evidently only a short time after conversing with Mercer); "Colonel Gould," actually Lieut. Colonel Charles Gold, one of the divisional artil-

lery commanders; and "Major M'Lloyd," actually William
Lloyd, commander of a foot battery, who shortly after speaking
to Mercer received a wound from which he died some five
weeks later.

Although Mercer's *Journal* is generally regarded as a classic
account of the campaign, it should be recognized as an account
of what he experienced and not as a flawless history. Mercer
admitted that his intention was to write only gossip for his
own amusement. Although written in its present form many
years after the event, it was based upon a journal he kept at the
time, noting down every evening the events of the day. Hardly
surprisingly, the three hectic days at the climax of the campaign left him no time for his usual daily record of events, and
he admitted that the turmoil of battle tended to confuse the se-
quence of events when he came to note them down some days
later—a refreshing candor not commonly found in campaign
journals. Consequently, Mercer's account concentrates upon
the incidents which made the most impression upon him, and
perhaps not surprisingly contains some errors.

A few points concerning the battle are worthy of note, not least
Mercer's admittance of disobeying orders and firing against the
French artillery, which was prohibited. Mercer does not mention
(indeed, probably never knew) that Wellington observed this
transgression and blamed Capt. Charles Sandham of the foot artillery, who with some difficulty proved his innocence.

Perhaps the most notable incident described by Mercer in
the entire battle is his renewed disobeying of orders to leave
his guns to shelter among the infantry during the French cavalry attacks. His stated reason is that he feared abandoning his
guns lest the sight of running gunners would cause two unsteady squares of Brunswickers to bolt. So G Troop remained
and manned its guns, which (according to Mercer) evidently
put heart into the wavering infantry, who remained steady and
joined in with musketry, devastating with Mercer's case-shot
the approaching French cavalry. Further details of the action
were recounted by Mercer when replying to the historian
Capt. William Siborne's questions about the battle. Mercer's
letter to him, which was dated 26 November 1834 and based
on material in his original journal, reveals that the position he
took up was protected by a fold in the ground, which had the

effect of forming a natural fortification, as if he were protected by a parapet (*genouillère*):

> The ground we were to occupy was two or three feet lower than that immediately in our front, so that the bank where this difference occurred *abruptly*, and along which ran a narrow open road, formed a sort of *genouillère* to our Battery . . . Our leading sub-division had scarcely arrived on the position, ere it became evident that the Duke's order [to take shelter among the infantry] could not be complied with, for a Column of Cavalry composed of Grenadiers à Cheval and Cuirassiers, had just ascended the Plateau and was advancing upon us at a rapid pace, so that there scarcely appeared time even to get into action, and, if caught in column, of course we were lost. However, the order was given to deploy, and each Gun as it came up immediately opened its fire; the two Infantry Squares at the same time commencing a feeble and desultory fire; for they were in such a state that I momentarily expected to see them disband. Their ranks, loose and disjointed, presented gaps of several file in breadth, which the Officers and Sergeants were busily employed filling up by pushing and even thumping their men together; whilst these, standing like so many logs, with their arms at the recover, were apparently completely stupefied and bewildered. I should add that they were all perfect children. None of the privates, perhaps, were above 18 years of age. In spite of our fire the Column of Cavalry continued advancing at a *trot* until separated from us by scarcely more than the breadth of the little road, but at the very moment when we expected to be overwhelmed, those of the leading Squadrons suddenly turning, and endeavouring to make way to the rear, confusion took place, and the whole broke into a disorderly crowd. The scene that ensued is scarcely to be described . . . [1]

It will be seen that there is a subtle change of emphasis between the two accounts of this action: Mercer's earlier statement implies that he held his ground because there was not time to take shelter, whereas the published *Journal* implies that he stood by his guns deliberately, to prevent the Brunswickers from bolting. Perhaps both are true, and indeed the two are not mutually contradictory. The most important consideration is probably that the young Brunswickers *did* stand, under the most trying of circumstances, whether from their own innate discipline or

---

[1]*Waterloo Letters*, ed. Major-General H.T. Siborne, London, 1891, pp. 217-18.

from the example set by Mercer's Troop; probably both contributed to this part of Wellington's line remaining in position. Certainly Henry Leathes (in a letter to Mercer, it is true) appeared
to confirm Mercer's version, concerning their move "to the post
of honour near the Brunswickers, which, by your coolness and
judgment, you maintained to the last struggle of that great
day."[2] (Leathes must not have held too high an opinion of the
infantry in question as he described them as "young sourkraut-
squares"!)

Desperate though the fighting was, Mercer tended to over-
state the losses of his Troop, both in men and horses. The first
muster roll taken after the battle confirms that 69 horses were
killed, less than Mercer implied, but still almost three times as
many as any other Troop. Similarly, he overstated the ammunition expended in the battle; Frazer's estimate was that G
Troop as a whole had fired 700 rounds—more than any other
Troop—not the 700 rounds per gun estimated by Mercer,
which is an obvious error. Leathes explained the shortages of
personnel at the end of the day: "You ask me about the loss in
men . . . I do not think it was very great: at the close of the action many had been despatched with the wounded, and others
sent off to try and bring up a fresh ammunition supply."[3]

Exact casualty figures are difficult to determine: For the entire horse artillery, a return made by Sir George Wood on 24
June lists three officers and 32 other ranks killed, 14 and 115
respectively wounded, and seven rank-and-file missing. The
principal query over casualties concerns G Troop, which in a
list prepared by Frazer on the day after the battle is shown as
having had 18 men killed. The Troop's first muster roll after
the battle, however, notes only three fatalities on the day: drivers Daniel Bradbury, James Crammond, and John Miller; two
more, gunner John Butterworth and driver William Mainwar-
ing were struck off the roll in October 1815 as presumed killed
at Waterloo, their bodies evidently not having been identified.
Presumably the contradiction is explained by the fact that
Frazer's figure of 18 refers to G Troop's entire casualties, as
the muster roll lists twelve men "sick absent" and four "sick"
(but presumably still with the Troop), most of whom were

[2]*Reminiscences of Waterloo*, H. M. Leathes, London, n.d., p. 17.
[3]*ibid.*, p. 19

probably suffering from wounds sustained in the action. Among those listed is gunner Philip Hunt, noted by Mercer as the Troop's first casualty, his left arm shattered by a roundshot. (He survived the injury and was discharged from the R.H.A. on 10 December 1815.)[4]

Even for officers, the casualty figures prepared immediately after the battle are not accurate. For example, two of the officers described as wounded in Frazer's list succumbed to their injuries: Lieutenant William Robe of H Troop, hit by a musket ball in the groin, died on the day after Waterloo, and Lieutenant Michael Cromie of D Troop, who lost both legs to a single roundshot, died two days later; while John Hincks of Mercer's own Troop was slightly wounded, but declined to be returned as such in the official documents. In later life Mercer claimed that he too should have been counted among the wounded, from an unusual cause: When Breton's horse was killed, its blood soaked Mercer's overalls to such an extent that when they dried they stuck to him, and the action of riding caused the hardened fabric to so cut him across the perineum that he had to ride almost sidesaddle for a time. Twice in later life the injury broke out again, once when he was commanding at Dover and once after retirement.

Following the battle, Mercer succeeded to the command of D Troop, replacing Major George Beane, who had been killed. Mercer thought that his services had been unfairly ignored, and indeed his subsequent promotion was not rapid (although promotions in the Ordnance services were notoriously slow, being dependent upon seniority). After a period on half-pay, and with the rank of brevet-major (granted on 12 August 1819), he was posted to Canada in 1824; promoted to lieutenant-colonel on 5 June 1835, he returned to North America in 1837 and commanded the artillery there at the time of the Maine boundary dispute with the United States. His colonelcy was granted on 1 April 1846 and he became major-general on 20 June 1854. After a period in command of the garrison at Dover he retired from active service, but as colonel-commandant of the 9th Brigade of Royal Artillery, he was never officially placed upon the retired list. Until his death at the age of

[4]For the casualty-returns, see "A Waterloo Letter: The Royal Artillery and its Casualties," Major P. E. Abbott, *Journal of the Society for Army Historical Research*, XLII (1964) pp. 113-20.

85 on 9 November 1868, he lived at Cowley Cottage, Cowley Hill, near Exeter.

The fact that he received little recognition for his Waterloo service continued to rankle, especially when officers who were his junior received preferment: "Such a thunder-stroke aroused me,"[5] he wrote, and began to petition for the award of the Companionate of the Order of the Bath; but despite these attempts continuing at least as late as 1857, he was unsuccessful. Mercer suspected that he was ignored as a consequence of remarks made by "jealous brother officers" during the post-Waterloo occupation of Paris, to the effect that G Troop's losses were Mercer's fault for not posting his unit under cover (when none existed, according to him).[6] Writing to Leathes in March 1859, Mercer declared that he was content, having got his battalion and "no longer coveting the C.B., which I could not value as a distinction, seeing the manner in which it has been lavished, and the unimportant services of the majority so decorated. 'Sour grapes?'—No."[7] Clearly he blamed Frazer particularly ("Fraser's neglect of us was unpardonable—his own old troop!").[8] Two days after the battle Frazer had written: "I find my late troop (G) has lost ninety horses, but it behaved so well, so *steadily*, that I am highly and justly pleased";[9] but the letter containing this remark, Mercer thought, was so unlike Frazer's usual form of expression that it must have been written with an eye to publication, and so different from the "praise" Mercer claimed was bestowed upon him by Frazer in the immediate aftermath of the battle. Despite Mercer's protestations of contentment, his belief that he had been deliberately and unjustly ignored still rankled 47 years after the event.

In later years, the lance Mercer acquired after the battle from its wounded French owner formed the most tangible relic of this momentous episode in his life. Having recovered the weapon from ordnance stores, where it had been used in the designing of the first lance issued to British cavalry, Mercer kept it in the hall of his house, carefully preserved in memory of, and respect for, the brave enemy to whom it had belonged.

[5] Leathes, p. 6.
[6] ibid., p. 7.
[7] ibid., p. 8.
[8] ibid., p. 13.
[9] ibid., p. 21.

Every year on the anniversary of the battle, Mercer planted the lance in his garden, stuck into the lawn and decked with roses and laurel. To the end of his long life, Waterloo remained the high point of his career, the single event which had made the greatest impression upon him.

PHILIP J. HAYTHORNTHWAITE
Lancashire, England
March 1995